D1414666

Midnight in America

CIVIL WAR AMERICA

Peter S. Carmichael, Caroline E. Janney, and Aaron Sheehan-Dean, editors

This landmark series interprets broadly the history and culture of the Civil War era through the long nineteenth century and beyond. Drawing on diverse approaches and methods, the series publishes historical works that explore all aspects of the war, biographies of leading commanders, and tactical and campaign studies, along with select editions of primary sources. Together, these books shed new light on an era that remains central to our understanding of American and world history.

Midnight in America

Darkness, Sleep, and Dreams during the Civil War

Jonathan W. White

The University of North Carolina Press CHAPEL HILL

*This book was published with the assistance of the Anniversary Fund
of the University of North Carolina Press.*

© 2017 The University of North Carolina Press
All rights reserved
Manufactured in the United States of America
Set in Espinosa Nova by Westchester Publishing Services

The University of North Carolina Press has been a member of the Green Press
Initiative since 2003.

Library of Congress Cataloging-in-Publication Data
Names: White, Jonathan W., 1979– author.
Title: Midnight in America : darkness, sleep, and dreams during the Civil War /
    Jonathan W. White.
Other titles: Civil War America (Series)
Description: Chapel Hill : University of North Carolina Press, [2017] |
    Series: Civil War America | Includes bibliographical references and index.
Identifiers: LCCN 2016024922 | ISBN 9781469632049 (cloth : alk. paper) |
    ISBN 9781469632056 (ebook)
Subjects: LCSH: Dreams—Social aspects—United States—History—19th century. |
    Dreams—United States—History—19th century. | United States—History—Civil War,
    1861–1865.
Classification: LCC BF1078 .W45 2017 | DDC 154.6/3097309034—dc23
    LC record available at https://lccn.loc.gov/2016024922

Jacket illustration: *Soldier's Dream* by John E. Bihler, 1865. Courtesy of the
Philadelphia History Museum at the Atwater Kent.

For Lauren,
who tolerates my frequent bouts of writer's insomnia
and for Charlotte and Clara,
who love to wake us up in the morning

While others are asleep I think.
Night is the only time I have to think.

—ABRAHAM LINCOLN

Contents

Illustrations

Preface

In the fall of 1861, Julia Ward Howe accompanied her husband, Samuel Gridley Howe, to Washington, D.C. The city, according to one Union volunteer, was "the dirtiest, dustiest, filthiest place I ever saw." The streets were crowded, the heat and humidity oppressive, and flies and mosquitoes buzzed in people's faces both indoors and out.[1]

Julia and Samuel found a room at Willard's Hotel, a few blocks down Pennsylvania Avenue from the White House. While New York City diarist George Templeton Strong believed that Beelzebub "surely reigns there," Willard's really was the place to see and be seen—all of the prominent socialites and military officers stopped there when they visited the nation's capital.

On November 18, the Howes escaped the bustle and filth of the city and attended a grand review of the Army of the Potomac just outside of the capital, in Virginia. Fearing a Confederate attack, Gen. George B. McClellan broke up the review, and the Howes and the other sightseers retreated back to Washington. During the long carriage ride, they sang war songs, including "John Brown's Body":

> John Brown's body lies a-mouldering in the grave,
> John Brown's body lies a-mouldering in the grave,
> But his soul goes marching on.
> Glory, glory, hallelujah,
> Glory, glory, hallelujah,
> His soul goes marching on.

The song continued for a few more verses and choruses, and soldiers near the carriage joined in the revelry. One of Howe's companions turned to her and remarked that she should write "some good words for that stirring tune," to which she replied, "I had often wished to do this, but had not as yet found in my mind any leading toward it."

But soon an inspiration would come to her. Before daybreak the next morning, Howe awoke from her slumber with words flooding into her mind. Still "in a half dreaming state," she "sprang out of bed," grabbed "an old stump of a pen" and some of the hotel's complimentary stationery, and frantically "scrawled the verses almost without looking at the paper."

Howe frequently composed her poems in this manner. "I had learned to do this when, on previous occasions, attacks of versification had visited me in the night, and I feared to have recourse to a light lest it should wake the baby, who slept near me," she later wrote. "I was always obliged to decipher my scrawl before another night intervened, as it was legible only while the matter was fresh in my mind." Once she finished writing out the verses, she returned to bed and quickly fell back asleep, thinking to herself, "I like this better than most things that I have written."[2]

Howe sold her poem to the *Atlantic Monthly* for five dollars, and it appeared on the front page in February 1862. The first stanza read,

Mine eyes have seen the glory of the coming of the Lord:
He is trampling out the vintage where the grapes of wrath are stored;
He hath loosed the fateful lightning of His terrible swift sword:
His truth is marching on.

Four other stanzas followed the first, filled with messianic and martial symbolism—things that she may have seen in her dreams—such as the "watch-fires of a hundred circling camps"; a "fiery gospel writ in burnished rows of steel"; a sounding "trumpet that shall never call retreat"; and finally soldiers who would follow in the footsteps of Christ in their resolve to "die to make men free." When sung to the tune of "John Brown's Body," the famous chorus would ring throughout the nation for many years to follow:

Glory, glory, hallelujah!
Glory, glory, hallelujah!
Glory, glory, hallelujah!
His truth is marching on.

While the content of Howe's dream is unknown, it may be fairly said that few other dreams have had so lasting and consequential an effect on American popular culture. The words that Howe's sleeping mind wove together that morning have become a timeless anthem, sung by Union soldiers during the Civil War, by civil rights activists a century later, by Americans reeling from the attacks on 9/11, and by many others from all walks of life and political creeds in American history.[3]

ALL OF US DREAM, and our dreams tell us something important about ourselves—our hopes and fears, our preoccupations, our desires, and our disappointments. Indeed, dreams are a fundamental part of who we are, and trying to understand them has always been important to Americans.[4]

Study of the Civil War through the dreams of those who lived through it has the potential to teach us a great deal about how Americans experienced the war. When we read accounts of people's dreams, we enter an intimate place that they intended only for themselves or for their closest loved ones. Their dream reports were often remarkably raw and unfiltered. Reading their dreams can therefore help us see what they saw, feel what they felt, and hear what they heard in ways that no other primary source can. One scholar of colonial New England states, "Dream reports often brought an individual's most closely guarded emotional and spiritual preoccupations to the fore, highlighting religious struggles, or enabling the historian to glimpse emotional experience that otherwise would be hidden from view." Even more poignantly, a physician who studies Vietnam veterans' nightmares writes, "No one who has not experienced war first hand can imagine exactly what it is like. I submit that the next most available way is to experience the war dream world, not as a clinical phenomenon to be reduced to psychoanalytic interpretation, but as human experience."[5]

The same can be true of other eras as well. Indeed, the Civil War placed new and unique strains on nineteenth-century Americans, and their nightly visions reflected those hardships. Sometimes the war intruded on people's slumber, vividly bringing to life the horrors of the conflict; for others, nighttime was an escape from the hard realities of life and death in wartime. The dreams of Civil War–era Americans thus reveal that generation's deepest longings—its hopes and fears, its desires and struggles, its guilt and shame. When Americans recorded their dreams in their diaries, letters, and memoirs, they sought to make sense of the changing world around them, and to cope with the confusion, despair, and loneliness of life amid the turmoil of a war the likes of which they had never imagined.

Americans North and South were absorbed with their unconscious lives during that great and awful conflict—reliving distant memories or horrific experiences in battle, longing for a return to peace and life as they had known it before the war, kissing loved ones they had not seen for years, communing with the dead, traveling to faraway places they wished they could see in real life.[6] Friends shared their dreams with one another and sought to discern their meaning. Some tried desperately to remember their dreams. Women North and South adhered to an old superstition that naming their bedposts when they slept in a new bed would cause them to remember their dreams, or make their dreams come true. "O my prophetic soul! I do believe in dreams!" wrote one Confederate refugee in her diary. In order to remember her dreams when she slept away from home, she followed the peculiar ritual: "As usual, I named the bed posts, and prepared to remember my dreams."[7]

The recording and retelling of dreams served as a way to connect distant family members, exposing a deep link between the battlefield and the home front, and enabling twenty-first-century observers to discern a new dimension in the relationship between soldiers and their families. Recent scholarship has emphasized the divisions that emerged between soldiers and civilians as "hardened" soldiers found it difficult to relate to those who remained at home.[8] However, the dreams related between family members and friends reveal an intimate way that families sought to bridge that divide. Many Americans saw dreams as a real, almost tangible connection to their loved ones. "I dreamed Wednesday night that you were in a battle that day and it seems you were," wrote a Virginia woman to her husband a few days after the Battle of Antietam. Such dreams, she said, were evidence that "there is some magnetic chain between us and I can almost always tell . . . when you are in danger."[9] In fact, even nightmares could bring distant husbands and wives closer together emotionally—perhaps because they helped soldiers and civilians to realize how precious and precarious their earthly relationships were in times of danger.[10]

Distant spouses relished hearing each other's voices in their dreams, and parents and children loved seeing one another in nighttime visions. The conversations they envisioned in their sleeping brains felt to them like real communication with those at home. General Benjamin F. Butler's daughter, who was in school in Washington, D.C., wrote to her parents in faraway New Orleans: "It is well that thoughts can travel over the space, and imagination picture you all, for otherwise it would be very lonely. It is my most pleasant relaxation from study to try to think of what you are doing or saying, and dreaming thus I usually fall asleep."[11]

Dreams often served as powerful motivators for Civil War–era Americans. Many both North and South believed that their dreams offered supernatural revelations for their lives, or gave guidance for actions they should take. Some men dreamed about enlisting and then resolved to do so. In one case, a Philadelphian decided to enlist in the Union army after dreaming about George Washington. "Genl Washington appeared to me looking me in the eye said as he raised his hand in a solemn manner, 'This country must and shall be free,'" he wrote in his diary. Washington vanished after making this statement, but the sentiment lodged itself in the dreamer's mind. "When I awoke and told the dream to my wife, I said that means for me to go and fight for my country and my flag." His wife replied, "Go and God be with you." The next day he enlisted in a Zouave regiment.[12] When the father of the country appeared to someone in a dream it certainly merited serious consideration—even action.

Many Americans believed that their dreams were windows into the future, and they took their premonitions seriously. At various points during the war, ordinary Americans sent dream reports to their leaders, believing that their nighttime visions might offer guidance to those in command of the Union and Confederate governments. Private correspondence also often included descriptions of prophetic dreams accompanied by interpretations of their meaning. During the Peninsula Campaign in May 1862, Varina Howell Davis closed a letter to her husband, "We have been so much together of late years that my heart aches when I can not kiss you good night, and feel that I have you to lay my hand on when I wake." She then added ominously, "God grant dreams may not be warnings" and "may God in his goodness shield you in this your time of peril, and once more bring you safe to the arms of your devoted Winnie."[13]

Dream sharing had been an important part of antebellum life, and it continued with even greater urgency during the war years. Historian J. Matthew Gallman argues that "citizens at home turned to familiar means, aided by detailed letters, to cope with the harshest wartime losses."[14] The reporting of dreams was one crucial part in this process. As a case in point, almost every morning before the war, Ellie Goldwaite used to tell her husband, Richard, about the dreams she'd had the night before. When Richard left to fight with the Ninety-Ninth New York Infantry, she continued the tradition—only now she had to describe them in her letters. Some of her dreams, as we shall see, were terrifying. Others were more lighthearted, if not downright silly. The most frequent involved her husband coming home. Richard often responded to his wife's letters by revealing his own dreams, although he assured her, "I don't believe in dreams." He playfully called her "a kind of Fortune Teller," and said he hoped her dreams of him coming home would come true.[15]

Other soldiers responded to dreamers at home in similar ways. One Michigan cavalryman chastised his sister, telling her "to think nothing" of her "nonsensical dreams." "The cause of such dreams is this," he wrote; "your anxiety works itself to such a pitch thus to the over burdened mind it presents itself in the shape of a dream. I do hope you will not be so superstitious as to let these naughty dreams trouble the peace of your mind in the future."[16]

But these naysaying soldiers were in the minority in nineteenth-century America. More Americans were like Varina Davis, Ellie Goldwaite, and the cavalryman's sister. Fascination—if not obsession—with dreams, spiritualism, and other religious experiences saturated the world of Civil War Americans.[17] One day in 1859, a group of schoolchildren in upstate New York "listened with breathless attention" as their teacher explained "the nature of dreams and their cause and effect." By the end of the war little had changed. "To-day, here in the City of New York," wrote Phineas T. Barnum in 1866, "dream books are sold by the edition; a dozen fortune-tellers regularly advertise in the papers; a haunted house can gather excited crowds for weeks; abundance of people are uneasy if they spill salt, dislike to see the new moon over the wrong shoulder, and are delighted if they can find an old horse-shoe to nail to their door-post."[18] Americans of all stripes were thinking about their nighttime visions. As we will see, many soldiers and civilians who claimed not to "believe in dreams" still saw them as important enough to record and disseminate. The dreamscapes of ordinary Americans thus reveal a great deal about how Americans understood and experienced life and death during the Civil War.

AS YOUNG BOYS, Civil War soldiers had dreamed of the glory of going to war. Upon learning to read in the 1840s, Sidney Morris Davis's "slumbers were disturbed by warlike dreams, in which General George Washington, surmounted by a cocked hat, and on horseback, was the principal figure." In 1861 he would join a Federal cavalry unit to fight like his childhood hero. When first seeing the elephant, one Pennsylvania volunteer reflected on how this moment fulfilled the dreams of his youth. After resting in some woods, the bugle called the men to action "and the enthusiastic dream of my Boyhood[,] a battle filed [sic] with all its glorious pomp and Stern reality[,] opened up to our view."[19]

Now that millions of men were off to fight, the war turned the American experience on its head. Both night and day were affected by the conflict. Sleep patterns changed from what they had been in peacetime, restlessness plagued civilians and soldiers alike, and the weekly rhythms of a peaceful Sunday all but disappeared. Union general George B. McClellan sought to preserve Sabbath observance among the troops, saying, "One day's rest is necessary for man and animals." But his efforts were largely in vain. "The Sabbath has passed without my once remembering that it is our day of rest," wrote New York surgeon William Smith on a Sunday in August 1862. "I do not recall that this ever happened before. But there is, practically, no Sabbath here." Wrote another Union soldier, "Queer enough it would seem were I at home to see a hundred or more men take their axes and picks and spades and work with them the whole Sabbath but in War there is *no Sabbath*. All days are alike to us."[20]

The decrease of regular rest during the war led to increasing exhaustion among the men of both armies. General McClellan had recognized the importance of rejuvenation for both man and beast, but such a luxury could not be granted to most soldiers (or animals) in wartime. The perpetual movement of the campaigns eventually took its toll on the armies. One German soldier stationed in Missouri remarked in 1862 that "all of us suffered from such sleep deprivation that whoever sat down for a moment fell asleep immediately and could be awakened only with great effort. Half asleep, the soldiers marched. My horse lowered its head and plodded with closed eyes between the foot soldiers, and my own head also bowed down, being jerked up every ten minutes whenever my bent-over head was threatening me to lose my balance."[21] Sleep needed to be protected by the officer corps, but it wasn't. While Ulysses S. Grant ostensibly appreciated "the restorative qualities of sleep" (so said one of his staff officers), his strategy for winning the war during the Overland Campaign of 1864 wreaked more havoc on soldiers' rest than did any other period of the war.[22]

The war also affected—and afflicted—the sleep and dreams of soldiers' families. Wives who remained at home often missed the comforts and protection of their husbands, and children could no longer look to their fathers to scare away the monsters in their closets or the boogeymen under their beds. After describing where she and all of her children were sleeping, and her one son who "groans in his sleep" because of an earache, one Iowa woman told her husband, "Wish you were here to keep off the 'boogers' though I am not half so big a coward as I used to be."[23] Although they could not be at home to protect their families, soldiers on both sides believed that they were fighting so that their children could sleep in peace at home. Such realizations could be particularly heart-wrenching during the holidays. *Harper's Weekly* regularly published Christmas prints by Thomas Nast that juxtaposed illustrations of children sleeping warmly in their beds with their fathers who were serving in faraway cold, snowy battlefields.[24]

Soldiers and their spouses were not the only ones to lose sleep during the war. Even battle-hardened politicians could be unnerved by battlefield losses. "This is my seventh sleepless night—yours too, doubtless," wrote *New*

York Tribune editor Horace Greeley to Lincoln a week after the Union defeat at First Bull Run in July 1861, "yet I think I shall not die, because I have no right to die. I must struggle to live, however bitterly."[25]

Greeley marked his melodramatic missive "Midnight" as if to underscore the extent of his nightly suffering. But so early in the conflict—and so far away from the seat of war—the wily editor could not yet comprehend what would be coming over the next four years. Civilians who visited the front, by contrast, sometimes found themselves tortured by actual visions of what they had seen. Walt Whitman would later compose a poem about his dreams of the dead men he had seen in hospitals around Washington, D.C. Union nurse Kate Cummings was similarly plagued by nightmares of the suffering and wounded and dying. "Oh I felt so sad!" she wrote, "visions of the terrible past would rise in review before me—the days, weeks and months of suffering I had witnessed—and all for naught. Many a boyish and manly face, in the full hey-day of life and hope, now lying in the silent tomb."[26]

Being surrounded by the ever-increasing presence of death, soldiers and civilians frequently employed metaphorical language of sleep. Soldiers "slept" or took their "final rest" beneath Southern soil. Similes such as "like a dream" are also ubiquitous in soldiers' letters and recollections. Such language was often the best way citizen-soldiers knew to convey an experience they'd never imagined having—or, as they often put it, "never dreamed of." But aside from a brief discussion of these similes and metaphors in the Epilogue, I am not interested in figurative language of dreams, such as the Confederacy's "dream of independence" or the slaves' "dreams of freedom." And while other scholars have written about dreams in American fiction, those sorts of dreams have very little place in this book. I am interested in discerning the meaning of actual dreams of actual people.

When I say the "meaning" of these dreams, I mean their significance in a historical sense. I am not looking for symbols in dreams, nor am I doing psychohistory, or Freudian, Jungian, or post-Freudian analysis. Some readers may believe that a book about dreams should necessarily rely heavily on modern psychological or psychoanalytical theories; however, I would suggest that there is no reason that a history of dreams should be based in such theories any more or less than any other type of history. If psychology is the study of the human mind and human behavior, then psychological theories could just as easily be applied to any other type of history as they could to a history of dreams. Moreover, dream theories are contested and constantly changing.[27] Grounding this book in current theories would run the risk of making it anachronistic as the theories evolve or are discarded. Finally, and perhaps most importantly, I believe that the use of psychological theories in other histories of dreams has made those books less accessible to both historians and general readers.[28] For these reasons—and a few others that are discussed in the Note on Method—psychological theories make a very limited appearance in this book.

Instead, I am looking for patterns and major themes that emerge from a wide array of dream reports to see what dreams tell us about the daily (and nightly) experiences of the Civil War generation. Americans of the mid-nineteenth century recognized that their dreams reflected something significant about their emotional states of being. Indeed, writing shortly before the war, Henry David Thoreau observed, "In dreams we see ourselves naked and acting out our real characters, even more clearly than we see others awake." Ideas like these were spreading throughout the culture. To be sure, many Americans still adhered to the idea that dreams might be supernatural revelations; but, as historian Andrew Burstein has shown, the word "dream" had become synonymous with "wish" or "hope" in the years just before the Civil War. Clearly Americans of this period recognized that a connection existed between their waking concerns and their unconscious mind-wanderings at night.[29]

That so many Americans recorded their dreams reveals how significant dreams were to members of that society. Soldiers and civilians often looked to dreamed knowledge for warning, guidance, inspiration, or self-reflection. But dreams did not only influence individual dreamers. During such an intense national upheaval, Northerners and Southerners alike also found shared meaning, solace, and comfort for their suffering in their sleep. In sharing their dreams with each other, dreams often became a respite from the war.

NIGHTTIME DURING THE CIVIL WAR might reasonably be considered the most sleepless period in American history. Americans North and South, both soldier and civilian, experienced perpetual exhaustion. Soldiers faced the even greater danger of a "sleep debt," which resulted from their spending night after night without restful sleep. Modern sleep research has found that it can take days to recover from the loss of just one night's sleep. But as the war dragged on, soldiers rarely had the opportunity to recoup lost sleep.

Sleep deprivation could have significant effects on soldiers' physical health, mental well-being, and combat effectiveness. Utterly exhausted soldiers often lost the ability to make sound judgments under pressure. During the Overland Campaign, a picket from New York "whose mind had suddenly left him under the great pressure of hard service and loss of sleep" shot and killed an officer who approached him at night before the officer could offer the countersign. The picket then became "a raving maniac." As historian Carol A. Reardon writes, loss of sleep "exacerbates a number of recognized symptoms of battle fatigue" and "can produce results on psychological and physical reaction-time tests equivalent to those registered by test subjects who were legally drunk."[30]

Soldiers were routinely court-martialed for drunkenness on duty during the Civil War, but some may have actually been sleep deprived rather than intoxicated. Pvt. John Daly of the Fifth U.S. Regulars, for example, testified at his own trial, "I staggered when I got up out of my sleep" but denied that he had had anything to drink. Rather, he claimed that he "was unwell and sleepy and had not slept the night before." Nevertheless, he was found guilty and sentenced to three months at hard labor. Pvt. John Wilson of the Second California Volunteers admitted to having a drink of liquor but claimed that lack of sleep and not intoxication explained why he fell asleep on guard duty. He had been a prisoner for the four days prior to his offense, he said, and had been unable to lie down and sleep in the crowded guardhouse. "In consequence of the state of my head from want of sleep I was completely unsteady," he claimed at his trial. Nevertheless, Wilson, too, was found guilty of drunkenness on duty and was sentenced to dishonorable discharge after six months at hard labor with an eighteen-pound ball and chain.[31] Both of these trials took place far away from the battlefield—Daly was in New Mexico, while Wilson was in California. The significance of these cases is that sleep deprivation was a universal problem during the war, affecting those both near and far from the scenes of combat.

Historians who criticize the poor judgment of officers on the battlefield should always consider the effects of sleep deprivation upon soldiers' capacities to think clearly. Bad decision-making and battlefield blunders must not simply be viewed within the context of "the fog of war," or the result of cowardice, incompetence, or indecision. Scholars must also pay close attention to the lack of sleep that Civil War soldiers had in the nights and even weeks before a battle. Consider one of the most notorious frontal attacks of the Civil War: Union general Ambrose Burnside's assault at Fredericksburg on December 13, 1862. Historian George C. Rable astutely points out that "loss of sleep was catching up with" Burnside and that he "was not in the best condition to launch a risky attack against the strongest part of the Confederate line."[32] Perhaps paying more attention to sleep, as Rable has done, can help better explain other actions—both great and small—on the battlefield.

Modern sleep research has also found that exhaustion and sleep deprivation lead to increased intensity of dreams, especially when sleep deprived persons finally experience a sound slumber. "When someone is sleep deprived we see greater sleep intensity, meaning greater brain activity during sleep; dreaming is definitely increased and likely more vivid," states one neurologist. This process is known as REM (rapid eye movement) rebound.[33]

REM sleep is the period in which people dream most often and most vividly. Usually REM is the fifth stage of sleep occurring in each cycle (following four non-REM stages, the first of which is nodding off). However, people who have been deprived of REM sleep often jump directly into the REM stage and begin dreaming as soon as they doze off (modern researchers call this a sleep onset REM period). Such a phenomenon is known to occur in children and adolescents, after sleep disorders, in some sleep disorders (such as narcolepsy), in situations of stress (such as postpartum), and in other situations, but it is not the typical state of affairs for human adults. However, it is likely that Civil War soldiers experienced dreams early in their sleep precisely because of how tired and stressed they were. In fact, soldiers often described dreaming the moment they fell asleep. One example will suffice to demonstrate the point here. During the Overland Campaign in 1864, two exhausted New Hampshire soldiers fell asleep next to each other during the fighting at Spotsylvania Courthouse—only to wake up a few minutes later when one of their comrades was shot and cried out in pain. The two awakened men looked at each other and recounted their dreams. Both had dreamed of going home to see their families, and one remarked, "I wish it were all real."

What seemed notable to these soldiers was not that they had dreamed, but that they had slept under fire. One of them wrote after the war that it "may seem incredible" to civilians that soldiers could fall asleep while under fire from the enemy. But the soldiers were "so completely worn out by toil, watching, and anxiety," he wrote, "that the moment we stopped and lay down we went to sleep in spite of every effort to keep awake."[34] From a modern scientific perspective, however, it may be more significant that they had dreamed. Their dreaming under fire reveals just how physically and mentally exhausted the troops had become. In their exhausted state, they almost instantly fell into stage REM, which, again, is normally a later sleep stage more conducive to blocking out the world.[35] Understanding this

"The Tired Soldier—A Sketch from Life at Petersburg during the Siege, June 19th, 1864." Courtesy of the Library of Congress.

modern sleep science may help explain why dreams were so meaningful to so many soldiers. Their utter exhaustion (and their frequent falling asleep in a sleep onset REM period) led to extraordinary, often scenario-like dreams—dreams that soldiers regularly described as "vivid" or "singular"— dreams that had emotional significance for the soldiers and that were therefore worth writing home about. Along these lines, it is worth noting that these two soldiers had both experienced pleasant dreams of home, with one of them even voicing his desire for the escape of sleep.

Understanding soldiers' and civilians' sleep patterns is thus essential to understanding their dreams. Chapter 1 of this book therefore begins by examining the sleeplessness of Union and Confederate soldiers. This brief survey covers the entire war rather than one battle or campaign. Scholars often emphasize the distinctiveness of the Overland Campaign—and it was distinctive; however, sleep deprivation was a problem in many other places and at many different times during the war.[36] Only after we have come to understand the utter exhaustion of the troops as described in chapter 1 can we turn to their dreams in chapter 2.[37]

Fortunately for us, Americans of the Civil War generation kept a remarkable record of their dream experiences. In the pages that follow, we will see a new side of the Civil War, a world in which a man from New York has no compunctions about telling his friends that he'd dreamed of nursing a baby; a woman in Texas openly shares her nightmares of childbirth; and a war correspondent tells his readers of an embarrassing bed-sharing incident with strangers, leading to outlandish dreams—which he also shares with the public.[38] Whether nighttime visions were uplifting or distressing, ordinary or bizarre, soldiers and civilians reported their dreams to one another, freely expressing their deepest and most intimate feelings, vulnerabilities, desires, aspirations, anxieties, insecurities, and hopes. Contrary to the arguments of other historians who have examined historical dreams, these dreams and dream reports did not necessarily conform to the cultural expectations of Victorian America.[39] Far from being straitlaced or puritanical, soldiers and civilians showed little reluctance to report their violent, racy, or embarrassing dreams. They were surprisingly candid and forthright. As a consequence, the dream reports in this book offer an extraordinary glimpse into the emotional world of Civil War–era Americans.

At the same time, the prevalence of domestic matters in soldiers' dreams reveals the cultural power of sentimentalism in nineteenth-century America. More than anything else, men in the field dreamed of those they loved back home, and they often woke up and penned affecting letters to their wives and sweethearts. Moreover, as we will see, when soldiers awoke in the morning they were often disappointed that their dreamscapes were not reality. Such emotions were experienced morning after morning by many men of both armies, countering the prevalent idea among historians today that soldiers had lost their ability to have sympathy and feel because they had become hardened to war.

Modern scholarship often focuses on the emotionally destructive effects the war had upon the fighting men in blue and gray as well as on their families and communities. In *Embattled Courage*, for example, Gerald F. Linderman argues that "soldiers suffered a disillusionment more profound than historians have acknowledged—or the soldiers themselves would concede." Linderman defines disillusionment as "the deeply depressive condition arising from the demolition of soldiers' conceptions of themselves and their performance in war."[40]

While there is certainly some truth about the hardness and trauma of the war in the arguments of Linderman and others, no matter how difficult, trying, or exhausting the war became, Civil War soldiers, as a whole, showed remarkable psychological strength and resilience.[41] Modern scholars have become interested in exploring the extent to which Civil War soldiers experienced symptoms akin to post-traumatic stress disorder (PTSD). This line of inquiry stems from our increased awareness of the psychological effects of warfare upon fighting men and women.[42] To be clear, *Midnight in America* is not a study of PTSD. To explore the disease among Civil War soldiers would require study of multiple symptoms, as well as a much deeper understanding of each individual soldier's background, personality traits, and postwar dreams and experiences.[43] But as persistent nightmares are a common experience among those who suffer from post-traumatic stress, this book may have something to contribute to that discussion.[44]

One recent study of PTSD maintains that soldiers "never" dream about war while they are in theater.[45] This is certainly an overstatement. Ironically, historians of the Civil War may err in the opposite direction, assuming that Civil War soldiers experienced bad dreams more than they actually did. James M. McPherson, for example, writes that "many soldiers fought battles over again in nightmares." Michael C. C. Adams similarly suggests that "nightmares" were "particularly common after major actions."[46] As we will see, however, pleasant dreams of home far outnumbered nightmares of battle.[47]

The study of dreams may speak to other historiographical debates as well. Historians often point to ways that the Civil War portended the great "total" wars of the twentieth century. The sleeplessness of soldiers may have pointed forward to modern warfare, but their dreams largely did not. Confederate civilians—especially women—may be an exception. As we will see in chapter 3, they often had frightening and traumatic nightmares of invading Yankee hordes. Yet even these terrible nighttime visions may point back in time as much as they point toward dreaming in future wars. During the American Revolution, for example, women in occupied Philadelphia dreamed of violent armed conflicts, of their city engulfed in flames, of starving children walking through a sea of blood, and of being hanged, among other terrifying things.[48] It seems there may be nothing modern at all about bad dreams of war.

Midnight in America

CHAPTER ONE

The Soldier's Rest

Wyman S. White was tired. The previous day the young private had sustained an injury when he fell from a fence. Now, one evening in early May 1862, he was ordered to stand on picket duty along a road in Falmouth, Virginia. This wet, cold night seemed like "the longest night I had ever experienced," he later recalled. The next day, White's captain volunteered the company to serve on guard duty in Falmouth for as long as the provost marshal might want while the captain would remain behind in a comfortable home that had been abandoned by a local Confederate family. "Of course the Marshal was pleased to have a permanent guard," wrote White. "In return it gave our captain a parlor for his quarters, a fine bed to sleep in, a good cook to cook his rations and bring them in to the dining room table, also the other colored girls to attend to his wants." White continued furiously, "To himself he appeared a king. To me it gave five weeks of steady guard duty two hours on and four hours off the beat night and day."

Some of the guards in White's regiment were posted at houses and "had very little to do but to take their meals which were provided by the people where they were on duty." At night these guards even got to sleep in easy chairs. Guards posted at hospitals had no duty after 9 or 10 P.M. But the men who had to serve on guard duty on the streets—like White—"did duty two hours on and four hours off, night and day."

White believed that the soldiers should have been rotated among these various posts, but his officers "did not see fit to be put to that trouble." So he was stuck in a street post from 8 to 10 A.M., 2 to 4 P.M., 8 to 10 P.M., and 2 to 4 A.M. day after day after day. His terms during the normal waking hours tended to be "very busy," but the graveyard shift was often slow and monotonous.

Every morning, White made it to bed by 4:30 A.M., but he was up again by 7 A.M. In any twenty-four-hour period, he never got more than three hours' sleep at a time. "The result of the loss of sleep was such that a few days during the last time I was so sleepy in the night from two to four o'clock when there was very little doing that I could not keep awake even while walking my beat. Often I came near falling." Once, while carrying his rifle at right shoulder shift, he lost his balance and sent his gun flying so that

1

"the bayonet stuck in the ground so as to stand fast with the butt of the weapon up."

For five weeks, White endured this outrageous and abusive duty. Finally, one day he told his lieutenant that "I must have sleep," and he was granted permission to sleep for a night. But his replacement claimed to be sick before the 2 A.M. shift, so the corporal of the guard aroused White from his sleep and ordered him to the post. White refused, saying he had been given the night off. Not knowing how to respond, the corporal asked another officer what to do. "Tell him to either go on his post or to the Guardhouse," the officer replied. When the corporal awoke White a second time to relay the message, White stated "that I would go to the guardhouse but not on the beat so I slipped my feet into my shoes, picked up my blankets and was ready to go."

The guardhouse was a two-story brick tobacco warehouse near the bank of a creek. Among the inmates were horse thieves, accused murderers, and rebel guerrillas. When he arrived, White found the floor "covered with sleeping men, most of them without blankets and the majority of them wore grey." He noticed a "long and narrow" counter, four feet high, that he determined was "the best place in the room for sleep." Finally, he received the "great boon" he had so long sought: "Sleep, Sleep, grateful sleep." He slept until ten the next morning. After a few conversations and a small breakfast, "I bunked down and was sound asleep again." He slept again until 3 P.M., when he was awakened by a guard who was loudly calling his name from the doorway.

Word of White's treatment traveled up the chain of command. Some officers were outraged; others feared they might get in trouble for mistreating soldiers on guard duty. To make up for the weeks of mistreatment, White was given another night off and then transferred to guard duty at a hospital, where he never had to stand at a post after 9 P.M. "So, as it turned out, I had no fault to find with my night's sleep in the guardhouse," White later recalled with some satisfaction.[1]

Wanting to sleep during picket duty or guard duty was common among soldiers in both armies during the Civil War, and exhausted soldiers often found it impossible to keep their droopy eyes open. Pvt. Grant Taylor of the Fortieth Alabama Infantry described the great lengths he went to stay awake one night during picket duty in May 1864. "I never was sleepier in my life," he told his wife, "and I had to stand up all night to keep from going to sleep and even standing I would sometimes dream."[2] One Vermont officer similarly noted, "I have seen the boys walking on their beat regularly when they were so completely asleep that they could not observe my ap-

"Sketches with Co. B, 8th Reg. Pa. Ma. under the Officers of the Old Southwark Guard." Courtesy of the Library of Congress.

proach till I spoke to them. They would mechanically execute their duty, but consciousness had fled."[3]

The most famous sleeping sentinel of the Civil War was Pvt. William Scott of the Third Vermont Infantry. Just a few short weeks after enlisting, on July 10, 1861, this "big, awkward country lad who had a heart as big as he was" found himself encamped near the Potomac River in Georgetown. On August 29, he volunteered to take picket duty for a friend. The next night he had to serve on picket duty again. Sometime between 3 and 4 A.M. on the morning of August 31, Scott was found asleep at his post near Camp Lyon. He was arrested and court-martialed for violating the Forty-Sixth Article of War.

The trial commenced at 10 A.M. on Tuesday, September 3. Scott pleaded innocent to the charge and offered no defense. He was quickly found guilty and sentenced to be shot to death on September 9.

Scott's regimental chaplain and 191 other officers and enlisted men sent a petition to the commanding general asking for clemency. On September 8, Gen. George B. McClellan wrote to his wife, "Mr. Lincoln came this morning to ask me to pardon a man that I had ordered to be shot, suggesting that I could give as a reason in the order that it was by request of the 'Lady President.'"

On the morning of September 9, the Third Vermont and several other regiments were drawn into a hollow square to witness Scott's execution. A firing squad of twelve men—reportedly including one of Scott's brothers—took its position, and the unfortunate prisoner stood awaiting the execution of his sentence. One witness wrote, "He was deadly pale and shook from head to foot and was almost unable to sustain his weight."

As the assembled troops stood watching, something unexpected happened. Rather than read the sentence of execution, an officer read a pardon. It stated that President Lincoln had "expressed a wish that as this is the first condemnation to death in this army for this crime, mercy may be extended to the criminal." The pardon noted Scott's "inexperience," as well as "his previous good conduct and general good character, and the urgent entreaties made on his behalf." But of greater importance, the message underscored that this "act of clemency must not be understood as affording a precedent for any future case. The duty of a sentinel is of such a nature, that its neglect by sleeping upon or deserting his post may endanger the safety of a command, or even of the whole army, and all nations affix to the offence the penalty of death."

Regimental officers recognized the importance of what had just transpired. "It is hard to make them realize the fact that the responsibility of a sentry is great—awfully great in an enemy's country," wrote an officer in the Second Vermont. "This, however, will do them some good."

Scott was released and returned to duty. The men gave a cheer for Lincoln that "made the land of Dixie ring for miles around." One Democrat in the brigade was so elated that he pledged "to vote for 'Abe' if he is ever [a] candidate again."[4]

At least 2,000 Union soldiers were court-martialed for falling asleep at their post, about ninety of whom were sentenced to be executed. Men with professional military experience on both sides believed that those who slept at their post should be shot as an example to other soldiers because sleeping sentinels put entire camps and armies at risk. Confederate president Jefferson Davis stated that "sleepless watchfulness should be required of" Confederate pickets, noting that without such vigilance the pickets would be "worse than useless to the commands which rely upon them for timely notice of the approach of an enemy."[5]

Union general William Tecumseh Sherman agreed. When forwarding to Washington the court-martial proceedings of Avery Sheridan, an Ohio soldier who had been sentenced to be shot to death in 1862 for sleeping at his post, Sherman included a petition for mercy that had been signed by the members of the court. But Sherman also asked Lincoln to ignore the petition. "I admit the appearance & manner of the youth appeal to all who see him," wrote Sherman. "Still the circumstances of his sleeping when the whole Army lay within sight of our Enemy, the importance of the Post, the factor which does not appear of Record that he could not have been fatigued, as he had not marched or worked in the trenches that day, and the necessity for an example in this too common an offense among volunteers deter me from joining in the Petition."

Sherman continued that if Lincoln decided to grant mercy, he hoped that the president would "do it in such a manner as will not tend to diminish the importance attached by all military men to this particular offence." Still, Sherman pleaded with the president to make an example of this soldier. The masses of the armies could only sleep soundly if they could be confident that their camps were being guarded by alert sentries:

> No body of men can be healthy & strong without natural sleep, and no man can sleep in the presence of an Enemy without the Sense of perfect security which can only be experienced when all know that the camp is guarded by vigilant sentinels. The Regular soldier has this feeling of perfect safety, whilst the volunteer is ever restless & uneasy because he knows that his comrades like himself are not ever watchful. This simple fact accounts in part for the vast amount of sickness & debility among our Volunteers and affords one reason why a superhuman effort should be made to correct the evil.

The general explained that the "known severity of the punishment" had caused him to "overlook many cases which came under my personal observation." And he knew it was "almost impossible to make volunteer officers report the cases which they discover." But now, he concluded, it was "full time that we begin to consider ourselves soldiers engaged in Real War." Only by protecting the sleep of the masses—by executing those who fell asleep on picket duty—could the Union army mobilize enough strong and healthy fighting men to actually defeat the Confederates.

Sherman was likely disappointed with what transpired next. Upon reviewing the case in Washington, Judge Advocate General Joseph Holt found a technicality in the record that invalidated the proceedings. Lincoln affirmed Holt's finding, and Private Sheridan was released.[6]

The outcomes of William Scott's and Avery Sheridan's cases were by no means unique. Of the ninety men sentenced to be executed for sleeping at their post, Lincoln commuted the sentences of each and every one of them.[7]

There is some irony in this. General Sherman is often credited with bringing modernity to warfare during the Civil War, but in the case of sleeping sentinels, it was Lincoln and not Sherman who pointed toward the future. Execution for sleeping at one's post was fast becoming a thing of the past.

Still, Sherman touched on a point that all soldiers had to learn. Discipline in the face of exhaustion and hardship was essential for an army to be successful in "Real War." Union and Confederate soldiers learned this lesson throughout the conflict. As much as they hated to see their comrades executed—and they really did abhor those scenes—they understood the necessity of punishing, even severely, those who let down their fellow soldiers. Charles Harvey Brewster captured this complexity in a letter to his sister shortly after William Scott was pardoned: "You sympathize a great deal with a young man that was sentenced to be shot, more perhaps than you would, if you had to sleep in camp and lie down at night, and sleep depending upon the vigilance of the Sentry's for your life and perhaps for the lives of the whole camp." Still, Brewster was "glad" that Scott had "been pardoned, as I had no doubt he would be, but the next one will not get off so easy there is to[o] much depending on sentinels, to have them get into the habit of sleeping on their posts."[8]

General Sherman was correct when he stated that officers would often choose not to report sleeping sentinels. Some officers hoped to avoid the situation altogether. One innovative and compassionate officer found a way to teach his men not to sleep at their posts. When a lieutenant in the Sixty-Fifth Ohio found four sentries asleep, he hid their guns and shouted, "The rebels are coming!" Lt. Col. Wilbur F. Hinman of that regiment later recalled, "The sleepers sprang to their feet in wild alarm and vainly scratched around after their muskets, only to find that they were being taught a lesson in the duty of soldiers." The lieutenant lectured the men but promised not to report them. Still, he "reminded them that the penalty for sleeping on post was death, which they seemed to have forgotten," and "they began to realize that it was something of a serious matter."[9]

The experiences of pickets like Wyman S. White, William Scott, Avery Sheridan, and the sleeping sentinels from Ohio reveal several harsh truths about sleep during the Civil War. First, extreme sleep deprivation pervaded the armies throughout the entire four years of the war, not only during the final year. Second, professional military authorities did not appreciate the importance of sleep. Today, we understand that the human body requires a fixed amount of rest in order for the brain's motor skills to function properly. In the nineteenth century, the army did not know any better. Professional military men thought that falling asleep on picket duty reflected the inherent weakness of a person's character, not the physiological limitations of the human body. If a sentinel fell asleep, that meant that he was ill disciplined. The army, therefore, did not yet realize that it was necessary to take steps to protect sleep.[10]

Within this context, Lincoln's pardoning of the ninety sleeping sentinels takes on a new meaning. Historians often treat Lincoln's pardons as evidence of the president's exceptional mercy toward simple-minded soldier boys. Private Scott, after all, was inexperienced and not yet ready for the stern realities of army life. But Lincoln's pardoning of these soldiers was more than just mercy—it was an act of justice. Military authorities were not protecting soldiers' sleep, so that job fell to the president. In pardoning soldiers like Scott and Sheridan and the eighty-eight others, Lincoln was not merely a softhearted president interfering with army discipline—he was also a wise commander in chief correcting a severe problem within the Union's system of military justice.

HISTORIANS HAVE UNDERESTIMATED the importance of sleep to Civil War soldiers. It is remarkable how often soldiers described their beds, or remarked on the quality of their slumber, in their letters and diaries. Soldiers intuitively understood that sleep was a common experience that civilians back home could relate to and understand. As a consequence, they frequently commented on their sleep habits (or lack thereof). For as far away as the battlefield might be from the home front, soldiers knew that they were going to bed at the same time as their loved ones, and it gave them a special connection to home. "Well it is after Tattoo and mighty cold both for the toes and fingers while you tumble into a warm bed I must roll myself in my blanket and sleep as soundly upon the bosom of Mother Earth," wrote one Massachusetts soldier to his sister.[11]

Soldiers longed to feel an intimate connection with those at home. Perhaps they could read the Bible together, as they had done at bedtime in peaceful evenings gone by. "The first of Jan I commenced reading the bible through," wrote one Confederate soldier to his sister. "I commenced in the 1st chapter of Genesis and read two chapters every night. So about dark if you would know what I'm thinking of turn to your bible and read with me. This is the 12th and tonight I read from the 23 and 24 chapters of Genesis."[12] Others strained to believe that they'd been thinking about the same thing at the same time as those at home. While we don't know the background to this letter, one Georgia soldier told his wife to tell their toddler daughter "that I dreamed of huging and kissing either that night or near about it. I believe as well as I can recolect it was that very same night. We were all lying in line of battle on a hill some 3/4 of a mile from these camps."[13]

Even more comforting was the realization that husbands and wives were looking at the same moon and stars before turning in. After surveying the destruction around Fredericksburg on Christmas in 1862, Mississippi soldier Franklin Lafayette Riley remarked in his diary, "There is some comfort (not much) in knowing that, if she is looking at the heavens to-night, she sees the same stars I do. So we are not far apart after all."[14] But others felt tremendous peace in those quiet moments. "It is a source of great comfort to me to look at the moon at night and think perhaps you are at that moment looking at the same object," a Georgia soldier wrote his wife. "Sometimes I become so spell bound that I see your Shadow, with children playing around you on the face of the moon. *Then how I do gaze!*"[15] A black sergeant fighting with the Third U.S. Colored Infantry similarly thought of his family as he stared into the night sky. "i look up at the stars and ask god to bless you and take care of you," he told his wife.[16] Such quiet moments helped soldiers cope with their separation from loved ones during wartime.

Some soldiers could only imagine what their wives and children were doing at bedtime. "I wonder how it is at Mt. Pleasant, and what my sweet Emeline is doing?" wrote Iowa soldier Jacob Ritner to his wife one rainy night at 8 P.M. in November 1862. "I expect the children are all in bed and you are sitting up trying to write me a letter. No, I expect you are in bed too, and taking a good sleep, without thinking about Jake, but maybe you are sick or some of the children, or somebody is there and you are all sitting around the stove talking, or perhaps you are down at Ma's or someplace." The mysteriousness of his wife's experience at bedtime was difficult for Ritner to bear. "I wish I knew all about it. Won't you write and tell me. Do, my sweet dear." When Ritner finally concluded his letter two hours later—at 10 P.M.—he closed, "I know you are in bed sleeping by this time and don't hear a word I say. If I was there I would jump in and give you a good hug and kiss and wake you up."[17] Thinking of his wife being out and about was difficult for this lonely soldier, but envisioning her asleep in bed was a sweet comfort.

Many soldiers' letters described their sleeping arrangements down to the minutiae. Some included drawings and sketches of their beds and tents. Such descriptions offered assurances to loved ones of their health and safety.[18] Many wrote home about the beauty of sleeping outside under the open sky. "My temporary quarters were in the loveliest grove of trees, and as I sat & nodded on that door step, the mocking birds sang all night like nightingales, in the sweet air & among the blossoming trees," wrote Thomas Wentworth Higginson. "Since then we have arranged our defences & sleep soundly."[19] Others enjoyed resting "in a beautiful clover field bordered by a wood" or pitching tents "in the most beautiful grove you ever saw."[20] "Our camp was lighted only by the stars and with no canopy but the sky," wrote one New Yorker who "slept as sweetly as ever on my own soft bed at home" as he did on a bundle of oats in the field.[21]

Some soldiers remembered their army accommodations for the rest of their lives.[22] "The first night in camp will doubtless long be remembered by many," an Illinois veteran recalled about a decade after the war. Those who tried to sleep on their first night in camp were often "cruelly defrauded out of so laudable a purpose by the many who, unrestrained, gave full vent to their joyous hilarity and ceaseless mischief, deluging the camp with fun and noises the most hideous and unearthly, as if a new Pandemonium had at once broken loose." This veteran remembered his first night in camp, when a man shouted, "Baa!" Another from a nearby tent responded in kind, and then another, until "the chorus" was "taken up along the line of tents from all parts of camp, and in ten seconds from the first yelp the whole crowd would be 'baaing' with the force of a thousand calf power."[23] This sort of raucous behavior was common among "green" soldiers. Another raw recruit wrote in 1863, "We could not sleep much—the natural excitement attendant upon our novel situation and the continual singing, hurrahing & general uproar prevented our feeling sleepy."[24]

Restless soldiers often came up with makeshift remedies for their insomnia. One Texas cavalryman found that washing his feet "caused me to sleep well."[25] Others needed something stronger. Col. Asbury Coward of the Fifth South Carolina Volunteers ingested morphine and lay down to dream of "Elysian fields with sunshine everywhere. Beautiful flowers sent their perfume on the wings of gentle zephyrs which fanned my brow and charmed me to sweet, restful sleep. A dryad, made of mist was bending over me."[26] To forget about the cold at night, another soldier would "reach out for a jug of whiskey and take a swallow and go back to sleep again."[27] But others feared the use of drugs. "If de Doctor put me to sleep," one former slave now serving in the Union army remarked about chloroform, "he never let me wake up."[28]

The darkness of night in the wartime South was brighter than most rural Americans had experienced at home in antebellum times, and they marveled at what they saw. One Union surgeon stationed in Hampton Roads, Virginia, observed "the whole horizon . . . ablaze with the camp fires of men." A British observer was struck by "the effect of the thousands of camp fires, or perhaps 20 miles long by 6 or 8 deep twinkling throughout the country." A Pennsylvania officer thought that the "camp fires of fifty thousand troops over the valley looked like the gas lights of a large city." Indeed, the sight of "a thousand Camp fires," observed one Indiana surgeon, "shine on the hills around."[29]

SOLDIERS' SLEEPING ARRANGEMENTS changed with the seasons. Whenever an army went on campaign—which typically occurred during the spring and summer months—soldiers used their blankets, knapsacks, cartridge boxes, or jackets for a pillow. Some used saddles or blankets wrapped around blocks of wood. As Spartan as these accommodations were, they represented the most comfortable ways to sleep on campaign. For instance, one Ohio soldier could find nothing but "a pile of broken rocks for a pillow." A few of his Confederate counterparts fared a little better with "roots for pillows." Even when they had a soft pillowcase stuffed full of clothes, soldiers and sailors might still complain. One sailor aboard the USS *Florida* wrote his wife that his pillowcase "had imbibed a quantity of No. Carolina filth" and was not "conducive to pleasant dreams when one is partial to clean bedding."[30]

The most common form of dwelling for the rank and file was the dog, or shelter, tent. Each soldier was given a piece of canvas measuring five feet two inches by four feet eight inches. The soldier then found a "chum" with whom to sleep, and each pair buttoned their two halves together, hanging them over a horizontal rope or stick. The tent was held up either by two vertical sticks or by the soldiers' upended muskets, stuck into the ground with fixed bayonets. One veteran quipped that they were called dog tents because they "would only comfortably accommodate a dog, and a small one at that."[31]

Dog tents were not the most stable source of shelter. In June 1863, one Union soldier wrote, "Some of the boys had their tents blown nearly down owing to the pins giving way." Nor could the canvas keep out the heat of the southern sun. "The sun is scarce an hour high yet," wrote one Yankee doctor, "but it already strikes through my tent with a furnace glow."

Another soldier wished that "the man who invented them had been hung before the invention was completed."[32]

During the frigid months of the year, when the armies could not risk a campaign, soldiers built winter quarters, which often consisted of log huts that could sleep four to ten men depending on the size. Unfortunately, soldiers might spend weeks building winter quarters and then be forced to abandon them the moment they were complete. After spending some time in November 1862 sleeping on the "wet ground in the open air," Confederate private William Cleg and his comrades felled some trees and built winter quarters. On December 17, 1862, Cleg wrote with disappointment that he had been ordered to pack up and prepare for an attack. "Every thing is now ready for a hasty move," he scrawled in his diary. "I am afraid we will leave our new huts but hope we will give the enemy an opportunity of forcing us from them."[33]

Union soldiers who happened upon abandoned winter quarters appreciated the luxury. "I am sitting in a former Confederate hut—a very comfortable place considered as soldiers' quarters, with a large stone fireplace in which the boys have built a big blazing fire, for the air is chilly," wrote chaplain Joseph H. Twichell in November 1862. The poor Confederates who had built such a "really palatial abode," as Twichell called it, must have sorely regretted having to give it up. But Twichell, too, could not get too comfortable. Two weeks later he wrote with disappointment that he would have to leave his quarters and depart for Fredericksburg.[34]

Even permanent residences were never really safe. When paymaster William Keeler returned to the USS *Monitor* after a brief hiatus, he found that "some evil disposed person . . . had appropriated my matrass, leaving a wooden gridiron for anyone desiring to experience a *cold* broil on the naked slats through the coming night." Upon realizing that another officer had not yet returned to the ship, he "rolled myself up in his blankets & woke the next morning to a shivering sense of a cold room, a cheerless aspect within and a furious snow storm without."[35]

Soldiers intuitively knew that their beds were never really their own. A Missouri soldier stationed near the Gulf Coast who slept "on some Matrasses that are stained with Blood" wondered grimly whether "some of my comrades have yielded up their spirit to god from off this verry Matress on which I sit."[36] Even more macabre, a young soldier named Willie Clark who rented a room at the Petersen boarding house across the street from Ford's Theatre, in Washington, D.C., continued to sleep on the mattress on which his commander in chief had died on April 15, 1865. In a letter written to his sister shortly after the assassination, he enclosed a piece of lace that had fallen from Mary Lincoln's clothes onto his bedroom floor. "It is worth keeping for its historical value," he told her. "I have a lock of Mr. Lincoln's hair, which I have had neatly framed; also a piece of linen with a portion of his brain."[37]

MOTHER NATURE WREAKED havoc on an army's sleep. Indeed, the extremes in southern weather—the heat and humidity of a Virginia summer or the steamy mornings on a Mississippi bayou—often cost Union soldiers a good night's rest. "All last night our boys lay out in the rain entirely unprotected and every man was as drenched as water could make him, yet their pluck is unabated," wrote Chaplain Twichell in May 1862. "I was thankful and amazed this morning to witness their spirit. I tell you, Father, I did not imagine before now, how much men can endure. . . . I woke this morning after a sound sleep, to find myself partially submerged in water, and at this present moment I have not a dry thread on me, yet I never felt better in my life." This sort of experience was not at all unusual for Civil War soldiers. A Wisconsin infantryman remarked after a cold midnight downpour in January 1863, "Its a good thing for me that I learned in my childhood to swim or I might have drowned this morning . . . when I woke I had to put my swimming powers to use to get out of bed."[38]

For some soldiers, the patter of a nighttime rain brought back memories of childhood and home; it also could drown out the usual sounds of camp life. Alabama soldier Hiram Smith Williams recorded in his diary one rainy night that "we smiled at the inclemency of the weather and sought our limbs to be soothed to refreshing slumber by the pleasant patter on the roof." Listening to these sounds brought back "glorious childish memories" to Williams's mind. He continued: "How many a night I have been soothed to the sound of sweet sleep of boyhood by the rain, and how well I remember it, in the dear, delightful place that ever has been, and ever will be, *home*."[39]

But when Williams did not have shelter, his feelings about the rain were less enthusiastic. Covered with only two blankets one stormy night—and sleeping on a steep hillside—Williams and his comrades "had to stick our heels in the ground to keep from sliding down." Between the crooked campground and the pouring rain, the men "could not sleep a wink." Still, Williams recognized at least one benefit in the rain—stormy weather could bring a brief hiatus from the war. "Thank Heaven the fighting has ceased for a time," he wrote, "and the tired soldier, even if he cannot sleep, can at least feel that he has a short respite from danger."[40]

Few men were cheerful on a wet morning. The "rain poured in perfect torrents," Charles Harvey Brewster told his mother in May 1862. "I wish you could have seen me last night but you can imagine yourself sleeping in a swamp under two umbrellas and in a harder storm than you ever saw. thats the nearest to it of anything I can illustrate our condition." During such torrents, canvas tents provided little actual shelter "and men awoke from dreams of home and other luxuries to find themselves wetter than if they had just emerged from the neighboring mill ponds." Following one heavy rainstorm, a Union soldier compared his tent to "fish nets or mosquito bars." And along with summer thunderstorms came "oppressive" heat and humidity that often made it difficult to be comfortable doing anything.[41]

The freezing temperatures of winter could be as detrimental to sleep as the heat of summer. "At three o'clock this morning I woke up nearly frozen," wrote Brewster in April 1862. On another cold night he awoke with his "feet in thin stockings stuck out of the end of the tent in the mud," but he was "too tired to be kept awake by any small miseries and drew in my feet and went to sleep again." Soldiers like Brewster grew weary of extreme weather with little or no shelter, especially when it seemed like they were doing so "for no possible purpose only to make ourselves just as miserable as can be for 24 hours, and then come back to camp again," as he wrote one cold February evening. "It is a perfect humbug. We could endure it cheerfully if it was for any good purpose but it is not and that makes it ten times worse." Confederate soldiers experienced the same frustrations. The Eighth Georgia Volunteers, camped out near the James River just south of Richmond in February 1863, slept during a snowstorm and by morning "were only indistinct mounds in the snow."[42]

Soldiers who did not have winter quarters came up with innovative ways to make camp life more comfortable during the winter months. Some soldiers used newspapers as extra insulation with their blankets, while one Pennsylvanian "kep my oald hat to sleep in."[43] But soldiers strove to find more efficient ways to keep warm. "I usually keep a fire all night," one soldier told his wife in January 1863, "and put a hot brick to my feet when cold."[44] Placing fires adjacent to sleeping men often proved dangerous. In December 1861, one Michigan infantryman wrote in his journal, "It was tedious last night. The ground froze deep & hard. I slept not more than 15 minutes all night. I sat down on a pole which was stuck up near the fire & was soon asleep. I was dreaming that I was in the warmest and downiest bed imaginable and God only knows what other charms would soon have been added if I had not tumbled off the pole & burned my new trousers. It was a pretty long night & required a great deal of walking to keep from freezing."[45]

Fire caused much greater calamities for others. One man in the Seventh New Hampshire recalled the frequency that soldiers used their stoves to warm their tents during the winter, although this "led to the accidental burning of many of our canvas homes." In a crowded tent, "some of the men would sometimes accidentally kick over the stove in the endeavor to move their feet while asleep," he continued, "and the straw with which the floor was covered would take fire at once." It was not uncommon for soldiers to hear a sentry crying, "Fire," and to look out "just in time to see a tent ablaze, and the occupants hardly awakened and out before it would be a total wreck, often losing their equipments, clothing, and arms, and sometimes personally escaping in a very scanty costume."[46]

Far more desirable were permanent structures. When given the chance, soldiers often slept in private homes or abandoned buildings. A small group of soldiers from the Eighth Georgia spent a night in the home of a Virginia Confederate but decided that the "snowy sheets and pillow slips" on the guestroom beds "were too nice for us, so we stretched off on the floor and were soon asleep."[47] This chivalric rebel courtesy was apparently quite common. On several occasions, different groups of filthy Confederates stayed with Eliza Fain of Tennessee. In February 1862 she described several "poor boys who are tonight laying on the floor in my room" because they felt "they could not sleep on a bed." In January 1864, two Texas soldiers "would not sleep in a bed" and instead slept "on the floor." And in January 1865 a large group of soldiers "slept on the floor in the front room."[48] Meanwhile, some other rebels in northern Virginia opted to sleep in a barn rather than in a home that was offered to them.[49]

If feelings of guilt kept soldiers out of offered beds, it did not prevent them from resting in abandoned structures. "Had a good nights rest last night," wrote a New York soldier stationed near New Bern, North Carolina, in December 1862. "When we camped, I took possession of an old and dilapidated house, formerly used as negro quarters, so that I had a floor to lie on once more." The next night, after a fifteen-mile march, he pitched his tent near wagons "so that I had my tent for a screen from the biting frost." It was "the sharpest & coldest night of the season," he continued. "In my very heart, I do pity the poor fellows who lie on the frozen ground by the thousands on all sides of me, wrapped in their blankets only—no shelter tents, even. A keen, sharp north wind creeps into every crevice, and through their blankets, chilling them severely."[50]

If the extremes in the weather were not enough to prevent a good night's sleep, nature could bring other unwelcome disturbances. Maj. Gen. Benjamin F. Butler's future son-in-law (and future governor of Mississippi) Adelbert Ames complained about a "disturbance at night that I have to endure." It was quite disgusting: "A large *rat* has taken possession of my tent—I ruling supreme during the day, and he during the night. He treats me very badly—wakes me up at night, runs through the mud and then drags his tail over my pillow, walks on my letter paper, makes his bed on me and pokes his nose into my private affairs, a course of conduct decidedly unkind, I think. I do not do so to him. For his rudeness I am feeding him—bread and butter spiced with arsenic."[51] Sailors aboard Union blockading vessels also all too frequently found themselves awakened by rodents nibbling at their fingers and pulling at their hair.[52]

Other animals, too, infested the closest of quarters. An Indianan awoke from a pleasant dream to find a six-foot black snake in his arms.[53] One Iowa officer was well pleased with his wall tent, thinking it "a splendid arrangement" where he "was going to have a nice sleep." But after two hours, he still could not close his eyes, for "every time he gets to sleep, a bullfrog jumps on to the bed and scares him out. There are half a dozen in here now, jumping around. The captain is getting disgusted with the whole thing and ha[s] concluded not to sleep *any*." The witness to this scene told his wife, "It is 10 o'clock and still raining like fury and bullfrogs are getting thicker, and I must quit and go to bed." Of greater courage—or perhaps just more exhausted—than his captain, he added, "I don't think any four-legged animal will keep me awake."[54]

Perhaps the most infuriating critter was lice. One Maine soldier wondered whether "a pair of them went into the ark with the rest of the animals of creation" or if "Noah had a few on *him* when he went in." Fleas, too, bothered this soldier. "The straw we sleep on breeds them fast," he told his sister. An Indiana officer whose clothes were infested by the little grey backs "on several occasions felt an uneasiness when awake, and in his dreams had been run over, stamped into the ground and horned and tossed in the air by ferocious herds of cattle, awaking in sweat and scratches of terror." Eventually he determined the problem, bathed, and "defeated" the buggers—but one comrade noted that this soldier "was pretty lice-entious at that time."[55]

Noises, distractions, nature, and impending battle all too often disturbed the soldiers' rest. Indeed, the cacophony of camp life could drown out the solitude that farm boys had grown accustomed to during antebellum life. The typical sounds of camp—the rain, the marching of soldiers, the neighing of horses, the clanking of tin cups, the crackle of a thousand camp fires, and "nine hundred men snor[ing] in concert"—became part of the soldiers' everyday experience, causing sleeplessness for many a volunteer throughout the war. "Did not sleep much," wrote one Massachusetts surgeon in December 1863. "Teams driving through the woods, bringing rations, and making a good deal of noise about it, more than usual it appeared to me." Even after the novelty of war had worn off, rowdy men still frequently cost their comrades a good night's rest. "Lost a good part of my sleep and all my patience by a lot of drunken officers," wrote Lt. Russell M. Tuttle. "When an officer gets drunk and at a late hour of the night goes into another's quarters, and tears around, it is, to say the least, in very bad taste." Another soldier similarly complained that officers "can make as much noise as they choose when they get drunk, but privates are not allowed to fart." Indeed, booze and women could sound the death knell of sleep. "For the first few nights we could get no sleep for the cursing of the men [and] screaming of women and the firing of pistols outside our Camp," wrote one soldier from the Thirty-Ninth Ohio Volunteers in May 1863.[56]

Soldiers who suffered from psychological afflictions, akin to posttraumatic stress disorder, could also cause their bunkmates to lose sleep. Pvt. Owen Flaherty of the 125th Illinois Infantry began to suffer a mental breakdown by the midpoint of the war. His messmate, John McVey, testified later that Flaherty "would talk to himself while awake, of his family, and would when asleep talk and tremble in his sleep to such an extent that I had to frequently get up and go some where else to get to rest."[57] In October 1864, a soldier in the Sixth Pennsylvania Cavalry was removed from camp for being "insane" after he "kept the camp awake all night barking like a dog."[58]

Nature and war often worked in tandem to deprive the troops of a good night's sleep. "After supper we lay down to sleep, soothed by the screaming of shell, cracking of rifles, buzzing of mosquitoes, and biting of wood ticks," wrote one officer with more than a hint of sarcasm. "The booming of cannon and whizzing of shell keep sleep away," he continued. "During the intervals of firing I hear the Rebel bands playing 'Dixie.' Frogs, whippoorwills, and owls put in the filling."[59]

Some sounds could keep almost any soldier up all night. One Marylander complained of the clamor caused by railroad cars that "pass within 40 feet of our quarters, every hour all night mak[ing] this awful noise as they approach & pass."[60] During the siege of Petersburg, Charles Harvey Brewster wrote that "we eat sleep and drink with the continual cracking of all sorts of firearms day and night." Bullets flying through the air could be a great danger to restless men at night as some "occasionally . . . thug into the body limbs or head of some poor blue coat for the men cannot be kept lying still but get up and move about with a most supreme indifference to these messages of death." On another occasion, Brewster was aroused from his sleep after midnight by the firing of guns. "Pop—Pop—Pop Pop Pop," he heard, and then the "regular roar of musketry." He and his comrades "sprang up and strapped on our knapsacks in quick time and the boys seized thier muskets with a firmer grasp and we were ready for them, but much to our regret they did not come." It turned out to have been other Union troops. Still, the episode underscored the danger to soldiers near enemy lines of being shot in their sleep.[61]

The sounds of fighting made interrupted sleep a normal experience for soldiers on both sides. With guns booming one night in May 1862, Chaplain Twichell wrote that "it took me [a] while to conquer my ears and get asleep. So frequent were the discharges that between them I had not enough time to march my drowsy powers so far into the dreamy realms, but that the next screaming shell would flank and hustle them back without ceremony." Fear of impending battle kept many soldiers from fully resting at night. "We never lay down with a certainty we shall not be roused to combat before the dawn again beams upon us," wrote Union general John White Geary. A Confederate soldier reported to his mother that his men only slept "an hour or two at a time, till this morning at half past three we were ordered to march." Sleeping soldiers might be rudely awakened by the sound of gunfire or cries of "the Yankees are coming." After long stretches of time, such stresses eventually took an emotional toll on some soldiers. Indeed, impending battle could cause unrest, even among the most battle-tested veteran. Even William Tecumseh Sherman felt "so restless and impatient that I could not sleep" at night before attacking Atlanta.[62]

Sunset could bring needed relief from combat. "Night mercifully put an end to the slaughter," recalled one Union soldier of Fredericksburg.[63] But the night after battle could still be one of the hardest times to sleep. Charles Harvey Brewster recalled listening "to the humming of minnie bullets about my ears, and again I have slept upon the battlefield among the dead and listened to the groans and shrieks of the wounded."[64] A soldier in Duryée's Zouaves wrote after Fredericksburg, "The bullets whizzed over our heads from the firing just in front of us. . . . I curled up in a heap to keep myself warm, and to keep on the board,—my share consisting of a space two and a half feet long, and one and a half broad. I could not sleep; and few there were who closed their eyes that night. As I lay I thought of the morrow,—how many of us would live to come out—of home, and eternity. But worse than all were the cries of the wounded lying between the lines without any one to help them."[65] Col. Joshua Lawrence Chamberlain of the Twentieth Maine had a similarly eerie experience at Fredericksburg, recalling years later,

> It was a cold night. Bitter, raw north winds swept the stark slopes. The men, heated by their energetic and exciting work, felt keenly the chilling change. Many of them had neither overcoat nor blanket, having left them with the discarded knapsacks. They roamed about to find some garment not needed by the dead. . . . Necessity compels strange uses. For myself it seemed best to bestow my body between two dead men among the many left there by earlier assaults, and to draw another crosswise for a pillow out of the trampled, blood-soaked sod, pulling the flap of his coat over my face to fend off the chilling winds, and, still more chilling, the deep, many-voiced moan that overspread the field.

Chamberlain recollected that the sound was "heart-rending; it could not be borne." At midnight he and a companion arose from their "unearthly bivouac" and walked about the field to see how they could help "these forsaken sufferers," although there was little that they could accomplish. After taking canteens from the dead to the wounded, repositioning soldiers with broken limbs, or simply listening to the final words of the dying, Chamberlain returned to "our strange companionship of bed," where he slept until "the sharp fire that spoke the dawn" caused him to lift "my head from its restful though strange pillow."[66]

Field hospitals rarely offered respite to wounded soldiers. Bed shortages were common. Even worse, the groans and moans of the most severely wounded caused other wounded soldiers to lose sleep. One Iowa soldier lying on a cot next to a dying comrade after the Battle of Belmont in November 1861 "could not rest for his moans from his pain and suffering."

Even after the war, this soldier remarked that "the memory of it to this day clings to me like a horrid nightmare." Sgt. Eli M. Tarbell of the Nineteenth U.S. Infantry noted that he "would rather hear the roar of artillery than the grones of thes poor Soldiers."[67]

Arriving at a general hospital could be an initial improvement over the conditions of field hospitals. Sergeant Tarbell was glad that upon his arrival at Cumberland Hospital in Nashville, Tennessee, he "got clean Cloths, Eat Supper & went to Bead in a nice Clean Sauft Bed." He noted that "it Seames Strang to Strip off & get into a nice Bed." Within days, however, Tarbell would come to loath this place.[68] Indeed, the sleep of the sick and wounded was often disturbed in general hospitals just as it was in field hospitals. One Illinois veteran at a hospital in Louisville, Kentucky, complained of the coughing man on the cot next to him. The cough "might well be compared to a fog-horn, or the hoarse tones of a thunder storm," he wrote. "'Twas not a small, hacking cough, escaping just beyond the lips, but deep and unfathomable; surging up from the lowest depths; wrenching every joint and muscle of the mortal system. That cough would long ago have wrecked any common craft, sailing on its tumultuous billows. . . . There was no let up to it at this time, and all night long it was cough, cough, cough—like the soughing of a steamboat, or the hoarse barking of a blood-hound."

If the mad cougher was not bad enough, this poor convalescent had a "lubberly fellow" on his other side "who appeared to care more for his rations than for the disease" with which he was afflicted. This oversized man would chatter on all day about his ailments, and at night would commence to snore "such deep, unearthly snores coming from the cavernous depths of a huge pair of lungs, rushing like a hurricane through a flabby glottis and distended nostrils, in tones as unmusical as the rasping of a saw or the hooting of a bazoon." A poor German soldier across the room would sit up in bed and "in accents of despair cry out, 'Schay, you dhare, stophs dat! me none at all schleps dees nicht.'"[69]

UTTER EXHAUSTION BECAME a common motif in soldiers' letters and diaries. "I was up all night last night, and of course will have to be up for many hours now," wrote Lt. Russell M. Tuttle before his regiment even left New York in August 1862. "When will I ever get any sleep! I don't know." During the Peninsula Campaign, a Union soldier remarked in his journal, "Without sleep for nearly a week and but little to eat, with plenty of work, has left me very tired to say the least." A New Yorker told his family that he went into battle "most d—d tired." Even the most hardened of veterans could become "senseless from fatigue" or "most broke down for the want of sleep." A Michigan soldier complained that he and his comrades were "all becoming pretty well worn out" as a consequence of the "night work" they were required to do night after night. Many found it "difficult to describe how tired and sleepy we all are," not having slept for four or five days in this particular soldier's case. Chaplain Twichell described his men before Gettysburg: "This morning we set out again after insufficient sleep on the soaked ground, under soaked blankets." Four days later, he wrote, "We are all tired out and had been allowed insufficient rest, never halting till dark and being aroused before sunrise almost every night." An Alabama soldier similarly told his mother after nineteen days of marching that "I am so near marched to death that I cannot write with any degree of intelligence, and having lost so much sleep, too." With all of the chores involved in keeping their horses, cavalrymen generally lost even more sleep than infantrymen.[70]

Men who reached these levels of fatigue "sank exhausted to sleep anywhere the body could find room to repose." Some men straggled out of camp at night to find better sleeping accommodations. In October 1863, one exhausted New Yorker told his wife he would pay twenty dollars for a bed to sleep in. During the final desperate days of fighting before the fall of Atlanta, Jacob Ritner of Iowa wrote, "I don't think I was ever so tired in my life. . . . And when we halted a little bit while about daylight I lay down right in the road and went to sleep." One night, Chaplain Twichell "was thoroughly tired out and found my cot and blanket delicious beyond description." After completing a seventeen-mile march through Georgia in May 1864, a Michigan soldier lay down in some dust "which was about a foot deep." "It was dark & I was tired," he wrote, "so that I did not much mind where I laid down." Upon awaking the next morning, however, he discovered that he "had been sleeping in a grave yard, with a grave as my pillow."[71]

Exhausted soldiers—wearied from day after day of campaigning—sometimes even found themselves asleep while marching or in battle. Such peculiarities were particularly common during the Overland Campaign of 1864, but they happened at other times as well. In December 1863, a Massachusetts soldier wrote, "I doubt if our ancestors at Valley Forge suffered more from cold than we did. . . . [I] often found that I had been sound asleep while my legs were trudging along."[72] Sometimes soldiers became so exhausted that they could not tell the difference between reality and a dream.

As one Georgia soldier approached a river, he "sat down to collect my thoughts and to be sure I was not dreaming."[73]

IRONICALLY, REPORTING ON LACK OF SLEEP could be a wonderful way for soldiers on the front lines to connect with their friends and family at home. Civil War regiments were usually made up of men from a community. If one did not sleep, others likely did not either. And describing their sleeplessness in letters home could add humor about neighbors to otherwise mundane or despondent correspondence. "Our mess now consists of John Willing, Dave & myself, Will Myers, Clay Bucher, and Cal Wirt, whom we received to day," reported one Maryland soldier to his uncle. "Six in a tent makes pretty tight sleeping & last night Will Myers Brother slept with us. I was on the outside & got pretty cool." But at 1 A.M. he woke up and "stepped between Dave & Willing where I soon was on the other extreme in a perspiration from the heat."[74]

Spooning was common among Civil War troops. One Indiana regiment adopted the motto, "*United, we sleep; divided, we freeze.*" For raw recruits, sleeping in such close quarters might be the most danger they faced in the field. "Slept cold all night. Came near Smothering at one time," wrote Lorenzo Vanderhoef of the Eighth Ohio Volunteers in May 1861. He explained that he pulled a blanket over his head and went to sleep, "but when I awoke was nearly suffocated." One tent mate "had rolled against me on one side," while the other had done so "on the other [side], in such a manner as to fasten me." Vanderheof "took a moment to loosen myself, but I felt as though I had escaped a death not at all pleasant."[75]

To be sure, nineteenth-century American men were used to sleeping in such close quarters. In the 1840s, Abraham Lincoln shared a bed with a stranger who later became his closest friend—Joshua Speed. During the war, Lincoln occasionally shared a bed with Capt. David V. Derickson of the 150th Pennsylvania Volunteers at the Soldiers' Home in Washington, D.C. Derickson, according to rumors, even made "use of His Excellency's nightshirts!"[76]

While not all soldiers bunked with their commander in chief, most did share beds or close quarters with each other. "Then a family bed for five was made on the ground," wrote surgeon William Smith, "a rubber blanket laid on the ground to shield from the water in the saturated earth, a blanket for a bed & others for cover and Colonel W., Quartermaster Butts, John and JA Brown and self, turned in a row. Myself the Alpha and the quartermaster the Omega of the row." By 9 P.M., Smith noted, "the quartet of snorers by my side have forgotten all toil and danger; and I only wait to finish this hurried record by the light of the bivouac fire, to join them in the land of forgetfulness."

But Smith did not sleep well that December night. He awoke shortly after 3 A.M. "from a sleep which was broken & disturbed all the night by the complaints of my uncushioned hip bones, and by the ceaseless stir and bustle of the camp." He heard the sounds of axes chopping firewood, men talking, singing, and shouting so that he was "almost entirely denied the benefit of 'nature's sweet restorer.'"

The next night Smith again found himself in his "family bed," and again, "All sleep has forsaken my eyes. I have wooed the sleepy God this hour past in vain; I cannot seduce her to my embrace again this morning." So he got up and sat by a campfire and thought "of those whom I cherish as my life, far, far, away, now doubtless sleeping sweetly on their soft, warm beds," wondering "if they ever dream of him who loves them so well, or in their waking hours, think of the hardships & frustrations he endures. Here & there a soldier, sleepless like myself, replenishes his campfire & seems like a morning specter in the distant glimmering light."[77]

Sometimes sleep in such close quarters led to quarrels. One night during the winter of 1862, James McClure Scott of the Tenth Virginia Cavalry got into a fistfight with his tent mate, John Collins. "They were sleeping together under the same blanket," wrote someone who had heard the story of this "famous fight" from an eyewitness. "Each woke in the night abusing the other for taking all the cover. From words they went to blows, rousing their comrades who grew interested in this trial of strength between two such athletes. John Collins was very strong but no match for Jim in quickness or dexterity." An officer tried to intervene but was stopped by another onlooker. "Jim knocked John Collins down 10 or 12 times before he'd give up, then they made friends, and in a very short time were asleep under the same blanket over which the dispute arose."[78]

Eventually, many soldiers became used to the incidents of camp life and the noises of war. "I don't care much now what I sleep on or under now," wrote a Union army surgeon on May 22, 1864. "When I am tired I can sleep wherever I am."[79] "It seems almost impossible that I have become so accustomed to the miseries of life and the solemn mysteries of death," observed Chaplain Twichell. "I can sleep the night through when the air is full of anguished cries."[80] Another wrote that he was "lulled to sleep by the braying of mules and snoring of teamsters."[81] After tattoo one night in May 1862,

"Army of the Potomac—Sleeping on Their Arms," *Harper's Weekly*, May 28, 1864. Courtesy of the Yale University Art Gallery.

General Geary listened as "the continued hum of camp is being hushed to sleep," as he told his wife. He continued, "The sentinels are pacing their lonely rounds, with ever and anon 'who goes there,' with an occasional discharge of a rifle at possibly a phantom."[82]

Some soldiers even grew to need such noises in order to sleep. One Union soldier remarked in 1863, "The silence was so unusual that many in camp, accustomed to hear the incessant reports of heavy guns and mortars, the hawl of shot and the bursting of shells, felt that there was something needed to make it possible to sleep soundly." Others became "nervous and restless" when "the regular nightly cannonade was suspended," remarking that the thunder of cannons had become "almost a necessity" to the weary men. One soldier asked, "What will the soldier do when he returns to his quiet country home, and hears only the shot of the fowling piece or the annual discharge of the immense brass six [pounder] on Fourth of July?" Similarly, a surgeon stationed near Petersburg in August 1864 wondered, "What shall I do when I can no longer be 'lulled to sleep' by the popping of musketry and booming of big guns?"[83]

Such questions must have seemed strange to those who slept at home in relative peace and quiet. But they became part of an ongoing dialogue between the battlefield and the home front that lasted throughout the war.

Soldiers found that writing about their sleep was one of the best ways to commune with those at home. Mothers and wives and children wanted to hear about such mundane—and relatively safe—matters. "Every night that I lay down I wonder where you are and what kind of place you have to sleep," wrote an Iowa woman to her husband.[84] And soldiers often obliged by using homely metaphors to help their families relate to their unusual slumbers. One Massachusetts soldier told his mother that he and his comrades "slept sound as pigs in clover." Another poor Union soldier who had no blanket still "slept like a log till the sun was up." A Michigan infantryman recalled making a bed of "Virginia feathers," by which he meant cedar boughs. A Confederate artillerist recalled burrowing into some leaves in "a big cavity made by the upturned roots" of a fallen tree and sleeping "like a bug in a rug." Biblical allusions also abounded between correspondents. "Unlike Father Noah," wrote one Maine volunteer following a nighttime downpour, "we have no Ark, nor even a tent or shelter." Another soldier slept on ground that was "harder than Pharaoh's heart," but noted that at least it "promotes early rising."[85]

Correspondence like this enabled civilians at home to empathize with the travails of the men in the field. "Fearful night," wrote Eliza Fain of Tennessee in January 1862, "poor soldiers how my heart feels for you this dreary night. Sleet falling until the ground is white and I am alone. . . . Where are my soldier sons this night? My heart is so grieved when I think of our poor soldiers who have to face the storm of rain, wind and sleet with but little to protect them from its chilling effects." Jane Thompson of Iowa similarly told her husband, "I think if I had known the nights that you were so wet that I would not have slept very much."[86]

Letters from the field often sought to assuage mothers like Fain or wives like Thompson of their grief and fear. Dr. William Child, a surgeon with the Fifth New Hampshire Volunteers, described his bed in great detail in a letter to his wife—it was a stretcher on which he had placed "some long shingles of oak," a "straw bed," and "five large army blankets." At the close of his letter, he wished his wife "good night" and asked her, "Where do you sleep?—Where do the children sleep? . . . Tell me all about it—won't you?"[87]

Dr. Child frequently told his wife that he dreamed of her, and he bid her "good night" in nearly every letter he wrote, once repeating the phrase four times. While he could not know the time that she would read his letters, in his mind, it was as though they were there together and he was wishing her "good night" as he readied himself for bed. In an attempt to feel the intimacy of married life at home, he slept with "your picture under my head and dream of home." He once wrote, "It is now evening. I can see the same stars you see." On another occasion, he implored her, "Kiss the babies— and tell them papa thinks of them every night after he goes to bed."[88]

Thousands of soldiers' letters closed by bidding the recipient a "good night" or "sweet dreams." Not uncommon at all was the closing of one of William Keeler's letters written belowdecks of the *Monitor*: " 'tis ten o'clock," he told his wife, Anna in faraway Illinois, "so a kiss & good night." Or as Col. William Roane Aylett of the Fifty-Third Virginia Infantry told his wife early in the war, "I sadly miss my beloved bedfellow."[89] Writing one mid-night in North Carolina in March 1864, a Confederate doctor assured a close friend back home that he still would spare an hour of his time to write her a letter, "for I know I shall sleep all the better for a bit of conversation with you; not the more soundly—no—but the more sweetly, for visions of friends whose kindness makes life dear to me, of the loved ones on earth, and the loved ones in heaven, will hover round my pillow." These "precious" dreams, he continued, "will make my chamber bright and solace me under a sense of separation from some whom I never can, and from others whom under the uncertainties of life, I never may see again on earth."[90]

Civil War soldiers and sailors wanted to continue their bedtime conversations with their wives and families and friends, just as they had done in peacetime. After a hard day of work, they longed to decompress and relax with loved ones, and to make sense of what had transpired throughout the day. But they were far away from home now. Those monologues in correspondence were the closest they could get to replicating a bedtime conversation. As one Georgia soldier wrote, "Every night when I lie down I think of my dear wife and child." Or, as another Georgian told his wife, "Good night, sweet one. Oh how I would be pleased to kiss your sweet lips to night!" Or, as an Iowa soldier wrote as he prepared to go on late-night picket duty, "Then I shall be thinking about you—perhaps you will be asleep in your warm bed, dreaming about me. . . . Good night dear." Or, as a Virginian told his sweetheart: "I was with you again in my dream."[91]

Soldiers' families, too, longed for a connection to their menfolk at bedtime. An Iowa woman told her husband that while everyone else in her home was asleep, "I could not go to sleep until I had a short talk with you." One Vermont woman asked her husband in 1864 whether he had "gotten weaned from a bed." "I have not," he replied. "I always think of a good bed at home with you when I lie down to sleep." A Georgia woman wrote to her husband at 10 P.M. one night, remarking, "Now perhaps your head is pillowed on a hard bed, and you are dreaming of home, of bright eyed Laura, and I dare to think of me too. Would I were with you, my own beloved, to press those lips that ever spoke words of love and affection with kisses that can but faintly express my love for you, but how many weary months must follow each other, ere I again am permitted to be near you and perhaps never." In like manner, a Pennsylvania woman told her husband that she was "restless" while he was away. "I cannot sleep no more," another Pennsylvania woman told the father of her child (but not her husband). "I shall sleep no more until I see you. And oh if I do it will be dreamy sleep I ashure you."[92]

CHAPTER TWO

The Soldier's Dream

More than anything else, Union and Confederate soldiers dreamed about home. "Last night I dreamed of being at home as I often do and sweet were the kisses what I took all around," wrote a New York soldier to his wife. A thirty-six-year-old Virginian similarly told his sixteen-year-old sweetheart, "I dream about you som times three or four nights in succesion. I dream som mighty good dreams about you." While many dreams of home were comforting or romantic, sometimes they focused on the mundane, or things that soldiers missed. Pvt. Chauncey H. Cooke of Wisconsin wrote to his mother from the Pine Woods of Georgia in 1864, "I dreamed last night about the cheese which you wrote about in the letter I got three days ago" and how much "I would like a taste of it."[1]

But pleasant dreams of home could lead to disappointment after sunrise. "I dreamed of huging and kissing you all night last night," wrote one Indiana soldier to his wife. "Oh, how happy I was but how bad I did feel this morning." After having a dream that "I am hugging you to my heart," one Connecticut volunteer told his wife, "then I awaken and find myself lying in this damd place. it makes me swear some, but that does no good." A private from Georgia experienced similar feelings. "Oh how disappointed I was when I awoke and found it a dream," he wrote in May 1862 after dreaming of his family. More than a year later he reiterated the sentiment. "Dear Malinda, I dream of you often and oh, what pleasure it is to be with you but when I awake [and] find its all a dream, how sad I feel."[2]

A delightful dream of home could lead to awkward and unintended closeness between tent mates. One Georgia soldier told his wife that he "dream[ed] of hugging you" but woke up "hugging the boys" in his tent. Such occurrences made this soldier "mad." "Darling I wish I was their to sleep with you tonight," he continued sorrowfully. "I now wold sleep warm and more than that I co[u]ld hug up with you. . . . I hope the time ant far off [when I] can sleep with you all the time." In like manner, Indiana lieutenant John Hadley received a rude awakening after dreaming that he had finally married his sweetheart. "I arrived and met you at the door and there was grasping of hands and touching of lips," he told her. "Leaning upon my arm we went into your chamber. . . . Like two weary, wandering souls

"The Soldier's Dream." This image, which appeared in *Harper's Weekly* on November 7, 1863, captured how many Americans viewed soldiers' dreams—as reinforcing traditional familial ties and religious beliefs. Collection of the author.

stepping into Heaven did we enter into the happiness of wedlock and as the evening wore away our cup of happiness seemed to grow fuller and fuller. You were leaning on my arm and we were strolling through the yard drinking each others' sighs and shaping our course for life." But soon Hadley "awoke and found nothing but the rough touch of Captain Banta."[3]

Dreams of home often revealed soldiers' deep-seated concerns for the well-being of their families. One Virginia Confederate was plagued by worried dreams about his pregnant wife and unborn child until he finally learned that both mother and baby had survived the delivery. Others had dreams about their families' health. "I have dreamed about you several times lately," Capt. Jacob Ritner told his wife back in Iowa. "I dreamed the other night that I had you in my arms and was kissing you. I thought you were just as pretty and sweet as ever, but that you looked pale and thin, like you had been sick for a long time." He then advised her, "I hope you have taken medicine and got over that bad cough."[4]

Unfortunately, visitations with loved ones in soldiers' dreams were not always pleasant, and soldiers' sleeping brains sometimes created scenarios that revealed unease about their family lives that might have been rumbling just beneath the surface of the soldiers' subconscious. Perhaps most tellingly, feelings of guilt often materialized in dreams, and remorse for secret sins sometimes manifested itself in soldiers' sleep. The most striking and common iniquity to appear in dreams was marital infidelity. Young men away from home feared that their wives and sweethearts might lose hope, or believe that their lovers had died, and fall into the arms of a sneaking coward at home.[5] Such worries that another man—or men—might disrupt their households caused some soldiers to write home about their concerns.

Soldiers were remarkably candid in bringing up their fears of abandonment and adultery. To soften the difficulty of the issue, however, they often situated it within a discussion of their dreams. Doing so enabled them to maintain a certain level of intimacy while broaching a difficult subject. In September 1862, New Hampshire surgeon William Child told his wife, Carrie, that in his dream she did not say she loved him "the first time you saw me," but soon thereafter "you kissed me—and told me you loved me." A year and a half later, his insecurities still revealed themselves in his letters and dreams. "I can not tell you how I desire to see you," he wrote in April 1864. "You seem more dear to me than ever. I love—love you. I dream of you almost nightly. . . . And nothing would cause me more misery than to feel that my wife should have no love for me—for then she certainly could not be happy." But she wrote to him infrequently, and her letters were rather short and perfunctory. By December 1864, he was feeling great trepidation about his marriage. "I have had terrible days and nights of doubt," he told her. "You never caressed—never kissed me of your own accord—and I felt that I was not the person who could command all your love for I was neither a hero or a genius—nor perfect." Then would come "the awful idea that perhaps you might love some man not your husband."[6]

It is little wonder that a vague word of a dream in one of Carrie's letters put Dr. Child on edge. "You say you had a dream about me," he wrote to her in January 1864. "Why did you not tell me all about or not say anything about it? You make me feel as though there was something very bad about me—or that you at least thought so." He then reiterated that he dreamed about her "often" and that they are "always good and pleasant dreams too."

Carrie apparently never revealed her dream. Two months later he again implored her to tell him. Again, she refused. A year later, in January 1865, he was still tortured by the dream. "Last night I dreamed of you a long and pleasant dream," he wrote. "You mentioned that you once dreamed of me— an unpleasant dream—awful dream, but you would not tell it to me. Why not? You always tell me just enough to excite my curiosity, then leave me to wonder."[7]

Other soldiers had dreams that explicitly exposed their fears of spousal infidelity, abandonment, or other marital difficulties. Capt. Thomas Jefferson Hyatt of the 126th Ohio Volunteers had several "very queer" dreams one night. "First I dreamed that we had been married some years, and the time had run out and we were about arranging another term," he told his wife. But then, "I dreamed you had abandoned me and had or was about to form an alliance with Lt. [Joseph C.] Watson of this Regt." At first Captain Hyatt was content with this new arrangement, "as I supposed I was free to go where I chose." But soon he "began to feel very badly, and could not think of the separation." His wife seemed "offish," and he grew jealous of how she looked at Lieutenant Watson. But eventually she began "to regret the steps you had taken and began to think I was a *little* better than your second choice. I just then awoke, and behold it was all a dream, and I was very glad of it."[8]

These kinds of dreams were ubiquitous. Despite his disbelief in dreams, Lt. Richard Goldwaite's unconscious nighttime wanderings revealed his longing for his wife—and perhaps also his fears that he might never see her again. He dreamed that "you came here to see me and we were a going to have a good time in my tent when night came and when I woke up in the morning and did not find you, I was mad enough to go over to Baltimore and get drunk."[9] Minnesota infantryman Duren F. Kelley dreamed that he saw his wife on a street back home but that she "seemed to take no notice of me and kept right on." South Carolinian Jesse W. Reid's wife "would hardly speak to me" in his dream. In like manner, New Yorker John Hartwell dreamed he came home but his wife "took about as much notice of me as you would if I had been out to get an armful of wood." But things only went downhill from there, likely revealing some of Hartwell's deepest anxieties. As the dream progressed, Hartwell saw his wife "take the hand of a finely dressed gentleman & jump into a carriage & ride away."[10]

Bad dreams of home often resulted from lack of correspondence with loved ones.[11] After not receiving a letter from his wife for almost two months, Wisconsin soldier Miles Butterfield had a "very strange Dream" that he could not get out of his mind, which he described in a twelve-page letter to his wife. Butterfield dreamed that he had gotten out of the service and gone home to see his wife and baby, but she refused to "take any notice of me." Eventually he learned that she "did not intend to live with me anymore," and she wanted him to get his furniture out of the house. He pleaded with her, but to no avail. He then walked into town and saw several friends, including one named Cram, who "all knew that you was going to leave me and they all looked at me so that I did not know what to do and then Cram told me that he had been living with you about 3 weeks and that he was not the only one that had been with you, but he was the one that you was going off with." Now Butterfield felt even worse. He returned home and told his wife he could "forgive all and live with you as before," but again she rejected him, and left town on a train. Suicidal thoughts now flooded Butterfield's sleeping brain. "I was going to wait until the next train come along and I would put an end to my Miserable life by lying down on the track and letting the cars run over me, for now I had nothing to live for as you and the Baby was gone, but I began to think how you had been acting, and concluded that I would go back and let you go, and thought that it was a good thing that you had gone as I did with one once before as you know." After several pages of this vivid description, Butterfield again asked his wife to send him more letters.[12] Clearly lack of communication from home was having a destructive effect on this soldier's psyche.

Other soldiers had similarly violent dreams about adultery—some of which, like Butterfield's, involved their wives cheating with multiple men. On September 4, 1861, William Harris Hardy dreamt that he had returned home to Mississippi and that his wife, Sallie, "received me cooly." He watched her get into "a buggy with a young man and left in a gay and fastidious manner." He followed them to a party, where he now saw her "in a fine glee, entertained by two nice-looking gentlemen." Sallie still ignored William, so that his "heart sunk, and the tears gushed forth from my eyes." She chastised him and "rejoined your two favorite beaux." At this point Hardy "became enraged and determined to settle the matter. I got my double barrel shotgun heavily loaded, and after killing both the young men, I drew a dagger and determined to terminate your life and my own with the same knife at the same time." But before he could execute "this horrible deed, I awoke." Hardy's "mind was contorted, my whole physical frame convulsed, and I almost crazy." Only after he had become convinced that it was a dream did he finally relax. Hardy attributed such a "terrible dream" to having heard of a comrade's wife being unfaithful, as well as being "tired and worn down, completely exhausted from a long and tedious drill."[13]

Such dream reports reveal the remarkable level of honesty that existed between husbands and wives who were so far apart during the war. Of course, the dreamers may simply have been trying to compel their spouses to remain faithful by sharing such dreams about infidelity—unsophisticated attempts at reverse psychology. But something more than manipulation seems to have been going on in these dream reports between spouses. Ironically, as soldiers and their wives alike were experiencing severe doubts about their partner's faithfulness, they still felt close enough to share their most intimate insecurities.

Some soldiers relayed romantic dreams to lonely spouses to reassure them of their love. "You are mighty mistaken when you think that, for you are not off of my mind one minute of the day," wrote a Georgia soldier. "I will tell you what I dreamed the other night about you. I dreamt that I went home and you would not notice me hardly for a long time, and I thought that I hugged you and kissed you. But when I woke I was a-lying all alone. That is no new thing for me to dream of you, for I dream of you nearly every night."[14]

In some cases, soldiers' own struggles with temptation were manifested in their dreams. A young private in the Twenty-First Missouri Volunteers confided in his diary that he saw "lovely Females" as he walked the streets of a small Gulf Coast town in Mississippi, and that he "feel like possessing their charms, but resolve not to do it. have a finer Point in view." That "finer Point" was probably his upcoming marriage. Nevertheless, such temptations may have infiltrated his dreams in the form of insecurity: "Carrie, last night I dreamed I was sitting beside you reading the Bible of Love & Marriage," he wrote. "I broached the subject in regard to *our* Marriage, you said you dident Know if you could or could not fulfill your vows, said there were two other men [who] loved you dearly & wanted to marry you, might pledge your affections to one of them. I replied as I awoke, when such was the fact, I wished to leave you in harmony, & my existence cease for ever."[15] Fortunately, this dream was not prophetic. As soon as his enlistment was over, he returned home and married Carrie Springer.

Not all soldiers had monogamous dreams, and many likely dreamed of multiple women back home. One Confederate officer dreamed of visiting a Miss Sallie. "She was standing on [the] porch," he wrote. "I cried out to Miss S., 'Here comes your sweetheart. She ran in the house. Met me at door. Went in and was having a nice time when awoke & 'twas all a dream." Two nights later he dreamed of a different girl. "Suddenly Miss Kate opened the door and came in looking beautiful as an angel. I spoke to her. Told me, she congratulated me on being married. Told the miss she was mistaken, but if she was willing I'd soon be. Don't remember her answer." Four days later, he dreamt that he was about to "pop the question" to a "Miss Frances."[16]

Confederate Hiram Smith Williams dreamed elaborate love stories with fictional characters. In one, a wealthy bachelor who lived on the banks of the Mississippi River saved a woman and her baby during a flood. In more than eleven hundred words, Williams described this escapade in great detail, until, in the end, the wealthy planter rescued the woman, married her, and "lived happily ever after." Such dreams could have emotional effects on the soldiers who dreamed them. After dreaming of an imaginary "fair lady last night," one Maine soldier "felt home sick all day as a consequence." A few months later, he wrote, "Occasionally I dream as you did of loving some fair one and the love I feel for her lasts me a whole day and makes a different man of me for that 24 hours."[17]

Most soldiers were modest—even shy—when describing romantic dreams to their wives and sweethearts. Confederate surgeon George W. Peddy of the Fifty-Sixth Georgia Volunteers told his wife of a dream he had of her the night before. "Honey, I wish I could tell you what a dream I had of you last night," he wrote obliquely. "I will tell you about it when I get to see you. Oh that I could realize such facts as the dream perpetrated!"[18] Giving slightly more detail, Dr. William Child of New Hampshire assured his wife on a cold night in November 1864 that he missed "home with its thousand comforts among which a comfortable bed—with a comfortable bed-fellow and warm—is not the least." He then told her that he "dreamed of home more than once in my restless sleep. It might cause you to laugh should I tell you what I dreamed—perhaps blush. I have concluded to tell you at another time if I should ever see you." Instead of sleeping with her, he lay on the frozen ground in a blanket next to a hospital steward. "You would laugh to see us in bed curled up like two pigs with our heads covered," he wrote.[19]

Other soldiers, by contrast, described explicit dreams that probably made their women blush and avert their eyes. Union general Godfrey Weitzel wrote a colorfully descriptive and romantic letter to his future wife, Louisa Bogen, on March 4, 1864: "I have pinched your picture and it does not holler. I have bitten it and it does not holler. I have kissed it and it does not return my kisses. I have hugged it and it does not return my hug. So just consider yourself pinched, bitten, hugged and kissed. I have been dreaming about you all last night. I was back at home and had only 12 hours to stay. You and I sneaked away from the rest of the folks and went upstairs to that little front room in your house and we had such a pleasant time. But alas! It was only a dream."[20]

For some soldiers, dreams of girls led to wet dreams. In one extraordinarily graphic letter, Lt. John Foster of the 155th Pennsylvania Volunteers encouraged his wife to masturbate by their fireplace after describing a dream he'd had about her in which he "was having the sensation, as my shirt fully attested."[21] Not all soldiers saw seminal emissions as a positive effect of dreams, however. A chaplain in the 145th Pennsylvania Volunteers noted a peculiar reason that two men in his regiment claimed for a discharge: "Both of them have been married for some years; and yet such are the pernicious effects of the early indulgences, that now they frequently have nocturnal emissions, foul dreams, etc.—besides rheumatism and general debility—such as renders them unfit for service."[22] While these soldiers may have believed that they had a legitimate disability, other soldiers realized that they could feign wet dreams (by masturbating) in order to get out of the service. One team of army surgeons, for example, found that three out of the four patients under their care who claimed to suffer from "spermatorrhoea" had actually produced "manufactured" evidence of the disorder.[23]

Nevertheless, most soldiers saw romantic dreams as a welcome comfort. Some even believed they could offer protection on the battlefield. One Georgia volunteer believed that if he dreamed of his sweetheart before a fight it was "a good omen" and he could go into battle "with the full relief that I will come out safe." He reckoned, "Maybe it is the spirit of my wee little sweetheart that hovers over me in battle and protects me from death or injury."[24]

Of course, not all dreams of love or lovemaking ended happily. Surrounded by ever-present threats of death, some soldiers' dreams of erotic desire were marred by funerals. Confederate soldier Hiram Smith Williams dreamed that he was in Mobile, Alabama, working at a theater. After performing his first piece, he walked outside and met "a lovely girl of some 16 summers, rather small of her age, but beautiful as a fairy." He watched her vainly attempt to reject the company of a persistent young man, so "I advanced by her side" and the young man "left us in a great rage." The beautiful young girl then put her hand on Williams's arm and looked at him with her "pair of large soul-mirrored eyes," saying, "I know you are a Theatre actor, and Ma tells me that actors are bad men, but I know you will protect me by your looks." At that moment, the scene changed. Williams now found himself walking down a suburban street near a large crowd that surrounded a private residence. "Impelled by curiosity, I went in and found it was a funeral," he wrote. "I went to the coffin, and there, beneath a thin gauze shroud, I beheld the face of the lovely girl whose protector I had been." She had a "single white rose ... entwined in her hair" and "looked surpassingly beautiful." So "deep a feeling pervaded my mind that with a cry of horror I awoke, and for an hour afterward, I lay and thought about this most strange dream."[25]

SEX, LOVE, AND MARRIAGE were not the only motifs in dreams that revealed anxieties about potential abandonment. Soldiers' deep-seated fears of being forsaken or forgotten appeared in dreams in a number of different ways. One soldier dreamed "that every friend I ever had had left me," except his little daughter, Kate. "She alone remained to comfort me. I could see her little, sweet face saying 'don't cry papa.' I waked with my face wet with tears." Some soldiers dreamed about the loss of their spouse or a child. Upon receiving word from his wife that his infant son was sick, one helpless Confederate soldier "dreamed about him several times and . . . was uneasy." Alexander Campbell of the Seventy-Ninth New York Infantry similarly "had a verry strange Dream" about his children dying. After describing the vision to his wife, he concluded that "it would not doe of one was to beleive dreams to be true. I hope that one of mines is not true." In other cases, soldiers dreamt that their children grew up while they were away at war, turning the child into an adult they did not know. Such homesick dreams could be very impactful for lonely soldiers, with one man writing that they gave him the "blues."[26]

Some soldiers feared that their friends and family would desert them in their cause. Lieutenant Hadley wrote his sweetheart about a dream he had during the long, hot summer of 1863. "Mary I am not a believer in dreams this I believe I have before told you nor do I attach any importance to their Revelations," he wrote, "but I had one the other night so singular so unlike any I ever before had in the service that I make no excuse for unfolding it to you." He proceeded to recount his dream in great detail. He was on picket duty, camped out in an abandoned Southern theater. "The war was over. Peace was smiling in the door of evry household. Our bloody hands had been washed in the waters of the Potomac. Our sabres had been returned to their scabbards. Our arms stacked on completely and honorably finishing our task we boarded the cars for *home*."

The nation was rejoicing, he continued. "There was singing and dancing and 'much merry making.' Evry heart danced light upon the expectations of soon seeing the 'loved ones at home.'" Soon Hadley and his comrades had made it back to Indiana, but the soldiers were "disappointed" by what they encountered. They expected to be greeted by "bright eyes" but instead they were shunned:

The hearts that we expected to see swell with gratitude for what we had done in restoring their Government were turned aside in cold and haughty indifference. The tongues, which we expected would be busy in welcoming us among them again were mute only in blaspheming the name of Soldier. Mothers were there, but they prefered the hand of the son who had stayed by her side. Sisters were there but they prefered the sosiety of brothers who remained dreaming behind & had not the tawny & worn look of the soldier.

Maidens were there whoes hearts had once been given, but were now reclaimed & posessed by those who hated the profession of war. Shuned and disowned by all we turned, enraged, heart-broken and distressed, from the mothers who bore us, from the board that had nourished us, from the friends that had once owned us; and when I awoke we were tossing on a bark which was bearing us to Sanfransisco.

When he awoke the next morning, Hadley assured his sweetheart, "Of course I don't believe anything it tells—glad I don't." He was confident that those at home would not succumb to the treasonable appeals of the Copperheads—nor lose heart in the war—and he told her that he would "sweat & march, & fight evryday with increased enthusiasm."[27] Still, Hadley's dream revealed some of the tensions soldiers felt with those they perceived as traitors at home. When things seemed to be going badly at the front—and peace sentiment gained traction among civilians—soldiers in the field, of both armies, worried that friends and neighbors at home might abandon the cause and neglect the soldiers. While Hadley professed not to have possessed such fears, his dream life revealed the grave concerns he harbored deep within.

Loneliness and lack of correspondence often spurred dreams of capture among Union and Confederate soldiers. For two weeks in August 1864 Vermont surgeon Melvin Hyde had a recurring dream "of being a prisoner every night" in "some gloomy dungeon drag[g]ing out a miserable existence." Immediately before and after his description of these dreams, Hyde implored his stepdaughter and wife to "write *oftener*." Such dreams became commonplace in both armies, reflecting one of the very real concerns facing soldiers. "Had a remarkable dream last night," wrote a Pennsylvania cavalryman in June 1863. "Dreamt I was taken prisoner near Phila. and the rebs entered the city and I escaped from them." Surgeon William Child similarly dreamed that the rebels were at his home in New Hampshire "and came near catching me." An Alabama soldier "dreamed last night of being in a little fight and thought I was taken prisoner." George Tillotson of New York feared that his ominous dream of capture would come true—so much so that he told his comrades it was bound to happen. One Federal officer even dreamed that he "was taken prisoner, [and] brought before Jeff. Davis in council."[28]

MEN WHO WERE actually captured and imprisoned had a unique wartime dream experience. Not surprisingly, undernourished prisoners of war often dreamed of sumptuous meals. A Union POW from Michigan, who was starving at the notorious Confederate prison camp at Belle Isle in Richmond, recorded in his diary, "Dream continually nights about something good to eat." Months later, when at Andersonville, he wrote, "In our dreams we see and eat bountiful repasts, and awake to the other extreme."[29] A Pennsylvania cavalryman at Belle Isle similarly remembered after the war that his "hours of slumber were full of dreams, and the burden of these visions was food—food!" In these dreams the cavalryman "was always sitting down to tables that groaned under the choicest viands, and, although I appeared to partake freely of these, I never seemed to be surfeited." Many of these dreams took him to a particular boarding house in Pittsburgh "with the kind, motherly face of Mrs. Cook beaming on me" from the other side of the table. But when morning came and he awoke, "everlasting hunger was upon me, from which there was no escape."[30]

Such dreams were ubiquitous among prisoners of war—and also generally unique to them. Union and Confederate soldiers on the battlefield rarely reported dreams about food, but prisoners often did. Dreams, in a very real sense, became a form of escape for POWs from the harsh realities of prison life. A New Yorker who had spent time at Andersonville recalled, "Dreams of home and of home comforts, especially the favorite dishes that had been prepared by the hands of a doting mother, a pet sister, or a loving wife, were of nightly and even daily occurrence." Another New Yorker there similarly wrote, "I wash every day in well water but am getting thin, weak and ragged. I often dream of eating roast beef or oysters, and can actually taste them in my sleep." But these dreams always left the prisoners feeling empty. Men would "lay down in vain hopes that sleep might come to us, but our hunger was too intense," recalled Ezra Hoyt Ripple of Pennsylvania. "After a while I did drop off, but only for a time, and during that time I dreamed of home and of eating, eating without satisfaction, and then I awoke to face the miserable reality." Sometimes prisoners' dreams could be torturous. A Massachusetts prisoner at Andersonville dreamed of "any quantity of ham & eggs" but he "could not eat any for I was in the bull pen: I didn't think much of that you better believe." When this soldier died about two weeks later, one of his comrades remarked on the "poor fellow, literally starved to death, no disease about him, but reduced to a living skeleton."[31]

Several prisoners at Belle Isle "often dreamed of eating and woke up to go through the motions frothing at the mouth." On one occasion, these poor men "begged the guard to throw over pieces of a cow that had been delivered of a calf three days before, some of which they devoured raw."[32] After the war, John McElroy of the Sixteenth Illinois Cavalry described how he endured "torturing dreams" of food almost every night at Andersonville. In fact, he wrote, he had "hundreds" of dreams of a banquet he'd enjoyed in St. Louis before the war:

> I saw the wide corridors, with their mosaic pavement; I entered the grand dining-room, keeping timidly near the friend to whose kindness I owed this wonderful favor; I saw again the mirror-lined walls, the evergreen decked ceilings, the festoons and mottos, the tables gleaming with cut-glass and silver, the buffets with wines and fruits, the brigade of sleek, black, white-aproned waiters, headed by one who had presence enough for a Major General. Again I reveled in all the dainties and dishes on the bill-of-fare; calling for everything that I dared to, just to see what each was like.

After dreaming of these luxurious days gone by McElroy would then "awake to find myself a half-naked, half-starved, vermin-eaten wretch, crouching in a hole in the ground, waiting for my keepers to fling me a chunk of corn bread."[33]

Dreams of hunger and home around the holidays could be particularly affecting for prisoners of war. A POW from the 118th Pennsylvania Volunteers who was held at the Confederate prison at Florence, South Carolina, dreamed one Christmas eve "of feasting on all the good things in the way of food that I had ever heard of or eaten." Confederate cavalryman William Downer of the Sixth Virginia Cavalry, while imprisoned at Camp Chase in Ohio, dreamed on Christmas morning in 1864 that he "had been exchanged and reached home in safety." His wife had prepared a "large loaf of bread" that "was on the table smoking and a large pint of butter setting in the middle of the table." Downer envisioned himself seated at the table and, "oh; how I enjoyed it. I really thought the best I had ever eaten." His children were gathered near him at the table and on the floor and his wife sat "at the head of the table looking upon me with delight not eating a mouthful." After such a long time apart she was too preoccupied with him to eat, while in his dream, he could not help but notice the food. Such a "pleasant dream" made Downer feel "truly happy" until he awoke and realized that it was "nothing but a dream." "Oh; what a disappointment," he wrote, "when I raised my head up in my bed and realized [it was] nothing more than a dream." It would be another seven months until the war would end and Downer would return home.[34]

Other types of dreams were also unique to the POW experience, thus revealing what appears to be something of a psychological transformation in soldiers from combatant to captive.[35] While soldiers in the field dreamed of capture, those in prison dreamt of POW exchanges. Capt. J. Madison Drake of the Ninth New Jersey Volunteers would retire at night "to again dream of 'freedom.'"[36] Following the breakdown in prisoner exchanges, the morale of some prisoners deteriorated, sometimes revealing itself in their dreams. One prisoner at Macon Prison, in Georgia, dreamed that he was in a New York saloon with Abraham Lincoln, Secretary of War Edwin M. Stanton, and Maj. Gen. Benjamin F. Butler, about twenty years after the war: "Butler asked Lincoln if he knew what had ever become of those officers and men of ours who were confined in Georgia in 1864. Of course 'Abe' referred the matter to Stanton, who confessed he had lost track of them. They then concluded it would be judicious to send commissioners south to learn what had been the fate of these forgotten fellows. So 'Abe' sent his commissioners to Georgia, who after a diligent search returned with the intelligence that the poor fellows had all died in prison—the last one about two years ago." Not only was the dream "quite interesting to the dreamer," but it also caught the attention of other POWs who heard about it. "When we hear that our poor men at Andersonville (Ga.) are dying at the rate of 40 or 50 a day, there is a sort of gloomy humor about this curious dream, which excites some feelings other than those of mere curiosity," wrote a fellow prisoner. "I hope the dream may never come to pass, but sometimes it seems among the possibilities of the dubious future."[37]

Sometimes dreams of exchange incorporated other themes of soldiers' dreams, including concerns about spousal infidelity. Congressman Alfred Ely of New York was captured by the Confederates during the First Battle of Bull Run in July 1861 and spent six months as a prisoner of war in Richmond. One night in late October, he dreamed that Confederate authorities had directed his release and sent him home to Rochester but that he was chaperoned by a Confederate officer.

On our way there he took occasion to speak of my wife, and to say that he had formed a high opinion of her during his stay in Richmond, and that it would not be strange if, upon his arrival at my house he should *supplant* me in her favor altogether. Wondering what chance he had had of *making her acquaintance while in Richmond*, it occurred to me that all the letters which she had addressed to me while there had *passed through his hands*, as officer of the post, with the privilege of *reading them all*, and the idea that it might be the means of *my ruin* so appealed to my bump of *combativeness* that I hurled him a volley of invectives, accompanying it with violent gesticulations of anger.

This dream so captivated the dreamer that he awoke all of his fellow prisoners around him and they "laughed at me most heartily." But Ely may not have seen humor in that moment. According to some contemporaneous Confederate accounts, Ely was known to be "disturbed" and to cry "like a child" during his six-month captivity in the South.[38]

Some prisoners' dreams naturally reflected the squalor of prison life. Union prisoner of war John Ransom dreamed that "the rebels were so hard up for mules that they hitched up a couple of grayback lice to draw in the bread."[39] Other dreams captured the hopelessness many POWs felt. Death was omnipresent, in daylight and in darkness. After three months at Andersonville, Corp. Samuel J. Gibson of the 103rd Pennsylvania Infantry wrote in his diary,

> I am not a believer in *dreams*; but I had a singular one last night which has oft been repeated; it may mean something, or it may mean nothing; I thought I was in a steamboat in a deep & *muddy* river, the water ran wildly; I thought the Boat I was on was sinking & I sprang from the Hurricane deck upon the hurricane deck of another Boat, which to my horror I found was also sinking, springing from this upon some pieces of broken wreck, I got safely to shore dry shod, while many of my comrades went under.

This recurring dream continued to plague Gibson's thoughts by day. Two weeks after first recording it in his diary—and as he was recovering from a bout of scurvy—Gibson mused that he hoped he would "outlive this misfortune of being a Prisoner but I am not made of *iron*; still I consider myself pretty tough." Then, explicitly referring to his dream, he wrote that he "will try to keep my head '*Above water*' but I am seeing my dream verified every day; by seeing scores of my fellows carried out dead." True to his dream, Gibson survived the war, but not before seeing many comrades buried far away from home in Georgia.[40]

When the chances for exchange seemed bleak, prisoners thought increasingly about escape. The freedom that escapees felt when they got outside of the confines of prison—and the hope of returning to their comrades or their homes—caused a marked change in POWs' dreams. "We are now 131 miles from our starting point having been out 13 nights," wrote Maine officer Charles Mattocks during an attempted escape from the Confederate prison at Columbia. "We begin to feel the want of sleep. Although we get tired, it seems almost impossible to sleep much by day. I dream of home or of reaching our lines every night. . . . Visions optimistic begin to loom up, perhaps yet to be wrested from us." John Ransom of Andersonville had a similar experience during a failed escape, perhaps because he now had the comfort of sleeping on "a soft bed" of spruce boughs. "A change has come over the spirit of my dreams," he wrote in his diary, reflecting the positivity that entered his subconscious as the prospects for freedom seemed high.[41]

If not all soldiers attempted actual escape, many dreamed of it. And for many who were stuck within the confines of a prison, sleep became a time to let their minds escape to happier times at home—just like their counterparts in the field. One Union prisoner of war hoped to forget reality and to "dream of something pleasant to remember the next day." A Confederate inmate at Elmira dreamed of "happier scenes" back in Louisiana. Many prisoners dreamed of their families. New York congressman Albert Ely recorded in his journal while a prisoner of war: "I slept soundly last night, and woke only once from a dream of my wife and children, and the disappointment in not seeing them for a time overcame my feelings."[42]

THE VIVIDNESS OF WARTIME dreams made an indelible mark on nearly all who kept a record of them. Nightmares of battle could be as jarring as dreams of home were pleasant. An Alabama soldier wrote that his dreams of battle "frighten me more than ever the fight did when I was wide awake," while a Massachusetts infantryman lamented that "the minute I get into a doze I hear the whistling of the shells and the shouts and groans" of the wounded. "To sum it up," he concluded, "it is *horrible*." While recuperating at a hospital in St. Louis in April 1862, Lt. Col. James O. Churchill described several "unnatural dreams" in a letter to his parents. "I would be in battle and charge to the mouth of a cannon, when it would fire and I would be blown to pieces," he wrote. "One night I dreamed that two officers came and sat by me; by their shoulder-straps I saw they were colonels. I swallowed them both and they passed down and into my fractured leg, took out their

"The Dream of the Soldier." *Le Rêve* [The Dream] (1888), by the French painter Edouard Detaille, was available in various formats in the United States in the late nineteenth and early twentieth centuries. Collection of the author.

swords and commenced hewing their way out." These dreams were so disturbing that Churchill would wake up violently and unset his broken leg.[43]

Some of these nightmares could be mentally scarring or cause depression. After a cold rainy night in which he "did not sleep well," one Indiana soldier "woke from a dream crying." For the entire day he then had "the blues." A Massachusetts officer told his wife that staring death in the face every day was giving him the blues and causing night terrors. "I get so worked up the other nights I could not sleep and grate drops of swett roled of from me," he told her.[44]

Of course, not all nightmares had to do with battles. In March 1862, long before seeing any significant action, Kentucky Confederate Edward Guerrant had a nightmare "of fire & destruction, blasted hopes & ruined fortunes" and that "some friend of mine was in great danger." In August 1863, Guerrant suffered through a "fearful" and terrifying dream in which he married another man's wife. "Cannot account, rationally, for such singular dreams," he wrote in his diary. "Made me miserable." In May 1864, Guerrant had bad dreams of "a long arduous journey" in which he killed a man.

But perhaps the most terrifying dream came in February 1865 in which he "Dreamed I was *forgotten* . . . and was miserable."[45]

Some soldiers had recurring nightmares of battles they had survived, illustrating the guilt they felt for surviving when so many others had perished. Capt. Henry T. Owen of the Eighteenth Virginia Infantry wrote his wife in December 1863 about a dream he had about Gettysburg that tormented him night after night. Standing amid an immense line of troops, and looking off into the distance, he "saw the dim outlines of lofty hills, broken rocks and frightful precipices which resembled Gettysburg." He and his men marched forward, "fighting that great battle over again." But in his dreams something was different. A "thin shaddow" kept placing itself between Owen and the Union troops amassed along Cemetery Ridge. No matter how he tried to get around it, it kept getting in front of him. "Nobody else seemed to see or notice the shaddow which looked as thin as smoke, and did not prevent my seeing the enemy distinctly thru' it." Finally, when the guns had ceased firing, the shadow spoke to him in biblical cadences. "I am the angel that protected you," it said. "I will never leave nor forsake you." Owen awoke and "burst into tears," wondering why he should be afforded such protection while so many of his comrades had died.[46]

Dreams of battle could be revealed as soldiers talked in their sleep. One Union soldier overheard his tent mate "evidently chasing a rebel in his dream," while another slumbering artillerist shouted, "By detail, load; two, three, four! Sponge; two, three, four! Ram two, three! Ready, fire!" An Illinois officer working in an army hospital similarly overheard one convalescing veteran: "His dreams were vocal ones, and it would have puzzled the most rapid short-hand reporter to have followed the vagaries of his wandering and somnolent senses. At times he was at work upon the farm, driving oxen or horses, and then engaged in some fierce brawl."[47]

Soldiers sometimes tried to wake up their comrades from a bad dream. One Vermont musician described his brother having a nightmare around 11 P.M. one night in late March 1865 when they were sharing a bed, adding that it was "no uncommon thing for him." He continued: "As usual I began to punch and shake him, but no ordinary shaking would bring him out of it. In my intense desire to shake him out of the night mare I forgot that he was on the front side of an elevated bed only wide enough for two to lie on, and when I gave him an extra nudge, off he went to the ground meeting 'terra firma' on his hands and knees and terribly frightening the occupants of the lower bunk. . . . He took all the blankets with him and I found myself all of a sudden in a very lonely condition without covering or bed fellow." Fortunately, "the fall did him no injury and it is needless to say the fall brought him out of the night mare." The men all thought it "a comical affair and we laughed long and well."[48]

A man in the Fifth New Jersey Volunteers gave his comrades "considerable trouble by getting the night mare rather too often," recalled one veteran of the regiment. During one of these "spells" the dreamer evidently thought that "he was [being] attacked by a party of Rebs." He jumped out of his bed, grabbed "a large Bowie knife that lay under his head," and went tumbling over the other men who were sleeping around him. As quickly as they could, his comrades threw cold water into his face to wake him up. But before he fully came to, the boys also seized his knife and pistol, "not wishing to wake up some night and perhaps find him at work on our scalps, dreaming that we were Indians."[49]

Sometimes a soldier's vocal dream of battle could cause a stir throughout camp. A veteran from the First Maine Heavy Artillery recalled that some of his comrades would "holler in their sleep." During "joyous dreams" a soldier might call out, "Hurrah!" to which "immediately a dozen or two of men, more asleep than awake, would stand up and yell, 'Hurrah!'" Not all of the boys were so quick on their feet, as he remembered it. "Some stupid fellow, slower than the rest, would raise himself up on all fours and yell out, 'Where is old Bobby Lee.'"[50]

Just past midnight on August 26, 1862, the men of the Twenty-Eighth New York were roused from their beds and ordered "in a great hurry" to go on picket. Rumors around camp held that the commanding general had awakened "from the effect of a very disagreeable dream, which he imagined the forerunner of impending danger, and in consequence of this dream" the soldiers were awakened and marched more than a mile "in the almost impenetrable darkness, through thickets of bushes, over rocks, across ravines" until they encountered another body of Union troops sleeping on the ground. An officer from the Twenty-Eighth posted a few guards and "the remainder of the men once more sunk on the ground to sleep and the residue of the night passed without further alarm."[51]

Enlisted men with vocal dreams could likewise cause a false alarm. One night, a soldier in the Eighth Vermont yelled out in his sleep, "The rebels are coming!" His entire camp fell into a frenzied panic. The regiment formed and awaited a Confederate attack for thirty minutes while the colonel investigated the cause of the alarm. When the source of was finally determined, the colonel dismissed his men, telling them to "go back to sleep like good little boys." The noise of two oxen "bellowing" through the parade ground of the Twelfth Wisconsin Infantry caused one sleeping soldier to dream that the camp was surrounded by rebels. After he shouted, "My God! we're all surrounded!" his comrades began "a hurried search for trousers, and a seizing of guns" before the mistake was realized.[52]

It seems quite likely that war brought about an increase in violence in the dreams of some citizen-soldiers—even in noncombat dreams. One Wisconsin soldier dreamed of murdering a fellow Union soldier in order to steal his furlough.[53] Commissary Sergeant Alexander Paxton of the Fourth Virginia Infantry kept a dream journal over the first two months of 1864. As is common, Paxton's dreaming mind meandered in illogical ways, jumping from scene to scene, often in an incoherent manner. Many of his dreams included friends and family, or ordinary activities, such as eating meals, walking with friends, going to church or the post office, and riding horses. In one, he dreamed, "My sister Emma didn't want to kiss me because [I] had a big mustache." But other dreams reflected his work as a soldier. In some he weighed meat or doled out rations. And his dreams frequently exhibited violent themes and actions. Some involved fistfights with other individuals. On January 7, 1864, he dreamed that he "slapped a nigger up stairs & had to explain." The following night he dreamed he got a local teacher "on the ground and was choking him," after which he dreamed he got into a fight with a fellow member of his regiment. "I choked him no blood shed tho'." Later that month, he dreamed that a Confederate officer insulted him, so "I slipped off and knocked him over with my fist, then I made a quick time getting away as he had a sword." The fight continued, and the officer "cut me on [the] head and arm with [the] sword," but then Paxton seized the sword and the officer had to flee. Sometimes violence even involved animals. While picking potatoes in one dream, Paxton wrote, an "old sow knocked me down and was chawing at me at wonderful rate."

On a number of occasions, Paxton dreamed of battle. On January 12, 1864, he dreamed he was shot by the enemy, but he was almost instantly transported to another scene in which he was riding in a canoe. The next night, "Was in a fight. Some 'shelling' and they burst near me. Didn't fancy it much. Didn't get hit. Was making a speech somewhere. Was rolling out the ideas. Old Irish woman had my speech, copy of it. Gave it to me. Was going to college or school somewhere. Studying (don't remember). Also had a tooth pulled. Came out easy." In another, he captured several Yankee prisoners. And in yet another, he was shot in the right foot and used "a gun for a crutch." Paxton also dreamt of a macabre scene that was experienced by many soldiers in the grim aftermath of battle—that he went scavenging over a battlefield "hunting wounded friends" and looking for a "good Yankee overcoat."[54]

Dreams of battle often terrified recruits who had not yet seen the elephant. In 1861, Sidney Morris Davis, a young Pennsylvanian planning to enlist in a cavalry unit, tried to sleep on a steamer on his way to Pittsburgh to muster in. For hours he lay awake. Finally, about midnight, he fell into "a troubled, feverish sleep." Davis saw "long lines of battle, clouds of dust and smoke" and he could hear "the thunder of cannon and the tramping of squadrons of cavalry." He "awoke with a start" and sat up so quickly that he banged his head against the ceiling "with such a force that it seemed to rebound back upon the pillow, making sparks of fire fly from my eyes." A "sense of relief came over me as I thought it was only a dream after all," he wrote, "but I dared not close my eyes again for fear the terrible vision would return to haunt the portals of my brain."[55]

Unlike Sidney Davis, Col. Asbury Coward of the Fifth South Carolina Volunteers feared that "the battle would be over before I could get there." Like Davis, he dreamed about battle in northern Virginia before the First Battle of Bull Run took place. But the effects of his dream were quite different. After equipping himself, he "spent a fitful night, dreaming of a battle being fought while I galloped toward it at top speed but never seemed to reach it." When he arrived at Manassas Junction the next morning, he found the tents empty. "Feeling that my dream was prophetic, I hurriedly put my new saddle and bridle on Pythias and rode towards Bull Run." Fortunately—from his perspective—he had not yet missed the fight.[56]

The war quite literally intervened in some soldiers' dreams in other ways as well. While sleeping through a cannonade, one soldier in the Twelfth New Hampshire dreamt that he was watching "a Fourth of July Celebration at home." More ominously, in December 1864, a Maine soldier dreamed about pickets firing shots around him. "The thing finally almost became a nightmare," he wrote in his diary, "when one of the shots woke me up. Sure enough the pickets had been firing occasionally for an hour or more. I got up at once and went out to find that there was more disturbance in camp than I had dreamed of." In this case, the dream was not as frightful as the reality. But this moment did underscore the connection between battle and some soldiers' bad dreams. Indeed, many battle-hardened soldiers hoped that an end to the fighting would restore their sleep to antebellum norms. "My sleep is generally broken and I am troubled considerably with night mares," wrote one Vermont soldier in April 1865. "I will surely be glad when I am done soldiering."[57]

Bad weather could similarly cause unpleasant dreams. "We had a tremendous Thunder shower last night," wrote Massachusetts soldier Charles Harvey Brewster. "I lay dreaming and I thought it was cannon. I thought we were marching towards it, and could see the smoke and I wondered why the balls did not come, finally I woke up and there came a clap precisely like the firing of cannon, and I expected to hear the long roll, but when I heard the rain pattering on the tent I concluded that it was all right." One freezing night in December 1864, a Kentucky Confederate dreamed "of fighting a fearful battle with icicles, in which I was transfixed, bayonetted through & through, one was thrust in my eye, one through my knees, & arms, & breast, & back, & sides." Meanwhile, a soldier from the Thirteenth New Hampshire Volunteers, sleeping on the cold, wet ground without a tent, dreamed that he was "sailing in a boat, the boat capsizes, he is just on the point of sinking, and falls to screaming for help—when he wakes to find himself half buried in water near a foot in depth, and coming up about his ears."[58]

An accidental shooting invaded the dream life of Sgt. Elijah P. Marrs, a former slave who enlisted in the Twelfth U.S. Colored Heavy Artillery in September 1864. During his first night at the Taylor Barracks in Louisville, Marrs occupied the top bed in a three-tiered bunk. "During the night the man who occupied the middle one accidentally discharged his revolver. The ball passed downward, striking the man below in the head and killing him almost instantly." The poor deceased man was then robbed of the three hundred dollars he had received as a substitute. "This was the experience of the first eight hours of my soldier life," recalled Marrs after the war, "and it naturally caused my mind to revert back to my old home and to those I had left behind." After a while, Marrs finally dosed off again, "only to dream of what had happened in the former part of the night, with other horrible things, and was only too glad to waken in the morning and find them not true."[59]

Fear of injury often played out in soldiers' sleep. Soldiers were cognizant of the danger of being run over by horses. With this in mind, surgeon Abner Hard of the Eighth Illinois Cavalry dreamed one night that he was being trampled by a horse. Awaking with a start, he sprang to his feet and hit his head on the crossbeam of his tent, bringing the whole tent down upon himself and his tent mates. "For a few moments, consternation seized them," he recalled after the war, "but no one was seriously injured, and order being again restored, a little sleep was obtained."[60]

As in Surgeon Hard's case, the actions of one soldier could easily affect the sleep and dreams of another. While sitting in his tent eating crackers,

Robert Gould Shaw noticed the regimental drummer "groaning in his sleep" nearby. "I couldn't help imagining that his groan always came in just as I took a bite of toast, or a large gulp of coffee," Shaw wrote to his mother on Christmas Day 1861. "This diminished my enjoyment; and when he suddenly said, '*Martha! there isn't any breakfast*,' I was certain that my proceedings were influencing his dreams!" More dramatically, during the Gettysburg campaign, Pvt. William S. Keller of the 147th Pennsylvania Volunteers "went to sleep . . . dreaming that he was engaged in a hand to hand encounter with the enemy." In his sleep, he swung his arm wildly, striking Capt. Nelson Byers "a severe blow in the face which soon brought the Captain to his feet." Before awaking, however, the force of the blow caused Byers to dream "that he had been struck by a rebel shell."[61]

Many dreams were downright bizarre. The chaplain for the Fifty-Eighth Indiana claimed that sleeping on a cot with folding legs "made me dream of a broken leg." A South Carolinian who had just gorged himself on "a bale of wild onions" dreamed that when he went to visit a former love interest he found her father "perfectly nude—scabs, scales, and dirt covered his entire body, and in this predicament he ushered me into the presence of his daughter." A Wisconsin soldier dreamed that "there was a million angels in rebel uniforms, poaching eggs for me." After eating "poor quality" ginger cakes, a Georgia infantryman reported a series of dreams he had one night to his wife. First, he was an instructor at a female military academy, then he became a member of the Confederate Congress, then an army surgeon, then he saw British minister Lord Lyons, and finally he went home and impregnated his wife. This last dream made him want to laugh. "Of course you will not let any one see this," he then wrote her. "You understand me."[62]

Other soldiers dreamed about the ordinary—but significant—aspects of life. During the night before the state and local elections in Indiana in 1864, chaplain John J. Hight of the Fifty-Eighth Indiana dreamed "that I voted . . . just as I would have done had I been at home—for all the Union ticket." By 1864, nineteen Northern states had passed legislation that permitted soldiers to vote in the field, but Indiana was not one of them. It likely grated on Hight that he could not exercise the citizen's highest privilege while he was risking life and limb in the army. Thus, such a momentous concern as politics made its way into his sleep. In this dream, Hight voted for the Republican candidates on the state and county tickets except for Col. Conrad Baker. "He once insulted me in a small matter, and has never made any apology," wrote Hight. "I bear him no malice, but I cannot vote for him under present circumstances—even in dreams."[63]

Politics and the changing nature of the war affected Confederates' dreams, even when they could not fully recognize how. On January 14, 1863—just two weeks after Lincoln issued his Emancipation Proclamation—an Arkansas soldier wrote to his mother of a strange dream he'd had: "I dreamed last night of being at Aunt Polly's, at a big dinner. I thought things didnt go on right; I thought I had to eat by the side of a negro and he had a plate to eat on, and I had none." One would think that the meaning of such a dream would have been obvious to this soldier, especially because his other letters attest to his political awareness, and he occasionally mentioned Lincoln. But he continued, "If you can interpret that dream you may do it for I cant." Still, he felt confident that he had nothing to fear. "I dont think it will ever come to pass; I know it will never be that way at aunt Polly's house. I think a heap of aunt Polly and I know if the feds do whip us, she will not allow the negroes to eat at her table with white folks."[64]

The war brought about significant changes in American society—things that were largely beyond the power of individuals to control. Nevertheless, soldiers' sleeping brains often sought to bring peace and order to the war-torn country. For all the variety of dreams that soldiers recorded in their letters, diaries, and journals, perhaps none were more affecting than their dreams of the war's end. Soldiers longed to return to life as it had been in peace. Chaplain Joseph Hopkins Twichell of the Seventy-First New York Infantry, after seeing an old college friend in the field, "passed the evening deliciously rambling in our talk over past, present and future, and went to bed to dream of Yale." Even more poignantly, George W. Peck of the Tenth Wisconsin Infantry dreamed that all of the bullets used in the war were made of India rubber "and war was just fun." "There was no more blood," he continued. "There was no one killed, no legs shot off, and men on each side, when not fighting with harmless missiles, were gathered together, blue and gray, having a regular picnic, and every evening there was a dance, the rebels furnishing the girls." After a while, the Union and Confederate soldiers began to mix their sides with "as many blue-coated Yankees among the gray rebels as there were rebels among the Yankees, and after awhile it seemed as though all were dressed alike, in a sort of 'blue-gray,' and then they disappeared, and I recovered my senses." Such safe interactions between Union and Confederate soldiers must have become increasingly frequent in soldiers' dreams. One night Union army surgeon J. Franklin Dyer "dreamed among other things that in conversation with a Rebel, I told him that if we could not whip them in two years we would acknowledge their independence, but can't say that I acknowledge that when awake."[65] It seems likely that dreams like these stemmed from the conflict between soldiers' internal yearning for peace and their willingness to fight out the war until it was won.

Confederate soldiers, of course, experienced similar nocturnal emotions. "I dreamed of seeing you the other night at home," one Georgia soldier told his wife. "I thought peace was made and I had landed home. I was so glad. But I woke up and found it all a dream. When I went to sleep again I dreamed the same dream only I thought I was home on sick furlough. I hope I may get home someday."[66]

THIS BROAD SURVEY of soldiers' dreams reveals something noteworthy about the effects of the war upon the troops. To be sure, many soldiers suffered from nightmares and night terrors (others are discussed in chapter 5), but more bad dreams appear to have been caused by lack of correspondence or fear of infidelity than by the experience of combat. So great were these domestic travails that some soldiers even dreamed about not receiving letters from their families.[67] And letters from home could ameliorate the effects of bad dreams. As one Minnesota soldier even told his wife in November 1863, "Another letter from you at last, which somewhat relieves me from the gloom of that horrible dream."[68]

Of even greater significance, however, is that most soldiers reported happy, peaceful, and romantic dreams of home. Far more common than nightmares of battle were soldiers like John Jones of the Forty-Fifth Illinois, who told his wife of a dream in which she "gave me a most enrapturing kiss." Or William Wallace of Wisconsin, who slept with pictures of his wife and children under his pillow so that he might dream of home. Or a Mississippian who wrote happily to his future wife after awaking from a dream, "My soul thanks the great Giver of all good that He has endowed us with the faculty of dreaming, that the overwrought, wearied soul may wander a season, through the mystic regions of the Dream-land . . . of another and happier world." Or Henry Graves of New York, who saw dreams of home as "angels of mercy" sent to the "soldier mortal." Or Sam Farnum of Rhode Island, who told a friend in November 1862, "I have dreamed often enough of sisters but of picket duty & fights I have never had the luck to dream."[69]

To be sure, the dream reports described in this chapter may contain some bias, since most of them were recorded in correspondence with loved ones. Nevertheless, the candor of soldiers' letters to their spouses and friends is remarkable. When they had a bad dream, they often shared it. Scholars who want to chronicle the "dark side" of the Civil War in dreams can easily find evidence for it; nightmares were certainly discussed by some soldiers and their nurses.[70] But the dream lives of soldiers—on the whole—do not appear to have been dark or terrifying. Some soldiers even awoke from their dreams in laughter.[71] And those who awoke in sadness often did so because of the closeness they had felt to their families while they were asleep. Their dreams had been happy; waking up led to a bitter parting. Indeed, one Confederate soldier wrote from Johnson's Island Prison in October 1863, "We lie down to rest at night to visit perhaps the beautiful and magic world of dreamland, which mocks us with its unattainable witcheries."[72]

On the whole, thoughts and dreams of home helped sustain soldiers in their cause, giving them visual reminders of what—and who—they were fighting for.[73] In their dreams, their homes were places that did not change—they offered hope and familiarity, as well as the promise of eventual peace and happiness. In short, most soldiers delighted in their dreams of home.[74] The dreams of Civil War soldiers—both Union and Confederate—thus reveal an intense intimacy between soldiers and their families. Sharing their dreams with one another helped sustain them through long periods of separation and anxiety and sadness. Rather than growing distant and uncommunicative, soldiers strove to maintain strong lines of communication in their letters, even when doing so meant divulging embarrassing secrets or insecurities. "Do you like to have me tell you my dreams?" one Union sailor playfully asked his wife. "If I cant see you during the day it is at least pleasant to see you in my dreams."[75]

CHAPTER THREE

Civilians' Dreams

During his harried flight from Richmond in the spring of 1865, Jefferson Davis's weariness and utter exhaustion became more and more apparent. When his party stopped for the night at a home in Washington, Georgia, on May 3, Davis "went to bed almost as soon as he got into the house." One of his companions also "came into our house and went right to bed and slept fourteen hours on a stretch." A woman living in the home noted that Davis and his party were "all worn out and half-dead for sleep" after having traveled night after night on horseback.[1]

By now it was only a matter of time. One night in early May, Varina Howell Davis dreamed that their party would be captured while fleeing through Georgia. A day or two later, it finally happened. On May 10, Federal soldiers surrounded Davis and his entourage near Irwinville, Georgia. Varina covered her husband with a shawl and asked the Federals if she could take her "poor old mother out of the way" because she was "so frightened and fears to be killed." But a Union soldier noticed Davis's feet and then recognized the Confederate president. The Federals sent their prize to Fort Monroe, in Hampton Roads, Virginia. In addition to an impending incarceration and punishment, the rebel chief faced the humiliation of knowing that newspapers throughout the nation were depicting him as a fugitive coward dressed in drag.[2]

At Fort Monroe, Davis was placed in irons for five days; he faced sleep deprivation, his mail was censored, and initially he was not allowed to use silverware for fear that he might use it to commit suicide. One of his fellow prisoners in a nearby casemate, Alabama senator Clement C. Clay, described their captivity in "this living tomb" in a letter to his wife: "With a bright light in my room & the adjoining room . . . & with two soldiers in this room & two & a Lieutenant in the adjoining until about 30th June with the opening and shutting of these heavy iron doors or gates, the soldiers being relieved every 2 hours, with the tramp of these heavy armed men, walking their beats, rattling their arms & still more, of the guard (whose duty is to look at me every 15 minutes)—you may be sure that my sleep has been often disturbed and broken." Clay likened this treatment to "one of the tortures of the Spanish inquisition in this frequent, periodical & irregular disturbance of my sleep. During the 112 days of my imprisonment here," he continued, "I have never enjoyed one nights' unbroken sleep—yea, I have been roused every 2 hours, if asleep, by the tread of the soldiers, the clank of & the voices of officers," except for a handful of nights when he was "stupefied by heavy doses of opium," which were presumably given to him by army doctors. The sleep deprivation and lack of privacy made Clay feel "caged & baited, like a wild beast," and he lamented that he had "never known the feeling of refreshment from sleep arising any morning of my imprisonment."[3]

Jefferson Davis faced the same dehumanizing sleep deprivation. In September 1865 he complained that his "loss of sleep has created a morbid excitability" as well as loss of memory. To his wife, he wrote, "For say three months after I was imprisoned here two hours of consecutive sleep were never allowed to me, more recently it has not been so bad, but it is still only broken sleep which I get at night, and by day my attention is distracted by the passing of the Sentinels who are kept around me as well by day as by night." The constant light in his cell also affected his sleep.[4]

Despite all of these hardships, Davis wanted his wife and children to know that he dreamed of them during the little bits of sleep that he got. "In dreams you have lately come to me often in my prayers you and the children form the little group, spiritually, assembled in our Heavenly Father's name," he told Varina in September 1865. He wrote his daughter Margaret in May 1866, "In dreams you come to me the same gentle, loving child from whom I never received any thing which it is not happiness to remember." On a few rare occasions, Davis described his dreams in some detail, even though he professed not to put much credence in them. "Little Maggie appeared to me in a most vivid dream, warning me not to wake you," he wrote to Varina in August 1865. "You know how little I have been accustomed to regard like things," he continued. But in prison "such visions have been frequent, nor have they always been without comfort."[5]

In moments of exhausted delirium, Davis sometimes had difficulty differentiating between his waking moments and his dreams. Unable to sleep one night in January 1866, he sat down near the fireplace in his room. While staring at the fire he saw "a startling optical illusion, such you know as were common in fever." He thought he "saw little Pollie walk across the floor and kneel down between me and the fire in the attitude of prayer." Davis got excited and moved toward his daughter, at which point "the sweet vision melted away. I have not called it a dream because not conscious of being asleep, but sleep has many stages, and that only is perfect sleep which we call Death."[6]

Davis must have reflected on his own mortality while he sat in prison with multiple indictments for treason hanging over his head. During many "silent hours of the night" when he could not sleep, he thought of "the gallant Confederate soldiers, who at the close of the war had returned to ruined and desolate homes, to battle with poverty and all its attendant evils." Nevertheless, Davis's dreams appear to have been mostly peaceful and pleasant. "If I were a believer in dreams my days would be spent in reviewing the visions of the night," he wrote to Varina in October 1865. "In the broken sleep which I get, you and the children frequently visit me and generally I am happy to say with more pleasing aspect than in my wakeful reflections. Little Polly comes oftenest and usually with the gentle, thoughtful air of a woman." But sometimes while sitting in prison alone Davis's feelings of affection for his family overwhelmed him and made him "afraid to dream." To avoid bad dreams, he kept from drinking tea or eating food in the evening and sat up late reading "the dullest book in my possession." Still, he counseled his wife, "as long as your dreams continue to be pleasant, I do not warn you off of that fairy land."[7]

Varina's dreams of her husband, in turn, were pleasant and reassuring. "God has greatly blessed me with dreams for the last three weeks," she wrote to Jefferson in January 1866, but "I had a queer dream some days ago." She dreamed that the United States had gone to war "with England, indeed with all the world, and that we were in Canada, and desperately poor." In the dream a man came to Davis and "offered you a command on the English side," but Davis declined to take the position. After the man departed, Varina "asked you to tell me what you felt, and you said I will never be goaded by want into performing the part of a Swiss or a Hessian." Varina "felt so proud and happy to see that no circumstance co[u]ld debase you." She then awoke and appended this dream to a letter she'd begun two days earlier. "Sometimes these dreams strengthen me—comfort me," she concluded, "—and I forget for an hour that I am alone."[8]

The communication of dreams like these became a way for Varina to encourage Jefferson to live with resolve and not to break under pressure or to compromise his principles. Dream reporting also enabled Varina to commune with her husband, and to remind him that she was with him in spirit even if they could not be physically present with one another. In earlier times, the Davis marriage had faced difficulties that had at times seemed insurmountable. But now that the war was over, the couple wrote affectionately to one another, using dream reports as a source of comfort and consolation. Indeed, Varina told Jefferson, "No bars or bolts can keep me from you in dreams."[9]

Despite such reassurances from his wife, the rebel chieftain's health rapidly deteriorated during his incarceration. "His nervous system is greatly deranged," wrote U.S. army surgeon George Cooper, "being much prostrated and excessively irritable.... Want of sleep has been a great and almost the principal cause of his nervous excitability." The tramping of the sentinels through his room at all hours of the night was the primary cause of this problem. "Prisoner Davis states that he has scarcely enjoyed over two hours of sleep unbroken at one time since his confinement," Cooper continued. The army had placed mats on the floors of his cell "to alleviate this source of disturbance, but with only partial success." Cooper concluded ominously, "Should he be attacked by any of the severe forms of disease to which the tidewater region of Virginia is subject, I, with reason, fear for the result."[10]

The *New York World*, a leading Democratic newspaper, likened Davis's treatment to ancient Roman "torment by insomnia," like that endured by "Caligula roaming through the vast halls of the palace of the Caesars night after night with bloodshot eyes, sleeplessness, and driven by sleeplessness to insanity." The editors of the *World* then asked, "And in what light are we, this triumphant American people of the nineteenth century, to appear before posterity weighted with the damning image of our most conspicuous enemy thus tied by us to the stake and tortured by us with worse than Indian tortures unto death?"[11]

After spending four and a half months in a casemate with a window overlooking the moat at Fort Monroe, Davis was transferred to Carroll Hall, where he dwelled for the remainder of his two-year imprisonment. There, he wrote, his "sleep was less disturbed than formerly." During the summer of 1866, Union military authorities instituted other changes in Davis's sleeping arrangements and his health continued to improve. Two army surgeons reported in August "that he had been free from neuralgia for some time past and slept quite well at night" and that his health was showing marked improvement. The army even permitted Davis to move his bed to the middle of his cell, away from the drafty walls, and ordered "a heavy and dark blanket to be hung at the door, to darken the room and stop the draught."[12] Thenceforth Davis slept more soundly.

"Why He Cannot Sleep," *Harper's Weekly*, July 7, 1866. Collection of the author.

While Democratic papers like the *World* showed sympathy for the captured rebel president, Republican newspapers interpreted Davis's sleeplessness quite differently. "Several times Mr. Davis has passed sleepless nights," reported the *Philadelphia Press*, "caused, no doubt, by reason of his past misdeeds and crimes that cry to Heaven for vengeance."[13] On July 7, 1866, *Harper's Weekly* even printed a full-page cartoon by Thomas Nast entitled, "Why He Cannot Sleep." Like the Ghost of Christmas Past in Charles Dickens's *A Christmas Carol*, this dark and sensational image depicted the beleaguered Confederate leader slumped in his bed and haunted by the figure of Lady Liberty, who was directing Davis's mind to nightmares in the form of dead and suffering Union soldiers at prisoner of war camps and blood-soaked battlefields.[14]

CHRISTMAS MORNING DOWN SOUTH

Master Jeff Davis finds a pretty present Santa Claus has left at his bed side for him.

"Christmas Morning Down South." The influence of the devil over Jefferson Davis became a common trope in Northern iconography of the Civil War era—just as it had been with figures like Benedict Arnold during the American Revolution and would later be for John Wilkes Booth. In this image, an apparition of Satan infiltrates Davis's sleep and dreams. Courtesy of Special Collections/Musselman Library, Gettysburg College.

The difference between Davis's actual dreams—which were pleasant visitations with his family—and how newspaper editors and readers *imagined* his dreams, underscores the deep value that nineteenth-century Americans placed in dreams and visions. The depictions in the popular press revealed the depth of emotional guilt that Northerners believed the ex-president ought to bear as a consequence for his leadership in the rebellion. Gone was the feminized dandy captured in women's attire. No longer did Northerners wish simply to lampoon or ridicule Davis. Now they wanted to punish him. If Federal attorneys were moving too slowly in the prosecution of the nation's greatest traitor, then public opinion could at least be satisfied to believe that Davis's conscience was holding him accountable. Nowhere was guilt more deeply felt than in a person's sleepless nights and tortured dreams. And Northerners would have to content themselves that such a punishment was sufficient for the time being.

It is unknown whether Davis ever dreamt of his potential prosecution or execution while he sat imprisoned at Fort Monroe, but his vice president, Alexander Stephens, did. Similarly plagued with poor sleep while imprisoned at Fort Warren in Boston Harbor, Stephens lay awake at night "thinking of my imprisonment, and brooding over my suspense." It is little wonder that he had nightmares about Federal retribution. "Had bad dreams," he wrote in his diary on September 24, 1865; "dreamed of seeing several people hanged."[15]

If Davis ever had dreams like Stephens's, he never said so. Instead, he only reported comforting dreams in his letters. And Varina responded in kind, hoping to encourage her suffering husband in this time of great trial. Dreams for the Davises became an escape from reality, a way to commune during a period of separation, and a means of encouraging each other to persevere. In their dream reporting, the Davises followed the cultural scripts of mid-nineteenth-century America perfectly—using their dream reports to uplift and encourage one another so that they might survive a dark period of suffering.

Dreams served similar purposes for many Northern and Southern civilians during the war. But unlike the Davises, ordinary civilians were much more candid, often sharing both good and bad dreams in their letters. Such dream reports had the potential to demoralize or discourage individual soldiers, just as they did with Dr. William Child of New Hampshire as described in chapter 2. Nevertheless, women back home often could not resist the temptation to share disturbing visions with their menfolk. A dark or scary dream could cast such a shadow over a lonely woman at home that social convention was powerless to persuade her to keep it to herself. In this way, the private dreamworlds of Civil War–era Americans—and the desire to maintain a real emotional connection with their spouses—often held more sway over women than the social pressure to unequivocally support the war effort.

UNION AND CONFEDERATE women mobilized themselves in support of their respective war efforts. Whether serving as nurses, in sewing circles, or for large organizations like the U.S. Sanitary Commission, many white women cast their energies firmly with their cause. Nevertheless, women had real reservations and concerns about sending so many men off to fight, and this reluctance often revealed itself in the unconscious wanderings of their sleeping minds. The dream reports of women on the home front reveal the tensions they faced when their husbands, brothers, sons, and fathers were off fighting the war. These women longed to support their respective war efforts—and to support their menfolk who enlisted in their cause. Yet they also felt a strong, natural desire for their loved ones to be at home, where they would be safe.[16] So frequently were women's letters despondent in their tone that public speakers and essayists urged wives to write only encouraging letters to their husbands, never focusing on suffering or hardships during the war. On some occasions, Union military authorities even confiscated dispiriting letters from home before they could reach their intended recipients.[17]

Just as with some soldiers, the Civil War caused civilians to have bad dreams; and the dream lives of civilians at home could be as intense as those of soldiers in the field—perhaps even more so. After having a nightmare, civilian dreamers had to decide just how much they would reveal to their soldier-correspondents. Wives longed to share their bad dreams with their husbands—they wanted to receive comfort and support, just as they would have after a bad dream in prewar days. But now they felt hesitant to divulge dreams that might discourage the soldiers and undermine morale. Civilians understood that their dreams revealed something significant about their emotional states of mind, and they feared that sharing distressing dreams with men in the army might have a tangibly deleterious effect on the war. Dreams, in a very practical sense, could have the power to induce action on the part of soldiers—perhaps even desertion or resignation. Despite these misgivings, women North and South often erred on the side of disclosing too much to their husbands rather than too little. They wanted to keep the lines of communication open, and they hoped they could at least be comforted through letters from loved ones who were hundreds of miles away.

Lonely wives often experienced nightmares that could be nearly debilitating. Quite often such bad dreams were directly related to husbands' service in the war.[18] On May 12, 1863, Kate Peddy of Georgia wrote her husband, "Nearly every night I dream of you being in trouble, and it must be the case. I have been so uneasy for fear you would come off by yourself, and so many Yankee scouts prowleling around." In October, things were not much better: "Honey, I am tolerably well to night," she wrote, "but I am tormented with the most frightful dreams you ever knew and wake up scared almost to death." The following month these nightmares continued: "At night I am tormented with the most frightful dreams I ever had & nearly always something about your being wounded or sick. I wake screaming, then I am nearly tired to death. I can't sleep well no time."[19]

For whatever reason, Kate Peddy was either unable or unwilling to share the actual content of her dreams. All we can tell is that her husband's absence and proximity to danger, in conjunction with the stresses of raising their child alone, made her deathly afraid in her sleep. Other women were more forthcoming in their dream reports, sharing greater detail about the dreams that so disturbed them. Many of these dreams resulted from fears that women had of abandonment—either from their husband's death or because their husbands might simply prefer military life to matrimony.[20] In Iowa, Dollie Vermilion wrote her husband that she dreamed of him almost every night and that he was "always well and cheerful and bright, and I am so happy for a moment while the dear vision lasts." But, she continued, "I can't help longing to see you, to hear your voice, to feel your kisses on my lips, *to live with you again, all your own Dollie*, and I can't help telling you when I write to you." Still, she worried about the effects of her dream reports on his morale. "Sometimes I fear my letters do you harm rather than good, and I don't want to do you harm," she wrote. And in another letter in which she described "how desolate I feel" when she would wake up in the morning, she told him, "It is my *heart* that speaks like that. Don't blame me, dearest. Sometimes I am patriotic, and I feel that it would be a glorious thing to live, or die, in defense of a country so just and holy. But my heart is truer than my head."[21]

Some women were gradually able to overcome fearful feelings—even in their dreams. In upstate New York, Cora Benton "felt depressed in spirit" when her husband, Charlie, left to become a soldier in August 1862. One night in November of that year she "dreamed you had been in battle, and after the company had got back to camp, I rushed in to find *you gone—dead* and *buried* on the field, without one look, one word. I was frantic with grief, and although I know 'twas but a dream, it seemed so real I have not been able to throw off the influence during the day." It was "hard enough to bear your absence during waking hours, not to be thus harassed while sleeping," she wrote to Charlie the next morning. "Every time I dream of you, they are always hurrying you away before I can get to you to speak with you. Oh! it was *cruel* not to let you come to me." Cora then closed her sorrowful letter, "Good Night, dear, *dear husband*; may the time speedily come when my good-nights will not take days to reach you. 'Oh! My *lonely, lonely, lonely* pillow.' "[22]

Bad dreams continued to haunt Cora over the ensuing months. In January 1863, she told Charlie she was "having troubled dreams of you." In February, she dreamed that he looked older and had "two deep wrinkles across your fore head." The two embraced and "fondly kissed" and fortunately in this dream "you were not hurried from me as in previous dreams."[23] But in August the bad dreams returned. After waking up one morning, Cora felt "rather sad" and ready to cry. She had dreamed of hugging Charlie and asking him when he was coming home, but he replied in a frustrated voice, "It is always so—just as I get a little contented, you spoil it all." He began to sing a camp song "to forget home and wife." "Your voice was very sweet," she told him in a letter, "but each line went like a sword-thrust to my heart; and begging your forgiveness for giving you pain, I stood up weeping from the pain you had given me, and I you."

This "vivid" dream threw "a shadow over my heart all day," Cora wrote, and she interpreted it as a sign that her letters were not supportive enough of Charlie's service to the nation. Indeed, she took her dream to be a "warning to me to write differently to my husband than I have done" so that she would not make him discontented in his military service. But in her heart of hearts she could not help herself. "I want to see you so much," she quickly added, and "I can't hardly help saying so, and telling you how my heart aches."[24]

Over time, Cora became more active in civic life and economic matters. She still desperately longed for her husband's return, but she also found ways to occupy her time and better her family's living conditions. (In April 1864, for example, she founded a small school for local children.) When Charlie advised her on what to do about a physical ailment, she playfully replied, "You forget you don't take care of me much now, and I am not quite as dependent as I used to be on you. There will be two heads [of household] after this—do you understand, darling?" It is little wonder that a change also came about in Cora's dreams. Never again did she report a nightmare or troubled dream. "I had a very precious dream of you Friday night, and it seemed so real I felt happy all day yesterday," she wrote in May 1864. "I saw you plainly, and was sitting in your lap with my head on your shoulder, resting as I'd like to be this hour. It seemed very natural, and I'd like to dream so every night." She continued: "I am sure of one thing—I must work while you are gone in order to live at all, and I am willing to do so, while I keep well. It is needless to say I am weary of living as we do, and I wish the time was up for you to be away. I dreamed it was, last Friday night, but that did not make it so. We will try to be patient, and do our separate works faithfully, till God says it is enough, and we go hand in hand together again."[25]

Cora Benton's development into a more independent woman manifested itself in her dream life, and she revealed that growth in her letters to her husband. It may seem ironic that her dreams would become more positive at the very point when the war was becoming most destructive and dangerous—the summer of 1864—yet it may be because she was becoming more autonomous and self-reliant. As desperately as she longed to be with Charlie, she now knew a sense of autonomy and confidence that she had never known before. It is little wonder that she could write in her final letter to her husband in June 1865—reflecting on the hardships she had faced and overcome throughout the war—"I am not crushed, but sit here tonight stronger than when you left me."[26]

Like Kate Peddy, Cora Benton, and Dollie Vermilion, many wives chose to share their feelings honestly rather than keep them to themselves. "Grant I dreamed last night that you was dead for ceartain," wrote Malinda Taylor to her husband in the Fortieth Alabama Infantry. "I thought I went crazy and that will bee the way it will turn out if it is the case. I believe I had rather dye and leave my sweet little ones in the hands of a merciful God and go with you. I feel humbled down in the very dust this morning."[27] In like manner, a Texas woman told her husband about "some *very* pleasant dreams" she'd had about him over the course of a few nights, "but last night I cried in my sleep until I felt bad from it when I awoke—I was in great trouble." Indeed, women like this one were often surprisingly forthright with their husbands about their disturbing dreams. "I have some dreams about you sometimes some bad," she told him a few months later. "You know how superstitious I am about them."[28]

Ellie Goldwaite of New York dreamed almost nightly of her husband coming home from the war. In the morning she would check her dream book to look for symbols or find meaning. Reporting her dreams was a way to show affection to her husband. Sometimes she even used nonsensical dreams to let him know how much she missed him. One night Ellie dreamed that she was in a schoolhouse that was "full of honey bees and that I was throwing snow balls at the bees." Her very next dream involved her husband, Richard, being in a sour mood. After describing these two dreams in a letter, she playfully told him that if he was cross with her when he came home from the war, "I will snow ball you till you get pleasant again."[29]

Ellie's most terrifying dreams involved going to church, for these, she believed, portended battle. "Dick, I dreamed last night that I was going to church with your mother and three men came and gagged me and took me to prison, or I thought that it was a private mad house anyway," she wrote. Ellie awoke crying and it "haunted me all day . . . as if it were a reality." "Dick, church is trouble," she continued. "I do not like to dream about it. I dreamed about church the time of the Battle of [Big] Bethel."[30]

Such emotion-laden dreams as these again underscore the tensions that plagued many women both North and South as they struggled with their natural desires for their husbands to be home and their patriotic duties to send men off to fight. Reporting dreams was something like a hobby in antebellum days—a morning routine that generally had little consequence.[31] Dream reports during the war years, however, carried much greater significance. Soldiers' wives struggled with determining how selective to be when describing their dreams to their husbands so as not to discourage the men who were fighting. Yet they appear to have shown little reticence in sharing their bad dreams. Dream reports—to an extent—may reveal a limitation in these women's civic commitments. They shared their deepest emotions even if doing so might demoralize their kin.

In contrast with these ordinary women, Confederate first lady Varina Howell Davis may have better understood the importance of keeping bad dreams to herself—or at least not sharing them with her husband. Throughout the war, Mrs. Davis doubted the Confederacy's chances for success, and her indiscretions even made their way into the newspapers in the spring of 1862. She learned from these mistakes (at least temporarily; her lack of patriotism again appeared in the papers in 1864), and displayed prudent selectivity in her dream reports to Jefferson. During the summer of 1862 the Confederate first lady "suffered for three days with a nervous attack" and her restless sleep was filled with disturbing dreams about her husband. In one dream—which she did not share with Jefferson—she dreamed that "Mr Davis had been taken alive in battle by lopping off his hand, and while fainting he was secured." Such a nightmare must have terrified the Confederate first lady as Union soldiers were closing in on the Confederate capital during the Peninsula Campaign. Varina's dream mirrored the fears that many wives felt when their husbands marched off to war. In this case, however, she did not wish to discourage her husband, who was so desperately trying to steer the ship of state. Her dream only survives because she shared it with another intimate friend.

Varina did share other, less traumatizing dreams with her husband. "I have slept so little since I heard of the fighting," she told him during the Peninsula Campaign. "I will go to bed now and dream of you. I dreamed that you and I were saying good bye before a great multitude, and you kept returning, and clasping to your breast, and I running back to kiss you and the people laughing, yet I could not forbear, nor you." She then signed off, "Good night sweet, sweet Banny, may God bless you and keep you safe for Your devoted Wife."[32] Curiously, this 1862 dream mirrored another one she'd had during the Mexican War in September 1846, in which she and Jefferson kissed one another several times while they "were taking leave before a multitude."[33] The embarrassment Varina felt in her 1862 dream—as evidenced by the onlookers laughing—may have been the result of her much more public position at the time (she was often criticized by Richmonders during the war), whereas during the Mexican War she was an ordinary officer's wife. Nevertheless, Varina's reporting of this dream in 1862 offered love and encouragement to a man who was trying to lead a nation through a war for independence.[34] She may have had private misgivings about Confederate independence, but she knew that her dream reports could have public significance—even when reported privately. She therefore reported her dreams carefully and selectively, paying heed to the needs of both her husband and her nation.

CIVILIANS IN BOTH the North and the South frequently experienced the inverse of "the soldier's dream of home." While soldiers regularly dreamed of going home, women and children often dreamed of their menfolk coming home. Lonely women desperately longed to have these dreams, and some would do whatever they could to induce them. One night in 1863, Dollie Vermilion of Iowa put one of her husband's letters under her pillow, hoping she would dream of him. Unfortunately, the technique didn't work. Instead of dreaming of her husband coming home, she "dreamed of a battle somewhere, all night" with the sounds of "drums beating, and cannon booming, and the shout of the distant soldiers." When Dollie awoke the following morning and wrote a letter to her husband, she told him, "It troubles me." Clearly Dollie's attempt to influence her dreams in a positive way had exactly the opposite effect. Instead of dreaming pleasant dreams of her husband coming home, her unconscious mind traveled to the danger he was experiencing—something that undoubtedly preoccupied her waking thoughts.[35] Other women had better luck. Sometimes simply receiving a letter from the field could cause a lonely wife to have pleasant dreams of her husband. After receiving one such letter, one Minnesota wife replied lovingly, "I read it with interest as I always do your letters & went to bed to dream of seeing you."[36]

Women's dreams of their husbands were common during the Civil War, and often quite enjoyable. On her fourth wedding anniversary in November 1864, one Pennsylvania woman "dreamed so sweetly of my husband that he had come home & we were talking."[37] Women on the home front sometimes even welcomed dreams that exhibited the effects of psychological stress. In April 1862, Minnesotan Lizzie Caleff was "disopointed" to wake up from a dream in which her fiancé, James Bowler, "came home" but "had changed in your looks [so] that I did not know you." Even though he appeared strange to her in the dream, she still wanted to see him that way. In November 1862, Lizzie and James were married, and the following year they had a baby girl. In December 1863, James told Lizzie to move the baby to another bed when he came home so that she would not "come between [you] an[d] me." This sentiment must have impressed itself on Lizzie's mind—perhaps causing her to worry that James would not love his child (even though James expressed great affection for both mother and baby in his letters). In January 1864, Lizzie again dreamed that James returned home, but in this dream he walked right past their baby's cradle without even stopping to look down at her. "That made me sort of spunky & I would not show her to you," Lizzie wrote. One might think that such a dream would have upset the young mother, but Lizzie still loved any opportunity to see her husband in a dream. After Lizzie showed her spunk in the dream, her baby cried—in real life—and awakened Lizzie, "spoil[ing] the rest of my dream."[38]

Just as with soldiers' letters, women sometime reported erotic dreams to their husbands. After receiving a "short *naughty* letter" from her husband in February 1862, Emily Harris of New Hampshire replied, "it made me dream of you evry night since." A few weeks later she described a dream in which "I laid my head on your shoulder and your cheek was laid on my head and I felt your warm breath just as I used to. And though it was all a dream I am thankful for it and if you never come back, [I] will never ask a greater blessing than such dreams as these." A few months later she wrote again, "If you were here to night you would see what I would do to you for dreaming so naughty about me. I would squeeze you harder than you ever got squeezed before" and "kiss your lips . . . just how I used to kiss your face all over even your blessed loving blue eyes." Dollie Vermilion similarly told her husband, "I dreamed last night that I saw you, and you laid your head in my lap, and I kissed you and petted you, and combed your head, and pulled out all your grey hairs. Oh, I *loved* you so much in my dream."[39]

Of course, not all dreams involving spouses were pleasant or reassuring. Just as fears of infidelity, anxiety about separation, and feelings of lack of control pervaded soldiers' dreams, so could they be found in the dreams of women. With young men away from home, surrounded by strange women—including prostitutes, nurses, and belles—women back home worried that their menfolk might give in to temptation.[40] After receiving a letter about her husband's illness in November 1864, Cornelia Peake McDonald, a forty-two-year-old refugee in Virginia, dreamed that her husband was engaged to another woman and that "preparations were going on for the wedding." She "saw him sitting alone at a long table covered with a white cloth. On the table, just before him was laid a large green wreath; nothing else was on it." While McDonald's husband was not unfaithful to his wife (as far as we know, at least), his devotion to his country—and poor health during very trying times—would cause her to lose him. Soon after McDonald had this dream, Angus McDonald died.[41]

Just as lack of correspondence caused some soldiers to doubt their wives' love and fidelity, women back home also longed for a word from the army to assure them of their husband's love. "What can be the matter that you don't write?" Kate Peddy of Georgia asked her husband in the Confederate army. "It has been nearly three weeks since you wrote a single line. I fear my dream is coming true that you have learned to love me less." Such doubts plagued many women for the duration of the war. "I dreamed you came home the other night, and I was nearly crazy with joy, but you seemed indifferent," wrote Peddy in December 1862 in an echo of the common soldier's dream. "I wanted to know if you did not love me. You said, yes, but did not love me as much as you did before you had learned to stay away. I awoke in great distress, and all the next day it would come into my thoughts oftener than I wished."

Like many husbands, George Peddy tried to persuade his wife not to put much stock in her dreams. "The deceptive dreams spoken in yours of my coolness towards you when I return home should not be entertained," he chastised her lovingly, "for I assure you the rapid march of time only increases my genuine affection for you. No circumstance can ever change my adoration for you so long as you remain constant, and even then I could not forego the joy of your love." Following another of her bouts of nightmares, George tried to encourage Kate by telling her that he had "so many pleasant dreams of you these nights."[42]

Other soldiers responded in kind, countering their spouses' dream reports of infidelity with loving reassurances. When an Irish woman in New York dreamt that her husband left her and married "a nigger winch," he playfully replied, "i amnot as yet i dunt now howe soon i may get one the[y] are [as] plnty [as] cattle around." He then assured her of his faithfulness, asking her to "give my love to the children and a bushil of kisses to each one and 2 bushil for your self." In like manner, a New Hampshire soldier comforted his wife, "I hardly know what to say to your dream. I will not say you was silly to tell me of it, but you *was* silly to dream any such things about your husband who loves you better than all the rest of the world. But

"The Soldier's Home, The Vision." While this print by Currier and Ives offers a sentimentalist depiction of a wife's dreams of her husband on the battlefield, it captures the real connection between correspondence and positive dreams that many soldiers and civilians experienced during the war. Courtesy of the American Antiquarian Society.

I have told this so many times that it seems like an old story, and I know that you do not doubt it."[43]

The fear of abandonment could come out in women's dreams in some of the strangest ways. Emma Crutcher of Natchez, Mississippi, wrote a bizarre letter to her husband, Will, in the Confederate army, telling him of the "maximized joy" she felt when she dreamed that he had been shot in the leg and had it amputated. "Now, thought I, he will never leave me again, for he will be of no use, in the army, and—if I die, he will never marry again, for no one but me would love a lame man—he is mine now." When she awoke in the morning, Emma breathed a sigh of relief that "it was not reality, lameness and all," but she assured him, "I had rather take you now, lamed for life, than wait for months and maybe years longer, with the chance of [not] having you back with me."[44]

While Emma Crutcher's dream may not have been the most romantic sentiment she'd ever expressed to her husband, it captured, in its own peculiar way, her love for him and her desire to never lose him. As unsettling as receiving such a letter must have been, at least Will could rest assured in his wife's abiding faithfulness to him. Still, most women did not welcome dreams of their husbands being wounded. When Hannah Long of Pennsylvania dreamed that her husband was sick and "wounded in the left arm and shoulder and face and was so poor that I could cary you in my arms," she awoke gasping for breath, calling the dream "dreadful." But, like Crutcher, she used such a nightmare to reassure her husband, "I am loving you with all my heart."[45]

Single women dreamed of lovers—real or imaginary—they longed to meet. Following an old superstition that sleeping with one's head on a "slice of bride cake" would cause an unmarried person to "dream of their future wife or husband," Kate Stone "slept on my paper and dreamed my best but to no purpose, 'nobody coming to marry me, nobody coming to woo.'" Lizzie Alsop of Fredericksburg had better luck in her dreams. "Last night I had such a delightful dream—of course Cupid presided," she wrote in her diary in February 1865. But then she added sorrowfully, "I wish it were indeed only a reality." The lack of eligible bachelors in the Confederacy may have had curious effects on the unconscious imaginings of Southern women. After a Virginia girl was rudely awakened by a rat that scurried around on her bed, she "dreamed that a rat was escorting me about the yard discussing moonlight, music, love and flowers, so that I felt very stupid all day."[46]

CIVILIANS OFTEN DREAMED—both literally and figuratively—of going to the front. Some women had been dreaming eagerly of war since before shots were even fired. In 1859, Elizabeth Oakes Smith of Virginia had a prophetic dream of the coming desolation: "I saw the immense camp of a vast soldiery—slaughter and demolition—sights to harrow up the soul—and then predicted—'there will be war—very soon will war come upon us—a terrible strife, which will last twenty years.'"[47] Ardent Confederate nationalists embraced the war in their daydreams and nighttime visions. Lizzie Hardin, a Confederate sympathizer from Kentucky, daydreamed in November 1860—just after Lincoln's election—that she was a Southern soldier fighting against the Yankee hordes. "After crossing another creek we began the ascent of an almost perpendicular knob and I tried to fancy how I would feel, belonging to a body of soldiers, ordered to charge up such a hill, under a heavy fire from the summit," she wrote in her diary. "Reaching the summit, I imagined myself in the much more pleasant position of firing down on the enemy, as they attempted to pass the road below. Then I tried charging down the knob, but noticing my accelerated speed, as I neared the bottom, I inwardly hoped I might not be received on fixed bayonets."[48]

Once the fighting began, however, Confederate and border region dreams of war were often less glorious and more steeped in the realities and anxieties of life during wartime.[49] In July 1861, a North Carolinian dreamed that he saw a great fire in the woods that made him think there would soon be "great trouble."[50] A few months later, Elizabeth Blair Lee of Washington, D.C., dreamed that the Confederates had captured one of the Federal forts around the capital. She dreamed herself onto Pennsylvania Avenue "in a scene of great anguish and trouble." "I tell you this," she wrote her husband, "to let you see how these terrible times haunt me."[51] A Louisiana woman whose husband was traveling "went to bed partially undressed to dream of Steam-boats blowing up."[52] Near the Yazoo Pass in Mississippi, planter William Cooper dreamed "of flood & planks to walk on . . . amid mud [and] water—& of my driving [a] wagon amid rain & high water with 2 mules . . . in flight from the enemies." In April 1862, a Georgia woman dreamed that her husband went insane. "I thought you would not speak to me," she wrote him the next morning. "I thought all you wanted to do was to fill up the roads with logs and brush so that Lincoln's Army could not pass through the country." The dream apparently terrified the woman. She continued, "It pestered me worse than any dream I ever dreamed before but I hope there is nothing of it." Following the death of a Confederate officer in 1863, Daniel Cobb of Virginia had nightmares of an army of men "without armes & legs" being pursued by another army. "I dream of the dead nightly and conversing with them," he wrote in his diary. A Virginia girl similarly "dreamed sad dreams about the boys and felt low-spirited all next day."[53]

Wartime loneliness and separation caused some civilians to have dreams about abandonment nearly identical to the ones experienced by soldiers. In April 1861 a delegate to Virginia's secession convention had a terrible nightmare that he was having a wonderful time at a party with his wife but that when "the party broke up and while I was getting my overcoat you started off with some other gentleman & left me alone." The delegate ran after his wife and called for her but she would not reply. All he could hear was her "laughing & talking in the midnight darkness up the street on your way home." He continued: "I went back, sat down & resolved never, never, to see you again, my sorrow & mortification knew no bounds, but my resolution was instantly fixed to fly & forever leave the Country. I would not submit to be disgraced & abandoned in that way." In the dream he arose and started to leave his hometown "finally & forever" when he awoke with his heart "jumping as if I had just run a race, & I was perfectly overwhelmed with alarm for a moment until I discovered that it was all a dream." Like so many soldiers who had frightening dreams of infidelity, this Virginia politician told his wife how lonely he was (they had been apart for more than two months).[54] Separation from home thus had similar effects on the emotional states of being of soldiers and civilians alike.

The stressful sleeplessness of wartime brought vivid dreams and emotional outpourings to many Southern households. During the Red River Campaign, in March 1864, Harriet Perry, a young woman in East Texas, told her husband, "My mind does not rest during the hours of sleep. I dream of you all the time. I never was so anxious to see you—I know you are suffering mentally and physically. I sympathise with you with all my heart, and would willingly share your privations and troubles, if it would lessen them and relieve you—My love for you was never so fond or intense as in these hours of danger and trial." Similarly, a Virginia woman was plagued by nightmares about her husband's sickness and death. "I was the most miserable being on earth," she wrote him one morning. "I thought it would kill me until I wakened up and found it all a dream. Oh, how glad I was when I waked up. I was going on at a dreadful rate when I woke up."[55]

Many nineteenth-century Americans believed that they could avoid bad dreams by controlling their diets. After dreaming in April 1865 that several loved ones had died, the wife of Union general Benjamin F. Butler wrote, "I have done eating their odious soups, and various other abominations. Coffee, bread, eggs and milk make up my diet. This will do away with dreams." Mary Chesnut of South Carolina blamed "war talk" and "eating macaroons unlimited" for her "fright and horror in the night," which awakened her husband with her screaming. It was, she said, a "nightmare in its worst shape." More successfully, Kate Stone of Louisiana wrote in her diary in 1864, "No knightly forms of soldiers brave disturbed our dreams after eating the white of an egg half-filled with salt."[56]

But in reality, Southerners could not avoid invading Yankee armies—even in their dreams. As early as the spring of 1861, Confederate women dreamed of swarming Union soldiers. In May 1861, Ada Bacot of upcountry South Carolina dreamed that a black woman came to her and "implored that I would protect her that the yankees were going to shoot her." Bacot was "much excited, & when I awoke found my self quite exhausted." In September 1863, Mary Chesnut recorded in her diary, "Tossing around in dreams, I could see marines falling in line, saluting Mr. Mallory, everywhere great guns firing, marine bands playing, &c&c." In like manner, Sarah Estes, a Tennessee refugee, dreamed in June 1862 that a unit of Federal cavalry approached her aunt Nannie's home, where she was staying. In the dream she beckoned her brother to flee. "He ran around the house but they rushed up and saw him trying to escape them and took him and my husband prisoner." As Sarah was feeling incredible distress, the scene suddenly changed. Thinking that her husband and brother had been taken to a prison in the North, she followed them "and the Yankee women laughed at my misery saying they felt no sympathy for a Southerner." She was "so unhappy" when she woke up, but believed that the dream had somehow been given "to comfort me and make me willing to go."[57]

On some occasions, dreams of war inspired dreamers to take actions in their waking moments. In June 1862, Louisiana refugee Sarah Morgan dreamed "of being shelled out unexpectedly and flying without saving an article." In the dream a friend and Confederate soldier, Will Pinkney, told her that Vicksburg had fallen. Pinkney said that he was to blame for the surrender and that the Southerners wanted to hang him for the defeat, while Northerners wanted to hang him for his treason. So in the dream "he was running for his life." Morgan continued, "He took me to a hill from which I could see the Garrison, and the American flag flying over it. I looked, and saw we were standing in blood up to our knees, while here and there ghastly white bones shone above the red surface." Morgan looked and saw crowds of people running. Pinkney told her that the town would soon be shelled. "Save yourself," he yelled to her. "But Will," she replied, "I must have some clothes, too! How can I go among strangers with a single dress? I *will* get some!" Pinkney then "smiled and said, 'You will run with only what articles you may happen to have on.'" At that moment the bombardment began. "Bang! went the first shell, the people rushed by with screams, and I awakened to tell Miriam [her sister] what an absurd dream I had had."

Whether absurd or not, Morgan's dream captured many of the fears and practical concerns that Southern refugees faced during the war—Yankee invasion, Confederate defeat, blood and death, threats to loved ones, loss of personal property, and a feeling of being overwhelmed by the chaos around her. Morgan had had a similar dream earlier in the war—a night or two before she fled her home in Baton Rouge in May. Now, a month later and experiencing life as a refugee, it is little wonder that she awoke that morning in June and "packed up a few articles to satisfy my conscience, since these men insist that another run is inevitable."

Life as a refugee would continue to invade Morgan's sleep during the war. In March 1863, she cursed her refugee status in her dreams. In July she dreamed that a Yankee officer told her all her belongings were lost.

She continued: "All kinds of troubles and annoyances followed, which I forget, until I found myself carrying somebody's baby over miles and miles of road, and at each mile, the baby grew larger and heavier, until I could scarcely carry it. I bent down to kiss its pretty cheek, and lo! instead, it turned to a great blood boil which burst on my lips." Morgan awoke "in horror" and murmured, "Bless that baby; my unfailing prophecy of trouble!"[58]

Some Southerners looked to their dreams for meaning about the war. Many believed that their dreams disclosed glimpses into the future. Some even had ideas in their dreams that they later found to be useful. One night a North Carolina attorney dreamed that he was deaf when the Yankees reached his home. Apparently he thought that was a good idea, for when the Union soldiers finally did arrive some time later he "played" deaf so that he wouldn't have to talk to them. Others grappled with the crumbling Confederate economy in their dreams. A South Carolina merchant—whose letters to his wife are filled with discussion of inflation and other fiscal matters—dreamed in early 1864 that somebody was choking him in an attempt to get what little money he had left.[59]

As the war dragged on, many Confederate civilians increasingly endured suffering both in waking and in sleep. "We lie down at night, only to dream of midnight murder, robbery, & burnings," wrote one Kentucky minister in his diary in August 1864. One night that autumn Virginia refugee Cornelia Peake McDonald woke up screaming after she had a frightening dream of her husband nearing death. Men also faced the harsh realities of war in their dreams. Two months after Richmond burned, Alexander Stephens dreamed he was in the former Confederate capital "roaming amid ruins" looking for a friend's house and for two of his former servants, Henry and Anthony. The houses he sought had all been "swept away by fire" and his servants were nowhere to be found.[60]

Dreams about slaves were not uncommon among Southerners during the war and its immediate aftermath. Indeed, Confederates could not avoid the impending social revolution within their society, even in their sleep. Even more importantly, their dreams reflected how they had internalized the ideologies of slavery. A dichotomy appeared in their dreams, with Confederates either viewing African Americans as an inferior race unworthy of respect and dignity, or as part of a paternalist system that truly benefited the slaves. Some dreams clearly reflected the former view. In chapter 2 we saw the Arkansas soldier who dreamed in January 1863 that his aunt Polly had allowed a black man to eat at her dinner table. In Mississippi, Sallie McRae wept for thirty minutes after dreaming that her mother gave her homespun dresses to the "niggers." Meanwhile, in Kentucky Ellen Wallace "could not sleep last night for thinking and dreaming of the [Union] draft which is to take place on Saturday." The thought of white men being conscripted "into Lincoln's Army side by side and shoulder to shoulder with the negro troops" was more than she could bear. "The master and his former slave must keep time to the same music, share the same rations [and] if there is any advantage the negro must have it," she wrote, clearly reflecting the images she had seen in her dreams.[61] As these dream reports reveal, prevailing views of race clearly infiltrated the dreamworlds of Southern whites during the war.

During the summer of 1865, while sleeping in a Yankee prison cell in Boston Harbor, Alexander Stephens had several dreams about his former slaves. Stephens's dreams reveal how paternalism was not simply a propaganda tool, but a set of beliefs some slave masters had truly incorporated into their thinking. Indeed, Stephens's nighttime visions reveal a sincere concern for the welfare and well-being of his former bondsmen. In one dream, Stephens saw that two young brothers, Henry and Anthony, "were in a bad condition" and "wanted to go back to Liberty Hall," Stephens's plantation in Georgia. "Poor Anthony!" wrote Stephens after waking up. "I fear he is in trouble." On another occasion, Stephens dreamed that he gave a coat to the little son of one of his former slaves.

On June 12, 1865, Stephens dreamed that he was in Atlanta on his way back to Liberty Hall. His former slave, Pierce, "joined me there; said he had come to go with me and we would spend the balance of our lives together; he intended never to leave me, I had been the best friend he ever had and he should never forget it." A month later, on the morning of July 8, 1865, Stephens awoke with his "eyes streaming in tears" after having a dream about his former slave, Bob. In the dream, Bob had prepared "a sumptuous dinner" for Stephens and several other slaves. "I was seated, talking to them about their new condition, contrasting it with their former; pointing out some of the evils they would most probably encounter, advising and instructing them how to act so as best to guard against these when I should be gone; impressing upon them the importance of industry, honesty, economy, obedience to the laws, with as few dealings with the vicious of their own and the like class of the white race as possible." Stephens lectured two of the slaves on "how to bring up their children," when he realized he "was about to leave them forever, never to see them again, and was giving them my last parting words." During this "valedictory, the fountains of the heart were broken up, and I was lecturing and weeping at once."

Stephens's dreams appear to reveal a genuine emotional connection to his slaves that contrasts with the dark prejudice he expressed toward African Americans in his infamous 1861 Cornerstone Address. These dreams may have been delusional fantasies, wishful thinking, or perhaps based in assumptions Stephens had about how his slaves felt about being in bondage. Taken in connection with the Stephens's political pronouncements, they seem to reveal how public and private views of slavery could be at times incongruous. The public Stephens championed white racial superiority, while the private Stephens cared deeply for those he saw as inferior.

Yet, while some of Stephens's dreams exhibited great affection for his former slaves, others reveal deep consternation about the societal changes that would accompany the postwar world. On August 22, he wrote in his diary, "It occurs to me that Harry's son, Tim, also appeared to me in my mental rovings during sleep last night. He was not the Tim, the little boy, I left at home; was about half-grown; was not docile and obedient as always heretofore but self-willed and obstinate."[62] Like other Southerners during the war years and in the months to follow, Stephens realized that, even if he were to return to his home in Georgia, things would never be the same. Indeed, though difficult for them to comprehend, Southern whites knew that the war had changed their society forever. "[I] woke this morning very sorrowful," wrote Sarah Lois Wadley of Monroe, Louisiana, a few months after Appomattox; "woke to find that my vivid dreams were only dreams of the past which can never return."[63]

LIKE THEIR SOUTHERN COUNTERPARTS, Northern women also dreamed of combat—but often in a different way: They went to the battle rather than the fighting coming to them. Because the war was more distant from daily life in the North, these dreams were often connected to news reports rather than direct contact with the war. In August 1861, a woman in Wisconsin told her mother that she was "anxious to get war news yet dread to hear it too. I get so nervous sometimes thinking of it that I cannot go to sleep and when I do it is only to be disturbed by dreadful dreams of battles." Two months later she similarly told her sister, "A great many of our neighbors and townsmen have gone to the war. O this dreadful war, I wish it could be over. It troubles me night and day. I have such awful dreams in the night and then when I read of battles it makes me so nervous I can hardly hold myself together."[64]

A Philadelphia woman recorded similar dreams and emotions early in the conflict. On September 16, 1861, Elizabeth Ingersoll Fisher heard "alarming war news, rumours of an impending battle, [and] that Washington is not safe." That night she experienced "bad dreams . . . about the War." She dreamt that she "was in battles and when I was awake could not help thinking of dreadful scenes that might be going on."[65] Fortunately, the rumors proved unfounded.

Women's dreams of battle could be quite intense, even for those who had never come close to combat. In September 1864, after reading about William Tecumseh Sherman's capture of Atlanta in the papers, another Philadelphia woman dreamed that she was fighting against several armed Confederates in a hotel. "I was lying on the floor to prevent their bullets striking me," she wrote. "I know I expected to be killed and I wondered if I would be much missed. I was just as cool as you please and wondered if everyone was as cool when in action," she told her husband proudly.[66]

Other women also experienced this sensation of fearlessness. Shortly after arriving in Beaufort, South Carolina, in March 1863, to teach former slaves how to read and write, Harriet Buss wrote home to her parents in Massachusetts about an impending attack on Charleston. "I dreamed a few nights ago of sailing right down through between the two forces during the conflict," she wrote. "I went the entire length of the opposing armies and back again, and the red hot shells were flying like rockets back and forth over my head, the contest was raging with all its power, but I felt not a particle of fear." After dreaming of war, some women wished they could play a larger role in the conflict. Illinois schoolteacher S. B. Dunn dreamed one night that she was at Union general Ulysses S. Grant's headquarters helping him capture the Confederate stronghold at Vicksburg. The next day she wrote, "I more than ever wish I was a man that I might fill one place left vacant by some brave soldier. At times when I first hear of the fearful loss of life in some engagements I can scarcely proceed with my duties in womans province."[67]

Feelings of distance from the armies could have a tangible impact on Northern women's dreams. Sometimes women felt utterly helpless in their sleep, such as Cora Benton (described above), who felt like she was being hurried away from her husband in her dreams. Jane Thompson of Iowa repeatedly worried about her husband's health and sent him letters asking him to resign his commission from the army. Most of her dreams were pleasant dreams of William coming home, although she had recurring dreams in late 1862 that he came "home sick but you would not let me come near you or do anything for you." In one particularly jarring dream, William was ill "and I started to come to you but I could not get started. I got to the cars and they were so full I could hardly get in but I did get a seat and then they were so heavily-loaded they could not run and it seemed as though I could hear you calling me to come to you quick." Jane "woke up crying" but was relieved "to find it only a dream." Still, her worries about William's health persisted, and she continually asked him to resign and come home. In this case—as with many other soldiers—William could not neglect his patriotic duty because of his wife's unpleasant dreams. He told her that it would be dishonorable and disgraceful to resign his commission, and he would not do so.[68]

Jane Thompson's dreams reveal the frustration of a woman separated from her husband, and also from the seat of war. She longed to see him and connect with him—on several occasions she wrote that she wished they could sleep together again—but he was always beyond her reach. Dollie Vermilion had a similar "mean dream." In it, her husband "had come home, but only stayed a few minutes. I thought you were in your shirtsleeves, and were so fat you could hardly walk."[69] If some Confederate women endured war dreams that brought the conflict too close, these Yankee women suffered from dreams that kept the war and its participants at a distance.

Indeed, Northern women appear to have had a propensity toward nightmares about things that were totally unrelated to the war, such as ghosts and haunted houses. One night in upstate New York, Ellie Goldwaite "dreamed that I heard two hard knocks and then there was a ghost come out of the corner and put her hands around my body right over my heart and I thought they was cold like death." The dream haunted her for days. "Dick, it was all a dream," she told her soldier-husband, "but I think that I can almost see that white ghost now and feel them cold hands over my heart." The next night she could not sleep in the same bed, and "sweat came on me like rain and I got so nervous that Mother had to leave her bed and come sleep with me." The following night she "went upstairs and I tried to be brave, but courage failed. It is only three nights ago I dreamed it." In Iowa in July 1863, Dollie Vermilion had several nights of dreams of her husband "being sick, and in danger, and about desolate, haunted houses, where I was lost and frightened."[70]

THE WAR INVADED the lives of Southern civilians in ways that it did not touch their Northern counterparts, and many Confederates hoped to escape from the realities of the war as they slept.[71] A nurse stationed at a military hospital in Richmond wrote to his wife back in Alabama one night in May 1863, "It is 9 o clock at night I am very tired—will go to bed and see if

I cant dream about you and our baby, and be happy, at least in my sleep." In like manner, while feeling particularly distraught about her relationship with a Confederate soldier, one Virginia girl wrote in her journal, "I shall have to have recourse to sleeping dreams." Many Confederate women dreamt themselves to faraway, peaceful places and times. A Maine woman, who had moved to Minnesota and then to Arkansas just before the war, dreamed in 1863 of visiting an expansive, wonderful North. Arkansas was a viciously contested area during the war, and she'd been forced to leave her home. Her dreams gave her respite from the realities of war. "Last night I dreamed of visiting Minnesota," she wrote in her diary. "How I got there I do not know. I entered the house to see Mother Gray and Lizzie looking as they did four years ago and pursuing their peaceful everyday duties just as calmly. I looked all over the house and went to the stable to see the favored white cow whose pasture reaches to the Pacific Ocean. The dream is so real today that I seem to have seen them since four years."[72]

Kate Peddy of Georgia, who suffered a long spell of nightmares during part of the war, told her husband in early 1865, "I had such a sweet dream a few [nights ago]. I thought that again we wander[ed] as we used to in our garden in the early days of our married life. I felt again the thrilling pre-shure of loving arms folded around me, and saw the tender smile of love kindle in those eyes, ever beaming with inteligence. Oh! I was so happy by your side." In her dream, the earth "seemed clothed with bea[u]ty and the sky appeared bluer than ever to me with a few rosy clouds floating through the air like cars of happy spirits." But then she awoke, and the "stern reality" of his absence again set in.[73]

Others visited places they had never been, or spoke with people they'd never met. Sarah Morgan, a young Confederate woman whose house in Baton Rouge was pillaged by Yankee soldiers in August 1862, recorded scores of dreams in her diary throughout the war. "I wanted to have a splendid dream last night, but failed," she wrote in September 1862. While we have already seen how the war sometimes intruded woefully on her sleep, Morgan still relished going to dreamland. When asked once whether she dreamed, she mused,

Dream? Dont I! Not the dreams *he* meant; but royal, purple dreams, that De Quincy[74] could not purchase with his opium; dreams that I would not forgo for all the inducements that could be offered. I go to sleep, and pay a visit to heaven or fairy land. I have white wings, and with another, float in rosy clouds, and look down on the moving world; or I have the power to raise myself in the air without wings, and silently float where ever I will, loving all things, and feeling that God loves me. I have heard Paul preach to the people, while I stood on a fearful rock above. I have been to strange lands and great cities; I have talked with people I never beheld. Charlotte Bronte has spent a week with me—in my dreams—and together we have talked of her sad life. Shakespeare and I have discussed his works, seated tete-a-tete over a small table. He pointed out the character of each of his hero-ines, explaining what I could not understand when awake; and closed the lecture with "*You* have the tenderest heart I have ever read, or sung of" which compliment, considering it as original with him, rather than myself, waked me up with surprise.

Morgan saw long-gone kin in her dreams, and wandered through gardens in paradise. In one dream she beheld "the vastness of eternity." In another she saw "a Something too great, awful, and mysterious for me to comprehend, though I struggled to understand." Such dreams were a release from the diffi-culties of life in the occupied South. "Dreams! who would give up the blessing?" she confided in her diary. "I would not care to sleep, if I could not dream."[75]

But at times Morgan's dreams reflected her greatest fears—fears that, ironically, had nothing to do with the war. "O what a dream I had last night! I have not yet recovered from my terror," wrote Morgan melodramatically in her diary. "I dreamed that I was to be married. Awful, was it not?" In her waking hours, Morgan had no desire to settle down. Elsewhere in her di-ary, she playfully referred to her "old maid project" and "the pleasures of single blessedness." Her nightmare of a wedding thus reveals how des-perately she sought to avoid marriage, and also how frequently the subject must have intruded on her mind. In her dream, she could see herself walk-ing down the aisle, her hand on the arm of the groom; four bridesmaids and four groomsmen followed close behind. "A silent horror crept over me," she wrote. But before she could reach the altar, "With a gasp of terror the phantom of myself disappeared from before my distended eyes." The scene had changed. Now it was a few moments before the wedding, and she was in a room with her mother and sister. "O mother I cannot! Save me!" she cried. "I'll die! Save me! tell him I am crazy! It will be true, for I shall be crazy if you force me into it!" But her sister replied, "Too late. The supper table is spread, and looks beautifully, too. They say the church is already crowded. Would you have them disappointed? Dont make your eyes red; you have just half an hour."

Morgan continued to plead with her sister to save her, revealing her strong will and how little social convention may have mattered to her: "Again I pleaded wildly; in my agony I threw myself on the ground, and besought her to tell him I could not marry him; that I had only discovered I hated him at the last moment. 'And if you refuse, I will solemnly swear that when the clergyman asks if I Will, I will answer No! with an energy which will startle him, and scandalize the congregation!' I burst forth, rising from my knees with a determined air." Morgan wailed and cried and pleaded. But her dream quickly changed again. Suddenly she found herself next to an unknown corpse. "First I dreamed of a wedding, then a funeral," she wrote gleefully. "One destroys the other; neither will follow." She hugged herself and cried for joy: "Saved! saved! . . . Thank heaven I am saved! Blessed be heaven, I am not married! Free! free!"

In her "ecstacy of joy," Morgan was awakened by a servant who was calling her for breakfast. "A tame ending," she wrote, "but my horror at the thought of marrying that man has not yet deserted me. I am glad I did not, even in my dreams. And his name was John! Bah!"[76]

Sarah Morgan's richly textured nightly escapes from the realities of war are unique in the historical record. Few could evade the war the way Morgan could. Indeed, for many civilians, the realities of war often permeated even the pleasant dreams wives had of spending time with their husbands. Sallie Lovett of Rocky Mount, Georgia, described the war as "only a bad dream" within her sweet dreams about her husband. She wrote to him in May 1862:

> Honey, sometimes when I am asleep and dreaming I think you are sleeping with me and I am hugging you and when I wake I have a breathless pillow hugged up in my arms and sometimes when I am dreaming I think this war is only a bad dream. And, oh, I think I am so glad it is only a dream, and I think I am getting close to you and I wake myself hugging up sis or a pillow and so many more. Last night I dreamt you had come home on a furlough and I thought I was the happiest person you ever saw. I do hope that dream will soon come to pass. Honey, I don't know what I would do with myself if I was to see you coming. I think I would run plum out of my skin to meet you.[77]

The war's appearance as a dream within a dream underscores the all-encompassing nature of the conflict for Southern civilians—even for those who were far away from the battlefield. Few moments—waking or sleeping—were free of apprehension.

Civilian men away from their families could also understand these emotions. After nearly two months apart from his wife—and eleven days since her last communication—Georgia congressman Warren Akin wrote his wife a heartfelt letter that captured many of the anxieties facing Southern civilians:

> I try to feel patient and hope on, but I get very *anxious* to be at home sometimes. I had a delicious dream about you last night. I dreamed I was home and you had your arms around me. When I waked up how sorry I was it was a dream. Is it not strange that things in dreams seem to be so real and produce such an effect on one? Nothing ever seemed more real in my waking hours than my dream last night. It is the first time I have dreamed about you since I left home. I have not, that I remember dreamed of home or any one there, and it seems strange that it is so, when I go to sleep thinking about you and wake up thinking about you. But I dream very little about any thing, and often dont sleep much. I wake up and roll over and over, but cant sleep.[78]

Awaking from a fearful dream reinforced traditional religious practices for many distraught Christians, causing them to fall to their knees in their darkened bedrooms. Eliza Fain of Tennessee awoke with a start one night shortly after the Battle of Chancellorsville. "I rose from my bed, kneeled and poured out my soul in prayer to my Father that he would give to us a time in which we might cradle and save our wheat," she wrote in her diary. "I feel he has heard me." On another occasion, Fain awoke at 3 A.M. feeling "so troubled" that "I slept no more but spent the time in prayers to God for his protection and care over my dear son" who was serving in the army.[79] If bad dreams could potentially undermine the war effort by demoralizing civilians and their soldier-correspondents, such dreams might also serve a different sort of public purpose by making individuals more reliant upon their Heavenly Father through prayer.

CHAPTER FOUR

African American Dreams

Harriet Tubman was a Moses for her people. Born into slavery in Maryland about 1820, she escaped from bondage in 1849 and devoted her life to helping other slaves do the same. For the next eleven years she worked as a conductor on the Underground Railroad, ultimately assisting some three hundred slaves in their quest for freedom. She continued her work during the Civil War, acting as a scout and spy for the Union armies. By the time of her death in 1913, she had attained a level of celebrity unusual for a black woman in the Jim Crow era.

Despite her renowned and tireless efforts on behalf of her people and her nation, Northern white society sometimes looked quizzically at Tubman's adherence to African religious beliefs. "She is the most shrewd and practical person in the world," wrote Francis B. Sanborn in the *Boston Commonwealth* in July 1863, "yet she is a firm believer in omens, dreams and warnings."[1] Such commentary by the Harvard-trained educator treated Tubman's belief in dreams as an unusual cleavage of African superstitions.

Prior to her escape from slavery, Tubman "used to dream of flying over fields and towns, and rivers and mountains, looking down upon them 'like a bird,' and reaching at last a great fence, or sometimes a river, over which she would try to fly, 'but it 'peared like I wouldn't hab de strength, and jes as I was sinkin' down, dare would be ladies all drest in white ober dere, and dey would put out dere arms and pull me 'cross.'" When Tubman made it to the North she claimed that "she remembered these very places as those she had seen in her dreams, and many of the ladies who befriended her were those she had been helped by in her visions."[2]

In 1858 or 1859, Tubman had a recurring dream in which she was in "a wilderness sort of place, all full of rocks and bushes." Out of the rocks a serpent raised its head, at which point the head became transfigured into "the head of an old man with a long white beard." The face gazed at her "wishful like, jes as ef he war gwine to speak to me," at which point two other younger heads rose up next to the first. A "great crowd of men rushed in and struck down the younger heads," but the old head kept staring at her wishfully. Soon thereafter she met John Brown and recognized his face from her dreams. When news of Harpers Ferry came in October 1859, she knew the two younger heads were those of Watson and Oliver Brown, his two sons who had been killed there.[3]

Shortly before the Civil War—probably sometime in 1860—Tubman was staying at the home of Henry Highland Garnet, a black abolitionist and minister in New York City. Coming down for breakfast one morning, she told Garnet of the dream from which she'd just awoken. She sang out in a loud voice, "My people are free! My people are free!" According to an early biographer, "She came down to breakfast singing the words in a sort of ecstasy. She could not eat. The dream or vision filled her whole soul, and physical needs were forgotten." An incredulous Garnet replied that neither he nor she would see the end of slavery in their lifetimes. "Oh Harriet! Harriet!" he told her. "You've come to torment us before the time; do cease this noise! My grandchildren may see the day of the emancipation of our people, but you and I will never see it." But Tubman was unmoved. "I tell you, sir, you'll see it, and you'll see it soon. My people are free! My people are free."[4]

Harriet Tubman's sleep and dreams have captured the imagination of Americans for more than a century. Accounts of her dreams have appeared in newspapers, children's books, and adult nonfiction. Some writers have compared Tubman to Joan of Arc. Others point out that her dreams often warned her of impending danger. One fugitive slave in Canada said in 1860 that "Moses is got de charm," and that "De whites can't catch Moses, kase you see she's born wid de charm." The black abolitionist William Wells Brown, who was critical of the excessive enthusiasm of black religious culture, acknowledged that Tubman believed that she possessed "the charm" and that it "nerved her up, gave her courage, and made all who followed her feel safe in her hands."[5]

Tubman's first biographer, Sarah Bradford, took special notice of Tubman's dreams and other religious practices in her two biographies of Tubman, which were published in 1869 and 1886. The biographies had several important differences, though. The first book contained much more language directly attributed to Tubman, whereas the second had more of Bradford's own narrative voice. Tubman biographer Jean Humez noticed how much Bradford's account changed from the Civil War era to the Gilded Age. The 1886 biography, she said, had "the effect of censoring aspects of Tubman's personality and politics," rendering Tubman "less salty and more saintly." Humez surmises that Bradford "censored Tubman's life story" in the later biography "at least in part for fear of marring the image of a saintly African-American heroine that she was trying to construct for white readers in a post-Reconstruction era of virulent racism."[6] In other words,

Tubman had to be repackaged for new and different times; the biographer was aware of her audience's changing sensibilities.

Tubman's most significant twentieth-century biographer, Earl Conrad, almost completely discounted Tubman's supernatural visions and dreams, seeing them as a result of her perpetual drowsiness. Tubman apparently had narcolepsy and had a tendency to fall asleep at unusual times, even in the midst of a conversation. Conrad attributed these "sleep attacks" to a head injury Tubman had suffered when a teenager. As an avowed atheist and Marxist in the 1930s, Conrad sought to diminish the importance of Tubman's "forebodings, omens, warnings and signs" to her life story. He did not want to write "the biography of the Supreme Being," he said, but rather that of an extraordinary woman. "God is too often given credit for achievements when human beings, who receive too little out of life, should receive such credit," he wrote in a private letter while he was working on his book.[7]

In his biography, *Harriet Tubman*, published in 1943, Conrad treated Tubman's dreams "in the figurative sense," and Conrad's Tubman was not "gifted with unusual psychic powers."[8] Rather, the "dreams revealed to her fellow blacks a restlessness which, they knew, was likely to burst forth one day in the form of escape or some other type of outbreak." In describing them, Tubman was merely exhibiting "a naturally developing sense of poetry, [and] an actual facility for composing it. The world was in her mind, and if she could not get up in the public square and denounce it, she could express her criticism through relating these dreams of swift deliverance, martyrdom, bloodshed." The dreaming, Conrad concluded, "was parent to the later acts of disciplined revolt."[9]

Conrad's materialist interpretation of Tubman's dreams probably says more about Conrad than it does about Tubman, and it immediately engendered controversy. The daughter of Tubman's "favorite niece," Alice Brickler, criticized Conrad, saying, "I may be wrong but I believe that every age, every country and every race, especially during the darkest history, has had its unusual Souls who were in touch with some mysterious central originating Force, a comprehensive stupendous Unity for which we have no adequate name. Aunt Harriet was one of those unusual souls. Her religion, her dreams or visions were so bo[u]nd together that nobody, and I certainly should not attempt it, could separate them." Brickler told Conrad that Tubman believed it was "God's voice which spoke to her in a dream and she never failed to obey her Master." She concluded, "It was her dreams which saved her life often."[10]

The tension between the white Conrad and African American Brickler captured a divide that had been emerging between many white and black Americans since the mid-nineteenth century. Whereas dreams and visions had been an important part of white and black religious experiences during the antebellum period, they were diminishing in white Christian practices by the time of the Civil War. Still, dreams remained a distinctive and essential component of African American life and religion past the midpoint of the nineteenth century. White biographers therefore sometimes treated slaves' dreams—like those of Harriet Tubman—as African "superstitions," or tried to explain them away as Conrad had done.

Twenty-first-century biographers still tread lightly over the subject of Tubman's dreams, hoping not to offend the sensibilities of modern readers—either those who believe in the spiritual power of nighttime visions, or those who don't. In one of the more recent Tubman biographies, Kate Clifford Larson exemplifies this tendency. "While a modern physician might attribute her seizures to physical causes," writes Larson, "for Tubman herself, as well as for [her contemporaries], Tubman's powerful faith lay at the root of her outbursts, visions, sleeping spells, and voices." Buried in a footnote one hundred pages later, however, Larson sheds more light on her interpretation: "While it is not my intention to minimize Tubman's spirituality by reducing it to merely a manifestation of her illness, it is important to view the two, her illness and her spirituality, as perhaps symbiotic."[11]

Clearly the dreams of slaves like Tubman continue to fascinate and perplex readers. Indeed, part of Tubman's hold on the American imagination was her ability to foresee the future through dreams. From children's books to adult nonfiction, Tubman's reputation has remained that of a spiritual seer who appeals to audiences of all races. And yet white biographers from Sarah Bradford to the present have often been vexed by how to portray this heroine. Larson's careful treatment of Tubman's dreams exemplifies the difficulty. Understanding how best to analyze other slaves' sleep and dreams can be just as complicated and contentious—and, in fact, it has been since before the Civil War.

NIGHTTIME WAS A RESTLESS TIME for slaves. After dark, slaves often did things that might earn them stripes from the overseer's lash if they were caught. Some slaves taught themselves to read at night. Others worked in the dark, making things that they could sell to earn some money for themselves or even to purchase their own freedom.[12] But some slaves were not even permitted the luxury of working for themselves at night, particularly during busy harvesting seasons. One free "Creole mulatto" from New Orleans testified in February 1864 that the "hours of labor on sugar plantations are from fifteen to eighteen hours per day for the year; at certain seasons they are obliged to labor a great part of the night; they are usually called at 3 or 4 A.M." The labor that slaves performed both night and day took a toll on their health; some remarked that they were often too tired to even stand.[13] Abolitionist Theodore Dwight Weld complained that the system of slavery did not permit the slave certain basic liberties, such as the freedom "to rest when he is tired, to sleep when he needs it."[14]

Paternalistic white Southerners believed that they provided suitable working and living conditions for their slaves, but the reality did not generally match the perception in the planters' minds.[15] Things only deteriorated further during the war. A Treasury Department official noted in June 1862 that slaves in the Sea Islands of South Carolina had "unsuitable" "bedding and sleeping apartments" because their masters had fled and taken the good things with them.[16]

Some slaves were so psychologically tortured by their existence that they could not sleep at night. The horrors and realities of slavery made indelible marks on the minds of slaves, sometimes keeping them from sleeping, and other times infiltrating their dreams. This process began as early as the Middle Passage. From the moment of their capture in Africa, slaves began having sorrowful dreams. At night on one slaver in the eighteenth century, African captives awoke from dreams of home making "a howling melancholy kind of noise, something expressive of extreme anguish."[17] Such torturous dreams continued in the New World for African captives and their descendants. One young slave boy in Arkansas spent "many a sleepless night ... in tears, because I was a slave. I looked back on all I had suffered—and when I looked ahead, all was dark and hopeless bondage." Even after he had escaped he would "frequently ... dream" that he had been recaptured and taken back into bondage in the South. So real did these nightmares feel to him that he would wake up sobbing and in great distress.[18] Terrifying dreams of enslavement like this one reveal some of the lasting psychological effects that could be experienced by slaves, including emotional stresses that might persist long after a slave had become free.[19]

If, as we saw in chapter 3, nighttime could be a time of metaphorical escape for some white Southerners, it could be a time of actual escape for slaves. They recognized that darkness was the best way to conceal their absconding, and many followed the North Star to freedom.[20] On the Underground Railroad, sympathetic whites helped fugitives continue their long journeys

THE
SLAVE'S DREAM

Words by Wm. C. Caroll.

I had a dream, a happy dream, I dreamed that I was free,
And in my own bright land again there was a home for me;
Savannah's tide rushed bravely on, I saw wave roll e'er wave
And when in full delight I awoke, I found myself a slave.
And when in full delight I awoke I found myself a slave.

I never knew a mother's love, though happy were my days;
'Twas by my own dear father's side I sung my simple lays;
He died and heartless strangers came and o'er him closed
    the grave,
They tore me, weeping, from his side and claimed me as a
    slave.
They tore me, weeping, from his side, and claimed me as a
    slave.

And this was in a christian land, where men oft kneel and pray
The vaunted home of liberty, where whip and lash hold sway.
O, give me back my Georgian cot, it is not wealth I crave,
O, let me live in freedom's light, or die if still a slave.
O, let me live in freedom's light, or die if still a slave.

"The Slave's Dream." This poem, likely written by a white person, captured the "delight" that many slaves experienced when they dreamed of becoming free and the profound sadness they felt when they awoke from such dreams. Courtesy of the Library of Congress.

in the dead of night. One former Kentucky slave owner named Thome would "get out of his bed in the middle of the night to help runaway slaves [get] out of the reach of their masters, give them clothes and money, and sen[d] them across the Ohio river." During the Civil War, many slaves continued to escape in the dark, but now they only had to make it as far as the Union military lines. So frequent were these nighttime flights that one Federal officer in Missouri noted, "The Negroes who do enlist [in the Union army] generally escape at night; not one in twenty, attempts to get away in the day time." Recognizing this hard truth, the Mobile *Advertiser and Register* warned its readers that if they did not keep proper watchfulness over their slaves, "It may happen some morning that somebody will wake up a nigger or two poorer than when he went to bed."[21]

Of course, slaves had a metaphorical dream of freedom, but many, like Harriet Tubman, had literal dreams of freedom as well. William Wells Brown "would dream at night that I was in Canada, a freeman, and on waking in the morning, weep to find myself so sadly mistaken." A twenty-year-old Tennessee slave, anticipating a whipping for having stayed at his wife's plantation too long, lay down to sleep during his six- or seven-mile journey back to his own plantation. "When he awoke," a newspaper interviewer reported in 1845, "he concluded from what he had dreamed, that that was the time for him to make his escape from bondage, and accordingly arose and turned his face to the *North*, and commenced his perilous journey." In 1865, an ex-slave in Georgia wrote to Abraham Lincoln telling him of a dream in which "I saw a comet come from the North to the South and I said good Lord what is that? I heard a voice 'There shall be wars & rumors of wars.'" This dream, he told the president, was the result of seventeen years of prayer for freedom and he believed that it was "you [who] was made known to me in a dream." Being able to let Lincoln know about this dream filled this man's soul with joy despite the fact that his "master threatened my life if I should talk about this."[22]

Indeed, some slaves were whipped for their visions and dreams of freedom. Ex-slave Minnie Fulkes of Petersburg, Virginia, described slave meetings where "the slave dat knowed th' most 'bout de Bible would tell and explain what God had told him in a vision (yo' young folks say, 'dream') dat dis freedom would come to pass; an' dey prayed for dis vision to come to pass, an' dars whar de paddy rollers would whip 'em ag'in."[23] Another slave named Ajax in Leesburg, Virginia, was whipped to death for having "a very remarkable dream or vision" in which "he conceived himself transported into the midst of the infernal regions" where he "saw his master and overseer . . . suspended by their tongues." Upon hearing of this, Ajax's master "hated him for his dream" and, in a fit of rage, whipped Ajax to death.[24]

Many slaves looked to their dreams for guidance when planning an escape. Some even received instructions in their dreams. About 1864, Harriott McClain, a slave near Henderson, Kentucky, found herself locked in an upstairs room for attempting to escape. One night she "received directions through a dream in which her escape was planned." She told her daughter "about the dream and instructed her to carry out orders that they might escape together." Harriott's twelve-year-old daughter, Adah, followed her mother's instructions. She brought a knife from her mistress's pantry and used it to pry open "the prison door." Her mother then "made her way into the open world about midnight," and Adah followed some time later. "Under cover of night the two fugitives traveled the three miles to Henderson," where they hid in someone's home "until darkness fell over the world to cover their retreat." Federal soldiers helped them cross the Ohio River into Indiana, where they settled and lived in freedom.[25]

Unlike these successes, some dreams portended disaster for slaves who wished to flee from bondage. Prior to an attempted escape in 1836, one of Frederick Douglass's companions, Sandy Jenkins—"a genuine African, [who] had inherited some of the so called magical powers, said to be possessed by African and eastern nations"—began to have dreams about their plans of escape. On a Saturday morning, Sandy approached Douglass and told him, "I dreamed, last night, that I was roused from sleep, by strange noises, like the voices of a swarm of angry birds, that caused a roar as they passed, which fell upon my ear like a coming gale over the tops of the trees. Looking up to see what it could mean," he said, "I saw you, Frederick, in the claws of a huge bird, surrounded by a large number of birds, of all colors and sizes." The birds were "picking" at Douglass with their beaks, "while you, with your arms, seemed to be trying to protect your eyes. Passing over me, the birds flew in a south-westerly direction, and I watched them until they were clean out of sight. Now I saw this as plainly as I now see you; and furder, honey, watch de Friday night dream; dare is sumpon in it, shose you born; dare is, indeed, honey."

Sandy's dream dampened Douglass's mood, but he attributed his concern to general excitement and anticipation of their impending escape. Five men planned to flee together, but Sandy backed out at the last moment. On the morning of the escape, as Douglass was spreading manure in a field, he "had a sudden presentiment, which flashed upon me like lightening in a dark night."

He turned to Sandy and told him, "*Sandy, we are betrayed*; something has just told me so." Sandy instantly replied, "Man, dat is strange; but I feel just as you do." Within thirty minutes, Douglass and his companions—excepting Sandy—were arrested and taken to jail. Someone had ratted them out.

Not all aspects of Sandy's dream came true. Douglass was not sold to the Deep South—although he considered himself "in the hands of moral vultures, and firmly held in their sharp talons" as a "fulfillment of Sandy's dream." Sitting in jail, Douglass and his companions wondered who the informant was. "Several circumstances seemed to point SANDY out, as our betrayer," he later recalled. "His entire knowledge of our plans—his participation in them—his withdrawal from us—his dream, and his simultaneous presentiment that we were betrayed—the taking us, and the leaving him—were calculated to turn suspicion toward him; and yet, we could not suspect him. We all loved him too well to think it *possible* that he could have betrayed us. So we rolled the guilt on other shoulders."[26]

Other fugitives had realistic and menacing dreams of recapture. During an attempted escape, William Grimes fell asleep "in an old log . . . and dreamed they had caught and was tying me to be whipped; and such was my agony, that I awoke, from a dream, indeed, but to reality not less painful." Grimes stayed in that place for three days until "I became so pinched with hunger, that I thought I might as well be whipped to death as to starve; so I concluded to give myself up."[27]

Even after crossing over the Ohio River or the Mason-Dixon Line, a fugitive's mind could never truly be at ease. "Two or three nights in succession I dreamt that I was taken by my master," wrote Kentucky slave Francis Frederic about his escape, "and all the details of the capture were so vividly depicted in my dreams, that I could scarcely, when awake, believe it was all a vision of the night." Similarly, Virginia slave Madison Jefferson told a newspaper reporter that long after arriving in Canada he still frequently dreamed "that he was again in the hands of his master." He would awake "in sudden alarm" and find "his pillow wet with tears from the anguish on his mind." Only when he was fully awake would he become "convinced him of his safety, his mind would be filled with thankfulness and praise to his great Deliverer." Although the war brought a greater promise of freedom through the presence of Union troops, it did not necessarily alleviate the stresses on slaves that led to such terrible dreams. One contraband woman who doubted the power of Federal soldiers to protect her had nightmares of recapture, telling a Northern journalist in 1862, "I doesn't want to go Souf again." It seems likely, though, that positive dreams increased during the war. About 1864, one Georgia slave allegedly "had a dream last night . . . that Massy Lincoln's soldiers had set us free."[28]

Persistent nightmares reveal how some escaped slaves may have never fully escaped from the experiences of bondage. Separation from loved ones, in particular, caused some of the most painful dreams. John Brown, a Georgia slave who had been bought and sold at a New Orleans slave pen when he was a child, later wrote, "I cannot think of it without a cold shiver. I often dream of it, and as often dwell upon it in the day-time." Lewis Clarke, a Virginia slave who was sold away from his family when he was only seven, wrote that his "thoughts continually by day and my dreams by night were of mother and home." After being separated from his mother, South Carolina slave Caleb Craig reported having "visions and dreams of her, in my sleep."[29]

Painful dreams of lost loved ones tortured many slaves in their sleep; but in some cases, they also motivated the enslaved to overcome their circumstances. Charles Ball, a Maryland slave who was sold to a planter in South Carolina in 1805, could barely sleep on the night he was sold. He passed the time thinking of "my wife and little children, whom I could not hope ever to see again," and also "my grandfather, and of the long nights I had passed with him, listening to his narratives of the scenes through which he had passed in Africa." When Ball finally fell asleep, he was "distressed by painful dreams. My wife and children appeared to be weeping and lamenting my calamity; and beseeching and imploring my master on their knees, not to carry me away from them. My little boy came and begged me not to go and leave him, and endeavored, as I thought, with his little hands to break the fetters that bound me." Ball "awoke in agony and cursed my existence." Later, when Ball had a vivid and detailed dream about his wife and children, he determined that "I should again embrace my wife, and caress my children."[30]

Solomon Northup, the talented New York violinist who was kidnapped and sold into slavery in 1841, "continually" thought about his family. "When sleep overpowered me I dreamed of them—dreamed I was again in Saratoga—that I could see their faces, and hear their voices calling me." But when he awoke "from the pleasant phantasms of sleep to the bitter realities around me, I could but groan and weep." Like Charles Ball of Maryland, Northup would not allow his spirit to be broken, and his dreams spurred him on to find a means of escape.[31]

Despite the pain that many felt when dreaming of long-gone loved ones, some slaves believed that these dreams offered hope for the future. One slave named Charlotte had lost her children, grandchildren, and great-grandchildren to the auction block. When, about 1859, her "last grandarter" was sold, she felt like her "heart would break." In 1860, "she dreamed . . . about wading to her knees in blood." Charlotte believed that "the Spirit of the Lord told her" to share this dream with her church, perhaps so that it would encourage her coreligionists. "Joseph was sold into Egypt," she reminded them; "they meant it for evil but the Lord meant it for good and he became a king, and so it would be with them yet." One night Harriet Jacobs saw a vision of her two children in "a streak of moonlight" that appeared on the floor in front of her. "They vanished; but I had seen them distinctly," she wrote. "Some will call it a dream, others a vision. I know not how to account for it, but it made a strong impression on my mind, and I felt certain something had happened to my little ones." Indeed, she would learn later that something tremendous had happened that day—her children's freedom had been purchased.[32]

Of course, not all former slaves had only negative dreams about their past lives. Many years after emancipation, eighty-two-year-old Robert Toatley of South Carolina dreamt about the way that slave children ate at his plantation in antebellum days. "After all de grown niggers eat and git out of de way, scraps and everything eatable was put in them troughs." The cook would blow a horn and, "quick as lightnin' a passle of fifty or sixty little niggers run out de plum bushes, from under de sheds and houses, and from everything where" and would "eat just lak you see pigs shovin' 'round slop troughs." "I see dat sight many times in my dreams," Toatley mused, "old as I is, eighty-two years last Saturday."[33]

African Americans who had been manumitted and colonized to Liberia also sometimes dreamed wishfully of the places and people they had left behind. Writing from Africa in 1859, Rosebell Burke wrote to her former mistress, Mary Custis Lee (Robert E. Lee's wife), "I have thought and dreamt much about you lately. I hope you have got over your rheumatism, and that many troubles of which you spoke in your last letter." Similarly, another ex-slave wrote to her former mistress from Liberia, "I wish that I could see your faice for I cannot take rest of nights Dreaming A bout you. sometimes I think I am thire [back in Virginia] and when I awoke I am hear in Liberea & how that dos greave me but I cannot healp my self[.] I am verry fraid I shal never see you faice a gain but if I never Do I hope I shal meat in the kingdom."[34]

THE PATTERNS THAT EMERGE in the dreams of American slaves reveal several important aspects of African American religious beliefs in the nineteenth century. Southern slaves, according to one ex-slave from Nashville named Ellis Ken Kannon, "wuz natur'ally superstitious en b'leeved in dreams, ole sayings en signs." Many slaves believed that dreams were signs from God. Ex-slave Patsy Hyde, also of Nashville, once dreamed "dat a big white thing wuz on de gatepost wid' a haid." She told her mother, who replied that "Gawd wuz warning us."[35]

Following her taking of a series of interviews with ex-slaves in Augusta, Georgia, in the 1930s, Louisa Oliphant of the Federal Writers' Project compiled a list of slave folk remedies and superstitions. Among the superstitions were a number related to dreams:

> To dream of muddy water, maggots, or fresh meat is a sign of death.
>> To dream of caskets is also a sign of death. You may expect to hear of as many deaths as there are caskets in the dream.
> To dream of blood is a sign of trouble.
> To dream of fish is a sign of motherhood.
> To dream of eggs is a sign of trouble unless the eggs are broken.
>> If the eggs are broken, your trouble is ended.
> To dream of snakes is a sign of enemies. If you kill the snakes, you have conquered your enemies.
> To dream of fire is a sign of danger.
> To dream of a funeral is a sign of a wedding.
> To dream of a wedding is a sign of a funeral.
> To dream of silver money is a sign of bad luck; bills—good luck.
> To dream of dead folk is a sign of rain. . . .
> To dream of crying is a sign of trouble.
> To dream of dancing is a sign of happiness. . . .
> To dream that your teeth fall out is a sign of death in the family.
> To dream of a woman's death is a sign of some man's death.
> To dream of a man's death is a sign of some woman's death.[36]

These sorts of beliefs were prevalent throughout the South, revealing a widespread dream culture among slaves. Dreams of snakes were particularly common, as we saw with Harriet Tubman. But other slaves had dreams of serpents as well. "I sho do believe in dreams," said Annie B. Boyd, an exslave from Hopkinsville, Kentucky. She recounted once having a dream "dat somethin was chokin me en I pulled at my dress en a big snake dropped out of my boosom [and] rolled down on de bed." She woke up a moment later and "sho nuff dar war a snake on de floor by de bed." After she killed it she came to the realization that a friend of hers would turn against her in a few days. But "by killing de snake I knowed dat I would conquer dat enemy."

Slaves throughout the South had the same beliefs about snake-infested dreams. Susie Branch of White Bluff, Georgia, explained that dreams of a snake "mean yuh got a enemy. Not many nights ago I dram bout a snake an uh sho wuz sked when uh wake up." Similarly, Mini Dawson of Pin Point, Georgia, said, "Ef yuh dream ub a snake dassa enemy neahby too."[37]

In 1831, former Virginia slave Austin Steward "was continually being startled by frightful dreams" of birds and snakes just before he went to Canada to work in the abolitionist movement. In one he "saw a monstrous serpent as large as a log stretched across the road between Rochester and the Genesee River"; in another, "I thought myself in the air so high that I could have a full view of the shores of Lake Ontario, and they were alive with snakes; and then I saw a large bird like an eagle, rise up out of the water and fly toward the south." His dreams may have been a premonition of the bad things that would soon take place in his life. Upon getting to Canada, he found that the financial backers had embezzled the funds for a free black settlement.[38]

Perhaps the most consequential vision of a snake was had by Nat Turner, who, in 1828, "heard a loud noise in the heavens, and the Spirit instantly appeared to me and said the Serpent was loosened, and Christ had laid down the yoke he had borne for the sins of men, and that I should take it on and fight against the Serpent, for the time was fast approaching when the first should be last and the last should be first." Turner knew exactly what this meant—he was to exterminate the white race and end human bondage. After receiving several other visions over the ensuing years, Turner set out on his work. In August 1831, he led a band of some fifty or sixty slaves through Southampton County, Virginia. Over the course of their thirty-six-hour rampage, they butchered nearly every white man, woman, and child they met, sparing none on account of age or sex.[39]

Like Turner and the others who knew what dreams of snakes meant, slaves professed to understand the meaning of their dream symbols even though most slaves and ex-slaves could not read dream books. Tom Wylie Neal, an ex-slave from Arkansas, knew the common belief that to dream of the dead meant there would be rain. "He don't believe in dreams but some dreams like when you dream of the dead there's sho' goner be falling weather," recorded one Works Progress Administration (WPA) interviewer.[40]

Unlike Neal, however, many slaves firmly believed that their futures had been revealed to them in their dreams. Slaves also widely believed that dreams of livestock portended death, just as Louisa Oliphant's compilation claimed. Lizzie Farmer, an eighty-year-old ex-slave from Texas recalled once dreaming about "a big black hoss" that came into her yard and would not leave. When she opened the gate to let it out, it went into her house. "Right after dat my son died," she recollected in the 1930s. "I saw dat hoss again de other night. A black hoss allus means death. Seeing it de other night might mean I'se gwineter die."[41] In like manner, an ex-slave from South Carolina had a dream about several uncles "skinning a cow and cutting her open." In the dream, women and children were sitting around the men crying. The girl told her dream to her mother, who replied that "it was a sign of death to dream about fresh meat." "Sure enough," the former slave continued, "that very evening Uncle Peter Price died. I used to dream so much that the old heads got so they took special notice of me and nearly every time it would come true."[42]

Lou Smith, an eighty-three-year-old ex-slave living in Oklahoma, knew as "a young woman" that she would be lonely in her old age. "I seen it in my sleep," she said. "I dreamed I spit every tooth in my head right out in my hand and something tell me I would be a widow. That's a bad thing to dream about, losing your teeth."[43] Another former slave attested to the belief that a dream of a wedding was a sign of a funeral, and vice versa, because, as he explained, "ez de man an' 'oman is united ez one in marriage so will dis body leab de earth ter be ez one wid Gawd."[44]

Determining the origins of these dream symbols and interpretations is complicated. Some appear to have clear African antecedents. For example, Arthur Glyn Leonard, a former British army officer, found in early twentieth-century Nigeria, "When a man dreams that he has been sick or unwell, his life is sure to turn out a long one; but if he dreams of health, it means that he will no longer live."[45] This sort of "reverse" trend, or paradoxical logic, was common in African American dream beliefs—such as dreaming of a wedding/funeral, or man/woman.

The origins of other symbols are more ambiguous. Many have both African and European roots.[46] Writing a decade before Louisa Oliphant compiled her list of slave superstitions and dream beliefs, folklorist Newbell Niles Puckett completed his doctoral dissertation at Yale University on "Folk Beliefs of the Southern Negro" (1925). Puckett found an incredible continuity between interpretations of symbols in dreams in Europe and those of former slaves in the United States.

In Scotland a dream of fresh fish means the arrival of children in the world. . . .

In Europe a dream of eggs indicates a quarrel. In Herefordshire a dream of spoiled eggs indicates a death in the family. . . .

Dreams of snakes are a sign of enemies ... while catching a snake on
the end of your fishing line is indicative of enemies trying to entrap
and kill you. The widespread idea of killing the first snake to kill
your principal enemy seems to be European in origin. ...

The signs relating to dreams of the dead have a similar distribution. In
this case the chief interpretation among the Negroes is that a dream
of the dead is a sign of rain, a belief of distinctly English origin. ...

Of European and also African incidence, and hence widely distributed,
is the idea that a dream of losing a tooth (or having a toothache)
indicates coming death.[47]

The commonalities between Puckett's list, Oliphant's compilation, and
the vast number of slave narratives are telling. The symbol of the snake—
which is by far the most common symbol in the reported dreams of slaves—
has clear African *and* European origins. Again writing of Nigeria, Arthur
Leonard found, "A snake seen in a dream implies a host of enemies seeking
to destroy the dreamer's life."[48] Drawing on this work, Puckett concluded,
"In England a nightmare of fighting with and conquering serpents denotes
victory over your enemies, but among the Ibos of Africa a dream of snakes
also indicates enemies. ... While it is well-nigh impossible to explain why
serpents should so universally be the symbol for enemies, yet this belief
coming from two distinct sources might well be expected to persist in the
Negro South."[49]

These African and European dream beliefs thus commingled, causing a
unique spiritual commonality between slave and slave master.[50] In fact,
Southern whites and blacks often had the same superstitions and dream culture. "To dream of the dead is said to be a sign of rain," wrote former Confederate vice president Alexander H. Stephens in his diary in 1865, in an
echo of the slave belief that dreams of death would lead to "falling weather."[51]
White Southerners also borrowed the slaves' idea that dreams ought to be
interpreted in reverse. North Carolinian William Dorsey Pender told his
wife in April 1863 not to be concerned about a dream in which she was riding in a hearse. "I thought dreams were interpreted by contraries," he wrote
her, "that hearses indicated a wedding or something of that sort." Similarly,
a Virginia politician told his wife in 1861 not to be worried about her nightmares: "Dreams always go by contraries, and are therefore always reversed."[52]

Dreams of snakes were both ubiquitous and commonly understood
among both whites and blacks to refer to enemies. The white colonel of
a black regiment "dreamed that I was walking through the forest when a

hideous copperhead sprang out of the bushes and fastened its fangs in my foot." In his dream he "immediately sought for alcoholic drink or stimulant, but finding none experienced all the horrors of death from poison." As the venom passed through his veins, chilling his blood, he awoke in something of a panic. "That same day I learned that an enemy had done me a great injury," he wrote in his diary. "Shortly after I dreamed that I had a terrible battle with Aleck Wible and today sure enough we had a severe contest with language only, but had I not been for[e]warned in my dream, it might have led to an essay with arms."[53] Similarly, after having a bizarre dream about a "monster" snake, an Ohio cavalryman worried, "I hope it dont mean any harm."[54]

Some Confederate civilians sought the meaning of dreams from their slaves. On the cold night of January 19, 1863, Lucy Breckinridge of Virginia dreamed about peaches. She described the vision to her slave, Dolly, who replied in rhyme that "to dream of fruit out of season is trouble without reason." Lying in bed, Lucy tried "to establish the fallacy of it," but "the truth of it was most painfully impressed upon my mind by looking around and finding my precious Luna frozen." Dolly's *exact language* was repeated elsewhere in the South. The concept of a dream that violated nature being a symbol of trouble (in this instance, fruit out of season) was not necessarily of African origin, however. In the second century A.D., a dream interpreter from Ephesus known as Artemidorus wrote that things dreamed of "that are out of season, are bad." Artemidorus's ideas were published in America as early as 1767.[55] Thus, it is unclear from what tradition—European or African—Dolly would have learned the symbolism. From Lucy Breckinridge's perspective, though, this wisdom had come from Africa.

In fact, there was a market for African dream interpretations among white dreamers in nineteenth-century America. *The Complete Fortune Teller and Dream Book*, an antebellum text allegedly written by an African slave who escaped from Virginia to Boston known as "Chloe Russel, A Woman of Colour," sold in several editions. Russel's work contained many of the same dream symbols as the others described in this chapter. For example,

Death—To dream you see a corpse, is a sign that you will either be married or assist at a wedding; if you dream you are dead yourself, is a sign of success in all your undertakings. . . .
Eggs—To dream of eating them signifies getting children, and breaking them some affront. . . .

Fish—To dream you are a fishing and catch none; you will never be married to the person you court, if you catch them you will be successful in love, and enjoy many happy days. . . .

Horses—To dream you see horses, it denotes intelligence; black horses death: white horses, marriage; if riding, you will change your situation. . . .

Serpents—To dream of serpents, signifies private enemies. . . .

Teeth—To dream your teeth drop out, is a token of losing some near relation. . . .

Wedding—To dream you are at a wedding, portends sickness, or the death of a near relation.[56]

It is unclear whether *The Complete Fortune Teller and Dream Book* was really written by an African slave, or whether white publishers knew they could make a profit selling a book purportedly written by an African fortune-teller to superstitious white consumers. The dream interpretations in this book thus may be of either African or Anglo-American origin. Either way, the salability of a book like this one reveals the clear interest white readers had in African understandings of dreams.[57]

THE PLACE OF DREAMS in American Christianity was hotly debated by ministers of the Gospel in the nineteenth century. Some white preachers believed that their dreams could serve as revelation akin to scripture. "I know the word of God is our infallible guide, and by it we are to try all our dreams and feelings," stated the white Methodist minister Freeborn Garrettson, but "I also know, that both sleeping and waking, things of a divine nature have been revealed to me." But publications such as the *Connecticut Evangelical Magazine* rebutted this position. "No person is warranted from the word of God to publish to the world the discoveries of heaven or hell which he supposes he has had in a dream, or trance, or vision."[58]

Some white divines relied on visions and dreams as a confirmation for their call to the ministry. Baptist preacher Jabez Swan of Connecticut recollected his call to the ministry in the 1820s in his memoir. "God finally attacked me with dreams, which were terrible," he wrote. His various dreams—of bridling an enormous white horse, or of wrestling with a demon—confirmed for him that "with God's help I could throw the Grand Enemy; but it would take a God to hold him." Itinerant Methodist preachers often enthusiastically shared their dreams in sermons in the eighteenth-century and up through the Second Great Awakening.[59] Eighteenth- and nineteenth-century Quakers were also particularly open to the incorporation of dreams into their worship of God.[60]

By the mid-nineteenth century, however, such dreams as confirmation of conversion or a call to Christian ministry had been relegated primarily to African American communities. White evangelicals increasingly labeled such adherence to "superstitions" and dreams as a perversion of the Gospel. One Presbyterian minister in Georgia lamented in 1842 the role of "superstitions brought from Africa" in Southern African American worship:

> *True religion* they are inclined to place in *profession*, in *forms and ordinances*, and in *excited states of feeling*. And *true conversion*, in *dreams, visions, trances, voices*—all bearing a perfect or striking resemblance to some form or type which has been handed down for generations, or which has been originated in the wild fancy of some religious teacher among them. These dreams and visions they will offer to church-sessions, as *evidences* of conversion, if encouraged so to do, or if their better instruction be neglected.... Intimately connected with their ignorance, is their *superstition*.... They believe in second-sight, in apparitions, charms, witchcraft, and in a kind of irresistible Satanic influence. The superstitions brought from Africa have not been wholly laid aside. Ignorance and superstition render them easy dupes to their teachers, doctors, prophets, conjurers; to artful and designing men.... A plain and faithful presentation of the Gospel, usually weakens if not destroys these superstitions.[61]

A Methodist missionary similarly bemoaned in the 1840s that slaves more often became "serious" about their religion and prayers not as "the result of preaching, but most commonly a 'warning in a dream.'"[62] So, too, a Moravian minister "regretted" that African Americans based their "conversion so much on dreams, visions and other fantasies."[63]

Historians have used evidence like this to show a marked contrast between black and white Christianity in nineteenth-century America. Persons of African descent came to the Christian faith through a period of "intensive prayer and the interpretation of dreams and visions, rather than the formal catechism associated with the institutional Christianity of the Roman Catholic and mainline Protestant churches," writes one scholar. "The framework for this Lowcountry Christian practice came from West-Central African and West African initiation societies, revealed in part by the stages of seeking in which the initiate endured seclusion in the wilderness and returned after a dramatic spiritual transformation."[64]

Ironically, many white Christian missionaries in the nineteenth century criticized what they perceived as the ignorance of black slaves for their belief in dreams, not realizing that those beliefs had European as well as African roots. In fact, some of the slaves' dream practices may have even been instilled in slaves by their masters and white missionaries in the eighteenth century. As early as April 24, 1742, the *South Carolina Gazette* censured the way that white missionaries Christianized Southern slaves, noting that "instead of teaching them the *Principles* of *Christianity*," preachers were "filling their heads with a parcel of *Cant-Phrases, Trances, Dreams*, Visions and Revelations."[65]

Thus, while dreams diminished as an important part of the conversion experience for many literate whites as the nineteenth-century progressed, they continued to play such a role for many blacks. One slave saw a vision in which God provided a safe path through "a sea of glass" that "was mingled with fire." Many saw heaven and hell, or had out-of-body experiences. One woman dreamed she saw "three suns rising in the east," while a voice spoke to her, saying, "The Father, the Son, and the Holy Ghost." Others saw angels or the devil, or deceased relatives. One even "came face to face with God" in a dream. These dreams served as confirmation for slaves and free blacks that their salvation was secure. "I have seen many visions," declared one ex-slave. "This is why I believe in God more strongly. Everything I have asked him to show me he has shown."[66]

Such dreams gave slaves a sense of autonomy in their religious lives that they lacked in their daily work and social interactions. Visions from God freed them from traditional religious hierarchies and ministerial authority, giving the enslaved man or woman a direct connection to a higher authority than any temporal power they encountered on earth. If white clergy by the time of the Civil War found much to criticize in slave religion, the slaves themselves found much spiritual comfort in these special revelations from God.

By the time of the Civil War, the difference between white and black Americans regarding dream practices may not have been so much the interest in and interpretation of dreams, but their public uses in religion. As white evangelical denominations—particularly Southern Baptists and Methodists—sought to appear more respectable in American society, they modified some of their beliefs and practices.[67] These changes likely included a sharp decrease in public use of dreams in Christian worship. This is not to say that white Christians outright rejected that dreams could carry spiritual meaning—far from it. But after the Second Great Awakening, white men and women more often shared their dreams with one another quietly, in letters and publications, or over the breakfast table, not in public places of worship.[68] Dreams for slaves, however, remained part of their public rituals and professions of faith. Thus, as the nineteenth century progressed, Afro-Christian dream culture seemed increasingly alien to whites—especially Northern whites. It is little wonder, then, that upon reaching the South, many Union soldiers had quizzical, if not downright negative reactions to slave preachers and prophets.

Some Union soldiers saw slaves' fascination with dreams as a curiosity. Charles Thomas Ackley of the Seventh Iowa Infantry told his wife about an Alabama slave preacher he met in the South: "They say he preached well for a man that could not read," wrote Ackley. "I have been reading to him. He wanted to hear Joseph's dream and I commenced and read two evenings to him. He can remember well and the boys can't beat him on an argument."[69] Others saw slave beliefs in dreams as far more spiritually dangerous. In June 1862, Capt. Dana King of the Eighth New Hampshire Volunteers encountered an "old patriarch" contraband who "appears perfectly sane as he employs all his low cunning in avoiding all work. His feet resemble a pair of brindled puppies. They show the effects of a bastinado. He is a very devout Baptist, having been 'converted,' as he says, 'from the errors of Methodism two years ago.' He sees visions, dreams, of course; is a corrector of the Scriptures, knows palmistry—all of which is a sable lie."[70]

CHAPTER FIVE

Dreams of the Dying

In the wee hours of the morning of May 2, 1863, during the Battle of Chancellorsville, Confederate general Thomas Jonathan "Stonewall" Jackson's sword was leaning against a tree. Then, without any *apparent* cause," it fell to the ground "with a clank." Col. A. L. Long of Robert E. Lee's staff picked up the saber and handed it to Jackson. But the incident "impressed me at the time as an omen of evil," Long later recalled, "an indefinable superstition such as sometimes affects persons on the falling of a picture or mirror." Long was "haunted" by ill feelings all day and suspected that something bad would soon befall the general.[1]

Later that day, Stonewall Jackson led a devastating assault against superior Federal numbers. But the attack had begun too late in the day for him to complete his work, so that evening he rode out to survey the situation to see if a night attack was possible. On his way back toward the Confederate lines, nervous North Carolinians opened fire on Jackson and his men, mortally wounding nine or ten men and hitting Jackson three times. The general's left arm was amputated at 3 A.M. on the morning of May 3 and was buried. Over the next few days, Jackson passed in and out of delirium, and faced restless nights with labored sleep. After he contracted pneumonia, his suffering only increased.

By May 10, it was clear that he would die soon. Jackson slipped in and out of consciousness; the loud ticking of the clock in the bedroom where he lay apparently sounded in his ears like cannon-fire and the crack of muskets. "Push up the columns!" he ordered in a dreamlike state. "Hasten the columns! Pendleton, you take charge of that! Where's Pendleton? Tell him to push up the column!" His mind moved through the previous few battles of the war in reverse chronological order: Antietam, Second Bull Run, the 1862 campaign in the Shenandoah Valley, and First Bull Run. He traveled further backwards in time. He was now an instructor at VMI, now with his friends and family, now in the Mexican-American War, now a cadet at West Point. Finally, his mind took him back to his childhood, to the place where he had been raised—Jackson's Mill and the West Fork River. "Let us cross over the river," he said, "and rest under the shade of the trees." With that, he died. Jackson's wife, Anna, later remembered, "All at once he spoke out very cheerfully and distinctly the beautiful sentence which has become immortal as his last."[2]

Stonewall Jackson's deathbed scene is one of the best documented and widely known of the war years, but it was by no means unique. Ordinary Confederate soldiers had similar deathbed experiences, returning to battle in their dying dreams. When Sgt. William McCoy of Charlottesville, Virginia, lay dying in May 1863, his family gave him morphine to help ease his pain, but which also caused him to speak in his sleep. The wanderings of his mind revealed a cognizance of the wounds he had received just two weeks earlier at Chancellorsville. One of his brothers wrote, "His dreams were decoherent and mostly of the battle field and his company; he drilled them sometimes calling 'Halt!' giving orders about taking out his piece; called the men's names very often. Once he said 'You must excuse me gentlemen, I can't engage in this game. I forgot I can't see nor use either hand nor walk a step; I am badly wounded.'" At one point, William called for his brother, "Charley, Charley McCoy," but when told that Charley was not there, he replied that he "thought some one said [Charley's] regiment had been ordered back."

As William drifted in and out of sleep, his thinking remained sharp. "His mind was perfectly calm and clear in the midst of all his suffering," wrote his brother shortly after he died. "We could wake him at any moment and he was perfectly himself, his manner, his language, his gentleness and politeness which he never forgot for a moment." And as death approached, he increasingly spoke of spiritual matters, both when awake and when asleep. "I do try from the bottom of my heart," he said once in his sleep, "to trust in God and in Jesus Christ." Some of his last words, also said in his sleep, were, "All for Jesus."[3]

Union soldiers had similar experiences. Frederick Reader of the 148th Pennsylvania Volunteers died at Chancellorsville while "dreaming in his dying moments of the battle he repeated, 'Major, we will stand up to them, won't we.'" And Pvt. Joseph H. Eaton of Vermont was mortally wounded a year later at the Wilderness in May 1864. As he died, "he went off into dreams and raved about his comrades and the battle."[4]

In the modern era, scientists and historians look cynically at such deathbed scenes. In an article debunking the "myth" of Robert E. Lee's deathbed speeches—in which Lee is supposed to have said, "Tell Hill he *must* come up," and "Strike the tents"—a team of neurologists, speech pathologists, and physicians concluded, "Deathbed speeches and final words are stage tricks, used to enhance drama and project the hopes and beliefs of the living." More importantly, they wrote, "such a phenomenon can be considered a sort of insurance policy for immortality—it matters little who initiates it, only that the beneficiary collects."[5]

But these views discount several important realities. While Lee's deathbed speeches were likely fabrications, other deathbed scenes are well documented. Stonewall Jackson biographer James I. Robertson writes, "Three people were in the room when Jackson died. . . . All attested to his final words." Moreover, the wide circulation of the story "within two weeks after his passing," writes Robertson, "gives it added authenticity and further protection against being termed a later fabrication."[6]

Some readers may still doubt the veracity of the recollections recounted in this chapter, especially since many of them were published decades after the war. But these stories were not mere insurance policies to make the living feel better about the spiritual state of the dead; nor were they merely "an important role in their work of preparation" for "the Good Death," as historian Drew Gilpin Faust suggests.[7] Both of these interpretations treat dying words, prophetic dreams, and premonitions as after-the-fact inventions perpetrated by the living. But these scholars underestimate the meaning of dying dreams to those who survived the Civil War. Many nineteenth-century Americans really believed that God revealed something about his providential designs in these deathbed moments, and such beliefs enabled Victorian Americans to find inspiration and hope in suffering and death. Indeed, the dreams of the dying reveal the persistence into the postwar period of antebellum understandings of death and providence, and the belief that soldiers' deaths were orchestrated by a higher power and were not without meaning.[8]

We will never know with certainty which of these dreams and presentiments actually occurred, and which, if any, were fabricated after the war. It is not implausible, however, to believe that most of these stories are true. Considering that human beings have on average more than eighteen hundred dreams per year, and these soldiers were often thinking about their own mortality over the course of several years, it is perfectly reasonable to expect that many would have dreamed that they were going to die. Of course, if they had such a dream and told it to a comrade—and the dreamer then died—it is little wonder such a dream would have seemed prophetic and would have later been remembered and preserved in the written record. Psychologist Michael Shermer writes (with intended irony, since he is an atheist) that since people have so many dreams in their lives "it would be a *miracle* if some death premonition dreams did not come true!"[9]

Hundreds—perhaps thousands—of soldiers and civilians claimed to experience prophetic dreams, visions, premonitions, visitations, or presentiments during the war.[10] Many of these supernatural occurrences foretold their own death or the death of a comrade or loved one. Some of these accounts appear in wartime writings; most, however, are found in postwar memoirs and regimental histories. Whether or not most of these prophetic visions actually occurred can never be known. Nor, at this point, does their authenticity really matter. Their significance lies in that so many soldiers remembered these moments in the postwar years. Long after the guns ceased firing, veterans clung to some of their antebellum conceptions of divine providence. To be sure, their views became less biblically orthodox over time. Nevertheless, a form of supernatural or providential thinking about dreams and premonitions persisted among many Civil War veterans well into the late nineteenth and early twentieth centuries.[11]

THE HUMAN TRAGEDY of the Civil War can be seen more clearly in the dreams of Civil War–era Americans than in any other surviving record. Indeed, as one scholar of traumatic dreams in another historical context argues, these dreams "testify to a past reality in a manner which perhaps could not be surpassed by any source."[12] Dreams reveal the ways that individuals sought to make sense of the world around them, or the chaos in their lives. Quite often dreams related to past events or present concerns in a person's life; but in some instances, nighttime visions became windows into the future. Prophetic dreams and presentiments (forebodings that were often experienced by soldiers at night, as they slept) expose an entirely different aspect of Civil War–era dream life, showing how the dreamers saw themselves and the meaning of their lives within the unfolding of larger events.[13] If most dreams reveal something about the dreamer's innermost thoughts, Americans saw prophetic dreams as a revelation given to them by an outside force. Because the dreamers perceived their visions and premonitions as authentic revelations, the dreams themselves tended to help reduce soldiers' fears about death, often giving them a sense of acceptance—sometimes even anticipation—for what was to come.[14]

Presentiments, premonitions, visions, and dreams of death were common among the fighting men of the Civil War. Soldiers often had a vague "presentiment of evil" during battle. Others saw "visions of home and friends" during a charge on the enemy. Still others "lost all consciousness of what was transpiring" around them.[15] The rush of battle could thus have a supernatural, dreamlike, or even out-of-body effect on soldiers, similar to what some psychiatrists today call dissociation. These sensations were sometimes experienced communally. Indeed, some regiments perceived communal premonitions. At various points in the war, soldiers in the Thirty-Third Iowa, Tenth Vermont, Twenty-Third North Carolina, Second Illinois, Sixth New Hampshire, and Twentieth and Thirty-Third Massachusetts seemed to experience this phenomenon.[16]

More commonly, soldiers experienced their own forebodings in the field. Sometimes these presentiments appeared to soldiers in a dream. One night, Confederate general Micah Jenkins had "a singular dream" that he could not get out of his mind. In the dream, he relived his entire life until he "came to a blank after the coming battle." "Why have I not forgotten this dream, as I have all the dreams I've had before?" he wondered. True to his prophetic vision, he died shortly thereafter during the Overland Campaign in May 1864.[17]

The regimental historian for the Twelfth New Hampshire Volunteers reported that at least twenty-five members of his unit had presentiments of their own deaths, or had family members who saw visions, had dreams, or experienced unmistakable feelings confirming the deaths of their loved ones. The wife of Pvt. John Merrill had dreamed for three years before the war of her husband being "surrounded by blood." She was so frightened by these visions that she would not allow him to ride in trains or work in dangerous places. When he enlisted in the army the dreams stopped, which she took to mean that he would be killed in battle. He was.[18]

On the night before the Battle of Gettysburg commenced in July 1863, the wife of Lt. Charles Emery of the Twelfth New Hampshire heard three or four loud raps at her front door. No one else in the house awoke, so she quietly went downstairs. At the door stood the specter of Lt. Henry French, a childhood friend of her husband's who had also joined the Twelfth. He silently and swiftly moved past her, down the hall. Startled, she followed him into the sitting room, but when she got there he was nowhere to be seen. Instead, she saw two coffins in the middle of the room. She slowly approached the open boxes. Inside one she saw "the pale face and lifeless form of Lieutenant French." When she peered into the other she found it empty, but she noticed a "small stream of blood" running out of the foot of it. She took this to mean that Lieutenant French would die immediately, but that her husband's time had not yet come.

When Mrs. Emery awoke the next morning she felt "it all seemed so real and so little like a dream." A day or two later, word of French's death arrived in their village. And following the Battle of Cold Harbor, in June

1864, her husband, Charlie, died as well. She made it to the hospital before he expired. "Just as he breathed his last, a stream of blood ran from off the foot of his bed upon the floor, just as I had seen it run out of the foot of the empty coffin," she later remembered, "and the realization of my vision was then and there sadly and solemnly consummated."[19]

Families throughout the North and South experienced similar signs and premonitions regarding the deaths of loved ones. On May 28, 1864, Martha Jackson awoke to the song of a mourning dove on her window-sill. She immediately knew that her husband had been killed in battle. According to a descendant, "She rose from her bed, dropped to her knees to pray, and wept softly, lest her grief be seen by her family and be considered impetuous and a product of superstition." She then made a note of her "revelation" in her Bible. In like manner, a black woman living near Ford's Theatre in 1865 said that "dogs howled and chickens were crowing for days before Lincoln's death, and when a large picture of Lincoln fell off the wall and a bird flew into the room, she just knew someone was going to die in the neighborhood."[20] The fiancée of an Ohio soldier similarly had a presentiment that her lover would die in battle. She sent him a letter to that effect, and he told a friend that he, too, had "a dread presentiment of it myself, but my country is in peril." He fell during the Atlanta campaign.[21]

Special revelations such as these could be difficult for soldiers and their families to ignore. Robert Gould Shaw asked a fellow officer in the Fifty-Fourth Massachusetts "if he believed in presentiments, and added that he felt he would be killed in the first action." When the other officer replied that Shaw should "try to shake off the feeling," Shaw quietly said, "I will try."[22] Of course, Shaw did fall in his regiment's first action in July 1863 during the famous assault on Fort Wagner in Charleston Harbor.

PREMONITIONS AND PRESENTIMENTS had varying effects on soldiers' morale. Many responded courageously. Shortly before dying at White Hall on December 16, 1862, Sgt. William T. Fowler of the Twenty-Third Massachusetts had a presentiment that he would be killed. He "refused an offer of duty at the rear," telling his commanding officer, "If I took it and saved my life so, I should never hear the last of it." Capt. William Pattangall of the First Maine Heavy Artillery similarly "had a strong presentiment that he should be killed in the first battle" but still "went boldly into the thickest of the fight and died like a hero." Soldiers in the Fifteenth Illinois, Seventy-Fifth Indiana, Twenty-Sixth New York, Ninety-Third New York,

141st Pennsylvania, and Twentieth Tennessee similarly chose to continue fighting despite a presentiment of death.[23]

In some cases, presentiments led men to act recklessly. In September 1863, Col. Thomas Owen of the Third Virginia Cavalry had a presentiment "that he should be very badly wounded in one of his legs and either lose the limb or his life." His friends urged him to be cautious, but instead "he exposed himself in the most reckless and unnecessary manner saying if he was destined to be shot he would be and if not, he wouldn't." In fact, he was not wounded for some time, but on May 7, 1864, he had a finger shot off at Todd's Tavern while "directing the fire of the regiment." Another Confederate, after having a presentiment that he would be killed, "went on the field as though it had been a gala day of review." He fought valiantly and was shot twice, once in the shoulder and once through the heart. "Thus was the gallant soldier's presentiment fulfilled," recalled one witness. "He walked up to what he believed to be inevitable death with laughter in his voice and a smile upon his lips." An even more tragic incident occurred in the 123rd New York Infantry. Sgt. James Cummings turned "melancholy and sad" after having a "feeling that he would not survive the next battle." He told a friend that he would rather be killed on the battlefield than linger with some disease in a hospital. At the Battle of New Hope Church, while most of the men lay hugging the ground, Cummings stood up amid the firing and told a comrade, "I don't think there is any more danger in standing here than lying in the mud, I have had enough of that." He was wrong. Within a minute a bullet struck him in the forehead.[24] Instances like these add a new layer to how we understand recklessness, which traditionally is seen as the result of a person having too much confidence in himself and not enough fear of surrounding danger.[25] In these cases, however, soldiers placed confidence not in themselves but in an external power that they could not overcome. Recklessness was the result of fatalism.

Presentiments and prophetic dreams caused some soldiers to become shrouded in gloom. Joel Hollingsworth of the 124th Pennsylvania Volunteers "awoke from a troubled sleep" and told his comrade that "if I had a good excuse for staying out, I would not go" into the next battle. But he did not have an excuse and his "presentiment that I would be killed or wounded" proved true. He was shot in the foot the next day, but he survived the war. Allen Pierce of the Seventh Rhode Island became "sick and discouraged" after he had a presentiment. His captain "took pity on him" and allowed him to assist the company cook rather than go into battle. But the higher power could not be thwarted. While Pierce was out gathering firewood away from the fighting a cannonball shattered his leg and he died shortly thereafter from infection. Upon watching so many of his men die in battle, the colonel of the First Maine Heavy Artillery was "besieged" by "sombre presentiments" and "surrounded by phantoms" until he was finally felled by a rebel bullet on August 17, 1864. During that summer outside of Petersburg, another soldier thought he looked like a "doomed man" marked for death. The colonel of the Fifty-Seventh New York similarly appeared "unusually depressed" after having a presentiment that he would be killed. Following his death at the Wilderness, a comrade recalled that "his low spirits and unhappy appearance made me feel very sorry for him."[26]

Yankee officer Nathan W. Daniels wrote in his diary, "Have the blues like Lucifer today. If there is any truth in Presentiments then have I one now, an oppressive feeling, as though some great calamity was suspended over me, affects me." Before the Battle of Fort Fisher, an officer of the 112th New York "had a gloomy presentiment that if he went into that battle he should not come out alive." He paced around looking "sad and abstracted," but when the charge began he moved forward "with a smile on his face, and cheerful words to his men" and marched two hundred yards before being hit by a rebel bullet. Another Yankee veteran anxiously washed his face one morning after having a vision of his impending death, telling his comrades that with a clean face he would "make a better looking corpse."[27]

Because of their emotional toll, soldiers could often perceive when a friend had had a vision of impending death. Some comrades deduced this from the tone of a soldier's letters or from his strange behavior in camp or in battle.[28] Two days before the Battle of Shiloh, Lt. Col. Edward Ellis of the Fifteenth Illinois addressed his regiment with a moving speech. "He prophesied the coming battle, exhorted us all to do our duty in every emergency," recalled one man. "He closed with an affecting appeal which brought tears to many eyes. Did he then have a presentiment of his fate? Brave and good man!" Ellis would fall at that place of peace.[29]

Some men turned cowardly and, going against cultural norms, vainly sought to avoid their fate. During one battle, a soldier in the Ninety-Seventh New York "lay upon the ground and did not fire" after he had a presentiment. Still, a bullet found him. An artillerist who had previously shown no fear had a presentiment in 1864 and "became a coward." During battle, he hid "in the rear" by the caissons, but he could not escape his destiny. According to another man in the regiment, "Death searched him out and found him" while he was "leaning over a fire, frying pan in hand, preparing his supper."[30] Fearing that they would be perceived as cowards, some men chose to keep their forebodings to themselves.[31]

Soldiers' courage—or lack thereof—was often rooted in their interpretation of supernatural revelations. Sgt. Edward B. Herbert of the First Maine Cavalry had "always" been eager to enter the fray until he "had a presentiment that he would be shot." He asked to be permitted to dismount during an engagement, but his superior officer refused, and poor Herbert "went to his doom." Unlike Herbert, most soldiers knew they could not accept a place in the rear. Prior to the Battle of Chickamauga, Capt. William Lease of the Thirty-First Indiana had a presentiment that he would be killed on the first day of the fight. He gave his pocket watch and a message for his wife to his colonel, who tried to persuade Lease that this was "some kind of foolish hallucination." The two men discussed whether Lease could go to the rear, but Lease declared "that he would die before he would go back dishonorably." Prior to one engagement, Charles Crommett of the 112th Illinois had a presentiment that he would "be hit." His captain ordered him to "exchange places with a horse holder," but Crommett "had not the moral courage to leave the line in time of action—staid—and lost a leg."[32]

A few men thought they could avoid the fate portended in a premonition. Pvt. Robert McKinney of the 141st Pennsylvania had a presentiment that he would be killed at the Battle of Chancellorsville. By the end of the day, he thought he had beaten the odds. As his regimental historian recounted after the war: "After the fight was over he went up to Lieutenant Clark, and placing his hand upon his shoulder said, 'I had a kind of presentiment when I went into this fight that I should be killed, but I guess I am all right after all.' Just at this moment he stopped talking and Lieutenant Clark turned and saw a hole entirely through his head made either from a stray grape shot or a piece of shell. It was so sudden, says Lieutenant Clark, that he did not fall at once, and I could hardly believe he had received his death hurt."[33]

The wide range of soldiers' reactions to threats—or perhaps more precisely, the perception of an impending threat—should not be surprising. Human beings naturally respond to crises in different ways depending on their personal temperament, past experiences, or belief system.[34] Nevertheless, it is telling that the majority of these soldiers chose to prioritize courage and honor, faithfulness to their comrades, or self-sacrifice for their cause, above their natural instincts for survival. Soldiers who experienced a dream or foreboding of death more often than not accepted their fate and prepared for the inevitable. They did so for several reasons. First, they saw themselves as participating in something that was more significant than their individual identities—a righteous cause in which it was fitting to suffer and die. Along these lines, their calm resignation in the face of death fit the mold of what historian Frances M. Clarke calls an "exemplary sufferer" in Victorian America, demonstrating their moral strength and virtue. They could entrust their individual fates to providence because they knew that God was overseeing everything that went on in the war.[35] Second, many believed that they were powerless to prevent the future event that had been revealed to them. Finally, some possessed a Christian faith that they would soon be in a world free of suffering and sin. As historian Mark S. Schantz argues, America's antebellum religious culture helped prepare the men of both North and South for the carnage of the Civil War.[36] There was no reason to play the coward in the minds of these men who had had the future revealed to them. Their fate could not be avoided, and something better awaited them anyway.

PROPHECIES, PRESENTIMENTS, AND DREAMS of death caused soldiers to grapple with the gravity of their tenuous situations. Sometimes this manifested itself through expressions of denial. One of the most common ways that soldiers responded to a comrade who had a presentiment was to laugh at him. The boys of the Ninety-Third New York Infantry had such a reaction to David Van Buren after he reported "a dream, in which he saw himself in battle and that he was slain, being the first one to fall." When he related his dream, "His comrades tried to divert his mind and laugh him out of it, but he could not shake off the feeling." When the Battle of the Wilderness began, Van Buren grabbed his gun courageously and was one of the first men to fall, "thus verifying his dream." Soldiers in the Ninety-Sixth Illinois, 140th and 147th Pennsylvania, and Twelfth Wisconsin responded similarly to comrades who had presentiments of death.[37]

In some cases, soldiers sought to encourage their comrades. One night, Pvt. Charles Walker of the Twenty-Second Massachusetts Volunteers dreamed that he "lost an arm, near the shoulder." His comrades "tried in vain to cheer him up" but "nothing could drive away his dreadful presentiment." According to his regimental historian, his "state of mind affected his body" and he died a few days later. In a few cases, soldiers taunted their suffering comrades. Pvt. James Sleeper of the Eleventh New Hampshire Infantry came out for roll call one morning shortly before the Battle of Fredericksburg in December 1862 "feeling pretty low-spirited." When asked what was the matter, he replied, "During the night I had a presentiment that I should be killed in my first battle." Lt. Charles E. Bartlett curtly replied, "I shall go through the whole war, and come out without a scratch." The Eleventh's regimental historian concluded, "And, strange as it may seem, both were right." Sleeper was wounded on December 13 and died the following day. Soldiers in the Second Pennsylvania Reserves threatened to shoot a comrade who always shirked during battle because of a presentiment he'd had. When they finally forced him into a fight, "he fell dead with nine of the enemy's balls in him."[38]

Many soldiers who had prophetic dreams and presentiments began to order their worldly affairs. Officers frequently told their comrades how to dispose of their bodies once they had fallen. Prior to being killed at Gaines Mill on June 27, 1862, Capt. William Partridge of the Fifth New York Infantry saw a vision of "John Brown with outstretched arms ready to receive him." Knowing that he would soon die, he gave directions for the disposition of his body after he was killed. Some officers expressed their desire to have their corpses sent home, while others ordered their men to bury their bodies in the field where they fell. Soldiers also often prepared packages for their loved ones, or wrote letters or instructions to be sent home upon their demise. Outside of Petersburg on March 25, 1865, Pvt. John Smith of the Tenth Vermont dreamed that he would be killed that day, and he asked a friend to send home his ring and a few other things. True enough, Smith was killed, and his friend took the ring from his finger to send home.[39]

Of course, not all dreams and visions proved accurate. One Virginian imprisoned at Johnson's Island in Ohio dreamed four times that his friend Willie Mitchel was still alive. The prisoner made several inquiries but could not learn of Mitchel's fate. After the fourth dream, he wrote, "let us see how much reliance may be had in dreams." In this instance, not much. Willie Mitchel, a seventeen-year-old private in the First Virginia Infantry, had been killed two months earlier at Gettysburg.[40]

Shortly before the Battle of Gettysburg, one young Pennsylvania soldier announced that he'd had a presentiment and expected to survive the war. "I would like to sing again in the choir of the old church on the hill and somehow I feel that this desire of my heart will be realized," he told his comrades. His dream would not come to pass; he fell a few days later on July 2, 1863. In other cases, soldiers lived to see peace. A Texas cavalryman wrote in his diary on February 17, 1862, that he did not expect to return home, but he survived the war. Prior to the Battle of Chancellorsville, Lt. William S. Batchelder of the 118th Pennsylvania Volunteers "labored all night with a harrowing presentiment that during the day he would certainly be killed." On other evenings, he had been "haunted with horrible dreams of frightful gaping wounds, so shocking and repulsive as to be beyond the reach of surgical skill or careful nursing." The "shrieks and pains of death and wounds" that he heard in his nightmares would awaken him with a start. When he fell back to sleep "these distressing scenes repeated" themselves. Nevertheless, he, too, survived the battle and the war.[41] As might be expected—and for reasons discussed below—dreams and forebodings that came to pass far outnumber those that did not in the historical record.

THE EVER-PRESENT THREAT of battle made it almost inevitable that soldiers' dreams of combat might come true. "Now and then a gun with the scream of a shell from the hostile works mixed with our drowsiness and made our dreams prophetic," wrote Union chaplain Joseph Hopkins Twichell.[42] Examples abound of actual dreams that were fulfilled.

Some prophetic dreams were fairly inconsequential. Sgt. T. J. McCall of the Fifteenth Pennsylvania Cavalry had identical dreams on consecutive nights about the capture of a train he was detailed to guard. "I told the boys about it, but they did not believe it would come true, but the second morning I saw it fulfilled," he wrote. "This was the only dream I ever had that came true." Other dreams had great meaning for the dreamers. Col. C. W. Heiskell of the Nineteenth Tennessee Volunteers dreamed before the battle of Corinth that "I met my brother who was a soldier in the Federal army face to face in battle. After the war we met, and I told him of the dream. 'Why,' he said, 'I was in that engagement.' And indeed we were, no doubt, not 500 yards apart in the fight."[43]

Before being killed near Vicksburg, Capt. Caspar Schleich of the Fifty-Fifth Illinois "felt one of those mysterious presentiments which sometimes seem to beckon soldiers across the silent river." Schleich "dreamed that I stood facing a rebel about fifty yards away when he shot me through the heart, and as he shot I sprang up in the bed, and I fear, greatly disturbed you," he told his bunk mate. At breakfast, he reported to his men, "Boys, I am glad I ate with you this morning, for I am going out here to be killed by these rebels, and I want you to bear witness that I desire to be buried here on this sand ridge." The chaplain of his regiment later recalled, "As in his dream he had stood facing a rebel soldier about fifty yards away, just long enough to be shot through the heart, and the spirit of my brave and beautiful captain had gone back to God who gave it."[44]

In the spring of 1862, Pvt. Henry C. Miles of the Thirty-Sixth Illinois Volunteers "dreamed a dream, which was very singular from the fact that it was twice repeated, and literally fulfilled in the main point." The first

time the dream occurred, Miles dreamed that the Confederate forces attacked his company, "and at the first fire" two brothers in the unit named
William and Alexander Stitt "tried to run away but were shot dead by the
file closers." This dream garnered significant attention and the two brothers
became the butts of "considerable chaffing for a day or two." A while later,
Miles had a similar dream. This time when the Stitt brothers tried to run
they "were shot by the Confederates and either killed or badly wounded."
Shortly thereafter, Miles had the dream again, except this time the two
Stitt boys were seriously wounded while the regiment was retreating. On
March 7, 1862—the day after this final dream—a number of men from the
Thirty-Sixth were sent out as skirmishers, where they encountered a for-
mation of Confederate infantry. They fired one volley and then commenced
to retreat. At this point the Confederates began a pursuit. "It was on this re-
treat that the dream was fulfilled," recalled one veteran from the regiment.
The two Stitt boys were wounded, one badly enough that he could no longer
serve in the army.[45]

Sgt. Washington Mackey Ives of the Fourth Florida Volunteers recalled
the night of May 27, 1863, when he shared a blanket with two lieutenants,
one on either side of him. About midnight, he woke up and saw the two
officers sitting by a fire near his feet, talking to one another. "They had each
dreamed that they would be killed that day and had decided to talk it over,"
wrote Ives. "I endeavored to cheer them, insisting that no confidence could
be placed in dreams, but my efforts only confirmed them." Both men gave
Sergeant Ives instructions of what to do with their belongings after they
were killed.

At sunrise, the men arose and packed up their camp. Within an hour or
so the first officer was killed. In the afternoon, they found the other officer
dead, leaning against a log where he had crawled and taken off his belt and
shoes. "The dreams of the two young officers who had met death impressed
me very seriously," wrote Ives. Ives himself was fortunate to escape a similar circumstance: On July 10, 1863, he and two other officers awoke "at the
same moment" and "looked into each other's faces and related our dreams
of being mortally wounded." This time all three men "passed through the
war without having a bullet enter us."[46]

In early 1862, one Alabamian noticed a soldier who "went to sleep ... a
few days ago and slept one whole day and night before they could finally
wake him." When the man awoke, he reported that "he had dreamed the
first and second weeks in April there would be the biggest fighting that had
been since the War began, and the fourth week there would be another big

fight." He then dreamed that peace would come in May "and in four days from that time he should die." The man who heard and recorded this dream was struck by some of its accuracies: "On the fourth day from the day of his dream he died. One of those fights commenced the second day of April in Corinth."[47]

Some Americans interpreted their nightmares as signs of chastisement from God. Early in the war, Eliza Fain, a Presbyterian woman in Tennessee, "was aroused from my sleep with heavy foreboding of evil. As a nation how has the Bible been disregarded by our Northern brethren and of what grievous sins have we of the South been guilty. We are visited with the indignation of the King of Kings and Lord of Hosts. Our land seems to be doomed to the horrors of civil war."[48]

Other dreams brought healing after the death of a loved one. Visitation dreams from ancestors or the dead were common in some African and Native American traditions, often occurring during a time of spiritual enlightenment or personal difficulty.[49] During the Civil War era they sometimes brought closure to families who had recently lost a loved one. Still just a "beardless" teenager, William H. S. Jackson of the Sixth Georgia Infantry State Guard died at the Battle of Resaca, just over a hundred miles from his home, on May 15, 1864. After the battle, his comrades buried him in "a pine coffin constructed of rough planks torn from a bridge." In 1866, Jackson's father, Jethro, learned the location of his son's burial, but when he went to find it, he was unsuccessful. According to one observer, "the broken-hearted father returned home."

A few nights later, Jethro dreamed that his son came to him in his bed. "Father, I am buried under a mound which was thrown up by the Yankees after I was killed," said Jackson. "You will know the mound when you see it by the pokeberry bushes growing upon it. Go and take me up and carry me home to Mother." The elder Jackson was so impressed by the dream that he "returned at once to Resaca, taking with him one of the comrades who had buried his son." They found the mound with the berries growing on it, and, upon digging, discovered the pine coffin just a few feet beneath the surface. Within the coffin was the body of the boy, "fully identified not only by the coffin, but by his shoes, a recent gift from his father, and by the name marked on his clothing." His remains were then "carried home to Mother," just as the dream of Jackson had asked his father to do.[50]

THE NUMBER OF PROPHECIES, presentiments and forebodings recorded in postwar memoirs and regimental histories is astounding. Their ubiquity in the writings of ordinary soldiers and veterans reveals that they were experienced—and believed in—by a broad number of fighting men; they were not simply propagated by political, cultural or religious leaders; nor could they all have been after-the-fact inventions.[51] Aside from those detailed elsewhere in this chapter, they also appear in the memoirs and regimental histories of the First, Third, Fourth, and Sixth Alabama,[52] the Second Florida,[53] the First Georgia Regulars,[54] the Thirty-Sixth, Fifty-Fifth, and Ninety-Sixth Illinois Infantries, and Eighth Illinois Cavalry,[55] the Seventy-First and Seventy-Second Indiana,[56] the Tenth and Sixteenth Maine,[57] the Second, Seventh, Twenty-Seventh, Thirty-Sixth, Thirty-Seventh, Fifty-Fifth, and Fifty-Seventh Massachusetts,[58] the Sixteenth Mississippi Volunteers,[59] the Second Missouri Cavalry (CSA) and Twenty-Fifth Missouri (Union),[60] the First, Eighth, Thirteenth, and Fourteenth New Hampshire,[61] the Thirteenth New York State Militia, Second New York Artillery, and the Sixteenth, Nineteenth, Twenty-Sixth, Fortieth, Sixty-Second, Ninety-Third, 115th, and 121st New York Infantries,[62] the Second and 126th Ohio,[63] the Sixth, Twenty-Eighth, Seventy-First, Ninety-Ninth, 118th, 125th, 141st, 148th, 149th, 160th, and 163rd Pennsylvania Volunteers,[64] the Sixth South Carolina,[65] the Second and Eighth Vermont,[66] the Thirty-Second Virginia,[67] the Third, Sixth, and Twenty-First Wisconsin,[68] and the Union Navy.[69] Speakers at Memorial Day reunions—as prominent as Oliver Wendell Holmes Jr.—recounted them as well.[70] The prevalence of these stories across so many different regiments and states reveals that American conceptions of both providence and death may not have changed as much during the war as many scholars contend. Nor could their suffering have been meaningless if a higher power was so intimately involved.

While most of the dreams and presentiments in this chapter were recorded and published after the war, several were reported at the time they occurred. During the antebellum period, some Americans had prophetic dreams that predicted the coming civil war and the abolition of slavery. Several Quakers published such visions before the war, and again as a pamphlet in 1889. The latter publication, they hoped, would remind readers that "God by his Holy Spirit instructs his people, and that prophecy is not yet extinct."[71] In fact, soldiers and civilians alike looked to dream reports in newspapers for comfort and hope. One New Yorker clipped an article that contained a Confederate's prophetic dream about the end of the war and sent it to his wife. Perhaps, he wrote in May 1862, the war might be over by July.[72]

The reporting of a prophetic dream in a letter home might encourage civilians not to worry about the dangers of the battlefield. In one letter to his family dated July 30, 1861, South Carolinian Jesse W. Reid wrote, "I still have a strong presentiment that I will get home again, some time. It may be a good while, and there is no telling at present what I may have to go through before I come, if I do come, only that I will have to encounter war and its consequences."[73] True to his premonition, Reid survived the war.

In other cases these dreams portended utter sorrow. Confederate congressman Warren Akin of Georgia dreamed on February 2, 1865, that his son Elbert was "on the ground in blood. I know not how he came there. I ran to him and raised him up and a stream of blood ran out of his mouth. He seemed speechless, but not dead, and in much grief I exclaimed: 'O, my boy, my boy!'" Akin awoke "much distressed, and continued depressed in feeling for some days." He wrote to his wife that same day and told her about the dream. By the time she received the letter the dream had been fulfilled. On Wednesday, February 8, Elbert fell off of a pony and hit his head on the frozen ground. Someone rushed to him and raised his head up as "blood poured out of his mouth, nose and ears." He revived a little, but never spoke again. He died Saturday morning. "How mysterious are the doings of Providence," Akin concluded in a letter to a friend. "Yet, I know, he 'doeth all things well.' I can not see it, but I know it is so."[74]

Perhaps most bizarre, in September 1863, Mary Boykin Chesnut received a letter from her sister that described a dream about an old friend. The letter stated, "I had almost forgotten Boykin's existence. But he came here last night! He stood by my bedside and spoke to me kindly and affectionately, as if we had just parted. I said, holding out my hand, 'Boykin, you are very pale.' He answered, 'I have come to tell you goodbye.'" At that point in the dream, Boykin seized her hands with hands that were "as cold and hard as ice. They froze the marrow of my bones." She awoke and screamed so loudly that the entire household—even "the negroes from the yard"— came rushing into her room. "This may have been a dream," she wrote, "but it haunts me." After hearing this read aloud at the breakfast table, someone else interjected, "Stop," and then read from that day's *Richmond Examiner*. "Capt. Burwell Boykin McCaa—found dead upon the battlefield, leading a cavalry charge, at the head of his company. He was shot through the head." Mary Chesnut could only conclude, "Coincidences are queer sometimes."[75]

The obvious questions remain: Why were so many of these dreams, visions, and premonitions recorded in soldiers' and civilians' letters, diaries, reminiscences, regimental histories, and memoirs? And what did they mean to nineteenth-century Americans?

Some soldiers saw presentiments as a test of manhood. One Pennsylvania boy enlisted despite a presentiment "that I should be killed" (and he believed that "presentiments always fulfill themselves"). In his postwar recollections, he added, "This was a grim test to my patriotism, but I felt that my steps could not be retraced."[76] In a related way, others thought that having prophetic dreams gave them credibility with their comrades. "On several occasions during this campaign I have dreamed of and told the boys events that afterwards did really transpire," George Tillotson of New York boasted to his wife in August 1864.[77]

Prophetic dreams could offer comfort, a spiritual sense of communion with loved ones, and solace to those who were suffering.[78] Even men who claimed that dreams carried no meaning could not ignore their apparent gravity. Soldiers were forced to grapple with death and their need to reconcile themselves with God before it became too late.[79] The trials of war, in fact, could cause a change of heart among those who had scoffed at the idea of believing in dreams. One Missouri man who had "always ridiculed the idea of any one believing in dreams" was "now like a drowning man catching at a straw." When his daughter told him that she'd seen her sister in a dream, he anxiously asked, "How did she look? Was she well?" The old man's daughter concluded, "I can appreciate his feelings so well, that I have not the heart to laugh at him, for his inconsistency."[80]

Some soldiers sought to find rational explanations for premonitions. Confederate general Evander M. Law dismissed the idea of prophetic visions, pointing out "that the minds of men of a certain temperament, by brooding over a threatened danger, become morbid, and in this state are easily convinced that the worst will happen when the danger comes." True, he conceded, many prophetic dreams and premonitions had been recorded; but most had not come to pass and thus "are forgotten."[81] A Vermont infantryman wrote after the war that it was "usual for experienced soldiers to have an intuitive presentiment of important campaigns or battles in which they are to participate." This may have simply been because of the "unusual activity noticeable at headquarters, the going and coming of orderlies and messengers, and the ominous silence of officers when questioned concerning the future movements of the troops." The "suspicion" would ripen "into certainty" when the soldiers were ordered to prepare three days' rations. "They were sure then that a grand movement would soon follow; but where, not even the wisest old campaigner was able to predict."[82] Along these lines, psychologist Michael Shermer contends that human beings see patterns in the natural occurrences in their daily lives and impart meaning to those patterns as a way of making sense of the world or finding comfort in uncertainty. People naturally look for omens and signs when they feel helpless or in danger, and, Shermer notes, "levels of superstitious rituals" rise as "the level of uncertainty in the environment increases."[83] Soldiers who were constantly confronted with death and destruction, in this view, would naturally have looked to supernatural explanations for their experiences.

But others were less skeptical—or, perhaps, more believing. Confederate general John B. Gordon conceded that many soldiers may have had "misleading" presentiments; but these, he wrote, "were probably the natural and strong apprehensions which any man is liable to feel, indeed must feel if he is a reasonable.being, as he goes into a consuming fire." There were many other instances, however, which seemed verifiable to Gordon. These were "not the outpourings of a disordered brain," or "the promptings of an unmanly fear of danger or apprehension of death," Gordon wrote, for the men who had them were courageous in battle and had "minds thoroughly balanced, clear and strong." Nor did Gordon believe that presentiments were "mere speculations." On the contrary, they were "perceptions" of a coming reality, and their "conspicuous characteristic was certainty." The people who experienced presentiments gained "knowledge" that "seemed so firmly fixed that no argument as to possible mistake, no persuasion, could shake it."

Echoing Puritan beliefs from colonial New England, Gordon believed that the knowledge revealed in presentiments and dreams was evidence of the "immortality" of the human soul. "It was the whispering of the Infinite beyond us to the Infinite within us—a whispering inaudible to the natural ear, but louder than the roar of battle to the spirit that heard it."[84] Others, too, recognized presentiments as something beyond human beings' ability "fully to interpret them." Confederate chaplain Philip Daingerfield Stephenson had a presentiment "that I would not live to see my 19th birthday, Sept. 7, 1864. But I did! Although curious enough, just a day or two before, I was 'popped' in the shoulder by a spent bullet!" The bullet tore Stephenson's jacket and gave him a bruise on his shoulder, but he did not have to leave the field. "It fell at my feet mashed flat," he later wrote. "I picked it up, put it in my pocket and went on fighting, feeling that the presentiment was sufficiently fulfilled."[85]

We must be wary of too easily dismissing belief in prophetic dreams as a lingering premodern superstition. Historian Timothy J. Orr offers a compelling explanation. Dreams, Orr suggests, "are revelations of truths that the conscious mind refuses to accept." Pointing to the story of Mrs. Emery, the New Hampshire woman who dreamed of her husband's coffin in her parlor, Orr argues that she "refused to accept the possibility that her husband could die in the war. Thus, her 1863 dream was the response of her subconscious mind; it prepared her for the possibility of his death. Her dream did not predict the future so much as it revealed it." A historian of seventeenth-century New England discerned a similar purpose for prophetic dreams within early modern British and Anglo-American culture: "In a world filled with death and uncertainty, predictive dreams perhaps offered a measure of control, even as they sometimes repeated earlier traumatic situations; individuals anticipating a loss could grieve it in advance through the images they saw in dreams."[86]

Some Civil War–era Americans recognized these purposes in their prophetic dreams. After learning that her husband was ill and likely near death in October 1864, Cornelia Peake McDonald, a forty-two-year-old Virginia refugee, had several bad dreams about him that seemed to portend his death. She later wrote in her memoir: "Though in happier times, when my life was calm I paid no attention to dreams, only thinking them idle wanderings of the mind when the body slept; but Oh! I have since thought that they sometimes come as shadows of the event; as premonitions to prepare the anxious and expectant soul for grief and calamity."[87] Within weeks of having her bad dreams, she was a widow and refugee with eight children, but McDonald had at least been partially prepared for the coming tragedy by her dreams.

If dreams psychologically prepared Americans for suffering *during* the war, they played an even more important role in *after* it. Most dreams are fleeting and quickly forgotten, if remembered at all. But soldiers' dreams of death stuck with their comrades for the remainder of their lives. If an enlisted man emerged from his tent one morning and told his buddies that he would be killed later that day, and then he was, his friends never forgot the dream they'd heard recounted. Soldiers and their families thus continued to retell these wartime dreams and presentiments for decades after the war. In these cases, the remembering of impactful dreams helped preserve the memories of scores of dead soldiers who otherwise would have become nameless and forgotten.[88] The dreams and their dreamers became imperishable.

Prophetic dreams and presentiments—or those dark, sad moments when a wife could sense that her husband had been killed on a faraway battlefield— mattered in the postwar years because they confirmed for veterans and their families that their sacrifices on the battlefield had mattered. Remembering those dreams helped them understand that their suffering had not been meaningless because it had been superintended by a higher power. Even as late-nineteenth-century Americans moved away from orthodox Christian understandings of providence, they still believed that a spiritual force had overseen their lives—and their deaths.

CHAPTER SIX

Dreams in Popular Culture

Soldiers' sleep and dreams appeared in newspapers, prints, songs, and poetry. The most famous sleeping sentinel, Pvt. William Scott of the Third Vermont Infantry, became something of a celebrity in the Union. His story evolved into a powerful morality tale that not only taught soldiers to do their duty but also showed the nation that their commander-in-chief was a kind-hearted man. Newspapers throughout the country published stories on the subject of Lincoln's pardon. Most editors praised his decision but called for stern punishment against future offenders. In an editorial entitled "A Lesson," the Washington, D.C., *Sunday Morning Chronicle* implored soldiers to stay awake at their posts so that Lincoln would not be compelled to approve a sentence of execution in the future. A Vermont newspaper echoed this sentiment: "It is to be published for the benefit of all the troops that the pardon is granted because it is the first offense of the kind and an intimation will be given that the President will not interpose again." This prediction, of course, proved patently false.

The residents of Scott's hometown celebrated the news of his pardon, and Scott's father travelled to Washington to personally thank the president. For his part, Private Scott became the beau ideal of a soldier. He is reported to have said, "I will show President Lincoln that I am not afraid to die for my country." He did just that a few months later. On April 16, 1862, he fell at the Battle of Dam One, near Lee's Mills, Virginia, reportedly saying as he died, "Tell President Lincoln that I thank him for his generous regard for me, when a poor soldier under the sentence of death."[1] He is buried in the Yorktown National Cemetery.

Upon dying, Scott's star soared in the American firmament. In 1863, Francis De Haes Janvier published "The Sleeping Sentinel," a poem that instantly gained a wide readership throughout the North. On January 19, 1863, "the celebrated elocutionist" James E. Murdoch read "The Sleeping Sentinel" before an audience at the White House, which included the president and first lady. Later that day, Murdoch read the poem in the Senate chamber at the U.S. Capitol, again with Abraham and Mary Lincoln in attendance. A few weeks later, on February 5, Murdoch read it at the American Academy of Music in Philadelphia before a throng of three thousand.

In that same city, it was read "with gusto" before Union League clubs and the Chester County Soldiers' Aid Society. Enthusiastic crowds also flocked to hear it in Baltimore, Albany, Boston, and other cities.

Over the next few years De Haes Janvier's poem would also be read to soldiers in the field to encourage them to remain manly and faithful in their duties. On July 4, 1864, the commanding officer at Camp William Penn, Col. Louis Wagner, had "The Sleeping Sentinel" read to the black troops under his command as they were training to go into combat. Perhaps even more poignantly, the elocutionist Murdoch read it to the boys of the Seventy-Ninth Indiana when he visited the battlefield at Chickamauga in search of the body of his dead son, Capt. Thomas Murdoch, who had fallen in the action there.

The poem exulted in the "patriot armies" of the North that "swept forth . . . to make our country truly free." It traced Private Scott's life from the pure mountain air of Vermont to his selfless and patriotic enlistment.

> Without a murmur, he endured a service new and hard;
> But, wearied with a toilsome march, it chanced one night, on guard,
> He sank, exhausted, at his post, and the gray morning found
> His prostrate form—a sentinel, asleep, upon the ground!

Comparing the fatigued young soldier to the devoted but weak disciples of Christ who had fallen asleep in the Garden of Gethsemane shortly before the crucifixion, the poet notes, "Yet, Jesus, with compassion moved, beheld their heavy eyes, / And, though betrayed to ruthless foes, forgiving, bade them rise!"

The poem then shifts to the White House, where Lincoln, in a dark, secluded room, paces back and forth, contemplating the "civil discord" that was destroying the country. His heart was burdened with grief as the entire nation suffered ("And yet, amid the din of war, he heard the plaintive cry / Of that poor soldier, as he lay in prison, doomed to die!").

The poem then takes the reader to the army camp, where a manacled, ashamed Private Scott, "with faltering step, and pale and anxious face," walks to his execution. At that point, Scott sees a vision of "his distant mountain home," with his aged parents devastated "with hopeless grief." The firing squad approaches, and he awaits the sound of the musket fire that will send him to his "nameless grave."

> Then—suddenly and unexpectedly—the president arrived!
> He came to save that stricken soul, now waking from despair;

And from a thousand voices rose a shout which rent the air!
The pardoned soldier understood the tones of jubilee,
And, bounding from his fetters, blessed the hand that made him free!

The final seven stanzas recount Scott's death at the Battle of Dam One. As he lies dying, he prays to heaven that "God, with His unfailing grace, would bless our President!"[2]

Americans who read or heard "The Sleeping Sentinel" encountered a story of redemption. Lincoln, as a Messianic figure, saves the penitent young sinner (although in reality, Lincoln did not show up at the scene of the execution to save the boy from death). The soldier eventually makes the ultimate sacrifice, achieving martyrdom, and praising his savior's name as he expires. The lesson was simple and sweet: true comfort could be found in serving a cause that was greater than oneself. In many ways, this story mirrors the idea of Lincoln as the Great Emancipator—the president frees a man from his chains and then is blessed as a liberator. How fitting that the poem was introduced to the nation in January 1863, the time of jubilee. Of equal significance, by depicting Lincoln as a Christ figure, the poem also eerily foreshadowed the president's eventual death on Good Friday two years later.

"The Sleeping Sentinel" appealed to Americans of a sentimental age. Audiences throughout the North were moved, even to tears, when they read it or heard it performed. It should come as no surprise that the poet invented a dream or vision of Scott seeing his grieving parents at home in the moments before he expected to die. Such a dream was something that almost any reader could relate to—a common "lived, personal experience of war," to quote historian Alice Fahs. Within the genre of Victorian sentimental literature, "The Sleeping Sentinel" also played an important role in shaping and confirming the ways that Americans would view their soldiers. They were morally upright, patriotic boys whose thoughts were on God and family and country; they were noble volunteers and faithful members of communities willingly making sacrifices for their nation.[3] This allegory—which was rooted in a real life story—would have resonated with nearly any American between 1861 and 1865. Incorporating a dream or vision into the story only raised the stakes because dreams often carried portentous meaning for Americans of the Civil War generation.

Discussion of dreams—both actual dreams and fictional ones—in popular culture became a powerful way to shape public opinion during the war. Union and Confederates soldiers described their dreams in letters to hometown newspapers to encourage those at home to keep faith in their respective cause. Dreams in prints, songs, stories and poems also inspired their audiences to keep up the fight. Political cartoons featuring dreams lampooned and caricatured Union and Confederate leaders. And most importantly, images of "the soldier's dream" resonated with soldiers and civilians alike—sustaining them as they sacrificed their safety, comfort and happiness on the battlefield. Indeed, during the war years, the "soldier's dream of home" would stand out as one of the most powerful motifs to connect soldiers in the field with their loved ones at home.

THE CONCEPT OF "the soldier's dream" predated the Civil War. In fact, it was not an American idea at all. Stories of soldiers dreaming date to ancient times, and biblical commentaries recounted the story of Gideon overhearing two Midianite soldiers discussing the meaning of a dream. At least one Civil War–era commentary placed this story under the heading "The Soldier's Dream."[4] In antebellum America, however, the best-known and loved version of the trope was the Scottish poet Thomas Campbell's poem "The Soldier's Dream" (circa 1800). Excerpts from Campbell's verses appeared on stationery and letterhead during the Civil War, such as these lines from the second and sixth stanzas, which appeared on one envelope:

At the dead of night a sweet vision I saw,
    And thrice e'er the morning I dreamt it again.
But sorrow return'd with the dawning of morn,
    And the voice in my dreaming ear melted away.

In fact, Union and Confederate soldiers had been imbibing Campbell's lyrics since their childhoods. Campbell's poem appeared in American anthologies as early as the 1820s, and by the 1830s it was being read by children in primary schools.[5] In March 1852, *Godey's Lady's Book* produced a story by the English novelist Henry William Herbert as well as a print of a Scottish soldier dreaming of home in faraway Egypt. Upon seeing the print, two women composed their own verses, both entitled "The Soldier's Dream of Home," which appeared in the magazine seven months later.[6] About the same time, an unknown printmaker produced a full-color large-format print of a Scottish soldier sleeping in the foreground with the pyramids behind him and his family above him in a dream. Beneath the serene image were Campbell's words. Currier and Ives would borrow heavily from this template a decade later, replacing the soldier's green kilt with a blue woolen uniform, while the pyramids in the background became canvas tents (although the tropical trees curiously survived in the American version).

"The Soldier's Dream of Home," *Godey's Lady's Book* (1852). Collection of the author.

The Civil War took place during an age of Victorian romanticism when even the most experienced of soldiers could be moved to tears by a poem about dreams and family. In 1862, Confederate general J. E. B. Stuart copied Campbell's poem in its entirety and then added a few lines of his own in an album for a young woman in Virginia. Other soldiers similarly transcribed the whole poem—or several stanzas from it—in their letters home. They may have done so from memory, for Campbell's words had been set to music, and many young men of the era likely knew them by heart. (In fact, Abraham Lincoln had sung "The Soldier's Dream" as a young man.) Some soldiers sang it in their tents at night. For others, meditating on this poem was the best way to capture their emotions after a battle. Soldiers sought out stationery with Campbell's poem and brought the verses to the attention of their wives and sweethearts. "Is not this beautiful," wrote one Ohio soldier to his fiancée in April 1862.[7]

"The Soldier's Dream of Home." This print by Currier and Ives captures not only an idealized soldier's dream but also the real connection between correspondence and pleasant dreams of home, as a letter from his wife lays just next to the sleeping soldier's hand. Courtesy of the Library of Congress.

Missouri infantryman John C. Hughes was so moved by a piece of letter-head featuring Campbell's poem that he penned an affectionate letter on the subject to his wife on February 27, 1863. "O the sweete visions that I hav saw when all was still when the trobeles and hardships and bustels of war was forgoten in sweet repose," he wrote. But these dreams "onley serve to increac my sorrow when I awoke to a true sence of my condition." He described seeing his wife and four sons in his dream, but "when i would awake and find that it was all a dream i hav often bathed my pilow in tears and almost wished that I could quit this world of sorrows and disappointment and meat my friends on shoars of sweet deliverance." Hughes wished that "wars would ceac" and he could return to his home and family in times of peace. Then, he wrote, "could we realise those sweete visions of the night."

Hughes closed his letter with two stanzas from "Fare Thee Well," by Lord Byron, which he must have copied from a poetry book (because the spelling was accurate, unlike the rest of his letter). Following those eight lines of poetry, he added a few from the song "I'd Offer Thee This Heart":

but now my dreams ar sadly o'er
fate bids them all depart

and i must leav my nativ shore
in brokenness of heart

and O dear one when far from thee
i'll never know joy again
I would not that one thought of me
should giv thy bosom pain
i'd ofer thee this hand of mine
if i could lov thee less but heart
so pure as thine should
never know distress

The romanticism of these lines—which Hughes clearly knew by heart—reflects the anguish of a lonely soldier who knew he was nearing death. Suffering alone in a military hospital so far from home, his dreams of his family had become his most cherished possession. But soon they, too, would be taken from him. Sadly, Hughes died of disease less than two months after writing this letter on a hospital boat near Helena, Arkansas.[8]

Women writers on both home fronts also expounded on these themes during the war. South Carolinian Caroline H. Gervais wrote an oft reprinted poem called "In His Blanket on the Ground," about a weary rebel soldier who dreams of "home, and friends, and loved ones."[9] In Massachusetts, the Unitarian poet Caroline A. Mason's "The Soldier's Dream of Home" touched soldiers as deeply as Thomas Campbell's verses had:

Oh, my very heart grows sick, Alice,
    I long so to behold
Rose with her pure, white forehead,
    And Maud, with her curls of gold;
And Willie, so gay and sprightly,
    So merry and full of glee;
Oh, my heart *yearns* to enfold ye,
    My "smiling group of three!"

Union soldier H. B. Howe was so moved by this poem that he told Mason that his own family was "almost [an] exact copy of the picture you have painted." "Such lines," he continued, "carry with them many a blessing as they are read by the exiled soldier—self exiled as many of us are, away from home, kindred and friends, especially from the dear ones of his heart."[10]

It is little wonder that so many soldiers penned their own clumsy and often melodramatic lines about dreams, seeking to capture the emotions

Dreams in Popular Culture

of the more popular verses. One New York POW wrote a poem called "Prisoner's Dream" while imprisoned at Andersonville, although the verses do not survive. A Virginia physician similarly hand wrote a poem called "Soldiers Dream" in his account book.[11] Some soldiers published similar poems in hometown newspapers. Dozens of these verses are preserved in regimental histories, such as these few lines from a poem by a soldier in the Twenty-Fifth Massachusetts Volunteers:

> This letter will tell you, dear Kitty,
>   That I was not kilt in the fight—
> My mind is uneasy by dreaming
>   Of you and the childers all night.
>
> I send you but twenty-five dollars,
>   I dreamed that you wanted some things;
> I can't keep a cent in my pocket,
>   Because you know money has wings.[12]

Music also often incorporated dream-related themes, and songs about dreams were ubiquitous. Nonmilitaristic songs continued to focus on dreams, just as many had in the antebellum era. Stephen Foster's most popular song of the war years, "Beautiful Dreamer" (1864), had no content related to the war. But some of the most touching ballads related to the experiences of soldiers and their families. The beautifully illustrated "Soldier's Vision" featured an enlisted man dreaming of "my home and friends so dear"—the place where he could relive "boyhood scenes" and never again see "blood stained fields" or hear "the cannon's thunder roar." "I Dreamed My Boy Was Home Again" related the story of a "lonely, weary, broken-hearted" mother who had a bright, joyous dream of her son returning home. One of the most popular Northern war songs, "All Quiet Along the Potomac Tonight," described Union soldiers "peacefully dreaming" of home. In the Southern counterpart, "All Quiet Along the Savannah To-Night," a Confederate picket sees "visions of loved ones . . . back home in his dreams." Among the Confederate ranks "See Her Still in My Dreams" was also popular.[13]

"Mother Kissed Me in My Dream" was a widely reprinted Union song based on the account of a dying soldier at Antietam. One song sheet included a brief account of the story behind the song as well as a touching image of a faithful mother praying for her son and then visiting him as an angel the night before he died. The lyrics beckoned soldiers to do their duty on the battlefield while assuring them that their pain and suffering would

Published by Cha[s] Magnus, 12 Frankfort St N.Y.

MOTHER KISSED ME
IN MY DREAM.

The music of this song can be obtained at the extensive Music Store of
WM. A. Pond & CO. 547 Broadway, N. Y.

A young soldier who was severely wounded at the battle of Antietam, lay in one of the hospitals at Frederick. A surgeon passing by his bedside, and seeing his boyish face lighted up with a peaceful smile, asked him how he felt. "Oh, I am happy and contented now," the soldier replied, —"Last night mother kissed me in my dream!"

Lying on my dying bed,
　Through the dark and silent night,
Praying for the coming day,
　Came a vision to my sight;
Near me stood the forms I loved,
　In the sunlight's mellow gleam,
Folding me unto her breast—
　Mother kissed me in my dream!
　　　Mother, mother,—
　　　Mother kissed me in my dream.

Comrades, tell her when you write,
　That I did my duty well,
Say that when the battle raged,
　Fighting in the van I fell;
Tell her too, when on my bed,
　Slowly ebbed my being's stream,
How I knew no peace until—
　Mother kissed me in my dream!
　　　Mother, mother, &c.

Once again I long to see
　Home and kindred far away;
But, I feel I shall be gone,
　Ere there dawns another day!
Hopefully I bide the hour
　When will fade life's feeble beam—
Ev'ry pang has left me now—
　Mother kissed me in my dream!
　　　Mother, mother, &c.

500 Illustrated Ballads, lithographed and printed by
CHARLES MAGNUS. No. 12 Frankfort Street, New York.
Branch Office: No. 520 7th St., Washington, D. C.

"Mother Kissed Me in My Dream" song sheet. Courtesy of the Library of Congress.

The Soldier's Vision sheet music. Courtesy of the Library of Congress.

be alleviated by visitation dreams from their mothers, and the song quickly gained an audience among Northern soldiers. During the Battle of Gettysburg, a wounded private in the Eighty-Sixth New York sang it "to cheer his comrades" while they were resting near the Wheatfield on July 3, 1863.[14]

Singing or playing a song about dreams underscored the depth of feeling that the musician or singer had for his or her listener. When Union general Washington Elliott was ordered from Petersburg to the western theater in October 1863, the band of the Tenth Vermont Volunteers serenaded him with several songs, including "Ever of Thee I'm Fondly Dreaming."[15] Such songs often made an indelible impression upon the minds of the singers or of those who heard it. Years after the war, one rebel recalled a group of young women who had serenaded him and other soldiers one night. "With guitar and voice they repaid us very sweetly. 'Oh, I Have Had Dreams,' one of the songs sung, lingers in my memory yet."[16]

Both armies appreciated when the other played a beautiful song. During the Atlanta campaign, Yankee soldiers called out for a Confederate cornet player to entertain them with music. "He would play, but *he's afraid you will spoil his horn!*" replied the rebels. When the Union soldiers promised not to fire, the rebel soldier played "Come Where My Love Lies Dreaming" and "I Dreamt That I Dwelt in Marble Halls," along with a few other operatic numbers.[17] Despite these moments of peace and harmony, such truces could not last forever. At another point during the siege, a Union band played "a beautiful arrangement of *Auld Lang Syne*" that both armies could hear. "Did it cause the hostile troops to dream of the old times when our country was at peace, and Columbia was indeed a 'happy land'?" wondered one Union soldier in the trenches. "If so, the dream was roughly dispelled by a Battery of twenty pound Parrotts just at our right, which sent shell after shell whizzing over the Rebel works away back to the center of the city w[h]ere they exploded with a lurid flash, and a dull heavy report that came back to us after listening many minutes. So we reminded them of the past, so of the present. Let them decide which they like best."[18]

Sometimes the sentimentality of music even influenced soldiers' dreams. Writing two weeks after the Battle of Fredericksburg, surgeon William Child of the Fifth New Hampshire Volunteers told his wife, "The soldiers have gone to rest and to dream of home. Such is the scene from my tent door. I walk among the tents and hear the sweet notes of 'Sweet Home'— and think of my own home so far away—when shall I return—what changes may transpire—shall I ever return—are they all well there—do they think of me—will my children remember me—Oh a thousand thoughts come rushing in producing one of those thrills of emotion that I love so well." That night Dr. Child "dreamed of home every hour."[19]

WHILE PAINFUL OR TERRIFYING DREAMS sometimes emerged from the fears and anxieties that families experienced during the war, Northern printmakers created and sold images of idealized soldiers' dreams to reassure families of their soldiers' fidelity to home and country. Soldiers portrayed in deep, restful sleep could be found on envelopes, in pictorial newspapers, and on prints by firms like Currier and Ives. These images—with titles such as *The Soldier's Dream, The Soldier's Dream of Home, The Union Soldier's Dream of Home,* and *The Soldier's Dream of Peace*—depicted volunteers in slumber on the night before battle, faithfully serving their country but dreaming wishfully of home. Some prints also contained other, related themes of the

"The American Patriot's Dream." Courtesy of the Library of Congress.

era, such as *The American Patriot's Dream*, in which a dreaming soldier envisions his return home, not only victorious, but also promoted to an officer. In this case he longed not only to be reunited with his family but also to be successful in the glories of war.[20]

At least one modern scholar views these depictions of soldiers dreaming as part of "the myth of America" and "a cultural cover-up" because they offer "tidy depictions of men and women in their correct roles, spaces, and places" rather than portraying "the controversial activities of female reformers prior to the Civil War, which had fostered fears and anxieties about 'monstrous women.'" This scholar implies that these images functioned to keep women bound in subservience, concluding, "Perhaps the soldier's dream was, in part, a dream of postwar normalcy: average men living normal lives with normal wives."[21]

Such an anachronistic critique wholly misunderstands the Victorian culture of Civil War America—not to mention the perfectly natural desires of families separated by war. While patriarchy still reflected the nature of marriage as a public institution, it did not capture the private realities of many households. In the early nineteenth-century, American families became less patriarchal and more democratic. As one scholar explains, marriage was increasingly "characterized by a companionate relationship between husband and wife" and "attitudes toward children within the family became gentler." In other words, husbands and wives experienced marriage as a partnership based in romantic love, and they no longer tended to view their children primarily as sources of supplemental income, as had been typical in earlier times. As historian J. Matthew Gallman explains, "as the century progressed it appears that increasing numbers of married couples—especially in the northern states—embraced the notion that the ideal marriage should be a partnership grounded in love and respect, even when the legal system recognized no such equality."[22]

Within this context it is little wonder that soldiers and their wives longed for normalcy. In its most primal sense, normalcy meant survival. Most soldiers naturally longed for that, as did their loved ones. But even more, normalcy represented relief from the hardships and anxieties of wartime. With so many men off in faraway, dangerous places for years at a time with very little communication to and from home, it should not be at all surprising that images like "The Soldier's Dream" appealed to soldiers and their wives. In most cases, married soldiers wanted to be home with their families. They resonated with these images, therefore, precisely because the scenes on paper captured the daily experiences and expectations of Union and Confederate soldiers. In a practical sense, the concept of "The Soldier's Dream" became a comfort to lonely spouses who were separated by war. A twenty-first-century scholar who seems disappointed that the few "controversial . . . female reformers" were not more widely depicted in popular lithography either does not understand basic market forces (these prints were produced by commercial firms, after all) or nineteenth-century sentimentality and family life.[23]

Images and words depicting "The Soldier's Dream" emotionally affected both men and women during the Civil War. Families likely hung prints of dreaming soldiers in their homes to convince themselves that their soldiers' thoughts were on them. One soldier in the Ninth Vermont Infantry inscribed a copy of the Currier and Ives print *The Soldier's Dream of Home* to his wife.[24] Women taught the words of "The Soldier's Dream" to their children.[25] A Quaker family in Virginia—with both men and women participating—even did a tableau of "The Soldier's Dream" at their home in January 1865.[26] Indeed, rather than subjugate women by relegating them to the domestic sphere, such images were intended to boost the morale of those who remained at home. "Such scenes were meant to reassure families that their men in arms remained inspired, perhaps even protected and blessed, by thoughts of home and hearth," write historians Mark E. Neely Jr., and Harold Holzer. Historian Alice Fahs adds that "the image reassured the viewer that soldiers had not become killers, but instead remained connected to their homes. . . . The image at once reassures the viewer that soldiers have not fundamentally changed, and provides a narrative 'happy ending' to the war within the dream itself."[27] Indeed, images like these reinforced sentimental notions and understandings of what the war was about and how families ought to experience the war.

Even images of death could accomplish similar ends. In an 1864 print entitled *The Dying Soldier*, a wounded infantryman looks upon a locket and sees a vision of his wife and three children sitting sadly by the dinner table at home. As he peacefully expires, his final thoughts were on his family. "Such touching scenes may well have served to comfort untold widows in the months of their bereavement," write Neely and Holzer.[28] Indeed, wives wanted to know that their husbands had been true to the very end—true in every sense of the word.

Images of soldiers dreaming had an incredible mass-market appeal, appearing in newspapers and on prints, *cartes de visite*, song sheets, envelopes, and stationery. In one patriotic cover produced by Cutter, Tower and Company in 1862, a soldier, sound asleep beneath a billowing flag, dreams of returning home to the warm embrace of his family. In the foreground of the envelope sits an American eagle with the mottos "E Pluribus Unum" and "U.S.A." "The imagery of the envelope carries a double message," writes one scholar. Primarily, patriotic covers emphasized the importance of victory and reunion. But of equal importance, the image of "the soldier's dream" underscored what soldiers longed for in their family lives. Their wives were "to be virtuous and chaste, a source of encouragement to their absent husbands, and the mainstay of the home and farm during his time of military service."[29] Other postal covers featured less patriotic imagery, focusing instead on the soldier's desire to be home with his family.

Soldiers could relate to these mass-market appeals in large measure because the images captured the very dreams they were having in their tents and bivouacs at the front. "Did you ever see a picture called the soldiers dream?" a Confederate soldier wrote to his wife in October 1862. "I have seen it somewhere, possibly in an old magazine. The artist had certainly seen life in camps and had a wife and baby."[30] This soldier almost certainly was remembering the 1852 *Godey's* image a full decade later.

Indeed, soldiers truly believed that the commercial images of "the soldier's dream" captured the reality of their experiences. On August 13, 1864, while encamped near Atlanta, Lt. Russell M. Tuttle of the 107th New York awoke from a nap and, although his sleep had been "filled with dreams," he could

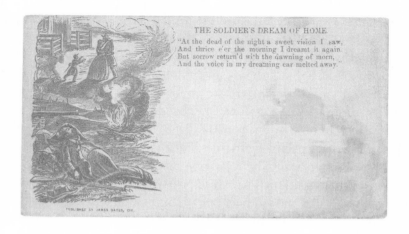

The prevalence of patriotic covers like these, which were printed in Cincinnati, New York, and Philadelphia, underscore how correspondents longed to include imagery related to dreaming in their regular correspondence. Collection of the author.

not remember what they had been. This realization caused him to ruminate on the many "Golden Dreams" that all of his comrades had in camp, around the campfire, while out on picket, in battle, or on the march. "Dreaming ever, and of what?" he wrote. "Almost always of home, of the glad return to old friends, and scenes which [are] to follow all this peril and hardship, which is to compensate for all we are now deprived of, which is to make substantial the honors gained in the field." He remembered seeing old British and French prints—with titles like *The Soldier's Return* and *The Soldier's Dream*—that featured affectionate reunions between husbands and their wives after war. "And I have read poetry picturing similar scenes," he wrote. "I can realize the sentiment of all this now, and I can tell you there is a deal of romance in these same visions of happier scenes that come to gladden the soldier with bright hopes." He continued,

> War and its havocs are always considered. The company that came out a hundred strong is to go back with but ten or a dozen, but the fond dreamer is always one of the fortunate survivors, and he trustingly dreams of the return home after years of service, with a little band of heroes, proud of their record in the field, grateful for the privilege of at last meeting their loved ones, and remembering with tender regret the comrades left sleeping their last sleep beneath southern skies. The picture is always bright, for the dreamer, never does it place him as one of those left behind, when the rest shall return. Never does death in the field of battle, or in the hospital find a welcome place in his vision. Alas! Then how many are disappointed. Yet strange as it may seem, few seem to be disappointed or surprised when they are called to be on the field. It may be different in hospital, but death on the battle-field when it really must come seems to be accepted as a matter of course, as no more than ought to have been expected, as with the most patient resignation.[31]

Soldiers like this one longed to have the idealized soldier's dreams. Like many people, they wished they could control their sleeping thoughts so that they could make a visit home. And when they were fortunate enough to travel those dreamy miles to see their families, they felt a kinship to other soldiers from generations gone by. "I dream the soldiers dream sometimes," wrote one Confederate soldier from Arkansas. "I wish I could dream it in reality."[32]

Confederate prisoners of war at Point Lookout, Maryland, clamored for images of soldiers dreaming. Prisoner James T. Wells of the Second South

Carolina Infantry recalled, "There were many portrait and landscape painters, and many fine pictures were produced there. One, 'The Prisoner's Dream of Home,' was greatly admired and coveted by many, but money could not purchase it from the owner." Perhaps to satisfy this demand, fellow prisoner John Jacob Omenhausser of the Forty-Sixth Virginia painted a colorful scene called "The Rebel's Dream in Prison." At least three versions of the image survive, depicting a handsome man surrounded by flowers, statuary, and two enraptured women, one of whom plays a stringed instrument. Omenhausser found eager buyers for his folk art among his fellow prisoners as well as his guards because the guards, like the prisoners, could appreciate the longing to be home.[33] As different as their experiences were as guard versus guarded, these Union and Confederate enemies had a shared experience of war.

In a remarkable way, therefore, images of soldiers dreaming of home humanized the enemy. An Indiana soldier described being in the "dilapidated old village" of Decatur, Georgia. Among the old wooden houses, he wrote, "Only a few of the citizens remain, and they are 'poor white trash.'" One caught his eye, however. A "pretty little girl, with bright black eyes and glossy curls" who "gazed upon us, from a window—a beautiful picture in a decayed frame." As he looked at this little girl among the ruins of her hometown, he recalled the children he and his comrades had left far away in the North. The thought caused a "tear to steal, unbidden, down the bronzed cheek." "These little episodes," he continued, "seemingly unimportant in themselves, often call our minds afar from the scenes of war. We dream, but we are awake. I often see a picture, 'The Soldier's Dream'; it is of home. We are not always asleep, when these visions come. Happy the remnant of us, who shall enter the promised land of a restored Union."[34]

While it is true that the Civil War took place during a time steeped in Victorian romanticism and sentimentality, to simply treat popular depictions of soldiers dreaming as mere outgrowths of that culture misses something important. The term "sentimentalism" implies an excessiveness in the expression of emotions, but as should be clear from the discussion of soldiers' dreams here and in chapter 2, Union and Confederate soldiers often *really dreamed* "the soldier's dream." Their dreams were not merely cultural by-products.[35] Dreams of home were ubiquitous, emotional, and often pleasant and reassuring.

Historians often see sentimentalism as on the decline in the period after the Civil War. In *Lincoln Dreamt He Died*, Andrew Burstein writes that "amid the sober and symbolic commemorations of men and battles destined to take place in the coming decades, it was the extravagance of nineteenth-century sentimentalism that disappeared as ground was ceded from the divine to the human."[36] This may have been true in some aspects of culture and society, but in the world of soldiers' dreams it was not. Popular depictions of soldiers' dreams continued to follow the sentimental mid-nineteenth-century pattern for several generations. World War I songs and postcards from America and its European allies continued to depict wives and children dreaming of their soldier-kin, or soldiers dreaming of loved ones. One postcard featured a poem entitled "Could I but Dream That Dream Again," with the lines:

> I told you of my love,
> You vowed by stars above
> You loved me only, loved me only!
> And now you've gone I'm lonely.

In another, a soldier's dream of "Coming Home" is depicted in cigarette smoke with a poem that concludes: "Oh! the longing and the dreaming, coming home! / Ah! Oh, the longing and the dreaming, coming home!" And a 1917 song entitled "The Dream of a Soldier Boy" contained this chorus:

> All the nations were kind to each other,
> Ev'ry law was a golden rule,
> Ev'ry mother and son
> Were together that day,
> And ev'ry gun was laid away.
> Ev'ry soldier was back with his sweetheart,
> All the world seemed to smile with joy;
> And God turned the trenches to gardens again,
> That's the dream of a soldier boy.

But these kinds of popular sentiments would not survive the Great War. Indeed, it was World War I, and not the Civil War, that shattered the sentimental popular depictions of soldiers' dreams in Western civilization.[37] By the 1940s, American soldiers would no longer be pictured dreaming wholesome dreams of home and loved ones. Now they would dream of sex, pinup girls, riding in first class travel (by bus and air), kicking Hitler in the rear end, and of other modern conveniences. Americans had been buying and selling "the soldier's dream" since the mid-nineteenth century—on postal covers and song sheets, and in newspapers. During the Civil War and World War I, these images had been meant to mobilize and encourage both soldiers and civilians. During World War II, "the soldier's dream" was more often used to sell things. Soldiers were often still depicted as dreaming of home and family, but the focus of the depictions had changed. Thus, a magazine advertisement for Camel cigarettes featured a soldier waking up in bed as his parents bring him a tray of food and cigarettes. An inset states, "A soldier's dream . . . even to the Camels!" In a General Electric advertisement, a soldier dreams of his wife "in the kitchen, after dinner." He tells her, "You're wearing some kind of frilly apron and you're up to your elbows in dishwater and maybe there's a smudge on your pretty cheek that you got from cleaning the stove." But she replies that she will "shatter your dream—in a nice way" by getting a G.E. dishwasher so that neither of them have to wash or dry the dishes.

In a series of Greyhound Bus ads, a soldier dreams during "the tense waiting hours between battles" of "home and the ones he loves." The advertisement continues, "Somewhere in the dreams of every fighting man are the trips he intends to make, one day, in the land he's fighting for— and, usually, *one very special trip with the girl who waited!*" Another Greyhound ad featured a soldier and his sweetheart watching a beautiful sunset above the message "These Dreams Will Come True." But if bus travel was too slow, the Air Transportation Authority had a message for soldiers in uncomfortable transport planes: "Dreaming of the plane you'll travel in tomorrow, soldier? Cruising up to five miles a minute, sound-proofed, air-conditioned, smartly decorated, with the softest seats known to the anatomy of man . . . and a good-looking stewardess to serve you piping hot meals when you're hungry!" Meanwhile, in an advertisement called "Here's what *one* leatherneck dreams about!" the National Dairy Products Corporation told readers, "Strawberry ice cream was a symbol, of course, to a hot, tired fighting man in a foxhole—a symbol of his home town and the corner drug store—a symbol of America." The dreams were still about home, but only indirectly. Now they were more about *things* at home—commodities that could be purchased and enjoyed. Family members were incidental in these dreams; the soldier's dream had largely become a marketing tool.

Still, the sentimentality—and perhaps sincerity—was not entirely gone. In an advertisement entitled "I had a dream in Africa last night," Stromberg-Carlson (a telecommunications company) urged Americans to "buy[] War Bonds till it pinches" and "giv[e] our blood to the Red Cross" so that the war could come to a speedy and successful conclusion. And in a touching ad entitled "I had a dream the other night," the Pitney-Bowes Postage Meter Company told the story of a father who was visited in his sleep by his son and two other boys from the neighborhood, all of whom had died or were missing in the war. The father admits his frustration with the war, saying, "Sure, I'll admit it—I've been sore at times, the way this war is being run . . . at all the damn dumb things that make it cost so much." Nevertheless, he calls on his readers to remember the sacrifices of those who have died. "Every day the war goes on we lose more than we ever can afford," he says. "Let's get the job done—fast! So all of us can start to live again!"[38] As in earlier times, a visitation dream could carry tremendous emotional power for those who heard the report of it.

THE DREAMS THAT were depicted in popular culture during the Civil War became part of a collective dream experience that contained public and often political significance. Soldiers' dreams in newspapers could help mobilize civilians at home. An unknown Confederate soldier convalescing at Hospital No. 8 in Raleigh, North Carolina, urged his fellow countrymen to continue the fight through the recitation of a dream he had one night in October 1863. He dreamed that he was chairing a committee to draft resolutions on the state of the Confederacy and that the resolutions "recommended reconstruction; in other words, unconditional submission." At that point, the dreamer heard the sounds of a "mighty wind; or the roaring of many waters." He looked around him and saw "many thousands of the noble dead, who have been slain in battle since the commencement of this revolution. . . . They shook their gory locks at me; pointing at their ghastly wounds and said:—can it be possible that we have sacrificed our lives on the altar of patriotism in vain? Must our blood that has been crying to you from the ground remain unavenged? Ye cowards! Shame upon you; a just God will forever frown upon you; posterity will curse your memory; and all the civilized nations of the earth will point the finger of scorn at you." Filled with dread, the dreaming Confederate dropped the resolutions, fled the meeting, and shouldered his musket to fight in the cause of Southern independence. He then awoke "and found it was all a dream."[39]

The foregoing dream, which was signed and attributed to a soldier who was convalescing in a particular hospital, was probably an actual dream. However, fabricated dreams of public figures also often appeared in the papers. Indeed, invented dreams of national leaders—both living and dead— could be used to teach citizens moral lessons, just as depictions of "the soldier's dream" sought to do. Whereas popular images of "the soldier's dream of home" were always positive and uplifting, politicians were often depicted in popular culture as having nightmares.

In January 1850, a story began circulating throughout the nation that Sen. John C. Calhoun had had a harrowing dream of George Washington. In the dream, the South Carolinian was sitting at his desk preparing to sign a document that would dismember the Union. Washington appeared to the disunionist and pointed out a black spot on Calhoun's right hand, calling it "the mark by which Benedict Arnold is known in the next world." Washington then showed him the skeleton of Isaac Hayne, a South Carolinian who had been hanged by the British during the American Revolution. The meaning of this fabricated dream was obvious to all who read it. In juxtaposing Washington's legacy with Calhoun's, readers could choose which side they would want to be associated with. A paper in Wisconsin remarked simply, "The allegory is certainly well carried out."[40]

Calhoun died on March 31, 1850, shortly after this fictitious dream began making the rounds in the papers, but as civil war seemed increasingly inevitable the South Carolina senator continued to appear as a symbol of treason in other fabricated dreams. About ten years after Calhoun's death—and just a few days after Lincoln won the presidential election of 1860—a story circulated in Republican newspapers about a dream involving the lame duck president, James Buchanan, and the long-dead South Carolina fire-eater. According to the story, an Arkansas Democrat dreamed that Buchanan descended into hell, where "Sheriff Calhoun" greeted him. Calhoun informed the outgoing president that he had arrived in hell just in time. "Why," continued Calhoun, "his Satanic Majesty has been dead these three hours, and we've just had an election for a successor to the deceased Devil. It was all a one sided affair. There was no opposition. I'm the Sheriff, and have come to notify you that you are chosen unanimously to the successorship of the dead Devil."[41]

As the war was rapidly approaching, invented dreams continued to appear in newspapers, poems and prints. On February 2, 1861, *Harper's Weekly* ran as a full two-page spread an illustration entitled *The Dream of a Secessionist, Washington and Valley Forge*. In it, a Southern fire-eater sits at his desk, holding the draft of an ordinance of secession, while a vision of Washington and his ragged army plodding through the snow fills the background. Such an image foreshadowed Lincoln's appeal to the "mystic chords of memory, stretching from every battle-field, and patriot grave, to every living heart and hearthstone, all over this broad land." Hoping that Northerners and Southerners might remember their common sacrifice of 1776, the artist implicitly reminded his audience of the shared dream of the Revolutionary generation—that of a common, united country.

"The Dream of a Secessionist—Washington and Valley Forge," *Harper's Weekly*, February 2, 1861. Collection of the author.

About the same time that *Harper's* published the image of Washington, a story entitled "Washington's Vision" appeared in other papers throughout the North. The story opened with Washington praying during the winter encampment around Valley Forge in 1777. As he was beseeching heaven, a beautiful woman and a series of angels appeared to the general, and they revealed threats that the new nation would face during its lifetime. "In UNION she will have strength," Washington interpreted the vision to mean, "in DISUNION her destruction." Upon reading the story, Edward Everett declared that it taught "a highly important lesson to every true lover of his country."[42] In reality, it was a feeble and unsuccessful attempt to stave off disunion and war.

Washington continued to be a central figure in fictional dreams during the war. In late 1861 or early 1862, a broadside appeared entitled "General M'Clellan's Dream," claiming that a godlike Washington had appeared to George B. McClellan in a vision one night at 2 A.M., revealing the Confederates' plans to the Union commander. A humble McClellan resolved to act quickly. While these two details—the general's humility and celerity—undermine the credibility of the story, the publishers claimed that McClellan's actions were "the best argument for its truthfulness." In fact, the story had been concocted by the same person who wrote "Washington's Vision." As

"The Emblem of the Free" or "The Traitor's Dream." Courtesy of the Library of Congress.

in his previous tale, the author hoped to use McClellan's "dream" to mobilize and unify the people—this time the people of the North against the South.[43]

Throughout the war, Northern writers and printmakers also invented dreams that skewered their rebel opponents. Several dreams attributed to Jefferson Davis circulated in Northern papers. In one poem entitled "Jeff Davis's Dream," a skeleton awakens the Confederate president and recounts all of the recent Confederate defeats and casualties. It chastises Davis for not fulfilling his promise to secure Confederate independence, and for making the cause of the South seem hopeless. "Ah, Jeff! little man of our trust and our hope," states the skeleton, "The future is dim with the shade of a rope." In a song by the same title, Davis sells his soul to the Devil to become "King, of the Southern Confederacy." The artwork acccompanying the song "The Emblem of the Free" features George Washington directing Jefferson Davis's attention to the suffering soldiers at Valley Forge while Satan crowns him king of the Confederacy. Soldiers performed these songs in camp and wrote their own bawdy parodies.[44] A patriotic cover also featured a caricature of Varina Howell Davis writhing in bed above the caption: "NIGHTMARE. Mrs. Davis dreaming she saw her husband with a rope around his neck." The purpose of these various (and sometimes vulgar) artistic creations was to humiliate the enemy and to galvanize Northern morale.

NIGHTMARE.
Mrs. Davis dreaming she saw her husband
with a rope around his neck.

"Nightmare. Mrs. Davis dreaming she saw her husband with a rope around his neck." This comical image, which appeared on a postal cover, reinforced for Northerners that the Confederate first lady suffered in her sleep as she dreamed about the punishment her husband would receive. Collection of the author.

Images of dreams also cautioned all members of society to remain faithful to their cause. "The Dream of the Army Contractor," a poem and print that appeared in *Vanity Fair* in August 1861, depicted a fat, wealthy army contractor being served wine from "the cup of Hell" by the skeleton of a soldier who had died in camp because of the shoddy food and equipment that had been provided by avaricious and unscrupulous army contractors. The contractor awoke in fright, leaving the reader to contemplate how his defrauding of the government was really harming the men in the field. Within a month of appearing in *Vanity Fair*, the poem would be reproduced in newspapers as far away as California. It would appear in print again in 1865 under the title "The Shoddy Millionaire's Nightmare."[45]

Of course, Lincoln was a prominent figure in Northern depictions of dreams. A cartoon published in *Frank Leslie's Illustrated Newspaper* on February 14, 1863, entitled "Lincoln's Dream; or, There's a Good Time Coming," depicted the president in a bout of fitful sleep, dreaming that he was chopping off the heads of his Union commanders—Irvin McDowell after First Bull Run, McClellan after the Peninsula Campaign, Ambrose Burnside after Fredericksburg. Next in line appear several cabinet members, including Secretary of State William H. Seward, Secretary of War Edwin M. Stanton, and Secretary of the Navy Gideon Welles, then Gen-

The Dream of the Army Contractor.

Old HUCKLEBURY, the Army Contractor, lay snoozily back in his chair,
After a sumptuous dinner, such as became a millionaire.
Wines were upon the table, gathered from sundry foreign lands,
A vulgar splendor of bottles bearing curious trade-marks and brands.

At first his dream was auriferous : he fancied himself afloat,
Hauling up gold-fish, hand over hand, into a rose-wood boat ;
And as the fishes went flippety-flop among the ebony thwarts,
Their scales in yellow dollars flew off, and he pocketed them by quarts.

But, lo ! a distressing circumstance alloyed the bliss of his dream,
His clothes were turned into army cloth, and they gaped at every seam ;
And the golden dollars fell clinkety-clank from tattered trowsers and coat,
And, where they fell, they burned round holes through the bottom of the boat.

Then, as the old Army Contractor sank, with a shriek, into the deep,
He felt the grasp of a skeleton hand that doubled him into a heap,
And he heard the croak of a skeleton voice—" Look here, old HUCKLEBUR-EE,
You never was born to be drown-ded, so come along with me !

" I am the bones of a soldi-er, as died in the sickly camp,
Reduced by the pizenous food and the clothes that didn't keep out the damp ;
Likeways the sperrits that to us was sarved, worse liquor never I see ;
The thirst was on me—I drank it, and died—and now you must drink with me !"

And then it brandished its bony hands, that skeleton yellow and dry,
Making the vitriolic parts of a deadly cock-tail fly ;
Then came the skeleton voice, again—" Drink, 'tis the cup of Hell !"——
O ! the pallid lips and the glaring eyes, as old H. awoke with a yell !

"The Dream of the Army Contractor," *Vanity Fair*, August 17, 1861.

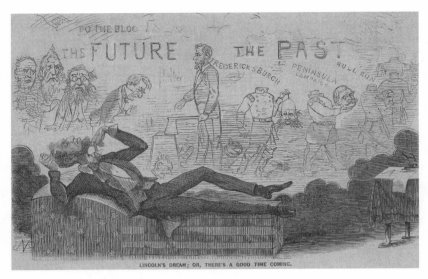

"Lincoln's Dream; or, There's a Good Time Coming," *Frank Leslie's Illustrated Newspaper*, February 14, 1863. Courtesy of the House Divided Project at Dickinson College.

COLUMBIA'S NIGHTMARE.

"Columbia's Nightmare,"
Fun, September 10, 1864.

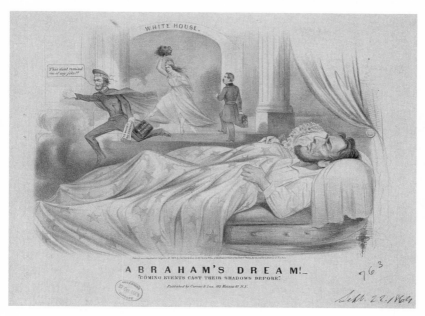

"Abraham's Dream!—'Coming Events Cast Their Shadows Before.'" Courtesy of the Library of Congress.

"Jeff Davis's November Nightmare," *Frank Leslie's Illustrated Newspaper*, December 3, 1864. Collection of the author.

eral Henry W. Halleck. The cartoon offered a dark commentary on Lincoln's inability to find an adequate military commander (not to mention suitable advisors). For the cartoonist—if not the American public—in early 1863, the future seemed a nightmare as hopeless as the recent past.

The language of dreams made frequent appearances during the presidential election of 1864—most of which were not sympathetic toward the incumbent. One print entitled *Abraham's Dream!—Coming Events Cast Their Shadows Before* depicted a sleeping Lincoln who dreams of being chased out of the White House by Lady Liberty (who is about to hurl the severed head of a black man at him) while General McClellan, the Democratic nominee for president, walks in the front door. In the September 10 issue of the satirical periodical *Fun*, a full-page cartoon featured an impish Lincoln crouched above the sleeping goddess Columbia as she writhes in her sleep. Lincoln's reelection, according to this British cartoonist, was "Columbia's Nightmare." Throughout the campaign, Northern Democratic newspapers predicted that Republicans might fine voters fifty dollars "for dreaming disrespectfully of Mr. Lincoln," and Democrats decried being called traitors for not believing "that all that Mr. Lincoln did, said and dreamed, was entirely right and proper."[46] An anonymous soldier letter to the *New York Sunday Mercury* during the election described Lincoln in even darker terms: "He has become a vampire that gnaws into the very bowels of the country—he is the nightmare beneath the horrors of which the nation groans in the agony of despair."[47]

But if Lincoln was anyone's nightmare, he was Jefferson Davis's. The Confederate president was fully committed to fighting for Southern independence, while Lincoln was equally—if not more—committed to stopping him. Lincoln's landslide electoral victory in November 1864 turned out to be the real nightmare for the rebels, for it spelled the doom of the Confederacy and set the stage for the ultimate extinction of slavery. A cartoonist at *Frank Leslie's Illustrated Newspaper* captured this pivotal moment in a cartoon entitled "Jeff Davis's November Nightmare," which appeared on December 3, 1864. In it, the sleeping rebel president envisions the Northern commander-in-chief sitting at the foot of his bed holding a newspaper that announces the Republican victory in the presidential contest. "Is that You, still there Long Abe?" asks Davis? "Yes!" replies Lincoln. "And I'm going to be Four Years Longer." As with so many other depictions of dreams in popular culture, this cartoon reassured Northern readers that peace and reunion were on the horizon. Unfortunately, it did not correctly predict how long Lincoln would live.

CHAPTER SEVEN

Lincoln's Dreams of Death

Some Americans began to see Lincoln as a messianic figure even before the first major land battle of the Civil War. In May 1861, a Rochester woman wrote to Mary Todd Lincoln about "a remarkable dream I had last night about Mr Lincoln" that she believed had "a significant meaning." In the dream she saw a raging storm with terrible thunder and lightening. It seemed, she wrote, "as tho the Heavens & Earth were coming together." When the storm ceased, she saw "very dark clouds sailing thro the horison" with Lincoln "standing erect in the firmament with a book in his hand." The sun was now rising from the east, shedding "a soft mellow light around about him." He walked south upon "dark & heavy clouds" above Washington, D.C., and "he was crowned with honors & coverd with Laurels, and looked very smiling." At that point the woman clapped her hands and sung out a verse:

A voice from the North has proclaimed the glad Morn
And Slavery is ended & Freedom is born
The fair sunny South is restor'd one more
Secession is ended & Slavery is ore.

Upon singing this verse she awoke and wrote it down before the words could escape her. In these "perilous times," she wrote, she hoped that her dream would be "a comfort" to Mrs. Lincoln.[1] This remarkable dream would prove prophetic in several ways. Before the Civil War began in earnest—and long before Lincoln would issue his Emancipation Proclamation—this woman envisioned Lincoln as a savior to the nation and a liberator for the slaves.

Other Northerners had less profound prophetic dreams about the president. Union soldiers sometimes dreamed about their commander in chief granting them promotions. Col. Nathan W. Daniels of the Second Louisiana Native Guards kept a record of many of his dreams in his diary, noting that a number of them came true. In September 1863, he dreamed of having conversations with Generals Ulysses S. Grant and Nathaniel P. Banks, as well as with President and Mrs. Lincoln. These, he hoped, were "a favorable augury." A few months later, when he had a positive meeting with Lincoln about an appointment in the Treasury Department, Daniels went back to his old diary entry and inserted, "the dream was realized in the months November & December 1863." Corporal George W. Peck of the Tenth Wisconsin was not quite as fortunate. He dreamt "that the President and secretary of war had got on to me, as it were, and had offered me high positions," but, unlike Daniels, Peck "would wake up in the morning the same red-headed corporal, and cook my breakfast."[2]

Confederates, by contrast, relished in their dreams of Lincoln's eventual demise. Early in the war, a Confederate woman who was imprisoned at the Old Capitol Prison in Washington, D.C., described "a vision" she had "last night" in which she saw Lincoln, Secretary of State William H. Seward, Secretary of War Simon Cameron, Union general Andrew Porter, "and others praying to Almighty God . . . for the mercy they denied to harmless women." In this vision, God answered: "Have I not said, as ye, mete it unto others, so shall it be measured unto you again? Depart from my sight, ye cursed, and take up your abode in the hell prepared for Abraham Lincoln and his government, and who assist him in his abominable persecutions."[3]

Dreams of Lincoln in eternal damnation must have been somewhat common south of the Mason-Dixon Line. On July 7, 1864, Richmond attorney George Dabney Wootton dreamed that he "died and went to another world." As he approached Heaven's gates, he asked Saint Peter "whether there were any lawyers in there." The apostle replied that he could not find any. Wootton then asked about the mayor of Richmond, Joseph Mayo. "Oh," replied Peter. "You'll find him in the other place." Wootton turned around and made his way to "a somber looking castle, over the entrance of which was painted 'Hell.'"

Upon entering, Wootton met Satan and saw "seats all around, some vacant and some occupied by lawyers." When Wootton went to sit in one of the seats, the Devil informed him that it was for Mayor Joseph C. Mayo. The next seat, he learned, was "reserved for old Ben Butler." Finally, he went for a third seat. "Don't take that seat," shouted the gathered assembly of suffering attorneys, "it is reserved for 'Old Abe,' the Devil's prompter." At that point Wootton "woke up shaking and shivering," but also wishing it "was not all a dream." Wootton told this dream to the members of the bar the next day while they were waiting for court to begin. A reporter nearby heard it and published it in the *Richmond Enquirer* the following morning.[4]

Northerners also dreamed about Lincoln's mortality, although their dreams tended not to wish for Lincoln's death. In December 1862, Henry Mosler, a correspondent for *Harper's Weekly*, "dreamed that Old 'Abe' was sitting in our room talking with my mother." His mother asked the president "how soon he thought the war would be over." Lincoln answered, "Not before I'm out.—meaning [the] Presidency."[5] In words very similar to ones Lincoln is said to have uttered, Mosler believed that Lincoln would live at least long enough to see the end of hostilities. This dream essentially proved true.

The circumstances surrounding Lincoln's death would haunt the dreams of some Americans well into the twentieth century—even people who were not alive when the tragedy took place. A young African American boy named John E. Washington grew up around the corner from Ford's Theatre "hearing wonderful stories about Lincoln, his family, and Booth, from the mouths of some who had really seen them, and from others who claimed they had seen their ghosts." One night when walking alone down the street by Ford's, Washington got spooked by the thought of ghosts. He "ran faster and faster" toward his home with his "eyes fixed straight ahead" while feeling "hot and cold chills from ghosts." Washington apparently did not feel any safer upon reaching home. That night he had a nightmare of John Wilkes Booth "chasing me with his dagger and pistol, over, under, and above the bed, and it was only when I escaped, by hanging from the ceiling in a spider web, and yelling, that I was suddenly awakened by my Grandmother, just as the dagger was approaching my heart."[6] John Washington's childhood love for Lincoln would eventually blossom into a book—part memoir, part history—about African American appreciation for the sixteenth president. Lincoln's death was a central moment in this boy's life—and dream life— just as it had been in the life of the nation.

"I HAD THIS strange dream again last night," Abraham Lincoln told his Cabinet on April 14, 1865—just hours before his assassination—"and we shall, judging from the past, have great news very soon." Lincoln said that this was "the usual dream" he had had "preceding nearly every great and important event of the war." The president was upbeat about the omen. "Generally the news had been favorable which succeeded the dream," he stated, "and the dream itself was always the same." Secretary of the Navy Gideon Welles asked Lincoln about the nature of this "remarkable dream," to which the president replied that it "related to the water." Lincoln then described his dream in some detail: He was on a ship—"some singular, indescribable vessel"—that was "moving with great rapidity [towards an indefinite shore]." (Welles later added the words "towards an indefinite shore" to the diary entry.) Lincoln told the Cabinet that he'd had this dream before the Confederate attack on Fort Sumter in April 1861, as well as preceding the battles of Bull Run, Antietam, Gettysburg, Stones River, Wilmington, and the surrender of Vicksburg on July 4, 1863. The president believed that the dream portended some good news involving Maj. Gen. William Tecumseh Sherman's army. General Ulysses S. Grant, who was attending the meeting, pointed out that Stones River "was certainly no victory, and he knew of no great results which followed from it." However that might be, Lincoln said, this dream preceded that fight.

Sitting at the Cabinet meeting, Secretary Welles did not think much of the dream. But two or three days later he remembered it and recorded it in his diary. "Great events did indeed follow," he wrote mournfully, "for within a few hours the good and gentle, as well as truly great, man who narrated his dream, closed forever his earthly career."[7]

The provenance for this dream is quite good. Several other witnesses to Lincoln's account also told this story. Less than three years later, Secretary of War Edwin M. Stanton recounted Lincoln's dream to English novelist Charles Dickens. Dickens, in turn, described it in a letter to the English biographer John Forster.

According to Dickens, Stanton had been late for the meeting, and Lincoln described the dream while they waited for him to arrive. When Stanton entered the room, Lincoln said, "Let us proceed to business, gentlemen." Stanton noticed something different about the president that afternoon. He "sat with an air of dignity in his chair instead of lolling about it in the most ungainly attitudes, as his invariable custom was; and that instead of telling irrelevant or questionable stories, he was grave and calm, and quite a different man." Upon leaving the meeting, Stanton said to Attorney General James Speed, "That is the most satisfactory cabinet meeting I have attended for many a long day! What an extraordinary change in Mr. Lincoln."

Speed agreed, and said that the entire Cabinet had noticed the change. "While we were waiting for you," Speed told Stanton, Lincoln told the Cabinet a story "with his chin on his breast": "Gentlemen, something very extraordinary is going to happen, and that very soon." Speed asked Lincoln whether it would be good news, but the president replied "very gravely": "I don't know. But it will happen, and shortly too!" Speed asked if Lincoln had some new information. "No, but I have had a dream. And I have now had the same dream three times. Once, on the night preceding the Battle of Bull Run." And one other time the night before another Union defeat (Dickens could not remember the name of the battle). Speed asked Lincoln about "the nature of this dream." "Well," Lincoln replied without lifting his head, "I am on a great broad rolling river—and I am in a boat—and I drift—and I drift!—but this is not business." At that point Stanton entered the room, and Lincoln said, "Let us proceed to business, gentlemen."[8]

Secretary of State William H. Seward's son, Frederick, was also present at the meeting representing the State Department, since his father had been badly injured in a carriage accident. In 1916, he published his own version of the dream—that Lincoln had felt "a vague sense of floating—floating away on some vast and indistinct expanse, toward an unknown shore." Lincoln, according to Seward, also mentioned "the coincidence that each of its previous recurrences had been followed by some important event or disaster, which he mentioned."

According to Seward, those in the room made "the usual comments." One thought it "merely a matter of coincidences." Another laughed and said, "At any rate it cannot presage a victory nor a defeat this time, for the war is over." Seward, taking the dream seriously, then suggested to the president, "Perhaps at each of these periods there were possibilities of great change or disaster, and the vague feeling of uncertainty may have led to the dim vision in sleep." "Perhaps," Lincoln replied, "perhaps that is the explanation."[9]

Like Stanton, General Grant related the story to a third party in 1867—but Grant's version was noticeably darker than those of the other eyewitnesses. According to this account, "a heavy gloom" rested upon Lincoln's "soul" as he convened the meeting. Lincoln told his advisors, "I feel some great disaster is coming upon us." He then proceeded to say he'd been "visited by a strange dream." In this version, Lincoln told his Cabinet that "news of disaster" had followed every other occurrence of this dream. "This same dream came to me last night in my sleep, and I feel as if some great calamity is to befall the nation, in which I am to be personally affected." Curiously, Grant's account made no mention of the content of the dream, just its negative foreboding.[10]

The story of the dream quickly spread throughout the country. It first appeared in the *New York Herald* on April 18, 1865, just three days after the president's death. When Lincoln's body traveled through Philadelphia on April 22 and 23, the women of St. Clement's Church built an anchor of white roses and violets, which they hung by Lincoln's open casket with a card that read, "'Before any great national event I have always had the same dream. I had it the other night. It is of a *ship sailing rapidly.*'—ABRAHAM LINCOLN." By May the dream had been reported in newspapers as far away as San

Francisco.[11] Clearly the story captivated the American imagination, perhaps because it confirmed something supernatural about Lincoln, his clairvoyant gifts.

When Welles published his memories as a Cabinet officer in 1872, he included the remarkable Cabinet meeting of April 14, 1865. Welles, who did not care for Grant, added a few sarcastic words to Grant's dialogue about Stones River—"that a few such victories would have ruined the country, and he knew of no important results from it." Welles also added a word of embellishment to Lincoln's description of the dream to make the shore seem more ominous—that the ship was headed toward "a dark and indefinite shore" instead of just "an indefinite shore," essentially confirming for his readers the negative premonitory nature of the dream (even though earlier in the paragraph Welles had quoted Lincoln as saying that "news would come soon and come favorably"). Historian Richard Wightman Fox suggests that this new detail signified a "shore [from which] there was no hope of return"—death.[12]

Welles's embellishments reflected a bit of artistic license. The story, after all, was worthy of a dramatic telling. Upon hearing of the dream in April 1865, George Templeton Strong wrote in his diary, "A poet could make something out of that." And, indeed, Charles Dickens and George Eliot later recounted the story to eager audiences. With each new telling, however, the story seemed to get darker and darker. One account in 1867, for example, took great liberties, stating that Lincoln's vessel "was swept along by an irresistible current toward a maelstrom, from which it seemed no power could save her. Faster and faster the whirling waters swept the fated ship toward the vortex, until, looking down into the black abyss, amid the deafening roar of the waves, and with the sensation of sinking down, down, down an unfathomable depth, the terrified dreamer awoke."[13]

The various accounts of the incident leave one important question unanswered: Who elicited the further explanation from the president? Over the next five decades, Lincoln's advisors jockeyed to place themselves at the center of this final conversation with the soon-to-be martyr. In the *New York Herald*'s report, the president volunteered the nature of the dream without being asked, while in each of the other three versions a different Cabinet officer was at the center of the dialogue with Lincoln. On the surface, Welles's account should be the most reliable since it was written in a personal diary only three days after the incident. Yet Welles changed his story over time (we have already seen three minor changes, noted above). Originally, Welles quoted Lincoln as saying that the dream "related to the water." In his 1872 memoir, he made an important emendation: "He said it was in my department—it related to the water." When his diary was finally published by his son in 1911, the diary entry now read, "He said it related to your (my) element, the water."[14]

Seward's recollections appear to be even less reliable. When Seward first published the story in a biography of his father in 1891, he gave credit to another anonymous Cabinet member, writing, "A third [Cabinet member] suggested, 'Perhaps at each of these periods. . . .'" But when he published his own memoir in 1916, Seward changed that important line to: "I suggested, 'Perhaps at each of these periods. . . .'"[15]

In the Dickens letter, Stanton gave credit to Speed instead of Welles for eliciting the dream from their commander in chief, but it should be remembered that Stanton was not present at the meeting when Lincoln told the story, and Stanton and Welles were not particularly fond of one another.[16] Grant's version never even got to the content of the dream.

We may never know with certainty who elicited the dream report from Lincoln, although the most reliable evidence would seem to suggest that it was Welles. At any rate, the infighting in the reminiscences of these Cabinet members reveals how important this dream was to Americans of the Civil War era. The dream—within the context of Lincoln's death—gave Lincoln an almost supernatural aura that offered comfort and hope to Americans. Perhaps he was a prophet receiving direct revelations from God.[17] It is little wonder that those who were closest to him wanted so badly to be remembered as being on intimate terms with him at this critical moment.

This dream has become so well known that it has appeared in children's books and movies, including in one of the opening scenes of Steven Spielberg's blockbuster film *Lincoln*. In Spielberg's version, Lincoln tells the dream to Mary in January 1865, just before the Union attack on Wilmington, North Carolina. Thus far, this depiction is historically accurate, since Lincoln (according to Welles, though not the others) had claimed to have the dream before the assault on Wilmington. Daniel Day-Lewis's Lincoln then describes the dream as viewers see a solitary figure of Lincoln on a *Monitor*-styled vessel (a very nice touch!), in what appears like dark 1920s film reel: "It's nighttime. The ship's moved by some terrible power, at a terrific speed. Though it's imperceptible in the darkness, I have an intuition that we're headed towards a shore. No one else seems to be aboard the vessel and I'm pretty keenly aware of my aloneness. I could be bounded in a nutshell and count myself a king of infinite space, not that I have bad dreams. I reckon it's the speed that's strange to me. I'm used to going a deliberate pace. I should spare you, Molly, I shouldn't tell you my dreams."[18] As with all accounts of Lincoln, the storyteller hopes to get a certain point across. In this case, the filmmaker seeks to convey Lincoln as a solitary, deliberate, and deliberative figure—a tormented leader, set apart. This version departs from Welles's original account, however, in that Lincoln did not describe his dream as a bad one.

LINCOLN'S DREAMS REVEAL a great deal about his mind and concerns; some of them also speak to his preoccupation with mortality. Historians and biographers have, in turn, been preoccupied with Lincoln's apparent obsession with death. Many writers have recounted the dream of the ship from his final Cabinet meeting. They also love to quote his prophetic public statement at Independence Hall in Philadelphia on George Washington's birthday in 1861—that he would rather be assassinated than sacrifice the principles of the Declaration of Independence.[19]

Lincoln's friends and associates frequently recounted statements he allegedly made to them portending his untimely death. One claimed to hear Lincoln say that he "may not live to see" the end of the war: "I feel a presentiment that I shall not outlast the rebellion. When it is over, my work will be done." Harriet Beecher Stowe, author of *Uncle Tom's Cabin*, heard Lincoln predict, "I shan't last long after it's over." Finally, he told friend and Illinois congressman Owen Lovejoy that the "war is eating my life out; I have a strong impression that I shall not live to see the end."[20]

Some of Lincoln's darkest dreams were about his children. "Did you ever dream of some lost friend and feel that you were having a sweet communion with him, and yet have a consciousness that it was not a reality?" Lincoln is reported to have asked an army colonel in May 1862. "That is the way I dream of my lost boy Willie." (Willie had just died on February 20.) The colonel later recalled that Lincoln was "deeply move[d]" and "his voice trembled" as he spoke of these visitation dreams. "He was utterly overcome," wrote the colonel. "His great frame shook & Bowing down on the table he wept as only such a man in the breaking down of a great sorrow could weep."[21]

As early as 1848, Lincoln had expressed deep concern over a dream he'd had about his eldest son, Robert, telling Mary, "I did not get rid of the impression of that foolish dream about dear Bobby till I got your letter written the same day." In June 1863, about a year after Willie's death, he sent a telegram to Mary telling her to *put 'Tad's' pistol away* because he'd had "an ugly dream about him."[22] (At the time, Mary and Tad were on a shopping trip in Philadelphia and Lincoln had permitted Tad to take his new pistol with him.) Pointing to this last dream, Richard Wightman Fox argues that Lincoln clearly believed that dreams had "some predictive capacity." "They weren't actual revelations of the future," Fox continues, "but they gave one a sense, however murky, of what might come to pass."[23]

Fox is probably correct about Lincoln's general view of dreams; however, there were some exceptions. In 1866, Mary Todd Lincoln told William H. Herndon that "Mr Lincoln had a dream when down the River at City point after Richmond was taken: he dreamed that the white House burned up." This dream appears to have caused Lincoln to fear that something had actually happened to the executive mansion. The next morning, Mary sent an urgent telegram to a White House maid, telling her, "Send a Telegram, directed to City Point, so soon as you receive this & say if all is right at the house—Every thing is left in your charge—be careful." She then returned to Washington and sent a telegram back to Lincoln: "Arrived here safely this morning, found all well."[24]

Of course, Lincoln's dreams were not always dark—some even revealed his sense of humor. Lincoln's private secretary John Hay recorded one such dream in his diary: "He was in a party of plain people and as it became known who he was they began to comment on his appearance. One of them said, 'He is a very common-looking man.' The President replied, 'The Lord prefers Common-looking people: that is the reason he makes so many of them.'" According to Hay, when Lincoln awoke, "he remembered it, and told it as a rather neat thing."[25] Writing in 1929, Lloyd Lewis wrote that this dream "thrived in American lore not so much for its humor as for its epitomizing of Lincoln's humanity." Of equal importance, it captured "the growing belief that Lincoln had loved the common people with something like divine attachment."[26]

The difficulty in understanding Lincoln's views about dreams, however, is that most of what we know about them comes from secondhand accounts—Lincoln's friends and former associates recounting what they claimed they'd heard him say. And these accounts are not always reliable.[27]

THE MOST FAMOUS of Lincoln's dreams and visions have a darker tinge to them. The first occurred sometime in 1860, although different versions of the story contain conflicting details.

In early May 1865, a brief story appeared in several newspapers claiming that after his election to the presidency in 1860, Lincoln had seen a peculiar double reflection of himself in a mirror at his home in Springfield. Upon seeing this strange double image of his face, "he thought he must be ill," for the second image "was perfect, but very pale." When Mary Lincoln saw how anemic he looked in the second reflection, she told him it meant he would be reelected but that he would not survive his second term.[28]

In June 1865, painter Francis Carpenter responded to this story, offering a more thorough account with some varying details. Carpenter claimed that he'd heard this story from Lincoln in June 1864, when Lincoln received word of his renomination for the presidency. According to Carpenter, Lincoln was reminded of "a very singular occurrence" that "took place the day I was nominated at Chicago, four years ago." Upon returning home on that May afternoon in 1860, Lincoln went into Mary's sitting room and reclined on a couch. As he looked across the room at a mirror, "I saw distinctly *two* images of myself, exactly alike, except that one was a little paler than the other." He got up and then lay back down and saw the same thing. "It made me quite uncomfortable for a few moments," Lincoln said, "but some friends coming in, the matter passed out of my mind." The next day Lincoln retried the experiment and attained the same result, determining "that it was the natural result of some principle of refraction or optics which I did not understand." Much later, he tried it again at the White House, but did not see the double image. In contradiction to the earlier account, Carpenter concluded, "He did not say, as is asserted in the story, that either he or Mrs. Lincoln attached any omen to it whatever. Neither did he say that the double reflection was seen while he was walking about the room. On the contrary, it was only visible in a certain position and at a certain angle, and therefore he thought could be accounted for upon scientific principles." Carpenter brought this up "to show upon what a slender foundation a marvelous account may be built!"[29]

Journalist Noah Brooks published a similar account in *Harper's New Monthly Magazine* in July 1865. Whereas Lincoln purportedly recounted the story to Carpenter in June 1864, Brooks claimed to have heard it shortly after the presidential election in November 1864. According to Brooks, Lincoln saw this vision on Election Day in 1860, not on the day he was nominated. In Brooks's account, Lincoln was in his own "chamber," whereas in Carpenter's he was in Mary's sitting room. In Brooks's account, Lincoln described "the tip of the nose of one [of the images] being about three inches from the tip of the other," a detail missing from Carpenter's account. But most importantly, in Brooks's version, Mary was greatly troubled by the vision and saw it as "'a sign' that I was to be elected to a second term of office, and that the paleness of one of the faces was an omen that I should not see life through the last term." According to Brooks (and in contrast with Carpenter), Lincoln would think of the vision every "once in a while" and it would "give me a little pang, as though something uncomfortable had happened." Nevertheless, Brooks concluded in general agreement with Carpenter: "The President, with his usual good sense, saw nothing in all this but an optical illusion; though the flavor of superstition which hangs about every man's composition made him wish that he had never seen it."[30]

Upon reading Brooks's account, Carpenter added a brief addendum to his own version of the story when he republished it in his 1866 memoir, *Six Months at the White House with Abraham Lincoln*. While Carpenter claimed to be "quite confident" that Lincoln had said the vision happened when he was nominated (since Lincoln had recalled the event to Carpenter on the day of his renomination in 1864), Carpenter conceded that "it is possible . . . that I am mistaken in the date." He also agreed that Brooks's depiction of Mary's fearful reaction to the dream "is undoubtedly correct."[31]

Lincoln's friend and self-appointed bodyguard Ward Hill Lamon also claimed to have heard about this vision from Lincoln "more than once," although Lamon almost certainly pilfered the story from Carpenter and Brooks. Lamon reproduced Brooks's account verbatim in his 1872 biography of Lincoln, incorrectly attributing the story to John Hay instead of Brooks.[32] Then, in his 1895 memoir, *Recollections of Abraham Lincoln*, Lamon recounted the story as though Lincoln had told it directly to him, although in this version he plagiarized significant amounts of Lincoln's dialogue from Carpenter's account. According to Lamon's *Recollections*, Lincoln recounted the vision in June 1864, at the time of his renomination, but the vision had occurred at the time of the election of 1860. Lamon thus split the difference between Carpenter and Brooks. But most importantly, Lamon attributed the premonitory interpretation of the dream to the president, not Mary. "To his mind the illusion was a sign," Lamon concluded, "the life-like image betokening a safe passage through his first term as President; the ghostly one, that death would overtake him before the close of the second."[33]

In *Recollections*, Lamon recounted a second dream that dealt with Lincoln's impending death. So real did it appear that Lamon called it "the most startling incident" of Lincoln's life. Lincoln allegedly dreamt it a few weeks before his assassination, but he kept it a secret until its mysteriousness overwhelmed him. One day in early April, according to Lamon, Lincoln approached a small group of friends at the White House, which included Lamon and Mary Lincoln. "The President was in a melancholy, meditative mood, and had been silent for some time," wrote Lamon. Finally, Mary aroused him to speak what was on his mind.

"It seems strange how much there is in the Bible about dreams," Lincoln said. "There are, I think, some sixteen chapters in the Old Testament and four or five in the New in which dreams are mentioned; and there are many other passages scattered throughout the book which refer to visions. If we believe the Bible, we must accept the fact that in the old days God and His angels came to men in their sleep and made themselves known in dreams. Nowadays dreams are regarded as very foolish, and are seldom told, except by old women and by young men and maidens in love."

Mary Lincoln was struck by Lincoln's dreadful solemnity and asked him, "Do *you* believe in dreams?" "I can't say that I do," Lincoln replied, "but I had one the other night which has haunted me ever since." After having the dream, Lincoln said that he had opened his Bible to the story in Genesis in which Jacob dreamed of a ladder ascending into heaven with angels going up and down it. Lincoln "turned to other passages, and seemed to encounter a dream or a vision wherever I looked. I kept on turning the leaves of the old book, and everywhere my eye fell upon passages recording matters strangely in keeping with my own thoughts,—supernatural visitations, dreams, visions, etc."

Lincoln "now looked so serious and disturbed" that Mary exclaimed, "You frighten me! What is the matter?" Lincoln replied that he should not have brought up the subject, "but somehow the thing has got possession of me, and, like Banquo's ghost, it will not down." According to Lamon, "This only inflamed Mrs. Lincoln's curiosity the more, and while bravely disclaiming any belief in dreams, she strongly urged him to tell the dream which seemed to have such a hold upon him, being seconded in this by another listener." Lincoln was hesitant to continue, but decided to describe the dream, "his brow overcast with a shade of melancholy." Lamon recounted Lincoln's words as accurately as he could remember them:

> "About ten days ago," said he, "I retired very late. I had been up waiting for important dispatches from the front. I could not have been long in bed when I fell into a slumber, for I was weary. I soon began to dream. There seemed to be a death-like stillness about me. Then I heard subdued sobs, as if a number of people were weeping. I thought I left my bed and wandered downstairs. There the silence was broken by the same pitiful sobbing, but the mourners were invisible. I went from room to room; no living person was in sight,

but the same mournful sounds of distress met me as I passed along. It was light in all the rooms; every object was familiar to me; but where were all the people who were grieving as if their hearts would break? I was puzzled and alarmed. What could be the meaning of all this? Determined to find the cause of a state of things so mysterious and so shocking, I kept on until I arrived at the East Room, which I entered. There I met with a sickening surprise. Before me was a catafalque, on which rested a corpse wrapped in funeral vestments. Around it were stationed soldiers who were acting as guards; and there was a throng of people, some gazing mournfully upon the corpse, whose face was covered, others weeping pitifully. 'Who is dead in the White House?' I demanded of one of the soldiers. 'The President,' was his answer; 'he was killed by an assassin!' Then came a loud burst of grief from the crowd, which awoke me from my dream. I slept no more that night; and although it was only a dream, I have been strangely annoyed by it ever since."

Mary Lincoln responded that the story was "horrid" and she wished Lincoln had not told it. "I am glad I don't believe in dreams," she said, "or I should be in terror from this time forth." Lincoln responded that it was "only a dream" and that they should "say no more about it, and try to forget it."

Lamon ventured that the dream was "so horrible, so real, and so in keeping with other dreams and threatening presentiments of his, that Mr. Lincoln was profoundly disturbed by it." Lincoln looked "grave," "gloomy," and "visibly pale" as he described his vision this first time, but then apparently later talked about it with Lamon "with some show of playful humor," telling Lamon that it was foolish to worry about the dream being prophetic: "Hill," said Lincoln, "your apprehension of harm to me from some hidden enemy is downright foolishness. For a long time you have been trying to keep somebody—the Lord knows who—from killing me. Don't you see how it will turn out? In this dream it was not me, but some other fellow, that was killed. It seems that this ghostly assassin tried his hand on some one else." Then, in a serious tone, Lincoln added, "Well, let it go. I think the Lord in His own good time and way will work this out all right. God knows what is best."

These are remarkable stories. Of the White House funeral dream, Lamon said, "there was something about it so amazingly real, so true to the actual tragedy which occurred soon after, that more than mortal strength and wisdom would have been required to let it pass without a shudder or a pang."[34] It is little wonder that the story has gained wide currency in American popular culture. Indeed, some of the best-selling writers on Lincoln spanning the twentieth and twenty-first centuries, such as Carl Sandburg, Philip Van Doren Stern, Richard Nelson Current, Gore Vidal, Stephen B. Oates, Jean H. Baker, Jay Winik, Doris Kearns Goodwin, Allen C. Guelzo, Harold Holzer, James L. Swanson, and Bill O'Reilly, have all repeated the dream.[35] The dream is told in detail in fantasy novels such as *Abraham Lincoln: Vampire Hunter* and *Lincoln's Dreams*.[36] In *Destiny of the Republic: A Tale of Madness, Medicine, and the Murder of a President*, Candice Millard writes that James A. Garfield asked his secretary of war, Robert Todd Lincoln, about this dream at Garfield's final Cabinet meeting—two days before Garfield was assassinated in 1881.[37] (What irony!) Historian Andrew Burstein even appropriated Lamon's story for the title of his book, *Lincoln Dreamt He Died: The Midnight Visions of Remarkable Americans from Colonial Times to Freud*.[38]

The dream has also appeared on television a number of times over the years, including in episodes of *One Step Beyond* (1960) and *Touched by an Angel* (1998), in documentaries on the History Channel and the Smithsonian Channel, and at least three made-for-TV movies: Gore Vidal's *Lincoln* (1988), *The Day Lincoln Was Shot* (1998), and the National Geographic Channel's *Killing Lincoln* (2013), which was based on O'Reilly's book.[39] It appeared in an article by Norman Vincent Peale that was then quoted on the floor of the U.S. Senate.[40] Finally, the dream appears in presidential trivia books and is a staple in the cottage industry of books about spiritualism, the paranormal, and dream interpretation, even appearing in a 1965 Nigerian dream manual.[41]

Some scholars have used the White House funeral dream to probe the inner psyche of Abraham Lincoln. Historian Christine Stansell, for example, uses the line "Nowadays dreams are regarded as very foolish, and are seldom told, except by old women and by young men and maidens in love" to depict Lincoln as something of a misogynist and racial bigot. She writes, "In his rich interior life as president, Lincoln often felt the urgency of dreams yet diminished their importance, noting their association with silliness and women (and, although he didn't say so, blacks)."[42]

But did Lincoln actually have the dream? We should be naturally hesitant to accept such an incredible story. The dream's provenance should cause even greater concern. The most frequently cited source is Ward Hill Lamon's posthumously published *Recollections of Abraham Lincoln* (1895). In

Recollections, Lamon claimed to retell the story "from notes which I made immediately after its recital" in April 1865. In truth, Lamon's daughter, Dorothy, probably inserted this line into her father's "recollections" when she compiled and published them after his death. Lamon made no mention of working from notes when he first published the dream in 1887 in the *Chicago Morning News*. Nor do any notes survive in his papers (although they do for other articles that he wrote).[43]

For years, scholars have treated Lamon's *Recollections* with reservation. Historian David Herbert Donald, for example, writes that one of Lamon's accounts of Lincoln at Gettysburg was "highly unreliable."[44] Similarly, Don E. Fehrenbacher and Virginia Fehrenbacher point out that "more than a little" of Lamon's "quotation of Lincoln was simply invented." The Fehrenbachers, in fact, demolish the credibility of Lamon's recollection in regard to the White House funeral dream:

> According to Lamon, Lincoln experienced this strikingly premonitory dream just a few days before his death, but he is quoted as describing it some ten days afterwards and as discussing it again at an even later time. There was no contemporary mention of the dream, not even after the assassination, by Lamon himself or by Mary Lincoln or anyone else who supposedly heard Lincoln's account of it. Furthermore, in fashioning the story, Lamon seems to have forgotten that Lincoln, who is quoted as saying that on the night of the dream he had been "waiting for important dispatches from the front," was actually *at the front* from March 24 to April 9, the day of Lee's surrender.[45]

Even more compelling evidence comes from Lamon's own hand. On April 27, 1865, Lamon wrote a letter to Secretary of War Edwin M. Stanton stating that he last saw Lincoln on April 13 (the day before Lincoln was shot), and that he had not seen the president "for three weeks [before April 13] because of an attack of the Rheumatism which prostrated me." This evidence is corroborated by a letter Lamon sent to Lincoln on March 23, which closed, "I would have called upon you in person on the subject, but for the fact that I am confined to my bed with an attack of the Rheumatism." In other words, Lincoln and Lamon did not see each during the period that Lamon claimed to have heard the dream.[46]

The Fehrenbachers' analysis about the chronology should have been enough to discredit Lamon's story, but even they did not dig deeply enough into the origins of the dream. Like most other scholars, they cited Lamon's 1895 *Recollections*. But earlier versions exist.

An abbreviated version of the White House funeral dream appeared as early as February 1874 in a small-town Maryland newspaper.[47] The full, detailed version (most similar to Lamon's) first appeared in an unsigned article entitled "President Lincoln's Dream" in the literary magazine *Gleason's Monthly Companion* in March 1880. The details in the 1880 version differ in several significant ways from Lamon's account in *Recollections*. First, it contains no chronological clues as to when Lincoln was supposed to have had the dream (compared to Lamon's version, which places it in April 1865). Second, Lincoln was in conversation with "Mrs. Lincoln and the children" in the 1880 version, not as Lamon described it, with "only two or three persons present," including himself. In the 1880 account, it was Lincoln's son, Tad, who implored him, "Do tell the dream, father," and who then called it "dreadful." Robert Todd Lincoln also made an appearance in this version, saying, "Well, father, I don't wonder that such a dream made an impression upon you." Third, in Lamon's account, Lincoln seemed unconcerned with assassinations, while Lamon portrayed himself as deeply concerned for the president's life. In the 1880 version, however, Lincoln "had an ever-present dread of the assassin's hand." Finally and most importantly, Lamon is nowhere to be seen in the 1880 version of the story.[48]

According to the 1880 version, Mary Lincoln's "first exclamation" after John Wilkes Booth shot her husband at Ford's Theatre was, "His dream was prophetic" (Lamon's version quotes this line as well, but does not connect it directly to the White House funeral dream). "This remark was not then understood," noted the anonymous author, which indicates that Lamon likely did not write the piece, since the 1895 version placed him in the room when Lincoln told the story. He certainly would have known the meaning of Mary's statement. But no contemporaneous evidence has Mary saying this when Lincoln was shot. In fact, in 1866, Mary told Lincoln's former law partner William H. Herndon that Lincoln "didn't in late years dream of death."[49]

The 1880 piece concludes, "Subsequently, the circumstances of Mr. Lincoln's dream was told to many in Washington, and formed one of the most impressive incidents connected with the tragedy which gave the nation its immortal martyr."[50]

A digital search of newspapers from 1865 indicates that the ship on the water dream had gained widespread attention within a month of Lincoln's death, but no such mention of the far more provocative White House funeral dream appeared. If it was all the talk around Washington, as the 1880 article intimates that it was, then surely it would have found its way into the press shortly after Lincoln's death.[51] In fact, the White House funeral dream was not widely circulated in newspapers and periodicals until the early 1880s, after the story appeared in *Gleason's Monthly Companion*.[52] Lamon almost certainly read it then.

All of this evidence suggests that this was a fictional piece written for a newspaper; it was later embellished by a literary magazine; it circulated through other newspapers in the 1880s; finally, Ward Hill Lamon appropriated and further exaggerated it in 1887 when he solicited newspaper editors around the country to purchase articles he would write about Lincoln. Finally, the story became enshrined in American memory when his daughter published Lamon's *Recollections* a few years later (and it should be recalled that either he or his daughter plagiarized the mirror vision at this time, too).[53] The dream is almost certainly a fabrication.[54]

Over the years, Lincoln's friends, family, and close associates recounted other improbable assassination dreams as well. For example, a similar White House funeral dream is attributed to Mary Todd Lincoln. In the 1940s, some descendants of the Todd family claimed that Mary "dreamed she descended the great staircase in the White House, looked into one of the large rooms and saw her husband's body lying in state" a few nights before April 14, 1865.[55] It seems likely that these descendants had read the account of Lincoln's dream in the newspapers and that over the ensuing decades the incredible story morphed into a dream of their direct relative, like a game of whisper down the lane.

And still more assassination "dreams" come from another of Lincoln's bodyguards. In his 1911 memoir *Memories of the White House*, William H. Crook claimed that on April 14 the president told him "of a dream he had had for three successive nights, concerning his impending assassination." This dream report put Crook in a state of "constant dread" so that he "almost begged" Lincoln not to go to Ford's Theatre that night. Crook asked if he could come to the theater to stand guard, but Lincoln replied, "No, Crook, you have had a long, hard day's work already, and must go home to sleep and rest. I cannot afford to have you get all tired out and exhausted." The president then said, "Good-bye, Crook."

This last statement lodged itself permanently into Crook's mind. Normally when Lincoln and Crook departed, the president would have said, "Good-night." But this time—April 14, 1865—was the first and only time that Lincoln said something different—"Good-bye." Crook claimed that when he learned of Lincoln's death a few hours later, "his last words [to me] were so burned into my memory that they never have been forgotten, and never can be forgotten."

On the surface, Crook's story seems unlikely to be true. It is possible but improbable that Lincoln would have remembered two different dreams from the previous night and then told one dream (the ship on the water) to his Cabinet, and another dream to Crook. Discrepancies in Crook's story make his account of a series of three assassination dreams even more unlikely. In an earlier memoir, *Through Five Administrations* (1910), Crook seemed much less adamant about his final farewell with Lincoln. Of the "Good-bye, Crook," he wrote, "It startled me. As far as I remember he had never said anything but 'Good-night, Crook,' before. Of course, it is possible that I may be mistaken."

Crook's description of Lincoln's dreams in *Through Five Administrations*, however, is what really casts doubt on his later story. Rather than mention the three successive nights Lincoln allegedly experienced assassination dreams, Crook instead recounted the ship on the water dream—and this, not as a witness to Lincoln's telling of the story, but as "a matter of record." And when Crook discussed Lincoln's fear of assassination in his earlier memoir, it was not because the president had had a series of frightful dreams, but because Crook "believe[d] that he had some vague sort of warning that the attempt would be made on the night of the 14th."[56] It seems that either Crook or his publisher decided that he should include a juicier tale for the 1911 edition of his reminiscences.

And still other fabricated Lincoln dreams of death surfaced in the twentieth century. A document appeared in a Lincolniana auction catalog in 1944 featuring a short note, dated April 11, 1843: "I dreamed last night I was dead," the note began. According to this short manuscript, Lincoln dreamed that he was too "long" for his grave site, so he "rolled out" of his coffin "to dig it longer"—at which point he grew "ancious of all the horrors of being buried alive," although his friends assured him that his "breathing would soon cease when they covered me up with dirt." The impression this dream allegedly made on Lincoln was so intense that he wrote it down in the morning, before leaving his room. "And even now, while writing, I shudder to think of it," concluded the note. When Roy P. Basler and his team gathered and edited Lincoln's writings in *The Collected Works of Abraham Lincoln* in 1953, they labeled this document a "forgery."[57]

Another dream that can be best described as an inadvertent fabrication appears in *The Destructive War: William Tecumseh Sherman, Stonewall Jackson, and the Americans* (1991), by Charles Royster. "On the last night of 1862, after news of fighting at Murfreesboro," writes Royster, Lincoln "dreamed of corpses on a battlefield in Tennessee, of gunfire in the night, of exhausted soldiers in the rain, and of crowds reading casualty lists posted at Willard's Hotel near the White House." Royster provides no citation for this remarkable story, but he likely discovered it in Stephen B. Oates's biography of Lincoln, *With Malice Toward None: The Life of Abraham Lincoln* (1977). The two accounts are nearly identical, with Royster only changing a few of Oates's words. Oates had written, "That night Lincoln tossed in fitful sleep, dreaming of corpses on a distant battlefield in Tennessee, of guns flashing in the night, of silent troops lying exhausted in the rain, of crowds reading casualty returns at Willard's Hotel."[58]

Oates's citations point to Benjamin P. Thomas's popular *Abraham Lincoln: A Biography* (1952), but Thomas's description is much less detailed: "Apparitions of dead and mutilated soldiers, of battle-spent men lying on the cold ground soaked by a winter rain, tortured the President's sleep."[59] Unfortunately, like Royster, Thomas did not cite his source.

There is good reason that Thomas provided no citation: He didn't have one. Thomas's description of this dream is vague; in fact, in Thomas's telling, it is not even definitively a dream. Instead, Thomas imagined this scene so that he could capture how Lincoln *must have felt* in the *nights* leading up to January 1, 1863, when he would issue his Emancipation Proclamation. Lincoln was war-weary and beleaguered. He knew that men were off fighting in Tennessee; he must have desperately wanted to know that they were victorious. *Certainly*, then, the president *must have* been tortured at night by visions of faraway battlefields; he must have restlessly twisted and turned in his bed sheets. With the flair of a novelist, Thomas thus rendered a compelling but fictional scene.

This bit of artistic license was not the only time Thomas took liberties in his biography. In fact, Thomas admitted to doing as much on at least four occasions. When describing how Lincoln wrote his famous memorandum on the will of God, Thomas surmised (in a private letter), "Lincoln must have been alone. He couldn't have thought out and penned such a memorandum except in solitude. But he was an extremely busy man. If he was alone, he must have written it late at night. Why was he up late and not working? He must have been waiting for news. What was his mood? Solemn, obviously, from the nature of the memorandum. Anxious, inevitably, with the enemy on Northern soil and a great battle impending." And so, having sufficiently entered Lincoln's state of being, Thomas wrote in his biography: "The lonely man in the White House found time for meditation as he waited for news night after night. With his strong sense of fatalism, he felt a Power beyond himself shaping the nation's destiny, and in an hour of anxiety he solemnly penned his thoughts." Thomas later admitted in private correspondence, "Those sentences are largely imaginative, yet I am convinced that they portray the situation accurately, and that something would have been lost in the telling without the use of imagination."[60]

Thomas's "use of imagination" took on a life of its own after he published his biography, and long after he died in 1956. Relying on Thomas's account, Stephen Oates mistook Thomas's story to be a literal dream. But even Oates was not content with the original—surely Lincoln must also have dreamt of actual corpses, guns flashing, rain pouring, and anxious crowds just around the corner at Willard's desperately checking the casualty lists. What started as an assumption—that Lincoln must have had a couple of sleepless nights—became an actual dream on a specific day: December 31, 1862. Royster then copied Oates, but gave the dream even more significance. Such dreams, according to Royster, "put Lincoln into combat" in ways that he could experience the terribleness of war almost as fully as the men he had called into action.[61] The myth of the dream, to borrow a turn of phrase from historian Joseph J. Ellis, grew "like ivy over a statue, effectively covering the man."[62]

WHY ARE SUCH specious dreams—particularly the White House funeral dream—so often included in the most widely read books about Lincoln? First, because they make for great stories. Americans want to read great stories about their greatest leaders—such as that John Adams and Thomas Jefferson both died on the fiftieth anniversary of the Declaration of Independence (which happens to be true). We are fascinated to *know* that one of our nation's most revered leaders envisioned his own assassination just days before it happened. The tragedy is gripping. It confirms America's providential place in history. And, as with any apocryphal story, it seems believable because it is in accord with Lincoln's life and character. But even more importantly, stories like these confirm the myths about Lincoln that Americans long to believe. In a sense, the fascination of American biographers and their readers with Lincoln's prophetic "dreams" may reveal more about Lincoln's admirers than about Lincoln himself.

Since his time on earth, Lincoln has been seen by many as a symbol of God's hand in American history. Some Americans, as we saw at the beginning of this chapter, dreamed about Lincoln's providential role in freeing the slaves as early as 1861. One Illinois Republican similarly declared at his state's Republican convention in 1864 that the "great man, old Abe Lincoln, is a special gift from God Almighty, and if we reject him in this Convention, we reject God Almighty." In his death, Lincoln almost universally assumed the status of a martyr. The timing of his death could not have been more prescient. Shot by John Wilkes Booth on Good Friday, he died the following morning. On Easter Sunday, Northern preachers seemed more preoccupied with Lincoln's death than with Christ's resurrection. A week later, Henry Ward Beecher declared at Plymouth Church in Brooklyn that Lincoln's name would be "an everlasting name in heaven" that "shall flourish in fragrance and beauty as long as men shall last upon the earth, or hearts remain, to revere truth, fidelity, and goodness."[63]

For some, Lincoln was elevated to the status of national deity—a Northern rejoinder to the Southern Lost Cause. In fact, Lincoln and dreams became a powerful component of what scholars call "the emancipationist" memory of the Civil War. Hezekiah Butterfield's 1884 poem, "Lincoln's Last Dream," celebrated Lincoln's triumphal entry into Richmond in April 1865 when "sable multitudes" rushed at him shouting "the name of 'Lincoln!'" In 1915, a black filmmaker, with the support of the NAACP, started work on a movie called *Lincoln's Dream* that was supposed to counteract the stereotypical depictions of African Americans in D. W. Griffith's racist blockbuster, *The Birth of a Nation*. In a model for a statue meant to commemorate Lincoln and emancipation, sculptor Harriet Hosmer placed a meditating figure of Lincoln above the words "God sent me a vision." The "vision" Hosmer concocted, as described by art historian Kirk Savage, featured "a seated 'African Sibyl,' dressed in a tiger skin, who twists up toward Lincoln while grasping an open book inscribed with Lincoln's words, 'If slavery is not wrong, nothing is wrong.' Clinging to the huge lower leg of this Michaelangelesque allegory of Africa is a nude black child with broken chains, who looks up toward the sibyl and Lincoln."[64] In order to perpetuate a particular understanding of Lincoln's role in history, the artist devised an actual vision from God—a dream, if you will—to guide the great statesman. Creating a providential dream could confirm Lincoln's status as a national martyr who had died in a holy cause. How fitting that in 1963, Martin Luther King Jr. would deliver his "I Have a Dream" speech in the shadow of the Great Emancipator.

In the years after the Civil War, communities throughout the country erected more than two hundred statues of Lincoln, while the nation built temples to his memory at his birthplace in Kentucky and in Washington, D.C. Lincoln's connection to divine providence would be renewed time and time again in public art, most often implicitly, but sometimes explicitly. Sculptor George Grey Barnard, for example, said that he pondered Lincoln's face for one hundred days and saw "the man of sorrows," alluding to an Old

Testament prophecy of Christ. "I sought the secret of this face in the marvelous constructive work of God," he wrote. When British playwright George Bernard Shaw saw Barnard's statue of Lincoln, he remarked that it was "the image of a saint."[65]

From the moment of his death, Americans began the process of myth-making about Lincoln, making him the nation's most exalted secular saint. When Secretary of War Edwin M. Stanton read the Gettysburg Address at a Republican rally in Pennsylvania in 1868, he declared triumphantly, "That is the voice of God speaking through the lips of Abraham Lincoln!" In a February 12, 1890, speech entitled, "Savior of the Nation," U.S. senator Shelby M. Cullom of Illinois praised the "great-hearted patriot, and martyr to the cause of union and liberty" who had been born on that day four score and one years before. "Never was a nobler man born of woman, and never throbbed a purer heart in human breast," Cullom declared. And "no man has ever existed on the American continent superior to Abraham Lincoln." Indeed, Lincoln "won immortality" when he "died with a martyr's crown of glory upon his brow." A senator from Iowa proclaimed in 1905 that Lincoln had been "transfigured" since his death (an allusion to Christ) into "some mysterious personality, in the hands of the higher Powers, with a supernatural commission to help and bless the human race." Finally, an Idaho senator declared at a monument dedication in Kentucky in 1911, "Sacred writers, had he lived in those days, would have placed him among their seers and prophets and invested him with the hidden powers of the mystic world. Antiquity would have clothed such a being with the attributes of deity. He was one of the moral and intellectual giants of the earth."[66]

Over time, the mythology surrounding Lincoln continued to grow. His lowly, humble, hardscrabble beginnings; his self-education; his diligence and hard work; his steadfast adherence to principle in the face of great adversity; his moral triumphs in freeing the slaves and restoring the Union; his martyrdom on Good Friday. All of these attributes are true. Yet somehow they have become larger than life; the whole has become greater than the sum of the parts. Lincoln has become the ideal national symbol—the perfect embodiment of the American Dream. "Lincoln the man was swallowed by the myth," write historians Harold Holzer, Gabor S. Boritt, and Mark E. Neely Jr., "a myth neither the passage of time nor the challenge of revisionist historians has been able to tarnish."[67]

Lincoln's prophetic dreams became an integral part of this process.[68] Indeed, accounts of his visions and dreams appeared in newspapers and books throughout the late nineteenth and early twentieth centuries. In 1892,

Lincoln's old friend from Illinois, Henry Clay Whitney, offered a positive interpretation of the ship on the water dream (which, it should be recalled, Lincoln believed portended "great news"). For Whitney, the dream foretold Lincoln's providential ascent into heaven. "His dream was consummated," wrote Whitney. "The storm-tossed vessel had reached 'a dark and indefinite shore;' and it was, indeed, 'Good news' to him, as would be manifest also to *us*, could we see with the eyes—could we discern with the wisdom—of Omniscience."[69]

Aging Civil War veterans also found solace and meaning for their own life experiences in their commander in chief's dreams of death. "Most dreams are of the earth," wrote one Illinois veteran in 1911, "in line with the current of our lives." But other dreams were "separate and apart; flashed upon the penumbra of our slumber world for a definite purpose." These "prophetic" dreams "savor of admonition, instruction, inspiration, or all together." The veteran conceded that "most men affect to laugh at them," but he firmly believed that deep down inside "all men believe—reticently and reluctantly perhaps, but they believe. No intelligent man questions the visions that crossed the disk of Abraham Lincoln's slumbers—that wonderful, startling portent of tremendous events." This aging veteran then reminisced about a dream he'd had ten years before the Civil War that portended that great and awful conflict. "I have forgotten a thousand of my idle dreams as completely as though they had never been," he wrote. "Not so this one—the token of a coming day!"[70] In a very real sense, the veracity of Lincoln's prophetic dreams lent credibility to his own.

"Lincoln the myth" is an important part of America's public memory. Within this context, it makes sense that Lincoln's portentous dreams have such wide appeal. For all that modern science and psychological theory have given us—for as rational as we believe ourselves to be—Americans in the twenty-first century want to believe that their dreams have significance and meaning, that something greater than themselves is superintending their lives, that fate is real, that ordinary human beings are capable of extraordinary greatness, and that their nation is the last best hope of earth. Americans who lived through the Civil War recorded and then communicated their dreams to one another as a coping mechanism for dealing with the deprivations and burdens of the war. In a very real way, this process helped enable the Civil War generation to sustain themselves and their nation through a long and bloody conflict. In the same way, the continued retelling of apocryphal stories is an essential part of our national identity. The stories have become part of who we are, and they affirm us as a nation.

It should come as no surprise, then, that the anonymous author of the 1880 article closed with the reflection that Lincoln's White House funeral dream was "one of the most impressive incidents connected with the tragedy which gave the nation its immortal martyr." Imagine that! A fictitious "dream"—a figment of an unknown writer's imagination—being put forth as one of the most significant incidents of the war years.

It was. And it remains so today because it affirms for us the greatness of one of our greatest leaders.

Epilogue

It Seems Like a Dream

"Thank God that I have lived to see this!" Abraham Lincoln remarked upon learning of the fall of Richmond in April 1865. "It seems to me that I have been dreaming a horrid dream for four years, and now the nightmare is gone. I want to see Richmond."[1]

The president seemed to be speaking for his entire army. "It seems like a dream that we are going to leave the field, and the past three years seem no less like a dream," wrote New England chaplain Joseph Hopkins Twichell when his term of service ended. "All its adventures and perils and grand events have a vague unreality attaching to them, as I try to recall the long months that have been made memorable to the country and the world, by them."[2] Other soldiers felt alike. "I cannot imagine that the war is over," wrote one New Yorker in April 1865. "It seems like a dream as I read the words of the general order that 'hostilities have ceased,' and that 'for us' Armies in the East, 'the war is ended.'"[3] Those who had languished in prisoner of war camps grasped the feeling even more acutely. "I could not take it all in," wrote one POW reflecting upon the moment he received his parole, "it seemed too much like a beautiful dream."[4]

But some southerners were unable to concede that the war was over and that they had lost. One Kentucky Confederate later wrote that news of Lee's surrender "came like midnight at midday. We never thought or dreamed of such a thing." At Appomattox Court House, Virginia, on April 9, 1865, one Confederate officer told Union general Joshua Lawrence Chamberlain, "You may forgive us but we won't be forgiven. There is a rancor in our hearts"—here the officer apparently flipped Chamberlain the middle finger—"which you little dream of. We hate you, sir." The gallant man from Maine quietly replied, "Oh, we don't mind much about dreams, nor about hate either. Those two lines of business are closed."[5]

But they weren't closed. Lincoln's assassination a few nights later shattered the North's joyous daydream and became the penultimate national nightmare. "It seems all a dream—a wild dream," wrote surgeon William Child of the Fifth New Hampshire Volunteers on April 14, 1865, shortly after leaving Ford's Theatre that tragic evening. "I cannot realize it though

I know I saw it only an hour since." Others who had not witnessed the devilish crime experienced feelings similar to Child's. "Though the capitol is so many hundred miles away," declared a Navy chaplain in a sermon, "the dread reality is as vivid to us as to them. . . . None of us can escape from its presence. It surrounds us every moment. . . . It haunts our very dreams; and when we awake to consciousness we hope sometimes that it may be only a dream."[6]

At least one American thought that his dreams might help lead to the capture of the assassin, John Wilkes Booth. On April 26, William Wadham of Cleveland wrote to Secretary of War Edwin M. Stanton telling him of a "singular" dream that he believed would reveal where Booth was hiding. "I Dreamed he was secreeted in a House in Washington in a Vault with an Iron Door," he wrote. The vault, according to Wadham, was hidden in the cellar, and the house stood to the northeast of the Capitol building. Above the front door of the house was a sign with the words "Rio. Phisco & Co." Wadham awoke from this dream, fell back asleep, and "had the same Dream again & [saw] the same words over the Door." He reminded Stanton that "in days of old God appeared to his Children in Dreams & Visions of the Night. I am a humble believer in Christ & a true friend to my Country and if it could be so that God would use me as an instrument in finding one of the Vilest of men I should be verry thankful if you should find him as I hope you will." Wadham told Stanton that he'd revealed this dream to his friends, and they had encouraged him to write to Washington about it.[7] (Unbeknownst to Wadham, Booth was discovered and killed the same day that he penned this letter—many miles south of Washington, D.C., in Virginia.)

The assassination of Lincoln caused Americans to reflect on the great changes that had taken place before their very eyes. For many, the language of "dreams" was the only way they could make sense of what had transpired. One Boston woman prayed, "Oh God! do let me wake from this night mare & find it all a dream."[8] Even some of Lincoln's political enemies reacted in similar ways. "It brought to mind Gray's 'Elegy,'" wrote Maria Lydig Daly, the partisan wife of a Democratic New York City judge, after watching Lincoln's funeral procession pass through her city. "How little did Lincoln dream of such an end when he used every possible engine of power and influence to secure his reelection, and how little did the friends of McClellan dream that they should ever have felt so much interest in him and so mourn his untimely and cruel death."[9] Former Confederate vice president Alexander Stephens had an even more heart-wrenching reaction upon learning of his old friend's murder. "Dreamed of home last night. O Dreams! Visions! Shadows of the brain! What are you?" he wrote from his prison cell. "My whole consciousness since I heard of President Lincoln's assassination, seems nothing but a horrid dream."[10]

In the immediate aftermath of the war, every aspect of the conflict seemed like it had been a dream rather than reality, from the ringing fire bells of secession down to the closing shots of the war. "The nation awoke from a dream of invincibility and easy triumph to find itself inextricably involved in a desperate and dubious struggle for life," wrote the irascible Horace Greeley in 1865, when describing the beginning of the conflict. Lincoln's private secretary John G. Nicolay explained the close of the war in similar terms: "The whole country seemed to awaken as from the trouble of a feverish dream, and once again men entered upon a conscious recognition of their proper relations to the Government."[11]

As the years went by, the fighting and battles of the war seemed increasingly distant and less real to those who had participated—"more like shadows" than a lived reality. "So many years have passed since the scenes were enacted which I shall try to recall, that, to the actors therein, they seem but dreams—airy structures in the deepest recesses of remembrance," stated one Union blockader in 1883. The former first lady of the Confederacy remembered the war in an almost identical way. In 1894, Varina Howell Davis recalled that living in the Confederate White House had seemed like a "troubled dream."[12]

Soldiers expected the war to remain with them in their dreams long after the guns ceased firing. After recounting some of the memorable horrors he had witnessed, Chaplain Twichell remarked, "Time would fail me to tell of all I have seen, but long after this war is over, if I live, my dreams will bring it back." Indeed, they did. Pvt. John Brown of the Fifteenth Pennsylvania Cavalry recalled years after the war a moment when he was holding on to two "spirited" horses while enduring hot enemy fire with "not even a tree" to protect him. "It was enough to demoralize a better man, or rather boy, than I was at that time," he wrote, noting, "I would rather be on the front line any time than hold horses just back of it. It gives some foundation for some very bad dreams all the rest of one's life."[13]

The trauma of war led to sleepless nights for many veterans in the postwar era. John A. Cundiff of the Ninety-Ninth Indiana Volunteers was haunted by his wartime experiences as he tried to adjust back to civilian life. Affidavits in his pension file revealed his erratic postwar behavior. "He has always claimed that the rebels had spies out to kill him," stated one affidavit. Cundiff "would take his gun and blanket and stay in the woods for days and nights at a time, and would leave the house at night and sleep in the fence corners." As the paranoia increased, Cundiff told one person that "two or three of his neighbors were rebels from the south . . . & that they were going to kill him but that he put his axe under his bed at night to defend himself."[14]

In his brilliant study, *Shook Over Hell: Post-Traumatic Stress, Vietnam, and the Civil War*, historian Eric T. Dean Jr. found a number of soldiers who suffered from postwar sleeplessness as a result of wartime trauma. Dean and other scholars have begun to examine whether Civil War soldiers experienced post-traumatic stress disorder (PTSD), but they have doubted that dreams could be used to determine whether Civil War soldiers experienced PTSD. In *Shook Over Hell*, Dean writes that "discussion or analysis of dreams is not common in Civil War materials."[15] In fact, soldiers talked a great deal about their dreams both during and after the war. But Dean is correct in this sense: postwar dreams of veterans are much harder to find. Once the war ended, soldiers stopped corresponding with loved ones, and descriptions of dreams resumed their place in unrecorded private conversations.

Some of the few postwar dreams of Civil War soldiers that do survive in the historical record give a rare glimpse into the psychological problems facing veterans. In 1866 and 1867, Pvt. Herman White of the Twenty-Second Massachusetts Volunteers, who had enlisted at sixteen years old and seen his brother die in battle, "dremp dreams of war & fighteing &c" and had his "sleep troubled by queer dreams."[16] A Maryland Unionist who saw very little action during his month in an emergency militia during the Gettysburg campaign, wrote in his diary in December 1864, "Slept well last night, but dreamed about being engaged in battles. I believe I have dreamed of something pertaining to fighting nearly every night this year."[17] Those two sentences comprise that soldier's entire explanation, but it is likely that his dreams were based on secondhand accounts of battle—or perhaps from subdued remorse for not fighting—since he faced no actual combat during his brief time in the service.

Nightmares of battle or of prison could be particularly disruptive for veterans who had survived the horrors of combat. Indeed, wartime experiences could make permanent impressions on the subconscious of a soldier. After surviving Andersonville and finally reaching home, Pvt. Wallace Woodford of the Sixteenth Connecticut would thrash his arms about in his sleep and dream that he was at Andersonville searching for food. Lt. Col. Newell Gleason of the Eighty-Seventh Indiana Volunteers began to lose his mind during the final year of the war. When he was finally admitted to an insane asylum ten years later, a physician noted that his sleep was "laborious" and "filled with dreams that seemed to make sleep exhaustive rather than refreshing."[18]

While touring several old battlefields in 1869, Massachusetts soldier Russell H. Conwell had similarly bad dreams. At Cold Harbor, he observed that many of the Union dead remained unburied. "Skeletons and ghosts haunt us in our dreams," he wrote, "and grinning skulls are all we can think of by day." At Fort Wagner, in Charleston, South Carolina, he observed skeletons washing up on the beach that "lay grinning upon the shore and filled us with sad sensations, which still haunt our dreams."[19] The veteran fiction writer Ambrose Bierce similarly suffered from "visions of the dead and dying" and "phantoms of that blood-stained period."[20] While many soldiers had pleasant dreams of home during the war, some had terrible nightmares of battle afterward.

Walt Whitman, who had served as a nurse in Washington, D.C., may also have been troubled by postwar nightmares. In a poem entitled "Old War Dreams," he wrote,

In midnight sleep of many a face of anguish,
Of the look at first of the mortally wounded, (of that indescribable look,)
Of the dead on their backs with arms extended wide,
    I dream, I dream, I dream.
Of scenes of Nature, fields and mountains,
Of skies so beauteous after a storm, and at night the moon so unearthly bright,
Shining sweetly, shining down, where we dig the trenches and gather the heaps,
    I dream, I dream, I dream.

Long have they pass'd, faces and trenches and fields,
Where through the carnage I moved with a callous composure, or away from the fallen,
Onward I sped at the time, but now of their forms at night,
    I dream, I dream, I dream.[21]

Some historians have focused on the disturbing nature of some soldiers' and civilians' wartime dreams. Charles Royster, for example, argues that dreams only increased the terribleness of the war for civilians. Writing in his prizewinning book *The Destructive War*, he says, "Dreams gave civilians sensations akin to those of soldiers: fright, rage, awe, gruesome suffering, watching events unfold apparently beyond control. Premonitions and intuitions of war or of war's episodes were ruled by violence, not by the mind to which the premonitions came. To imagine the end was not to fix the time of its coming. The last battle proved elusive; visions of death kept coming."[22] As we saw in chapter 7, however, Royster rooted this analysis partly in a fabricated dream about Murfreesboro that was attributed to Lincoln but that the president never actually had.

To be sure, some dreams caused civilians to feel pain and hurt over those they had loved and lost. "Last night I had such a strange troubled dream, that even the remembrance of it oppressed me when I awoke," wrote Lizzie Alsop of Fredericksburg in her diary in July 1865. She dreamed that she was "having a large party" in her parlor, and "in the midst of the laughing & talking, Col. [Stapleton] Crutchfield walked in"—a Confederate officer who had just recently died at the Battle of Sayler's Creek on April 6, 1865. He took her hand and she told him, "I am so glad you were not killed." But at that moment "the scene changed, and crowds of us were hurrying, hurrying on. I know not where—nor why—and again, it seemed that Col. Crutchfield & I were to be married, he so pale, so ghost-like, & all in black." The dream haunted Lizzie "all day" and she could not cast it from her mind.

Almost a year later, Lizzie again dreamed of the dead colonel. He "came and laid his hands upon my shoulders—& commenced talking—What he said I do not know, only that he looked into my eyes, and told me of his love." These dark visitation dreams bothered Lizzie. "Why is it I dream & think of him so often? Not because of any affection I bore him, but because of his early death & the sad associations connected with it, & with him, in his life. Yet who can tell 'what might have been.'"[23]

In like manner, Lincoln's private secretary John Hay had a melancholy dream of the war years shortly before his death in 1905. "I went to the White House to report to the President who turned out to be Mr. Lincoln," Hay wrote in his diary. "He was very kind and considerate, and sympathetic about my illness. He said there was little work of importance on hand. He gave me two unimportant letters to answer. I was pleased that this slight order was within my power to obey. I was not in the least surprised at Lincoln's presence in the White House. But the whole impression of the dream was one of overpowering melancholy."[24]

But not all postwar war dreams were unpleasant or discouraging. In 1872, less than a year before his own death, Lincoln's secretary of the Treasury,

Salmon P. Chase, had a "singular dream" in which Lincoln and Jefferson Davis had a "last battle." Davis was beaten and taken prisoner, but then Lincoln resigned his seat and Davis became president. The Union and Confederate Congresses then met and amended the Constitution to abolish slavery and grant suffrage to blacks; then Davis resigned and Lincoln was reelected. Lincoln then granted "Universal Amnesty" to the South and all southern congressmen were seated, leading to "general harmony & reconciliation."[25] The nation, in this dream, was finally restored and at peace—with black citizenship as well as the restoration of Confederates to their former place in the Union. Even more poignantly, such a dream seemed in line with Lincoln's vision of reunion.

Indeed, dreams often served a restorative function in the postwar years. The dreams that former Confederate vice president Alexander Stephens experienced in his prison cell at Fort Warren reveal the wide range of emotions and concerns facing the ex-Confederate leader in the immediate aftermath of the war. Some of Stephens's dreams exhibited his longing for his family. On July 17, 1865, he "dreamed of being at my sister Catherine's." It did not occur to Stephens's sleeping mind that Catherine had been dead for many years. "The dream was like my visits to her years ago, when most of her children were small. It was an exceedingly pleasant dream, notwithstanding I was weeping while talking to little Mollie in my lap. My tears were of pleasure, or at least, not of grief, when I woke. The time of my dream was when Mollie was about seven years old. She is grown." Upon waking and reflecting on this moving dream, Stephens was struck by how "far back on the dialplate of time" his "spirit [went] in its rovings."[26]

As we saw in chapter 3, Stephens had several dreams about the burning of Richmond, of people being hanged, and of his slaves, but not all of Stephens's dreams about wartime death and destruction unsettled him. On June 5, 1865, the former Confederate vice president dreamed that he was back home in Georgia when his little niece, Becky, ran into his room yelling, "The Yankees have come!" Stephens looked out the window and "saw them with guns," but, he wrote in his diary, "I was not discomforted, nor was the dream unpleasant. Becky did not seem frightened. I awoke. The vision was gone and I was laying on my bunk—far away from the scenes where my sleeping thoughts had roamed."[27]

During his imprisonment, Stephens thought often of his brother, Linton, who was a state judge back in Georgia. On August 21, Stephens remarked that he found it "strange" that he thought about Linton "more . . . than all other people and all other subjects combined, yet I have never once had a dream in which he figured prominently." Stephens occasionally dreamed of being at Linton's house, but they were in separate rooms and did not converse.[28] Clearly the waking Stephens longed to commune with his brother in his dreams, yet as a prisoner he felt so disconnected from him.

The next night Stephens had "a strange dream" of Linton. In the dream, Stephens was traveling on the front seat of a crowded omnibus. "I was expecting and looking for Linton," he wrote. "The consciousness of being a prisoner was in me, but what was the object of my movements or where I was going, did not seem to be in my mind. I had no idea about it." As the passengers were filling up the seats, he saw Linton standing about thirty yards in front of the bus. Linton "was greatly changed but I knew him. He looked tall and thin, taller and thinner, I thought, than I had ever seen him, and quite sunburnt, rather sallow than ruddy." And he was wearing the uniform of a Confederate colonel. Stephens was "delighted" to see his brother, but chided him for not coming sooner. Finally, when they were within earshot, Stephens simultaneously smiled and wept "as I bade him howdy." The vehicle kept moving, and before the brothers could greet each other, Stephens awoke. "For a long time I lay awake," he wrote in his diary. "This strange vision made upon my mind a deep and vivid impression which continues."[29]

A week later, Stephens again dreamed of his brother. This time "Linton seemed to be approaching my door hastily," he wrote in his diary. "I rose in great joy to meet him. As I seemed to rise, I awoke. It was a vision. He did not speak, nor did I. What to make of this, I do not know. I have not dreamed of talking with Linton since we parted at my gate. The whistle of the boat announces its arrival with the mail. May it bring me news of Linton if not Linton himself!"[30]

Stephens's dreams were very nearly prophetic. On September 1, Linton arrived at Fort Warren. Two weeks later, on September 15, Stephens told Linton about a presentiment that he'd had "that I should be released before long." Stephens was reluctant to reveal this to his brother, "for I thought he might consider it superstitious, and so it may be, but O my God, in Thy mercy make it true!" True, indeed, it became—although it took nearly another month. Finally, on October 12, Stephens was released from Fort Warren and began the long journey back to Georgia.[31]

The process of recording his prison dreams in his diary served several important functions for the former Confederate vice president. Perhaps most obviously, Stephens's dreams were a comfort and source of hope during his incarceration. Recording them allowed him to remember and reflect on happier times, and to visit with those he loved and longed to see. On occasion, his dreams reflected stress, anxiety and fear; yet his dreams more often served to point him toward a better future of reunion with those at home by bringing to mind the memories of those from his past.

Stephens knew that his relatives would one day read his diary. He wanted them to know that God had kept a providential and watchful eye over him during his time of tribulation. In this way his dreams could offer hope not only to Stephens but also to future, unknown readers. Of equal importance, Stephens's dream reports let his family and friends know that they had been his closest companions while he suffered a solitary existence in a Yankee bastille. They had been the instruments sent by God to sustain him. After dreaming of visiting with several loved ones on July 16, 1865, Stephens wrote, "It would be as impossible by language to convey an idea of the effect of this dream as it would be for me to reproduce in symbols strains of music which had just swept by, producing the sweetest harmony and the most soothing melody."

This metaphor was pregnant with meaning. Prison dreams were flashes of brilliance against a backdrop of desolation, conveying beauty and complexity, freedom and movement. They lifted a prisoner beyond the confines of the bars and chains that bound him, offering deliverance and psychological salvation. They were "the strains of a melody which had refreshed the spirit," Stephens wrote. Yet they were only a glimpse into a greater reality that the dreamer longed to see with his physical eyes. Like music in an era before recorded sound, they disappeared and could not be fully recreated by the dreamer, no matter how badly he might wish he could continue his dreams after waking.

As melody and harmony, dreams for Stephens were a mystic chord of memory, bringing together many notes into one glorious chorus. While he knew intellectually that his dreams were likely "nothing but the aberrations of my own mind," still, they seemed to be so much more: "special visitations; visitations of two kinds: social or every-day visits, and visits portending something that impress as presentiments."[32] Dreams, in other words, offered comfort in the present and hope for the future.

Veterans' dreams of war could also be hopeful, joyful, or romantic. Some soldiers relived their most glorious wartime experiences as they slept. In 1868, Confederate staff officer John Hampden Chamberlayne had several "death dreams," as he called them in a letter—not because they were frightening visions of his demise but because they involved comrades who had fallen in the war. "First I dreamed that I was again with Willy Pegram, in

Camp and march and battle—with him for days and with a strange sense, most indefinable but yet vivid, that I had lost him and found him again." On another night, he dreamed that he was sitting by a campfire in the Shenandoah Valley with "all I knew and loved in the army, Pegrams and Elletts, Cunningham and Crutchfield, Mann Page and John Reeve and Edmund Fontaine and many many others—whose names I need not repeat—and each one as I remembered him at his best, Willy Pegram as he was at Chancellorsville—Pelham and Fairfax as at Fredericksburg—A. P. Hill as when Harper's Ferry showed the white flag." Chamberlayne "thought twas the crisis of some great danger," but as each man arrived "to give his aid, we greeted, each other, with smiles and tears of joy—and always there was the same strange sense of reunion after deadly separation." He exulted in the feeling that "we were all again collected. And when the plans were laid, and all the orders given and received, me thought there was a pause, as before a great battle, and, while we whispered of old dangers we had shared together and rejoiced again to be comrades, the shade of [Stonewall] Jackson appeared, mounted, and in his faded old gray cap, with his look of melancholy abstraction gradually breaking up into the blaze that I saw once at Fredericksburg, as he recognized us, and the crisis in the coming struggle—He lifted his hand, and called out, forward." As Jackson barked this order, Chamberlayne's dream came to an abrupt end: "all vanished and I woke with a start and a great tremor; so lifelike was it, and so real and full of joy—I could scarcely believe, for a moment, but it was very truth." The dream remained "in my head" for the next two days at least, when he committed it to paper. He badly wished that the dream was a reality. "Would to God it were truth and I could follow those good and true and share their bivouac neath the flag, whether by Shenandoah or Potomac, James or Rappahannock."[33]

Chamberlayne's dream is tremendously significant. His mind was not filled with horrors of war, but with fond recollections of its most glorious and meaningful moments. He remembered each of his comrades "at his best"—not in anguish of death. And they "greeted each other, with smiles and tears of joy," feeling fondness in their "reunion," and rejoicing "again to be comrades." In 1867, Chamberlayne was penniless and had "suffered a complete physical and nervous breakdown."[34] But his dreams in 1868 were restorative. And it was happy memories of the war that his "death dreams" brought back to life.

Perhaps even more remarkably, some soldiers experienced a sort of physical restoration from battle wounds in their dreams. Col. Henry Shippen

Huidekoper of the 150th Pennsylvania Volunteers lost his right arm at Gettysburg on July 1, 1863. In the immediate aftermath of the amputation, he often inadvertently attempted to use his missing arm. "At home, I drove every day while regaining strength," he wrote. When a gust of wind would blow his straw hat off of his head, he would "involuntarily" attempt "to catch my hat with my right hand." Eventually these phantom feelings became less frequent (although he continued to feel his fingers in a partially clenched position), but his missing hand still came back to him in his dreams.

In 1906, Huidekoper wrote to S. Weir Mitchell, a Philadelphia physician who was conducting research on the neurological effects of amputations:

> I was 24 years old when I lost my arm, and am now 67. Almost two-thirds of my life has passed without thought of the possible use of my right arm, and yet never have I dreamed once, that I was not without two arms, and only last night I dreamt that I was holding a paper up with my two hands. When I ride, or drive, or cling to [a] limb on the trees, or write, in my dreams, I always have the use of both of my hands.... I write often in my dreams, but always with the right hand I used over forty years ago. To do this, I attempt to use the tendons which would hold and guide the pen, and this is done with so much fatigue ... that I suffer great pain in my finger tendons, even to wakening me up from the most profound sleep, because of the pain in the lost hand.

"Thus," he concluded, "in my dreams, I remain a man with a perfect frame, but while awake, I never think of myself otherwise than a one-handed being. And this after two-thirds, (and that of course the last two-thirds,) of my life had fully accustomed me to being with one hand only."[35]

This remarkable letter reveals several meaningful things about the dreams of aging Civil War veterans. Most notably, Huidekoper dreamed restorative dreams of a "perfect" body—one that he had not known for more than four decades. Despite the physical trauma he had experienced during the war, his dreams took him back to peaceful times. Equally significant, his dreams were of the mundane, not the frightful. He held a newspaper, rode in carriages or on horses, drove a plow, climbed a tree, and wrote things down with a pen (his letter, incidentally, was typed). All this, as he said, "after two-thirds ... of my life had fully accustomed me to being with one hand only." In his dreams, Huidekoper's body returned to a time before the war, when peace had reigned, and his body had been whole.

Note on Method

Several books have been published on dreams in the colonial and revolutionary eras. Two of these histories rely heavily on dreams that were reported in public speeches or were published by the dreamer. Using accounts of dreams in autobiographical narratives, Mechal Sobel argues in *Teach Me Dreams: The Search for Self in the Revolutionary Era* (2000) that dreams were a mechanism for achieving self-awareness, for refashioning images of oneself, and for dealing with threats. In like manner, in *Night Journeys: The Power of Dreams in Transatlantic Quaker Culture* (2004), Carla Gerona argues that Quakers from the mid-seventeenth century through the early nineteenth century saw dreams as powerful spiritual experiences that were useful for instructing and guiding society as well as for refashioning the Society of Friends.

Other books have relied on dreams that were not generally consumed by the public. In *Dreams and the Invisible World in Colonial New England: Indians, Colonists, and the Seventeenth Century* (2014), Ann Marie Plane shows how dreams and dream reporting helped shape the English colonial experience in New England, particularly as the colonists interacted with Indians, who had very different dream practices. Finally, in *Lincoln Dreamt He Died: The Midnight Visions of Remarkable Americans from Colonial Times to Freud* (2013), Andrew Burstein uses dreams to probe some of the ways that Americans from bygone eras were like or unlike twenty-first-century Americans (although, as I argue in chapter 7, Lincoln almost certainly did not dream that he died).

These books all offer unique insights into American history, from the colonial era through the nineteenth century; however, they also have their limitations. On occasion each of these authors attempts to interpret symbolism in dreams, which strikes me as beyond the historian's ken. Analyzing dreamers' interpretations of their own dreams is one thing, but to conclude that a white colonist likely wanted to have "a sinful sexual relationship with a black chattel servant" (says Sobel, and others concur) because he'd dreamed about a "black pott" in 1698 seems to stretch the bounds of credulity—especially since such analysis is rooted in a 1795 dream book that claim that "basins" represented "servant maids" in dreams.[1] Historians should be wary of accepting the interpretations of such dream manuals. Of one eighteenth-century dream book, Burstein rightly observes, "The level of absurdity is self-evident, and the genre hardly worth delving into at any length, other than to uncover examples of creative fraud."[2] Equally questionable is a historian who speculates that an evangelical woman who dreamed about an apple tree "longs for the fruit of the just nourished by the water of wisdom" simply because the woman would have been familiar with certain biblical passages about trees planted by streams of water.[3] The dreamers in these instances *may* have been thinking about trees of life or interracial sexual intercourse, but without stronger evidence historians should be hesitant to make such assertions. As noted in the preface, I have sought to avoid these sorts of judgments. In this book I only describe symbols in dreams in as much as the dreamers *believed* such symbols held certain meanings. I do not attribute any meaning to symbols for the simple reason that I do not believe that our dreams have universal (or even cultural) symbols.[4]

With a few important exceptions, I have also largely avoided dream reports that were published for public consumption. As the works by Sobel and Gerona ably demonstrate, such published dreams often served larger political purposes; they must, therefore, be read with some caution. Burstein also rightly points out that published dreams may have been "embellished in order to sell books."[5]

Most of the published dream reports in this study appear in the chapters on slaves and on dreams of death. Without published dreams, it would be impossible to find a large enough collection of slaves' dreams to analyze. I also use slaves' dreams from the entire antebellum period, not simply from the war years, for the same reason. I recognize that dreams in slave narratives are more likely to be embellished or fabricated than privately reported dreams since they served the public purpose of highlighting the evils of slavery; however, the similarities between published and unpublished dreams of slaves lend credibility to the published ones.

Deathbed dreams are also significant precisely because they were remembered, recorded and published in reminiscences and regimental histories years after the dreams took place. These dream reports may also have greater reliability than presumed. Although ostensibly published for public consumption, regimental histories and memoirs primarily served a private function for veterans. As historian Earl J. Hess notes, "above all else" the regimental historian and memoirist "wrote for himself and for his comrades."[6] These caveats aside, most of the dreams discussed in this book appear in the private correspondence and diaries of ordinary Americans because those dream reports reveal most genuinely the emotional states of mind and the deepest desires of soldiers and civilians at the time that the dreams took place.

Finally, all of these other books rely on very limited (although arguably adequate) source bases. Plane's book—which covers the "long seventeenth century"—consists of six topical chapters, each of which is "framed around a single dream text that embodies a central issue."[7] Gerona uses nearly three hundred dreams from Quakers in England from the 1640s to the early nineteenth century.[8] Sobel's research base for the period 1740 to 1840 consists of roughly two hundred published narratives, about half of which contain dream reports.[9] Burstein's book covers approximately two centuries and relies on 205 dreams.[10] Gerona, Sobel and Burstein thus provide about one dream per year; Plane utilizes significantly fewer, which is understandable considering the period she studies—and she fully acknowledges the limitations of her sample.

In all, I have unearthed more than four hundred dreams, nightmares, and presentiments from the Civil War era.[11] To be sure, this is a small sample when one considers that an ordinary individual has about five dreams per night—or 1,825 dreams per year.[12] Nevertheless, I believe my findings offer a reasonable snapshot of the sorts of dreams that ordinary Americans were having during the war. Easily discernible patterns emerged from a wide array of dreamers revealing a shared wartime experience for sleeping citizens and soldiers. In pointing out sample sizes, I do not necessarily mean to imply that "more is better." Nor do I wish to imply that these other scholars did not do due diligence—certainly more dreams will be available in the documentary record of the Civil War than from colonial or revolutionary America. But I do believe that having a larger sample for a shorter time period makes my conclusions less tentative than those of the other books.

I do not use the word "sample" in the foregoing paragraphs in a scientific sense; nor do I claim that the dreams I discuss in this book are necessarily representative of all the dreams of all the Americans who lived through the Civil War (that would be roughly 230 billion dreams I'd have to account for). This book is the result of several years of searching for dreams as diligently, as thoroughly, and as creatively as I knew how to do. Some readers might believe that nightmares and other bad dreams are underrepresented in the book, but, as I maintain at various points in the text, I believe that Civil War–era Americans were refreshingly candid and uncensored in their dream reporting, running counter to what we might expect from the Victorian era. As the preceding chapters reveal, spouses frequently divulged vivid and disturbing dreams to one another, seeking comfort or meaning from their faraway loved ones.[13] Indeed, they reported far more nightmares than I expected they would when I began this research.

Two other caveats should be addressed. First, other than in chapter 4, most of the dreams discussed in this book were dreamt by white Americans. For the sake of readability and flow, I generally do not specify the race of these dreamers ("Southerners," for example, refers to "white Southerners"). Second, there is a clinical distinction between bad dreams and nightmares. Bad dreams are often associated with interpersonal conflict, while nightmares are generally characterized by physical aggression or perceived threats. Nightmares also often lead the dreamer to wake up in great distress.[14] In this book, however, I sometimes interchange "bad dream" and "nightmare" in a colloquial sense since in most cases it would be difficult to determine with certainty that someone a century and a half ago had an actual nightmare.

LOOKING FOR DETAILED dream reports in personal writings is a bit like fishing— one faces long stretches of minimal activity that are punctuated by moments of great excitement. In searching for the dreams of ordinary Americans during the Civil War era, I relied heavily on published primary sources—in large part because I could more quickly find dream reports while more easily gaining a better sense of who the dreamers were and what they experienced during the war (by having access to entire collections along with the annotations and supplemental biographical information that is usually provided by editors).

My work was also furthered by the generosity of friends and scholars who sent me dreams they found while working on their own projects. These include Allen Guelzo and Pete Carmichael of Gettysburg College, Joan Cashin of the Ohio State University, Steve Knott of the U.S. Naval War College, Matt Gallman of the University of Florida, Michelle Krowl of the Library of Congress, Frances Pollard of the

Virginia Historical Society, Dick Sommers of the U.S. Military History Institute, Mike Gray of East Stroudsburg University, Sean Scott of the Indiana Academy at Ball State University, Anna Holloway of the National Park Service, Terry Alford of Northern Virginia Community College, Doug Wilson of Knox College, Nick Picerno of Bridgewater College, and especially Tim Orr of Old Dominion University.

Acknowledgments

First, I thank my wife, Lauren, for tolerating the many late nights I have worked on this project. When I started writing in May 2013, our newborn daughter, Charlotte, would lie next to me on the couch until 3 A.M. while Daddy worked and Mommy caught up on sleep. Now Charlotte is a big sister and I can no longer afford to stay up so late since I never know when I'll be greeted by Clara calling for us in the morning or Charlotte running into our room yelling, "Wake up, Daddy!"

I thank the scholars and friends mentioned in the Note on Method who generously pointed me toward a number of the dreams in this book. Christopher Newport University's interlibrary loan specialist, Jesse Spencer, tracked down many books, articles, manuscripts, and microfilm reels for me. My student research assistants, Erin Bello, Ben Coffman, Sarah Hopkins, Oliver Thomas, and Lizzy Wall, helped me locate several of the dreams discussed in this book; Daniel Glenn and Emily Risko assisted me with the page proofs and index. My mother-in-law, Leigh Kramer, read published collections of Civil War letters and diaries whenever she came to visit. I also thank my parents, Bill and Eileen White, for reading through almost everything I've written and for encouraging me to pursue my dream of becoming a historian.

Both the Department of Leadership and American Studies and Dean Bob Colvin of the College of Social Sciences at Christopher Newport University financially supported my research, as did the Office of the Provost through a Faculty Development Grant, which funded research in Philadelphia and Los Angeles. Throughout the past five years my department chair, Ben Redekop, has always managed to find extra resources to support my many research trips, for which I am very grateful. An Andrew W. Mellon Fellowship supported several trips to the Virginia Historical Society. And Harold Holzer sent me at least four score and seven books on Lincoln and the Civil War as he packed up his office at the Metropolitan Museum of Art, many of them proving timely additions to my library as I was completing this and other projects. Harold's generosity is unmatched, as he and Edith also send wonderful gifts for my children.

I thank Dana Shoaf, editor of *Civil War Times*; Clay Risen, editor of the *New York Times* "Disunion" blog; and the Abraham Lincoln Association for publishing earlier versions of this research.

Tore Nielsen of the University of Montreal and Deidre Barrett of Harvard University helped me understand the latest in sleep research. My colleague at CNU, Jason Hart, discussed recent scholarship in psychology with me and pointed me toward several helpful books and articles.

Finally, I am grateful to the friends and colleagues who read portions of the manuscript and offered suggestions for improvements. My undergraduate mentor, Mark

Neely of Penn State, read the entire manuscript, some chapters twice; Michael Burlingame of the University of Illinois at Springfield, Harold Holzer of Hunter College, Mike Parrish of Baylor University, and my CNU colleagues Liz Busch, Dustin Gish, Nathan Harter, Matthew Mendham, and Carl Scott all read chapter 7; Mark Schantz of Birmingham-Southern University read chapter 5; Christian McWhirter of the Papers of Abraham Lincoln read chapter 6; Tim Orr of Old Dominion University read chapters 1 and 2; Richard Boles of Oklahoma State University read chapter 4; Joan Cashin of Ohio State University and Judy Giesberg of Villanova University read chapter 3; Matt Gallman of the University of Florida read the preface (twice) and chapters 2 and 7; Mike Gray of East Stroudsburg University read a chapter on POWs that has since been dissolved and incorporated into several places in the book; Sean Scott of the Indiana Academy at Ball State University read chapters 4, 5, and 7; and LeeAnn Whites of the Filson Historical Society and Frances M. Clarke of the University of Sydney both offered helpful feedback on a conference paper I delivered at the Society of Civil War Historians meeting in June 2016. Pete Carmichael, the peer reviewers for UNC Press, and Mark Simpson-Vos offered expert feedback on the entire manuscript. All were extraordinarily generous with their comments, suggestions, and time.

Notes

Abbreviations

ALPLM	Abraham Lincoln Presidential Library and Museum, Springfield, Ill.
Court-martial case files	General Court-Martial Case Files, Record Group 153, Records of the Office of the Judge Advocate General (Army), National Archives and Records Administration, Washington, D.C. (Each case file includes an alpha-numeric case number.)
CP	The College of Physicians, Philadelphia, Pa.
CWL	Roy P. Basler et al., eds., *The Collected Works of Abraham Lincoln.* 9 vols. New Brunswick, N.J.: Rutgers University Press, 1953–1955.
CWM	College of William and Mary, Williamsburg, Va.
DU	Duke University, Durham, N.C.
FSA	Florida State Archives, Tallahassee, Fla.
GLI	Gilder Lehrman Institute of American History, New York, N.Y.
HL	Huntington Library, San Marino, Calif.
HSP	Historical Society of Pennsylvania, Philadelphia, Pa.
LC	Manuscript Division, Library of Congress, Washington, D.C.
LFFC	Lincoln Financial Foundation Collection, Allen County Public Library, Fort Wayne, Ind.
LV	Library of Virginia, Richmond, Va.
MDIHS	Mount Desert Island Historical Society, Mount Desert, Me.
MHI	U.S. Army Military History Institute, Carlisle, Pa.
NARA	National Archives and Records Administration, Washington, D.C.
NYHS	New-York Historical Society, New York, N.Y.
SCHS	South Carolina Historical Society, Charleston, S.C.
SHC	Southern Historical Collection, University of North Carolina, Chapel Hill, N.C.
TMM	The Mariners' Museum, Newport News, Va.
UAK	University of Arkansas, Fayetteville, Ark.
UIL	University of Iowa Libraries, Iowa City, Ia.
ULP	Union League of Philadelphia
UNH	University of New Hampshire, Durham, N.H.
UP	University of Pennsylvania, Philadelphia
UWM	University of Wisconsin-Milwaukee, Milwaukee, Wisc.
VHS	Virginia Historical Society, Richmond, Va.
W&L	Washington & Lee University, Lexington, Va.
WHS	Wisconsin Historical Society, Madison, Wisc.

| WML | Wood Memorial Library, South Windsor, Conn. |
| WPA | Works Progress Administration Slave Narratives, Library of Congress, Washington, D.C. |

Preface

1. Tappan, *Russell M. Tuttle*, 90; George Templeton Strong, diary entry for July 15, 1861, in Nevins and Thomas, *Diary of George Templeton Strong*, 3:164.

2. Clifford, *Mine Eyes Have Seen the Glory*, 142–44; Howe, "Reminiscences of Julia Ward Howe," 707; Howe, lecture at Detroit (1871), quoted in "Battle Hymn of the Republic" (1885), 88; "Battle Hymn of the Republic" (1862), 145.

3. See Stauffer and Soskis, *Battle Hymn of the Republic*; McWhirter, *Battle Hymns*. On creativity in dreams, see Barrett, "Creative Problem Solving in Dreams," in Barrett and McNamara, *Encyclopedia*, 1:182–86.

4. Plane, *Dreams and the Invisible World*, 156; Hall, *Worlds of Wonder*, chap. 2; Sobel, *Teach Me Dreams*, 3–4; Fischer, *Albion's Seed*, 519.

5. Plane, *Dreams and the Invisible World*, 71–72; Wilmer, "The Healing Nightmare," in Barrett, *Trauma and Dreams*, 86.

6. Antebellum America was a culture steeped in discussion of dreams. In one history of Southern evangelical women in the nineteenth century, 60 percent of the women studied recorded their dreams in their diaries. Friedman, *Enclosed Garden*, xiv. A search for dreams in fiction published between 1830 and 1865 in the Wright American Fiction database had 1561 hits. For an assessment of pre-Freudian dream beliefs in America, see Vande Kemp, "Dream in Periodical Literature," 88–115.

7. East, *Sarah Morgan*, 525; Simon, *Personal Memoirs of Julia Dent Grant*, 49–50.

8. See, for example, Ramold, *Across the Divide*; Jordan, *Marching Home*, chap. 2. Jordan's research is original and pathbreaking, but I don't believe the experiences of the veterans he describes necessarily represent those of most Union soldiers. Ramold's thesis, by contrast, is largely derivative of earlier historians, including Linderman, *Embattled Courage*, and Mitchell, *Civil War Soldiers*, chap. 3.

9. Mary Watkins to Richard Watkins, September 24, 1862, in Toalson, *Send Me a Pair of Old Boots*, 136.

10. See, for example, Allen and Bohannon, *Campaigning with "Old Stonewall,"* 130. Sweet dreams could have similar effects. See Ray, "Civil War Letters," 222.

11. Blanche Butler to mother, December 14, 1862, in Ames, *Chronicles from the Nineteenth Century*, 1:87; Emily S. Harris to Leander Harris, December 14, 1862, Harris Collection, UNH.

12. Miller, *"Punishment on the Nation,"* 15; Alexander Wallace Givens Diary (1862), ULP.

13. Crist et al., *Papers of Jefferson Davis*, 8:199.

14. Gallman, *Mastering Wartime*, 79.

15. Skipper and Taylor, *Handful of Providence*, 80–82, 180.

16. George W. Clark to sister, June 4, 1863, Clark Collection, GLI.

17. On spiritualism in the nineteenth century, see Taves, *Fits, Trances, and Visions*, 168–206; Faust, *This Republic of Suffering*, 180–85.

18. Richards, *Village Life in America*, 108; Barnum, *Humbugs of the World*, 295. See also Baer, *Shadows on My Heart*, 134.

19. Cooney, *Common Soldier, Uncommon War*, 1–2; Mannis and Wilson, *Bound to Be a Soldier*, 33. See also Linderman, *Embattled Courage*, 120.

20. Lowry, *Swamp Doctor*, 46; Martin and Snow, *"I Am Now a Soldier,"* 41; Scott, *Visitation of God*, 39–40, 55, 105–6, 144–45, 151–52; Knight, *Letters to Anna*, 117.

21. Quoted in Ferguson, "Furnace of Dreams," 37. On exhaustion of horses, see Gerleman, "Unchronicled Heroes," 68–69, 175–86, 195–97, 201–11, 252–54, 267–69, 308–13.

22. Porter, *Campaigning with Grant*, 54–55.

23. Larimer, *Love and Valor*, 166–67.

24. Rawlings, *Christmas Day*, 59–61, 90–92.

25. Greeley to Lincoln, July 29, 1861, Lincoln Papers, LC.

26. Cumming, *Journal of Hospital Life*, 196. See also Andrews, *North Reports*, 377, 548.

27. For critiques of dream content analysis and dream interpretation, see Lilienfeld et al., *50 Great Myths*, 104–8; Hobson, *Dreaming*. For criticism of several forms of psychological testing that could also be applied to dream interpretation, see Lilienfeld, "What's Wrong with This Picture?" 80–87.
For a helpful survey of how historians have written about dreams, see Gerona, *Night Journeys*, 15–21.

28. See, for example, Joanne Pope Melish's review of Sobel's *Teach Me Dreams* in the *Journal of the Early Republic*.

29. Thoreau, *Week on the Concord and Merrimack Rivers*, 314; Burstein, *Lincoln Dreamt He Died*, 170–71.

30. Reardon, *With a Sword in One Hand*, 108–9. Reardon offers an excellent discussion of combat stressors, 104–22.

31. Court-martial case files LL-826, LL-1066, and NN-880. Thomas P. Lowry tells me that some 323 cases of soldiers falling asleep involved alcohol. It may be that some of these were falsely accused of drunkenness. Soldiers were sometimes accused of drunkenness during battles when they may have in fact simply been exhausted. See, for example, Adams, *Living Hell*, 53–54; Rhea, *Spotsylvania Court House*, 165.

32. Rable, *Fredericksburg! Fredericksburg!*, 218–19.

33. Nicholson, "Strange but True."

34. Jackman, *Sixth New Hampshire*, 252–53.

35. The soldier's recollection of this experience replicates exactly what scientists are discovering in sleep labs today. See Nielsen, "Partial REM-Sleep Deprivation," 1083–89.

36. For a detailed discussion of how the Overland Campaign differed from previous campaigns of the war, see Reardon, *With a Sword in One Hand*, chap. 3.

37. Although not discussed at great length in this book, it should be noted that many civilians also faced extreme sleep deprivation during the war. Many Southern whites, for example, had lost significant sleep since the antebellum period due to fears of slave insurrection; such sleepless nights only increased when Union armies invaded the Confederacy during the war. Slaves lost significant amounts of sleep for a number

of reasons as well, including working at night to earn extra money as well as night-time flights toward the North Star.

38. Skipper and Taylor, *Handful of Providence*, 179; Johansson, *Widows by the Thousand*, 51; Andrews, *North Reports*, 476.

39. Burstein concludes, "Dreams conform to cultural expectations." See Burstein, *Lincoln Dreamt He Died*, 267.

40. Linderman, *Embattled Courage*, 240.

41. In contrast to the prevalent modern view that the war emotionally destroyed many soldiers, I find Walt Whitman's understanding of the common soldier much more compelling. Despite all of the awful suffering he witnessed in army hospitals and in the field, Whitman concluded that "the bulk of the average American People" was "animated in Soul by a definite purpose, though sweeping and fluid as some great storm—the Common People, emblemised in thousands of specimens of first-class Heroism, steadily accumulating." These sorts of men, Whitman said, were in every regiment, company, and file of men. See Whitman, *Memoranda During the War*, 4. Of course, heroism alone cannot explain the emotional and psychological strength of so many Civil War soldiers. A combination of other factors, including Americans' understandings of death in the antebellum era, religion, patriotism, their experiences with violence in both urban and rural life, nineteenth-century conceptions of courage and manliness, fear of Indian attacks during westward migration in the antebellum era, and the development of small-unit cohesion also all contributed to soldiers' emotional stability during the war. On these points, see McPherson, *For Cause and Comrades*; Schantz, *Awaiting the Heavenly Country*; Hess, *Union Soldier in Battle*, chaps. 5–6; Gallman, *Mastering Wartime*, 80–81; Foote, *Gentlemen and the Roughs*; Grimsted, *American Mobbing*; Gorn, "Gouge and Bite"; Lane, *Violent Death in the City*.

42. There almost seems to be a common perception among modern Americans that most soldiers return from war with PTSD; historians, too, may be reading too much of the diagnosis into the past. Victims of rape suffer from PTSD at a much higher rate (45.9 percent) than veterans. One study of Vietnam veterans conducted in 1983 found that 31 percent of the veterans had suffered from PTSD at some point in their lives, while 15.4 percent had "diagnosable PTSD" at the time they participated in the study. It is important to note that veterans with different war experiences and life backgrounds suffer from PTSD at far different rates. For example, 85 percent of American POWs held by the Japanese during World War II developed PTSD, whereas only 4 percent of the longtime captives at the Hanoi Hilton suffered from it. See Morris, *Evil Hours*, 42–50, 135, 157.

43. David J. Morris offers a helpful discussion of why people with differing backgrounds react to trauma in different ways. See ibid., 43–50.

44. Most of this book deals with wartime dreams and nightmares; in the epilogue I discuss several postwar dreams. Most of the modern research on PTSD nightmares looks at experiences after the veteran's term of service, which is an important difference from the focus of this book.

At the Society of Civil War Historians meeting in June 2016, historian Frances M. Clarke astutely cautioned historians against "imposing modern categories—especially PTSD—back onto the past." PTSD may eventually be discarded as a diagnosis, she points out, since, like some nineteenth-century diagnoses, it lacks "internal consistency, acting as a king of grab bag for symptoms . . . and thus a diagnosis that explains more about the society that invented it than about the experiences of those suffering from this alleged condition." She continues, "In the modern era, in other words, our diagnoses are no more stable than were those in the past, partly because the way we understand the workings of the human mind has changed considerably and will continue to do so."

45. Morris, *Evil Hours*, 128. I have been unable to find any systematic study of the content of American soldiers' dreams during their time at the front during any war. Studies of trauma and dreams in other cultures have found that war and totalitarianism had significant impacts on people's dreams as they experienced the trauma. A history of dissidents' dreams in Stalin's Soviet Union, for example, found that terror penetrated and influenced the innermost emotional spaces of those who suffered— even their dreams. See Irina, *Stories of the Soviet Experience*, 161–208. In the dreams of Germans from 1933 to 1939 that are cataloged in Beradt's *Third Reich of Dreams,* we see "the dreamer's anxiety, his helplessness, and the near absence of any wish to fight back" (quotation from the afterword by Bruno Bettelheim on 154–55). Beradt excluded violent dreams from her study.

46. McPherson, *For Cause and Comrades*, 43; Adams, *Living Hell*, 124; Hess, *Union Soldier in Battle*, 29.

47. Burstein found a similar paucity of nightmares among soldiers' reported dreams. See Burstein, *Lincoln Dreamt He Died*, 225.

48. Gerona, *Night Journeys*, 181–86, 189–93, 197–98.

Chapter One

1. White, *Diary of Wyman S. White*, 63–68. White's combined military service record at NARA does not indicate the dates of his injury or incarceration.

White's experience may not have been unique. One infantryman from Maine wrote caustically that enlisted men had to "sit up on guard [all night] so our officers won't have any nightmares." See Silliker, *Rebel Yell*, 245.

2. Blomquist and Taylor, *This Cruel War*, 254. Some pickets devised plans to get rest throughout the night, such as taking turns with their fellow pickets resting and staying awake. See, for example, Tappan, *Russell M. Tuttle*, 49. Thomas Wentworth Higginson maintained that black soldiers "make the very best sentinels I ever saw." While white soldiers saw picket duty "as a sort of play time" black soldiers realized it was "a serious matter. They will hardly even sleep in the daytime when posted at picquet stations," he wrote. See Looby, *Thomas Wentworth Higginson*, 131, 140.

3. Glover, *Sleeping Sentinel*, 27. For other soldiers' discussion of the discomfort of sleeping while on picket, see Blight, *When This Cruel War Is Over*, 135, 153–55; Silliker, *Rebel Yell*, 185.

4. Glover, *Sleeping Sentinel*, 14–22; Coffin, *Full Duty*, 85–90. On soldiers and politics, see Jonathan W. White, *Emancipation*.

5. Crist et al., *Papers of Jefferson Davis*, 8:81–82.

6. Sherman to Lorenzo Thomas, August 4, 1862, court-martial case file MM-567.

7. Lowry, *Don't Shoot That Boy*, 244; Lowry, *Merciful Lincoln*, 146, 207–8.

8. Charles Harvey Brewster to Mary, September 11, 1861, in Blight, *When This Cruel War Is Over*, 37. On the shame of being caught asleep at one's post, see Rattenbury, *From Wisconsin to the Sea*, 71–72.

9. Linderman, *Embattled Courage*, 55; Hinman, *Sherman Brigade*, 229.

10. Reardon, *With a Sword in One Hand*, 91–93, 110–12. There were some exceptions. Citizen-soldiers, like Col. Alvin C. Voris of the Sixty-Seventh Ohio Volunteers, by contrast, lamented having to order fatigued men. "O! wife, I do hate to drive tired men," he wrote. Quoted in Ramold, *Baring the Iron Hand*, 50. Jonathan Letterman, medical director for the Army of the Potomac, also tried to encourage soldiers to sleep on pine boughs to improve the quality of their sleep. See Meier, *Nature's Civil War*, 86–87.

11. Brewster to Mary, December 31, 1862, in Blight, *When This Cruel War Is Over*, 208.

12. Bonner, *Soldier's Pen*, 101. For another instance like this, see Scott, *Visitation of God*, 94.

13. Blomquist and Taylor, *This Cruel War*, 230. For a soldier who had an almost identical dream as one of his children at nearly the same time, see Mary Burnham to Erastus Burnham, December 12, 1864, Wood Memorial Library.

14. Rawlings, *Christmas Day*, 69.

15. Quoted in Berry, *All That Makes a Man*, 6. See also Kimmel and Musick, *"I Am Busy Drawing Pictures,"* 132, 137.

16. Tillman Valentine to Annie Valentine, December 26, 1863, in White, Fisher, and Wall, "Tillman Valentine," 181. See also Tappan, *Russell M. Tuttle*, 149.

17. Larimer, *Love and Valor*, 62–64. Women also wondered what their menfolk were doing as they lay down to sleep. See, for example, Diamond and Hattaway, *Forest Place*, 238.

18. Meier, *Nature's Civil War*, 104–6; Bonner, *Soldier's Pen*, 64, 114.

19. Looby, *Thomas Wentworth Higginson*, 111.

20. Messent and Courtney, *Joseph Hopkins Twichell*, 47, 50.

21. Lowry, *Swamp Doctor*, 41.

22. See, for example, Stewart, *Pair of Blankets*, which tells the story of a Confederate soldier who recovered blankets from the wreck of the USS *Cumberland* in 1862, used them for the duration of the war, and still had them hanging on his wall when he wrote his memoir nearly fifty years later.

23. Bennett and Haigh, *Thirty-Sixth Illinois*, 19–20.

24. Macsherry, *Pastime*, 117.

25. Johansson, *Widows by the Thousand*, 4.

26. Bond and Coward, *South Carolinians*, 95–96.

27. Quoted in Dean, *Shook Over Hell*, 80. A Confederate nurse similarly drank "a glass of cider" after "tossing about for two hours or more unable to sleep or rest" and almost immediately "fell into a delightful sleep." See Berlin, *Confederate Nurse*, 147–48. See also Meier, *Nature's Civil War*, 63.

28. Looby, *Thomas Wentworth Higginson*, 105.

29. Quoted in Dobak, *Freedom by the Sword*, 331; Preston, "British Military Observer," 57; McCalmont, *Extracts from Letters*, 49; Beck, "Letters of a Civil War Surgeon," 143. See also Robertson, "Indiana Soldier in Love and War," 257. On premodern darkness, see Bogard, *The End of Night*.

30. Bryan and Lankford, *Eye of the Storm*, 82, 149, 166, 206; Macsherry, *Pastime*, 152; Martin and Snow, "*I Am Now a Soldier*," 72; Hallock, *Joshua K. Callaway*, 52; Daly, *Aboard the USS Florida*, 34.

31. Billings, *Hardtack and Coffee*, 51–54.

32. Macsherry, *Pastime*, 118; Lowry, *Swamp Doctor*, 51; Wiley, *Life of Billy Yank*, 56.

33. Bonner, *Soldier's Pen*, 65–66. For a Confederate soldier's description of building winter quarters, see Evans, *16th Mississippi Infantry*, 53–54.

34. Messent and Courtney, *Joseph Hopkins Twichell*, 184, 189–90, 212.

35. Daly, *Aboard the USS Monitor*, 229.

36. Boney, *Land of the Vanquished*, 12.

37. Ferguson, *Land of Lincoln*, 128–29.

38. Messent and Courtney, *Joseph Hopkins Twichell*, 135; Henry H. Bennett, diary entry for January 14, 1863, H. H. Bennett Papers (MSS 935), Wisconsin Historical Society. Such poor sleeping conditions often led to illness among the soldiers, especially among new recruits. See Meier, *Nature's Civil War*, 47, 123–24.

39. Wynne and Taylor, *This War So Horrible*, 47. See also Tappan, *Russell M. Tuttle*, 112.

40. Wynne and Taylor, *This War So Horrible*, 61–62.

41. Bonner, *Soldier's Pen*, 100; Brewster to mother, May 31, 1862, in Blight, *When This Cruel War Is Over*, 141; Bennett and Haigh, *Thirty-Sixth Illinois*, 32; Lowry, *Swamp Doctor*, 31.

42. Blight, *When This Cruel War Is Over*, 84, 111, 138; Wilkinson and Woodworth, *Scythe of Fire*, 208; Poremba, *If I Am Found Dead*, 156.

43. Charles C. Perkins, diary entry for December 17, 1862, Perkins Diaries, MHI; Joseph A. Buckley to parents, November 9, 1862, in Henn, *Pike County*, 13.

44. Sawyer, Sawyer, and Sawyer, *Letters from a Civil War Surgeon*, 91.

45. Sears, *For Country, Cause & Leader*, 140–41. Remarkably, this soldier concluded, "I got through however & feel none the worse to day."

46. Little, *Seventh New Hampshire*, 11–12.

47. Wilkinson and Woodworth, *Scythe of Fire*, 136; Zettler, *War Stories*, 90–91.

48. Fain, *Sanctified Trial*, 34–35, 144, 292. Some soldiers were unwilling to sleep in private homes for fear that they would be discovered and captured. See ibid., 210, 239. In other cases, southern women felt unsafe after permitting Confederate soldiers to sleep in their homes. See Nelson and Sheriff, *People at War*, 272.

49. Anderson, "War Record," VHS.

50. Lowry, *Swamp Doctor*, 98–99. Abolitionist officer Thomas Wentworth Higginson was kept awake one night in March 1864 by a "furious wind." See Looby, *Thomas Wentworth Higginson*, 1.

51. Adelbert Ames to parents, January 21, 1862, in Ames, *Chronicles from the Nineteenth Century*, 1:6.

52. Merrill, "Men, Monotony, and Mouldy Beans," 51. For a Maine soldier whose sleep and dreams were disturbed by rats, mice, and bedbugs, see Jordan, *John Mead Gould*, 165, 463, 521.

53. Tatum, "Please Send Stamps," 217.

54. Larimer, *Love and Valor*, 63. See also Meier, *Nature's Civil War*, 57–58.

55. James M. Parker to sister, August 10, 1862, and December 13, 1864, James M. Parker Papers, MDIHS; McGee, *72d Indiana Volunteer Infantry*, 209–10, Meier, *Nature's Civil War*, 55; Poremba, *If I Am Found Dead*, 194.

56. Chesson, *Civil War Surgeon*, 133; Tappan, *Russell M. Tuttle*, 109; Ramold, *Baring the Iron Hand*, 70; Jones, *Tennessee in the Civil War*, 147–48; Lowry, *Tarnished Eagles*, 37. On snoring, see Looby, *Thomas Wentworth Higginson*, 236; Macsherry, *Pastime*, 129.

57. Pension file for Owen Flaherty, NARA. I first encountered this case in Dean, *Shook Over Hell*, 1–3.

58. Henry Inch Cowan to father and mother, October 5, 1864, Cowan Letters, UP.

59. Chesson, *Civil War Surgeon*, 18–19, 45; Meier, *Nature's Civil War*, 167n89.

60. Macsherry, *Pastime*, 117.

61. Blight, *When This Cruel War Is Over*, 114, 312, 315; Wiley, *Billy Yank*, 85–86.

62. Messent and Courtney, *Joseph Hopkins Twichell*, 121–22; John White Geary to wife, May 5, 1862, in Blair, *Politician Goes to War*, 42; Swank, *Confederate Letters*, 23; Wynne and Taylor, *This War So Horrible*, 68–69; Dean, *Shook Over Hell*, 64–65, 93; Sherman, *Memoirs*, 2:108.

63. Davis, *Camp-Fire Chats*, 293.

64. Blight, *When This Cruel War Is Over*, 224; Baker, *Confederate Guerilla*, 16; Hess, *Union Soldier in Battle*, 1, 22, 32–33.

65. Post, *Soldiers' Letters*, 172–73.

66. Chamberlain, *"Bayonet! Forward,"* 7–9. See also Dean, *Shook Over Hell*, 74. Soldiers regularly slept among the dead, sometimes even purposefully using them as pillows. See Hughes, *Philip Daingerfield Stephenson*, 59; Cockrell and Ballard, *Mississippi Rebel*, 261. Some soldiers found the aftermath of battle and ideal time to sleep. See, for example, Hartwig, "1st Minnesota Infantry," 43.

67. Broadhead, *Lady of Gettysburg*, 20; Smith, *Seventh Iowa*, 273; Rausch, "Civil War Medicine," 47.

68. Rausch, "Civil War Medicine," 47–48.

69. Bennett and Haigh, *Thirty-Sixth Illinois*, 288–89.

70. Tappan, *Russell M. Tuttle*, 18; Chesson, *Civil War Surgeon*, 25–26, 28; Crow and Barden, *Live Your Own Life*, 162; Bonner, *Soldier's Pen*, 91, 105, 174; Poremba, *If I Am Found Dead*, 194; Chesson, *Civil War Surgeon*, 124; Messent and Courtney, *Joseph Hopkins Twichell*, 245; Dean, *Shook Over Hell*, 47; Gerleman, "Unchronicled Heroes," 146–47. Some soldiers believed that sleeping on days of leisure was equivalent to throwing away free time. See Wells, *Civil War Time*, 61.

71. Fain, *Sanctified Trial*, 78; Meier, *Nature's Civil War*, 128–35; Hess, *Union Soldier in Battle*, 84–86; Barber and Swinson, *Charles Barber*, 147; Larimer, *Love and Valor*, 342; Messent and Courtney, *Joseph Hopkins Twichell*, 52; Poremba, *If I Am Found Dead*, 170; Guelzo, *Gettysburg*, 336. Some wounded men were so worn down that they fell asleep while being treated in a hospital. See Berlin, *Confederate Nurse*, 103.

72. Dean, *Shook Over Hell*, 48; Jackman, *Sixth New Hampshire*, 245, 252–53; Reardon, *With a Sword in One Hand*, 115.

73. Wilkinson and Woodworth, *Scythe of Fire*, 55; Zettler, *War Stories*, 53–54.

74. Macsherry, *Pastime*, 119.

75. Cincinnati *Western Christian Advocate*, January 1, 1862; Martin and Snow, *I Am Now a Soldier*, 14; Snell, *Dancing Along the Deadline*, 66–69; Gray, *Business of Captivity*, 62–63.

76. Pinsker, *Lincoln's Sanctuary*, 84–87; Johnson, "Did Abraham Lincoln Sleep with His Bodyguard?" For recollections of Lincoln's sleep habits, see Wilson and Davis, *Herndon's Informants*, 255, 331. After receiving bad news one night in 1863, Lincoln once allegedly remarked, "How willingly would I exchange places today with the soldier who sleeps on the ground in the Army of the Potomac." See Fehrenbacher and Fehrenbacher, *Recollected Words*, 113.

77. Lowry, *Swamp Doctor*, 80–82.

78. Anderson, "War Record."

79. Chesson, *Civil War Surgeon*, 160.

80. Messent and Courtney, *Joseph Hopkins Twichell*, 255.

81. Sneden, diary entry for April 4, 1862, in Bryan and Lankford, *Eye of the Storm*, 39.

82. Geary to wife, May 5, 1862, in Blair, *Politician Goes to War*, 42.

83. Smith, *Listening to Nineteenth-Century America*, 211; Chesson, *Civil War Surgeon*, 188. See also Jordan, *Marching Home*, 20–22. Other soldiers enjoyed resuming antebellum sleep patterns after the war. See, for example, Kallgren, *Abial and Anna*, 11.

84. Jane Thompson to William Thompson, September 7, 1862, in Riley, "Civil War Wife, Part I," 221–22.

85. Blight, *When This Cruel War Is Over*, 25, 135; Messent and Courtney, *Joseph Hopkins Twichell*, 25; Poremba, *If I Am Found Dead*, 140; Hughes, *Philip Daingerfield Stephenson*, 144; Silliker, *Rebel Yell*, 41. See also Lee, *Dear Isa, Dear Johna*, 23.

86. Fain, *Sanctified Trial*, 34; Jane Thompson to William Thompson, October 23, 1862, in Riley, "Civil War Wife, Part II," 304. See also Gwin, *Woman's Civil War*, 97.

87. Sawyer, Sawyer, and Sawyer, *Letters from a Civil War Surgeon*, 49–51.

88. See, for example, ibid., 60, 69, 93, 128, 144, 193, 201–7, 233, 261, 277, 299. Other soldiers also slept on pictures of their wives and children. See, for example, Johansson, *Widows by the Thousand*, 150. Men also eagerly awoke in the middle of the night if a letter arrived from home. See, for example, William G. Thompson to Jane Thompson, November 30, 1862, in Bearss, *William G. Thompson*, 83; Louis James M. Boyd to wife, January 28, 1863, Louis James M. Boyd Papers, FSA.

89. Daly, *Aboard the USS Monitor*, 242; William Roane Aylett to Alice Roane (Brockenbrough) Aylett, December 28, 1861, Aylett Family Papers, VHS.

90. Theodore Felix Keehln to Margaret Clewell, March 28, 1864, eBay auction 221564119004 (sold October 26, 2014).

91. Turner, *Southern Soldier's Letters Home*, 105; Cuttino, *Saddle Bag*, 213; Larimer, *Love and Valor*, 405; Kimmel and Musick, "I Am Busy Drawing Pictures," 130, 141. See also Maness and Combs, *Do They Miss Me*, 25–31, 34, 43, 46, 50–51, 59, 63, 72, 93, 154, 158–59, 169, 177, 180–81, 187, 210.

92. Jane Thompson to William Thompson, September 16, 1862, in Riley, "Civil War Wife, Part I," 229; Davis, *"Bully for the Band!,"* 196; Cuttino, *Saddle Bag*, 18; Longacre, "Come Home Soon," 398, 400–401. See also Johansson, *Widows by the Thousand*, 48; Sophia Stockett Sellman to John Henry Sellman, August 24, 1864, in Sophia Stockett Sellman Letters, LV.

Chapter Two

1. George Tillotson, to wife, January 9, 1862, in Bonner, *Soldier's Pen*, 52; M. B. Thurman to Jane Rosser, November 30, 1861, in Crewdson, *Love and War*, 26–27; Blaisdell, *Civil War Letters*, 178. See also William Ward Orme to Nannie, June 22, 1863, in Pratt, "William Ward Orme," 282; Evans, *16th Mississippi Infantry*, 5, 14, 25, 40, 55; Blair, *Politician Goes to War*, 195; Samuel Gilbert Webber to Nannie, December 21, 1862, Webber Letters, TMM; H. E. Coleman to wife, March 10, 1862, TMM; Miller, *"Punishment on the Nation,"* 93–95, 108, 134.

2. Ramold, *Across the Divide*, 45; Benjamin Hirst to wife, March 6, 1863, in Bee, *Boys from Rockville*, 88; Grant Taylor to wife and children, May 25, 1862, and November 15, 1863, both in Blomquist and Taylor, *This Cruel War*, 25, 196. See also Carmichael, "One Man's Turning Point," 68; Melvin J. Hyde to Alice L. Holcomb, March 4, 1864, in Chittick, *In the Field*, 72; Allen and Bohannon, *Campaigning with "Old Stonewall,"* 33–34; Rable, *Fredericksburg! Fredericksburg!*, 112; William H. Haigh to wife, June 1, 1865, Haigh Papers, SHC.

3. Walker, *Hell's Broke Loose*, 59; John V. Hadley to Mary Jane Hill, February 24, 1863, in Robertson, "Indiana Soldier," 229–30. See also Kundahl, *Bravest of the Brave*, 161; Wyatt Patterson to Lottie Dye, November 17, 1863, in the Patterson-Dye Correspondence, SCHS; Jabour, *Scarlett's Sisters*, 317n84.

4. McClurken, *Take Care of the Living*, 20–21; Jacob B. Ritner to Emeline, November 16, 1862, in Larimer, *Love and Valor*, 62–64.

5. Some poor soldiers returned home after the war to find these fears realized. See, for example, Bonner, *Soldier's Pen*, 220–21; Silber, *Daughters of the Union*, 105–13. For discussion of dreams of infidelity in the eighteenth century, see Ekirch, "Sleep We Have Lost," 375–76.

6. William Child to wife, September 22, 1862, April 1, November 20, 1864, all in Sawyer, Sawyer, and Sawyer, *Letters from a Civil War Surgeon*, 34, 211, 310–11.

7. Ibid., 201–9, 314. The Childs' marriage survived the war until Carrie died in 1867, at which point William married her sister. See also Gustave Cook to wife, December 10, 1862, Cook Collection, GLI.

8. Hyatt, "Captain Hyatt," 171.

9. Skipper and Taylor, *Handful of Providence*, 70. Other soldiers also dreamed of family coming to their camp for a visit. See, for example, William G. Thompson to Jane Thompson, October 20, 1862, in Bearss, *William G. Thompson*, 43.

10. Duren F. Kelley to Emma, December 24, 1863, in Offenberg and Parsonage, *Duren F. Kelley*, 83–84; Reid, *Fourth S.C.*, 46–47; Britton and Reed, *To My Beloved Wife*, 36–37.

11. Carol Reardon argues that lack of correspondence had a negative effect on soldiers' "sense of personal confidence and well-being." See Reardon, *With a Sword in One Hand*, 112.

12. Miles Butterfield to Libbie Butterfield, September 15, 1864, Butterfield Papers, UWM. For another bad dream connected to lack of correspondence from home, see Leander Harris to Emily S. Harris, September 6, 1863, Harris Collection, UNH. Other soldiers also mentioned lack of correspondence immediately before or after a description of a dream of home. See, for example, Silber and Sievers, *Yankee Correspondence*, 145; Allen and Bohannon, *Campaigning with "Old Stonewall,"* 14.

13. William Harris Hardy to Sallie Johnson Hardy, September 4, 1861, in Evans, *16th Mississippi Infantry*, 22.

14. Andrew J. Edge to Alpha Edge, March 17, 1864, in Lane, *Times That Prove*, 115.

15. Mathew Woodruff, diary entries for August 2, and September 22, 1865, both in Boney, *Land of the Vanquished*, 22, 40.

16. Alexander Sterrett Paxton, diary entries for January 20, 22 and 26, 1864, Paxton Papers, W&L. I thank Tom Camden and Seth McCormick-Goodheart for providing me with a copy of Paxton's dream journal.

17. Hiram Smith Williams, diary entry for April 19, 1864, in Wynne and Taylor, *This War So Horrible*, 49–52; Jordan, *John Mead Gould*, 76, 95.

18. George W. Peddy to wife, March 18, 1863, in Cuttino, *Saddle Bag*, 158.

19. William Child to Carrie, November 13, 1864, in Sawyer, Sawyer, and Sawyer, *Letters from a Civil War Surgeon*, 299.

20. Quoted in Lowry, *Story the Soldiers Wouldn't Tell*, 170.

21. J. A. H. Foster to wife, January 21 and March 1, 1864, in Powell, *Letters from the Storm*, 182, 193.

22. John H. W. Stuckenberg, diary entry for October 12, 1862, in Hedrick and Davis, *I'm Surrounded by Methodists*, 17. See also Berry, *All That Makes a Man*, 144–48.

23. William W. Keen, S. Weir Mitchell, and George R. Morehouse, "On Malingering, Especially in Regard to Simulation of Diseases of the Nervous System," *American Journal of the Medical Sciences* 48 (October 1864): 374–76. Not all medical experts at the time believed wet dreams were a legitimate excuse for discharge from the service unless its effects were "sufficiently decided and pronounced." See, for example, Ordronaux, *Hints on the Preservation*, 185; Bartholow, *Manual of Instructions*, 21–22. For a medical explanation of the physical and medical causes of wet dreams from the era, see Bartholow, *Spermatorrhoea*, 5–27.

24. McMurry, *Footprints of a Regiment*, 109.

25. Hiram Smith Williams, diary entry for March 22, 1864, in Wynne and Taylor, *This War So Horrible*, 38–39. See also Berry, *All That Makes a Man*, 6.

26. William Child to Carrie, April 1, 1864, in Sawyer, Sawyer, and Sawyer, *Letters from a Civil War Surgeon*, 211; Benjamin Franklin Jackson to Martha Jackson, August 12, 1862, in Jackson, *So Mourns the Dove*, 39; Alexander Campbell to wife, February 11, 1863, in Johnston, *"Him on the One Side,"* 127; Lee, *Dear Isa, Dear Johna*, 128; Levstik, "Albert Rogall," 34, 38, 40, 47, 54, 72; O. C. Shelton, diary entry for July 1, 1864, Shelton Family Papers, UIL; Emily S. Harris to Leander Harris, November 23, 1862, Harris

Collection, UNH; Taylor Peirce to family, April 21, 1863, in Kiper, *Dear Catharine, Dear Taylor*, 102; Drago, *Confederate Phoenix*, 30–32; Berry, *All That Makes a Man*, 225; Louis James M. Boyd to wife, February 2, 1863, Boyd Papers, FSA. For one soldier who dreamed that his children reverted to infancy, see Erastus Burnham to Mary Burnham, December 6, 1864, Burnham Collection, WML. On March 3, 1864, Burnham told his wife that he dreamed she had died, but believing that dreams should be interpreted as opposites, he wrote her, "that is a sure sign that you will be well." It was not unusual for soldiers to commune with deceased loved ones in their dreams. Like other dreams of home, such dreams could bring great joy during sleep and disappointment upon waking. See, for example, Lowry, *Swamp Doctor*, 32, 68; Barber and Swinson, *Charles Barber*, 99, 102.

27. John V. Hadley to Mary Jane Hill, August 23, 1863, in Robertson, "Indiana Soldier," 250–51.

28. Chittick, *In the Field*, 107; Matthias Baldwin Colton, diary entry for June 15, 1863, in Colton and Smith, *Column South*, 68; William Child to Carrie, September 19, 1864, in Sawyer, Sawyer, and Sawyer, *Letters from a Civil War Surgeon*, 261; Hallock, *Joshua K. Callaway*, 74; George W. Tillotson to wife, August 11, 1864, Tillotson Collection, GLI; Levstik, "Albert Rogall," 58, 60, 79.

29. Ransom, *Diary*, 21, 82. Convalescing soldiers also had dreams of food. See, for example, Rood, *Twelfth Wisconsin*, 347. On the reliability of Andersonville diarists, see Marvel, *Andersonville*, 323; Gray, "Introduction: Advancing Andersonville," in Futch, *Andersonville Prison*, xviii–xix.

30. Cooney, *Common Soldier, Uncommon War*, 478.

31. Merrill, *24th Independent Battery*, 251; Robert Knox Sneden, diary entry for July 1, 1864, in Bryan and Lankford, *Eye of the Storm*, 236; Snell, *Dancing Along the Deadline*, 77; Cozzens, "Survival in an Alabama Slammer," 56; Wilkinson, *May You Never See*, 286, 291, 294.

32. Northrop, *Chronicles*, 68. See also Shepherd, *Narrative of Prison Life*, 16.

33. McElroy, *Andersonville*, 341. The starvation endured by prisoners of war had permanent psychological effects on some of the veterans who survived. In the years after the war, Andersonville survivor Erastus Holmes of the Fifth Indiana Cavalry—a man who had lost almost half his body weight while incarcerated—was often afraid to go to sleep at night and on many nights would wake up and gorge himself with food. See Dean, *Shook Over Hell*, 85–86; Jordan, *Marching Home*, chap. 5.

34. Survivors' Association, *118th Pennsylvania*, 632; Swank, *Confederate Letters*, 165. See also Ransom, *Diary*, 29.

35. Deirdre Barrett found that the dreams of British POWs during World War II resembled those of other nonmilitary prisoners. She concludes that their "early capture" during World War II may explain "why their dreams resemble other prisoners more than other post-combatants." A study of five POWs during the Vietnam War, by contrast, found that prior to capture these soldiers frequently had "warning dreams" of being captured; while in prison they had "blissful dreams of gratification, power, and serenity." The soldiers remembered these latter dreams long after they'd had them and "would console themselves by dwelling on them." Only after their release from prison did the soldiers experience truly traumatic dreams of their expe-

rience in war. See Barrett, "Content of Dreams from WWII POWs"; Weiss, *How Psychotherapy Works*, 143–45. I thank Robert Shilkret of Mount Holyoke College for bringing this Vietnam study to my attention.

36. Drake, *Fast and Loose in Dixie*, 73.

37. Racine, *"Unspoiled Heart,"* 159–60.

38. Lanman, *Journal of Alfred Ely*, 202–3; Harry A. Bennett to John Bennett, August 8, 1864, Bennett Papers, VHS; Ujanirtus Allen to Susie, July 28, 1861, in Allen and Bohannon, *Campaigning with "Old Stonewall,"* 14.

39. Ransom, *Diary*, 72.

40. Samuel J. Gibson, diary entries for July 28 and August 12, 1864, in Gibson Diary and Correspondence, LC.

41. Racine, *Unspoiled Heart*, 236–37; Ransom, *Diary*, 147–48.

42. Partridge, *Ninety-Sixth Illinois*, 606; Ransom, *Diary*, 162; Gray, *Business of Captivity*, 63; Lanman, *Journal of Alfred Ely*, 31. See also the 1864 diary of Delos Phillips, MHI.

43. McPherson, *For Cause and Comrades*, 43; Charles Harvey Brewster to mother, June 2, 1862, in Blight, *When This Cruel War Is Over*, 145; James O. Churchill to parents, April 10, 1862, in *War Papers*, 1:164–65; Hess, *Union Soldier in Battle*, 29. See also Reid, *Practicing Medicine*, 66, 188; William Titus Rigby to brother, March 23, 1863, Rigby Letters, UIL; Davis and Swentor, *Bluegrass Confederate*, 549.

44. Dean, *Shook Over Hell*, 49; Meier, *Nature's Civil War*, 120.

45. Davis and Swentor, *Bluegrass Confederate*, 53, 318, 418, 644.

46. Quoted in Reardon, *Pickett's Charge*, 37.

47. Burstein, *Lincoln Dreamt He Died*, 213; Bennett and Haigh, *Thirty-Sixth Illinois*, 289. For ether-induced dreams, see Hess, *Union Soldier in Battle*, 34.

48. Davis, *"Bully for the Band!,"* 13, 48, 128, 223.

49. Donald, *Gone for a Soldier*, 15–17.

50. Shaw and House, *First Maine Heavy Artillery*, 189. For discussion of how these sorts of dreams, and the others that follow, may have resulted from battle fatigue, see Reardon, *With a Sword in One Hand*, 108.

51. Collier, *Chandler B. Gillam*, 232.

52. Carpenter, *Eighth Vermont*, 48–49; Rood, *Twelfth Wisconsin*, 138–40. For another similar example, see Hight, *Fifty-Eighth Indiana*, 332.

53. Peck, *How Private Peck*, 46. Soldiers' dreams sometimes reflected their frustrations with not receiving furloughs. One soldier in the 105th Illinois Infantry dreamt that he went home on furlough but did not have papers authorizing his leave, a crime for which he could be punished as a deserter. A Confederate dreamed that Robert E. Lee would not grant him a furlough since Lee himself "had not had one since *the war commenced*." See Lysander Wheeler to parents, August 16, 1863, Wheeler Collection, GLI; Toalson, *Send Me a Pair of Old Boots*, 168. At one point early in the war, Robert Gould Shaw dreamed "that this regiment was sworn into service for forty-seven years!" See Duncan, *Blue-Eyed Child of Fortune*, 103.

54. Paxton, various diary entries, January through March 1864, Paxton Papers. For a soldier who was awakened from a dream of home by pilferers, see Nisbet, *Four Years on the Firing Line*, 185.

55. Cooney, *Common Soldier, Uncommon War*, 17. See also Macsherry, *Pastime*, 176.

56. Bond and Coward, *South Carolinians*, 13–15.

57. Bartlett, *Twelfth New Hampshire*, 227; Jordan, *John Mead Gould*, 435; Davis, "*Bully for the Band!*," 241. For a similar account, see Hight, *Fifty-Eighth Indiana*, 205. For a soldier who dreamed himself to Grant's headquarters, see Peck, *How Private Peck*, 122.

58. Brewster to mother, April 6, 1862, in Blight, *When This Cruel War Is Over*, 107; Davis and Swentor, *Bluegrass Confederate*, 620; Thompson, *Thirteenth New Hampshire*, 283. See also Joseph A. Buckley to parents, December 5, 1862, in Henn, *Pike County*, 14.

59. Yacovone, *Freedom's Journey*, 474–75.

60. Hard, *Eighth Illinois Cavalry*, 122.

61. Duncan, *Blue-Eyed Child of Fortune*, 168; Schmidt, *147th Pennsylvania Regiment*, 351.

62. Hight, *Fifty-Eighth Indiana*, 161; Tally to Caroline Virginia Taliaferro Miller, April 24, 1863, in Everson and Simpson, *Far from Home*, 217–18; Peck, *How Private Peck*, 195–96; Ujanirtus Allen to Susie, December 23, 1862, in Allen and Bohannon, *Campaigning with "Old Stonewall*," 200.

63. Hight, *Fifty-Eighth Indiana*, 379. On the soldier vote of 1864, see Jonathan W. White, *Emancipation*, chap. 4. Politics was not an uncommon subject of Civil War–era Americans' dreams—even among women. See, for example, Hammond, *Diary of a Union Lady*, 262.

64. James M. Harrison to mother, January 14, 1863, Harrison Letters, UAK. I first encountered this dream in Manning, *What This Cruel War Was Over*, 82.

65. Twichell to mother, August 10, 1863, in Messent and Courtney, *Joseph Hopkins Twichell*, 258; Peck, *How Private Peck*, 199–200; J. Franklin Dyer, diary entry for April 23, 1863, in Chesson, *Civil War Surgeon*, 72. For a Wisconsin soldier's dream "that peace was fully restored to our country and the rebels cleaned out completely," see Thomas R. Sterns to wife, November 12, 1862, Sterns Family Papers, UIL.

66. Grant Taylor to wife and children, July 3, 1864, in Blomquist and Taylor, *This Cruel War*, 266–67.

67. See, for example, Joseph Jones to wife, September 7–9, 1862, Jones Collection, GLI; and George W. Clark to sister, June 4, 1863, Clark Collection, GLI.

68. James Madison Bowler to Elizabeth Caleff Bowler, November 14, 1863, in Foroughi, *Go If You Think It Your Duty*, 211.

69. John Jones to wife, March 12, 1863, Jones Collection, GLI; William Wallace to Sarah, December 7, 1862, Holzhueter, "William Wallace's Civil War Letters," 59; Burstein, *Lincoln Dreamt He Died*, 215; Henry Graves to wife, August 7, 1862, quoted in Burch, "Home Voices"; Sam Farnum to Frank, November 14, 1862, War Letters, 1861–1865, NYHS.

70. Adams, *Living Hell*, 114, 124–25.

71. George Hulslander to John Reeser, March 2, 1865, Gibson Collection, GLI.

72. Knight, *Letters to Anna*, 120.

73. Hess, *Union Soldier in Battle*, 124.

74. Only a few soldiers saw their dreams of home as unwelcome or as a sign of weakness because they took their focus off of the battlefield. See, for example, Ted Ownby, "Patriarchy in the World Where There is no Parting: Power Relations in the Confederate Heaven," in Clinton, *Southern Families*, 230; Davis and Swentor, *Bluegrass Confederate*, 526, 596; Jordan, *John Mead Gould*, 175; Burstein, *Lincoln Dreamt He Died*, 300n45. For analysis of why so many soldiers thought of their loved ones during battle, see Mitchell, *Civil War Soldiers*, 77.

75. Samuel Gilbert Webber to Nannie, December 22, 1862, Webber Letters, TMM. Soldiers and sailors also had similar dreams of home during peacetime. For an antebellum sailor's dreams of home, see William McBlair to wife, May 12 and 20, and September 25, 1857, and January 21 and February 3, 1858, all in McBlair Papers, TMM.

Chapter Three

1. Lane, *Times That Prove*, 245.

2. Cashin, *First Lady*, 161; James H. Wilson to Adam Badeau, May 13, 1865, in Jones, "'Your Left Arm,'" 243. For analyses of these prints of Davis, see Neely, Holzer, and Boritt, *Confederate Image*, 79–96; Silber, "Intemperate Men, Spiteful Women, and Jefferson Davis."

3. Eckert, *"Fiction Distorting Fact,"* xxv–xxvi.

4. Ibid., xxxi; Jefferson Davis to Varina Howell Davis, September 26, October 20, and December 2, 1865, all in Crist et al., *Papers of Jefferson Davis*, 12:29, 42, 67–68. Concerned about the welfare of her husband, Varina sent Davis an eye mask to wear at night. It is now in the collection at the American Civil War Museum in Richmond, Virginia, and I thank curator Cathy Wright for bringing it to my attention.

5. Ibid., 17, 27, 150.

6. Ibid., 113–14.

7. Ibid., 35, 114, 159–60. On Davis's treason trial, see Jonathan W. White, "The Trial of Jefferson Davis and the Americanization of Treason Law," in Moreno and O'Neill, eds., *Constitutionalism and the Civil War*, 113–32.

8. Crist et al., *Papers of Jefferson Davis*, 12:98. I thank Lynda Crist for providing me with a complete transcription of this letter.

9. Ibid., 79. On their early marriage difficulties, see Cashin, *First Lady*, 44–53, 71–73. Cashin argues that Varina learned that she would have to give in to Jefferson's will if their marriage was to survive. On the tenor of their correspondence during Jefferson's imprisonment, see ibid., 174–75.

10. Eckert, *"Fiction Distorting Fact,"* xxxv.

11. Ibid., xxxv–xxxvi.

12. Crist et al., *Papers of Jefferson Davis*, 12:55; Eckert, *"Fiction Distorting Fact,"* xxi–xl, xxxvii–xxxviii.

13. *Philadelphia Press*, July 29, 1865.

14. Some scholars have mistakenly identified this figure as Uncle Sam with the "features" of Abraham Lincoln. See Fischer, *Liberty and Freedom*, 327.

15. Avary, *Recollections of Stephens*, 511–12. On Stephens's lack of sleep while in prison, see 241, 320, 323, 370, 378, 381, 390, 437–38, 459, 466, 505. As a lifelong bachelor, Stephens had no one to confide in as Davis did. His dream reports in his personal diary would not have served the same function that the Davises did in correspondence.

16. On the tension Northern women felt between their duty to their country and their desires to keep their husbands home, see Silber, *Daughters of the Union*, 14–40. Silber suggests that as the war went on and women became more involved in civic affairs, women became less demanding of their husbands to return home. For Southern women's roles in public life, see Rable, *Civil Wars*, chap. 7.

17. Nelson and Sheriff, *People at War*, 234–35; Longacre, "Come Home Soon."

18. On the loneliness that was experienced by civilians during the war, see Paludan, *"People's Contest,"* 328–32; Silber, *Daughters of the Union*, 92. Quite naturally, children also dreamed about their fathers being in danger. See Larimer, *Love and Valor*, 296, 307–10.

19. Cuttino, *Saddle Bag*, 167, 183, 186.

20. On these fears, see Silber, *Daughters of the Union*, 91–105.

21. Dollie Vermilion to William Vermilion, March 9 and April 7, 1863, in Elder, *Love Amid the Turmoil*, 67–68, 75.

22. Cora to Charlie, November 6, 1862, in Taber, *Hard Breathing Days*, 18–19.

23. Cora to Charlie, January 20 and February 10, 1863, in ibid., 81, 101.

24. Cora to Charlie, August 23, 1863, in ibid., 224–25.

25. Cora to Charlie, April 17, May 22 and 29, and December 25, 1864, all in ibid., 314–16, 327, 331–32, 416.

26. Cora to Charlie, June 4, 1865, in ibid., 460.

27. Blomquist and Taylor, *This Cruel War*, 93. On other occasions, Malinda expressed her wish that Grant would desert and come home. See ibid., 308. Grant Taylor's death is discussed in chapter 5.

28. Johansson, *Widows by the Thousand*, 41, 88.

29. Skipper and Taylor, *Handful of Providence*, 75–76.

30. Ibid., 24, 27, 72, 95, 182. One early dream book stated that dreams of church meant the dreamer would "be disappointed in your expectations." See Gardner, *"Complete Fortune Teller,"* 276. Ellie may have been influenced by a similar interpretation.

31. For an insightful discussion of the ways that husbands and wives sought to maintain antebellum practices during the war, see Gallman, *Mastering Wartime*, chap. 3. These practices included dream sharing.

32. Varina Howell Davis to Jefferson Davis, June 3, 1862, and Varina Howell Davis to William Preston Johnston, June 5 and August 7, 1862, all in Crist et al., *Papers of Jefferson Davis*, 8:221–22. On Varina's tepid support of the Confederate war effort, see Cashin, *First Lady*, 1–6, 96–100, 107–9, 114–16, 123–33, 143–44, 148, 167.

33. Varina Howell Davis to Jefferson Davis, [September 1846], in McIntosh, *Papers of Jefferson Davis*: 3:53. For another woman who was more discreet in what she shared with her husband, see Gwin, *Woman's Civil War*, 139.

34. It should be noted that Varina and Jefferson's marriage was quite rocky at times, and she did not always share her views and feelings with him, even during the

war. Similar to this selective sharing of dreams in the summer of 1862, on August 13, 1862, she sent a lighthearted and superficial letter to Jefferson and a deeply revealing letter to another correspondent. See Cashin, *First Lady*, 72–73, 84–87, 130–33. Varina also understood how, in Cashin's words, "disappointing news from the battlefield profoundly affected his emotional state, and when he was unhappy, she looked after him." See ibid., 125.

35. Dollie Vermilion to William Vermilion, March 18, 1863, in Elder, *Love Amid the Turmoil*, 71.

36. Cuttino, *Saddle Bag*, 211; Elizabeth Caleff Bowler to James Madison Bowler, April 21, 1865, in Foroughi, *Go If You Think It Your Duty*, 290.

37. Mohr, *Cormany Diaries*, 454.

38. Elizabeth Caleff (Bowler) to James Madison Bowler, April 30, 1862; James to Elizabeth, November 14, 1863; and Elizabeth to James, January 8, 1864, all in Foroughi, *Go If You Think It Your Duty*, 83, 133–34, 211–12, 224.

39. Emily S. Harris to Leander Harris, February 1, March 16, April 7, and September 16, 1862, Harris Collection, UNH; Dollie Vermilion to William Vermilion, March 2, 1863, in Elder, *Love Amid the Turmoil*, 65. See also Henry Walker, "Power, Sex, and Gender Roles: The Transformation of an Alabama Planter Family during the Civil War," in Clinton, *Southern Families*, 180; Samuel Gilbert Webber to Nannie, December 22, 1862, Webber Letters, TMM.

40. On concerns about infidelity, see Silber, *Daughters of the Union*, 105–13; Paludan, *"People's Contest,"* 330–32.

41. Gwin, *Woman's Civil War*, 213–14. McDonald's husband had been a soldier early in the war; at the time of his death he was helping the Confederate war effort as a civilian.

42. Cuttino, *Saddle Bag*, 30, 136, 208, 282, 296–97. See also Culpepper, *Women of the Civil War South*, 146. For other examples of women who connected their dreams to correspondence from their husbands, see Isabel Shaw Brown to John A. Brown, June 13, 1864, in Lee, *Dear Isa, Dear Johna*, 63; Mary Eliza Rose to Charles Rose, n.d. [ca. summer 1863], Rose Family Papers, VHS.

43. Timothy F. Murphy to Betty Murphy, June 10, 1864, Murphy Papers, NHC; Leander Harris to Emily S. Harris, September 1, 1864, Harris Collection, UNH.

44. Miller, *Empty Sleeves*, 56–57, 91–92.

45. Salmon, *Common Men*, 283.

46. Berlin, *Confederate Nurse*, 34; Anderson, *Brokenburn*, 60–61; diary of Lizzie Alsop, February 17, 1865, Alsop Diary, VHS; Robertson, *Lucy Breckinridge*, 46, 167. See also Kallgren, *Abial and Anna*, 49; Phipps, *Genteel Rebel*, 51.

47. Quoted in Royster, *Destructive War*, 245.

48. Willet, "Our House Was Divided," 112. On Confederate women wishing they could fight, see Rable, *Civil Wars*, 151–53, 178.

49. George C. Rable argues that "the psychological assault [on Southern homes and families] began earlier and lasted longer than the physical destruction." See ibid., 154.

50. Pleasant H. Motsinger to brother, March 7, 1865, Motsinger Family Papers, DU. Motsinger reflected on this dream at the end of the war as Sherman's army

reached North Carolina. I thank Trudi Abel for supplying me with a scan of this letter.

51. Elizabeth Blair Lee to Phil, September 10, 1861, in Laas, *Wartime Washington*, 77.

52. King, *Northern Woman*, 165. This dream, which took place in December 1865, is part of a letter that reflects upon the devastation and hardships of the war.

53. Roark, *Masters without Slaves*, 87; Mitchell, *Civil War Soldiers*, 71; Crofts, "Southampton County Diarists," 594; Robertson, *Lucy Breckinridge*, 143. See also Burstein, *Lincoln Dreamt He Died*, 172; Cockrell and Ballard, *Mississippi Rebel*, 249–50; Baer, *Shadows on My Heart*, 293.

54. Tarter, *Daydreams and Nightmares*, 54–58.

55. Johansson, *Widows by the Thousand*, 235–36; Tarter, *Daydreams and Nightmares*, 59–60, 66–67. See also Davis, "Selective Memories," 742.

56. Mother to Blanche Butler, April 1865, in Ames, *Chronicles from the Nineteenth Century*, 1:110; Anderson, *Brokenburn*, 305; Woodward, *Mary Chesnut's Civil War*, 241.

57. Berlin, *Confederate Nurse*, 33; Woodward, *Mary Chesnut's Civil War*, 481; Jones, *Tennessee in the Civil War*, 87. See also Frank, *Civilian War*, 36.

58. East, *Sarah Morgan*, 128, 442, 525–26.

59. Jones, *Tennessee in the Civil War*, 214; Lehman and Nolt, *Mennonites*, 72; Jones, *Rebel War Clerk's Diary*, 1:56; Julia Crenshaw interview, WPA Slave Narratives; Drago, *Confederate Phoenix*, 46–49.

60. Birdwhistell, "Kentucky Baptist Pastor," 26; Gwin, *Woman's Civil War*, 211, 216; Avary, *Recollections of Stephens*, 163–64, 221. For a Confederate woman who could not find someone she was searching for in her dream, see Wiley, *Warren Akin*, 92, 101.

61. Roberts, *Confederate Belle*, 155; Willet, "Our House Was Divided," 218.

62. Avary, *Recollections of Stephens*, 204, 211–12, 315, 480, 505. On this aspect of paternalism, see Genovese, *Roll, Jordan, Roll*, 190–92, 206–7.

63. Quoted in Roberts, *Confederate Belle*, 177.

64. Hannah Aldrich to mother, August 21, 1861, in Krynski and Little, "Hannah's Letters, Part II," 296, and "Hannah's Letters, Part III," 42.

65. Elizabeth Ingersoll Fisher, diary entries for September 16–17, 1861, Fisher Collection, HSP.

66. Sophia Stockett Sellman to John Henry Sellman, September 6, 1864, Sellman Letters, LV.

67. Harriet M. Buss to parents, March 31–April 1, 1863, UP; Royster, *Destructive War*, 245.

68. Jane Thompson to William Thompson, September 11, 1862, in Riley, "Civil War Wife, Part I," 224; Jane to William, October 23 and December 8, 1862, in Riley, "Civil War Wife, Part II," 304, 311; William to Jane, November 25 and 27 and December 22, 1862, all in Bearss, *William G. Thompson*, 76, 80–82, 92–93.

69. Dollie Vermilion to William Vermilion, October 26, 1863, in Elder, *Love Amid the Turmoil*, 254.

70. Skipper and Taylor, *Handful of Providence*, 51–52; Dollie Vermilion to William Vermilion, July 5, 1863, in Elder, *Love Amid the Turmoil*, 153. See also Mary Hemsley to

brother, February 21, 1863, Thom Family Papers, VHS. In some cases, we know that civilians had nightmares but we don't know what they were about. See, for example, Baer, *Shadows on My Heart*, 281.

71. See, for example, Baer, *Shadows on My Heart*, 201.

72. Miller, "Alabama Merchant," 187, 198, 200, 206; Robertson, *Lucy Breckinridge*, 83; Virginia Davis Gray, diary entry for September 9, 1863, in Moneyhon, "Life in Confederate Arkansas," 53. On a particularly hot night, one Confederate woman "drempt I had found a cool spring of water." See Berlin, *Confederate Nurse*, 43. Confederates who left the South also had dreams of home. See, for example, James A. Fortune to Ann M. Bolton, July 5, 1861, Bolton Family Papers, VHS.

73. Cuttino, *Saddle Bag*, 304. Not all of Kate's dreams of her husband were bad. For positive dreams, see ibid., 132–33.

74. English essayist Thomas De Quincey (1785–1859), who wrote *Confessions of an English Opium-Eater* in 1822. For more on De Quincey, see Burstein, *Lincoln Dreamt He Died*, 108–15.

75. East, *Sarah Morgan*, 232–41, 254–55. Dreams of literary figures or other famous persons, such as the Prince of Wales, were not uncommon during the Civil War. See, for example, Berlin, *Confederate Nurse*, 31. Throughout the book we also see various dreams about Abraham Lincoln, Ulysses S. Grant, Robert E. Lee, and other leaders.

76. East, *Sarah Morgan*, xxiii–xxv, 301–2, 550.

77. Lane, *Times That Prove*, 100.

78. Wiley, *Warren Akin*, 80–81.

79. Fain, *Sanctified Trial*, 75–76, 295. See also Diary of Lizzie Alsop, June 8, 1862, Wynne Family Papers, VHS; Cuttino, *Saddle Bag*, 131.

Chapter Four

1. Quoted in Bradford, *Scenes*, 79; Sernett, *Harriet Tubman*, 134–35.

2. Bradford, *Scenes*, 79. For other instances of slaves "dreaming of flying over woods and rivers," see Sobel, *Teach Me Dreams*, 128–29; Johnson, *God Struck Me Dead*, 73, 91.

3. Ibid., 82–83.

4. Bradford, *Harriet*, 92–93.

5. Sernett, *Harriet Tubman*, 115, 121, 134–37, 145.

6. Humez, quoted in ibid., 138.

7. Ibid., 139–43.

8. Here I am quoting Sernett in ibid., 144.

9. Conrad, *Harriet Tubman*, 34.

10. Quoted in Sernett, *Harriet Tubman*, 142.

11. Larson, *Bound for the Promised Land*, 263, 381n83.

12. Christopher M. Span and James D. Anderson, "The Quest for 'Book Learning': African American Education in Slavery and Freedom," in Hornsby, *Companion to African American History*, 304; Blassingame, *Slave Testimony*, 688.

13. Berlin, *Freedom*, ser. 1, 3:521, 524. See also Berlin, *Generations of Captivity*, 176–77; Nolen, *African American Southerners*, 16, 81.

14. *American Slavery as It Is*, 144.

15. Roark, *Masters without Slaves*, 72; Johnson, *River of Dark Dreams*, 468n41.

16. Berlin, *Freedom*, ser. 1, 3:193.

17. Rediker, *Slave Ship*, 334.

18. Madison Jefferson interview (1841), in Blassingame, *Slave Testimony*, 224.

19. I am unaware of any scholarship that probes whether slaves suffered from post-traumatic stress disorder (PTSD) either during or after their time in bondage. Considering the prevalence of rape of slave women by their masters, and the fact that nearly half of female victims of rape suffer from symptoms of PTSD, it may be an avenue worth exploring in the future. Finding primary sources that would speak to these issues will not be easy, however.

20. Berlin, *Generations of Captivity*, 174; Blassingame, *Slave Testimony*, 222, 245, 283, 287, 298, 342, 464, 532; Larson, *Bound for the Promised Land*, 177.

21. Quotations from Innes, *Slave Life*, xiii; Berlin, *Freedom*, ser. 2, 241; Blight, *Slave No More*, 277n46. See also ibid., ser. 1, vol. 1, 140; ser. 1, vol. 2, 576; ser. 2, 235–36; vol. 3, 424, 518, 526; Johnson, *God Struck Me Dead*, 81–82.

22. Brown, *Narrative*, 83; Peter Smith interview (ca. 1845), in Blassingame, *Slave Testimony*, 246; George Washington to Lincoln, March 19, 1865, Lincoln Papers. See also the account of Daniel Taylor in "Buried Alive," *Harper's Weekly*, May 7, 1864.

23. Minnie Fulkes interview (March 5, 1937), WPA Slave Narratives.

24. Burstein, *Lincoln Dreamt He Died*, 212.

25. Adah Isabelle Suggs interview (ca. 1936–1938), WPA Slave Narratives.

26. Douglass, *My Bondage and My Freedom*, 238, 284–303.

27. Grimes, *Life*, 12.

28. Innes, *Slave Life*, 86–87; James L. Bradley autobiographical statement (1835), in Blassingame, *Slave Testimony*, 688; Cimprich, *Fort Pillow*, 22; Cedar Rapids *Evening Gazette*, May 30, 1887.

29. Deyle, *Carry Me Back*, 252; Caleb Craig interview (ca. 1937), WPA Slave Narratives.

30. Taylor, *I Was Born a Slave*, 1:276, 290.

31. Northup, *Twelve Years a Slave*, 47.

32. Schultz, *This Birth Place of Souls*, 99; Jacobs, *Incidents in the Life of a Slave Girl*, 164.

33. Robert Toatley interview (1937), WPA Slave Narratives.

34. Rosebell Burke to Mary C. Lee, February 20, 1859, in Blassingame, *Slave Testimony*, 106–7; Diana Skipwith to Sally Cocke Brent, May 7, 1838, in Miller, "*Dear Master*," 89. Nor were all slaves' dreams bad. See, for example, Ashton, *I Belong to South Carolina*, 199–200.

35. Ellis Ken Kannon and Patsy Hyde interviews (ca. 1936–1938), WPA Slave Narratives. See also Johnson, *God Struck Me Dead*, 147.

36. Louise Oliphant, "Compilation of Richmond County Ex-Slave Interviews: Folk Remedies and Superstition," WPA Slave Narratives.

37. Annie B. Boyd interview (ca. 1936–1938). WPA Slave Narratives; Branch and Dawson quoted in Archer, *Antebellum Slave Narratives*, 50. For a South Carolina

planter's dreams of snakes in 1856, see Genovese, *Roll, Jordan, Roll*, 425; for a Northern black woman's dream of snakes, see Humez, *Gifts of Power*, 93–94.

38. Steward, *Twenty-Two Years a Slave*, 183–84. Steward had other premonitions and prophetic dreams. See ibid., 118, 245–47.

39. Greenberg, *Confessions of Nat Turner*, 3, 46–49.

40. Tom Wylie Neal interview (ca. 1936–1938), WPA Slave Narratives.

41. Lizzie Farmer interview (ca. 1936–1938), WPA Slave Narratives.

42. Johnson, *God Struck Me Dead*, 78.

43. Lou Smith interview (ca. 1936–1938), WPA Slave Narratives.

44. Quoted in Puckett, *Folk Beliefs*, 499–500.

45. Leonard, *Lower Niger*, 146–47. I first found this work cited in Archer, *Antebellum Slave Narratives*, 49–50. On the difficulty of determining the origins of "magical beliefs," see Raboteau, *Slave Religion*, 33–35.

46. On the persistence of African religious traditions in the Americas, I believe the truth may lie in a middle ground between Butler, *Awash in a Sea of Faith*, chap. 5, and Frey and Wood, *Come Shouting to Zion*. For the purposes of this chapter, I do not believe enough sources exist to do the type of in-depth research on dream practices that other scholars have done when tracing other traditions from Europe and Africa to the New World, such as Fischer, *Albion's Seed*, or Thornton, "African Dimensions of the Stono Rebellion," 1101–13. Nor are there likely enough sources to do the sort of analysis that Ira Berlin so eloquently models in "Time, Space, and the Evolution of Afro-American Society."

47. Puckett, *Folk Beliefs*, 322, 498–502. I have rearranged the order of Puckett's findings to align with Oliphant's compilation.

48. Leonard, *Lower Niger*, 146–47.

49. Puckett, *Folk Beliefs*, 498. Puckett also pointed out that snakes were often symbols that a "conjure-doctor" might inflict illness on the dreamer. "The identification of the snake with the hoodoo-doctor (or with an enemy, as is most generally the case) may be of significance, since there is at least the possibility that while the snake has been dropped from actual voodoo worship, yet he still remains as a dream symbol of danger" (294). Some seventeenth-century Quakers also saw snakes as a symbol for a personal enemy. See Gerona, *Night Journeys*, 62. For other African interpretations of snakes in dreams, see Brown, *African-Atlantic Cultures*, 103. According to Sobel, "Numerous taboos of African peoples, and proscriptions of divinities and spirits, remained operative in America, coalescing into a vast body of superstitions and signs. Every black child and every white child raised by or with blacks learned much of the lore." See Sobel, *Trabelin' On*, 72.

50. Sobel, *Teach Me Dreams*, 47–48, 55–96, 213–14. On the emergence of Afro-Christianity, see Genovese, *Roll, Jordan, Roll*, 168–83, 209–79. For discussion of a "synthesis of Christian and African beliefs" during the American Revolution, see Gerona, *Night Journeys*, 180. During the colonial era, the dream practices of white colonists and Indians also commingled. See Plane, *Dreams and the Invisible World*, chap. 6, esp. 159–60, 170–71.

51. Avary, *Recollections of Stephens*, 483.

52. Hassler, *General to His Lady*, 216; Tarter, *Daydreams and Nightmares*, 60. Belief that dreams should be "interpreted backwards" had also infiltrated Southern white culture. For an example, see Burstein, *Lincoln Dreamt He Died*, 142.

53. Weaver, *Thank God My Regiment*, 124.

54. William McKnight to wife, January 25, 1863, in Maness and Combs, *Do They Miss Me at Home*, 49.

55. Robertson, *Lucy Breckinridge*, 98; Whitney and Bullock, *Folk-Lore from Maryland*, 13; Sobel, *Teach Me Dreams*, 37–38.

56. Gardner, *"Complete Fortune Teller,"* 276–81.

57. See also Genovese, *Roll, Jordan, Roll*, 217–18. The prevalence of dreams in antebellum slave narratives may have confirmed for white readers the legitimacy of the author as having been a *real* slave, while for black readers they confirmed the author's status as a Christian. Even fictional slave narratives, such as Browne, *Autobiography of a Female Slave*, incorporated dreams in order to make the story seem more authentic.

58. Both quoted in Hatch, *Democratization of American Christianity*, 10.

59. Denison, *Evangelist*, 54–55; Matthew Dennis, "Visions of Handsome Lake: Seneca Dreams, Prophecy, and the Second Great Awakening," in Plane and Tuttle, *Dreams, Dreamers, and Visions*, 237; Butler, *Awash in a Sea of Faith*, 236–41; Lyerly, *Methodism and the Southern Mind*, 9, 36–39, 115. For John Wesley's views of dreams, see Taves, *Fits, Trances, and Visions*, 52–58, 74. On the commonality of white and black views of dreams in the South in the late eighteenth and early nineteenth centuries, see Heyrman, *Southern Cross*, 61–62.

60. See Gerona, *Night Journeys*. For non-Quakers converting to the Society of Friends because of dreams, see 212–14.

61. Jones, *Religious Instruction of the Negroes*, 125–28. Jones continued, "The character of the Negroes both private and public in a state of freedom and in a state of slavery; their habits of thought, superstitions and manners, should be carefully studied by the preacher, so that he may adapt his preaching to them." Ibid., 261.

62. Quoted in Brown, *African-Atlantic Cultures*, 211. Another Methodist minister noted with satisfaction in 1833 that black preachers in Georgia were "prompt, evangelical and concise in speaking. No *dreams*, no *visions*, no *travels* were included." Quoted in Owen, *Sacred Flame of Love*, 40.

63. Renatus Shmidt, quoted in Sobel, *Teach Me Dreams*, 240.

64. Brown, *African-Atlantic Cultures*, 199. See also Chireau, *Black Magic*, 9, 123–28. On the role of visions and dreams in blacks' conversion experiences, see Raboteau, *Slave Religion*, 29, 268–71.

65. Quoted in Sobel, *Trabelin' On*, 102. See also Sensbach, *Rebecca's Revival*, 81–82, 87–88, 138. For examples of the public role of dreams for eighteenth-century whites, see Gerona, *Night Journeys*; Sobel, *Teach Me Dreams*, 13, 64–78, 149, 212–14. Eugene D. Genovese points out that early Christianity had borrowed from ancient pagan traditions in the same way that slaves absorbed aspects of Christianity. See Genovese, *Roll, Jordan, Roll*, 228–30.

66. Johnson, *God Struck Me Dead*, 61–101, 121–28, 140–71 (quotations 61, 67, 100, 140); Sobel, *Teach Me Dreams*, 45–47, 108–15, 128–32; Taves, *Fits, Trances, and Visions*,

109; Lee, *Religious Experience*, 14; Ashton, *I Belong to South Carolina*, 20, 45–46; Andrews, *Sisters of the Spirit*, 39–41, 54–57, 76–78, 82–84, 90–91, 135–38, 156. Philadelphia Shaker eldress Rebecca Cox Jackson recorded several dozen dreams that she imputed religious meaning to in her private writings. See Humez, *Gifts of Power*.

67. See Heyrman, *Southern Cross*; Lyerly, *Methodism and the Southern Mind*. Heyrman marks a significant turning point in this process as the death of Methodist leader Francis Asbury in 1816.

68. Dreams attributed to white people also often showed up in newspapers and periodicals to offer moral lessons to readers. These "dreams"—which were often fictitious—are discussed in chapter 6. Quakers still used dreams for public purposes well into the nineteenth century. See Gerona, *Night Journeys*. And, as we will see in chapter 5, white soldiers and veterans still often attributed prophetic meaning to dreams in published regimental histories. Clearly dreams continued to have significant meaning for both white and black Christians. My point here is that many whites ceased to give discussion of dreams a place in their public acts of worship, whereas dreams continued to be used in such ways by many African Americans—particularly slaves—in the Civil War era.

69. Ackley to wife, April 25, 1864, Ackley Civil War Letters, UIL. Of course, not all Union soldiers belittled slave preachers. See, for example, Genovese, *Roll, Jordan, Roll*, 268.

70. Stanyan, *Eighth New Hampshire*, 232–37.

Chapter Five

1. Long, *Memoirs of Lee*, 258.

2. Robertson, *Stonewall Jackson*, 701–53; Royster, *Destructive War*, 231. Previously, Jackson's father-in-law had predicted, "Jackson will perish in this war." See ibid., 214. Night attacks were rare during the Civil War. One Mississippi soldier once regretted that he could not command the sun to stand still in the sky as Joshua had in the Old Testament so that his men could have more soundly defeated a Union army. See Evans, *16th Mississippi Infantry*, 109.

3. Swank, *Confederate Letters*, 53–59, 63.

4. Muffly, *148th Pennsylvania*, 1011; Messent and Courtney, *Joseph Hopkins Twichell*, 300.

5. Rozear et al., "Lee's Stroke," 301–2.

6. Robertson, *Stonewall Jackson*, 921n61.

7. Faust, *This Republic of Suffering*, 19.

8. My findings here largely align with Clarke, *War Stories*, 4–5, 43–50, 61–62, 69–71; Woodworth, *While God Is Marching On*, 28–39, 108, 131–36, 226–30, 292–94.

9. Shermer, *Believing Brain*, 257.

10. Americans had similar experiences during other armed conflicts. For a discussion of signs and omens during King Philip's War in 1676, see Plane, *Dreams and the Invisible World*, 116–19.

11. My thinking on this point is influenced by Linderman, *Embattled Courage*, which contends that in the postwar period veterans recaptured some of their early

understandings of the war. Regarding Linderman's overall thesis, however, I find McPherson's critique in *For Cause and Comrades* more persuasive, with the exception of McPherson's argument that Union soldiers showed overwhelming support for emancipation, which I address in my work *Emancipation*.

12. Paperno, *Stories of the Soviet Experience*, 162.

13. In this chapter I discuss dreams, premonitions and presentiments together because in the early modern period there was "a less rigid distinction between waking and sleeping visionary experiences." See Plane and Tuttle, *Dreams, Dreamers, and Visions*, 5.

14. Patricia Bulkeley, "Dreams and Visions of the Dying," in Bulkeley, Adams, and Davis, *Dreaming in Christianity*, 71.

15. Burns, *Fifth New York Cavalry*, 41; Kidd, *Personal Recollections*, 409; Hight, *Fifty-Eighth Indiana*, 220.

16. Sperry, *33d Iowa*, 84–85; Haynes, *Tenth Vt.*, 251; Wall, *Pee Dee Guards*, 74; Bolton, *Second Illinois*, 30; Bruce, *Twentieth Massachusetts*, 241, 375; Boies, *Thirty-Third Massachusetts*, 48–49; Jackman, *Sixth New Hampshire*, 312, 321. It is perfectly conceivable that close-knit soldiers would experience similarities in their dreams, even at the same time. Families going through difficulty together sometimes have "shared images, ideas, and feelings" in their dreams. Scientists in the field of social neuroscience have also found that our nervous systems may "be less self-contained, more permeable than previously believed." See Edward Bruce Bynum, "Family Unconscious in Dreams," in Barrett and McNamara, *Encyclopedia*, 1:277; Walsh, *Cowardice*, 81–82.

17. Bond and Coward, *South Carolinians*, 133–39; Swisher, *Prince of Edisto*, chap. 12.

18. Bartlett, *Twelfth New Hampshire*, 340–53 (quotation 343).

19. Ibid., 346–49.

20. Jackson, *So Mourns the Dove*, 84; Washington, *They Knew Lincoln*, 32. For birds as signs of death in southern culture, see Lyerly, *Methodism and the Southern Mind*, 36; Heyrman, *Southern Cross*, 62.

21. Nixon B. Stewart, *Dan McCook's Regiment*, 131–32.

22. Emilio, *Fifty-Fourth Massachusetts*, 62, 67.

23. Emmerton, *Twenty-Third Mass.*, 127–29; Shaw and House, *First Maine Heavy Artillery*, 362; [Bacon], *William Kirkland Bacon*, 48–49, 80–81; Floyd, *Seventy-Fifth Indiana*, 139; Craft, *One Hundred Forty-First Pennsylvania*, 86; King, Gibbs, and Northup, *Ninety-Third New York*, 433–34; McMurray, *Twentieth Tennessee*, 112, 433; Barnet, *Martyrs and Heroes of Illinois*, 118–19.

24. Nanzig, *Virginia Cavalryman*, 185; Nanzig, *3rd Virginia Cavalry*, 47, 121; Crowley, *Tennessee Cavalier*, appendix, 7; Bauer, *Rice C. Bull*, 115–19.

25. Walsh, *Cowardice*, 5.

26. Robert M. Green, *One Hundred and Twenty-Fourth Pennsylvania*, 120–22; Hopkins, *Seventh Rhode Island*, 188; Shaw and House, *First Maine Heavy Artillery*, 141–42; Favill, *Diary of a Young Officer*, 289.

27. Weaver, *Thank God My Regiment*, 128; Hyde, *One Hundred and Twelfth N.Y.*, 142–43; Williams, *Leaves from a Trooper's Diary*, 47.

28. Barnet, *Martyrs and Heroes of Illinois*, 107–8; Strong, *121st Pennsylvania*, 132; Bennett and Haigh, *Thirty-Sixth Illinois*, 332; Denny, *Twenty-Fifth Mass.*, 330; Kimbell, *First Illinois Light Artillery*, 64; J. W. Merrill, *24th Independent Battery, N.Y. Light Artillery*, 33–34; Day, *One Hundred and First Ohio Infantry*, 21.

29. Barber, *Army Memoirs*, 49.

30. Hull, *Ninety-Seventh New York*, 90; Hughes, *Philip Daingerfield Stephenson*, 193–95.

31. Linderman, *Embattled Courage*, 24.

32. Tobie, *First Maine Cavalry*, 375; Smith, *Thirty-First Indiana*, 61, 63–64; Thompson, *112th Illinois*, 144.

33. Craft, *One Hundred Forty-First Pennsylvania*, 87.

34. Reardon, *With a Sword in One Hand*, 116.

35. See Clarke, *War Stories*, esp. chap. 3 and also 113. As the various examples in this chapter demonstrate, though, not all soldiers who experienced premonitions of death "suffered well" in the Victorian manner.

36. See Schantz, *Awaiting the Heavenly Country*. I find Schantz's explanation more persuasive than Faust's, who argues that soldiers' belief in the afterlife was rooted not in "Scripture or science" but in "distress and desire." See Faust, *This Republic of Suffering*, 187.

On fatalism and soldiers resigning themselves to accept their fate, see Rable, *God's Almost Chosen Peoples*, 140–43, 171, 175–76.

37. King, Gibbs, and Northup, *Ninety-Third New York*, 314–15; Partridge, *Ninety-Sixth Illinois Volunteer*, 442; Rood, *Twelfth Wisconsin*, 175–76; Robert Laird Stewart, *One Hundred and Fortieth Pennsylvania*, 428–29; Schmidt, *147th Pennsylvania*, 617–18; J. W. Jones, *Story of American Heroism*, 259, 676–77. For a similar reaction to amputations, see Brian Craig Miller, *Empty Sleeves*, 75.

38. Parker and Carter, *Twenty-Second Massachusetts*, 148; Cogswell, *Eleventh New Hampshire*, 145, 681; E. M. Woodward, *Our Regiment*, 200–201.

39. Davenport, *Fifth New York*, 468–69; Sanders, *Strange Tales*, 58–61.

40. Curran, *John Dooley's Civil War*, 209, 222.

41. Robert Laird Stewart, *One Hundred and Fortieth Pennsylvania*, 92; Lowe, *James C. Bates*, 70, 337; Survivors' Association, *118th Pennsylvania*, 185. For another false presentiment at Chancellorsville, see Muffly, *148th Pennsylvania*, 523–24.

42. Messent and Courtney, *Joseph Hopkins Twichell*, 115–16.

43. Kirk, *Fifteenth Pennsylvania Volunteer Cavalry*, 306; Worsham, *Nineteenth Tennessee*, 184.

44. *Report Proceedings Fifty-Fifth Illinois*, 193–94, 451–52.

45. Clark, "A Dream and Its Fulfillment" (1885), manuscript account in Brock Collection, HL. This story was also published by Clark as "Dreams That Come to Pass," 330–32.

46. "Officers' Dream of Death Fulfilled to the Letter," newspaper clipping in the Shaw Papers, FSA. I thank Krystal Thomas for providing me with a photocopy.

47. Benjamin I. Stubbs to Benjamin Franklin Jackson, April 8, 1862, in Jackson, *So Mourns the Dove*, 21.

48. Fain, *Sanctified Trial*, 31.

49. Genovese, *Roll, Jordan, Roll*, 217, 247–48; Anthony Shafton, "African American Dream Beliefs and Practices," in Barrett and McNamara, *Encyclopedia of Sleep and Dreams*, 1:19–20; Creel, *"A Peculiar People,"* 57; Plane, *Dreams and the Invisible World*, chaps. 5 and 6; Matthew Dennis, "Visions of Handsome Lake: Seneca Dreams, Prophecy, and the Second Great Awakening," in Plane and Tuttle, *Dreams, Dreamers, and Visions*, 230.

50. Pitts, *Gordon County*, 305–6; U.S. Census (1860), Spaulding County, Georgia, 28; combined military service record for W. H. S. Jackson, NARA; findagrave.com has a photograph of Jackson's grave at Oak Hill Cemetery in Griffin, Georgia, which confirms that his body was taken home. The dates on the tombstone are October 7, 1846, and May 15, 1864.

Other stories like this survive from the era, perhaps most famously the "Lost Children of the Alleghenies" who disappeared in 1856 and whose bodies were discovered because of a dream that revealed their location.

51. My thinking here is influenced by Clarke, *War Stories*, 53.

52. McMorries, *First Alabama*, 106; J. W. Jones, *Story of American Heroism*, 64; Gordon, *Reminiscences*, 60–61, 64–65.

53. Hartman and Coles, *Biographical Rosters*, 1:215; Fleming, *Memoir of Capt. C. Seton Fleming*, 53, 100–103.

54. McMurry, *1st Georgia Regulars*, 65, 194. For another similar case, see Stanyan, *Eighth New Hampshire*, 232–37.

55. Barnet, *Martyrs and Heroes of Illinois*, 163–64; Partridge, *Ninety-Sixth Illinois*, 442; Hard, *Eighth Cavalry Regiment Illinois Volunteers*, 280; *Story of the Fifty-Fifth Illinois*, 55.

56. J. W. Jones, *Story of American Heroism*, 120–21; McGee, *72d Indiana*, 181–82.

57. Gould, *First-Tenth-Twenty-Ninth Maine*, 501; Small, *Sixteenth Maine*, 69, 235.

58. Fitzpatrick, "Jubal Early and the Californians," 50–61; Hutchinson, *Seventh Massachusetts*, 135; Derby, *Twenty-Seventh Massachusetts*, 313; Burrage, *Thirty-Sixth Massachusetts*, 172; Sanders, *Strange Tales*, 26–30; Richard M. Reid, *Practicing Medicine*, 70; John Anderson, *Fifty-Seventh Massachusetts*, 144–45.

59. Cockrell and Ballard, *Mississippi Rebel*, 238–40.

60. McDonald, *14 Letters to a Friend*, 154; Neal, *Missouri Engineer*, 127. See also Crowley, *Tennessee Cavalier*, appendix, 7.

61. Stephen G. Abbott, *First New Hampshire*, 328; S. Millett Thompson, *Thirteenth New Hampshire*, 433; *Memorial Fourteenth New-Hampshire*, 234.

62. Bingham, *Little Drummer Boy*, 95, 99; Eddy, *Sixteenth New York*, 180–81; Hall and Hall, *Cayuga in the Field*, 165; Roemer, *Reminiscences*, 103; Moore, *Civil War in Song and Story*, 460; [Bacon], *William Kirkland Bacon*, 48–49, 80–81; Fred C. Floyd, *Fortieth New York*, 266; Clark, *Iron Hearted Regiment*, 190; Best, *121st New York*, 44.

63. Horace R. Abbott, *My Escape from Belle Isle*, 36–38; Sanders, *Strange Tales*, 22–24.

64. Washington Davis, *Camp-Fire Chats*, 289–93; *Indiana* (Pennsylvania) *Progress*, May 4, 1892; J. W. Jones, *Story of American Heroism*, 92; Moore, *Civil War in Song and Story*, 317; Survivors' Association, *118th Pennsylvania Volunteers*, 644; Wallace, *One Hundred and Twenty-Fifth Pennsylvania*, 191; Craft, *One Hundred Forty-First Pennsylvania*, 86; Nesbit, *149th Pennsylvania*, 86, 106; Kirk, *Fifteenth Pennsylvania Volunteer Cavalry*, 557; Rodenbough, Potter, and Seal, *Eighteenth Regiment of Cavalry Pennsylvania*, 25, 53.

65. Coker, *Ninth S.C.*, 100.

66. Zeller, *Second Vermont*, 215; Chittick, *In the Field*, 114; George N. Carpenter, *Eighth Vermont*, 175–76, 185–88.

67. John T. Parham, "Reminiscences of the Maryland Campaign of 1862," in Newsome, Horn, and Selby, *Civil War Talks*, 108.

68. Bryant, *Third Wisconsin*, 83, 378; *Proceedings of the Twenty-First Wisconsin*, 39–41; Sanders, *Strange Tales*, 12–14, 20–22, 30–32.

69. Parker, "The Navy in the Battles and Capture of Fort Fisher," in Blakeman, *Personal Recollections*, 114.

70. See, for example, Oliver Wendell Holmes Jr., "In Our Youth Our Hearts Were Touched with Fire," in Kass, Kass, and Schaub, *What So Proudly We Hail*, 694.

71. *Visions of Joseph Hoag*, 1; Gerona, *Night Journeys*, 249–52. For other antebellum dreams of the coming of the war, see Burstein, *Lincoln Dreamt He Died*, 192; Schantz, *Awaiting the Heavenly Country*, 97–98.

72. Barber and Swinson, *Charles Barber*, 46–50.

73. J. W. Reid, *Fourth S.C.*, 28. For another prophetic dream of a soldier coming home, see Burstein, *Lincoln Dreamt He Died*, 181.

74. Wiley, *Warren Akin*, 112–13.

75. Woodward, *Mary Chesnut's Civil War*, 440–41. See also Robertson, *Lucy Breckinridge*, 198. I have been unable to locate the original newspaper article.

76. Cooney, *Common Soldier*, 15.

77. George W. Tillotson to wife, August 11, 1864, Tillotson Collection, GLI. In this letter Tillotson also described a soldier who had a presentiment and hoped to avoid combat but was killed by a rebel bullet.

78. Avary, *Recollections of Stephens*, 346–47, 468.

79. Hughes, *Philip Daingerfield Stephenson*, 193.

80. Quoted in Culpepper, *Women of the Civil War South*, 146.

81. J. W. Jones, *Story of American Heroism*, 64.

82. George N. Carpenter, *History of the Eighth Vermont*, 152.

83. Shermer, *Believing Brain*, 59–110 (quotation 77); Plane, *Dreams and the Invisible World*, 116–17, 125.

84. John B. Gordon, *Reminiscences*, 61, 65; Plane, *Dreams and the Invisible World*, 39–40.

85. Hughes, *Philip Daingerfield Stephenson*, 193, 235.

86. Orr, "Outcome of a Maimed Consciousness"; Plane, *Dreams and the Invisible World*, 32.

87. Gwin, *Woman's Civil War*, 213.

88. On soldiers' fears of anonymous death, see Fahs, *Imagined Civil War*, 93–105; Faust, *This Republic of Suffering*, chap. 4; Mitchell, *Civil War Soldiers*, 60–64.

Chapter Six

1. Glover, *Sleeping Sentinel*; Stevens, *Three Years in the Sixth Corps*, 42–44. For Scott's full dying words, see Paschal P. Ripley to Lincoln, January 9, 1865, Lincoln Papers, LC.

2. De Haes Janvier, *Sleeping Sentinel*, 1–19; Philadelphia *Press*, April 29, June 9, 1863 and June 30, 1864; *Pittsburgh Daily Gazette and Advertiser*, November 6, 1863; *Milwaukee*

Sentinel, October 6, 1863; Fehrenbacher and Fehrenbacher, *Recollected Words*, 101. One witness to Murdock's reading in the Senate chamber wrote, "He read quite a number of pieces of patriotic poetry; most of them admirably well, but *agonized* too much over others, altogether over doing them." See Orville Hickman Browning, diary entry for January 10, 1863, in Pease and Randall, *Diary of Browning*, 1:612.

3. Fahs, *Imagined Civil War*, 92; Clarke, *War Stories*, 122, 145–46.

4. Hitchcock, *Analysis of the Holy Bible*, 158.

5. *The Wreath*, 147–48; Goodrich, *Fourth Reader*, 203–4; Sargent, *Standard Speaker*, 147.

6. Henry William Herbert, "The Soldier's Dream: An Incident of Egypt," *Godey's Lady's Book* (March 1852): 178–80; poems by J. L. Swan and Fanny Fales, "The Soldier's Dream of Home," *Godey's Lady's Book* (October 1852): 380.

7. Mauro, *Southern Spy*, 56–57; Robert Bruce Donald, *Manhood and Patriotic Awakening*, 92–93; McMurray, *Uncompromising Secessionist*, 65; Elias Winans Price to Henrietta McDowell Price, September 8, 1863, Price Papers, SHC; Lysander Wheeler to parents, March 15, 1863, Wheeler Collection, GLI; Burstein, *Lincoln Dreamt He Died*, 213; Burlingame, *Abraham Lincoln: A Life*, 1:245.

8. Clark and Clark, *Soldier's Dream of Home*, 78–83, 87. For another soldier who was moved to poetry by the thought of dreams of home, see Cincinnati *Western Christian Advocate*, January 1, 1862. For another soldier who used similar stationery, see Barber and Swinson, *Charles Barber*, 86.

9. Wharton, *War Songs*, 308–11.

10. Quoted in Fahs, *Imagined Civil War*, 106–7. The full text of the poem is available in Moore, *Lyrics of Loyalty*, 139–41, as well as a number of other books and periodicals from the period.

11. Northrop, *Chronicles*, 124; Clarke Account Books, CWM.

12. Denny, *Twenty-Fifth Mass.*, 102–3. The poem continues for another ten stanzas. For another example, see "To My Wife" in the Columbus *Crisis*, September 3, 1862.

13. McWhirter, *Battle Hymns*, 22; Everest, "Soldier's Vision"; Sawyer, "I Dreamed My Boy"; Fahs, *Imagined Civil War*, 118; Drago, *Confederate Phoenix*, 30.

14. Miles, *Photographic History*, 9:350. Several editions of this song are available at the Library of Congress and other repositories.

15. Davis, *"Bully for the Band!,"* 93.

16. Hughes, *Philip Daingerfield Stephenson*, 131.

17. Nisbet, *Four Years*, 303.

18. Tappan, *Russell M. Tuttle*, 149.

19. Sawyer, Sawyer, and Sawyer, *Letters from a Civil War Surgeon*, 75.

20. I have located about dozen visual images of soldiers' dreams from the Civil War years. Most are available in the catalog of the Library of Congress's Prints and Photographs Division. For another, see *The Soldier's Dream of Peace*, Civil War Broadsides, GLI. For a selection of patriotic covers, see Weiss, *Catalog of Patriotic Covers*, 213.

21. Hughes, *Spectacles of Reform*, 133–37.

22. Dennis E. Suttles, "'For the Well-Being of the Child': The Law and Childhood," in Stowell, *In Tender Consideration*, 46–47; Gallman, *Defining Duty*, 189–90; Mintz and Kellogg, *Domestic Revolutions*, 43–65.

23. On the power of sentimental literature in the Civil War era, see Fahs, *Imagined Civil War*, chap. 3; Clarke, *War Stories*.

24. Currier and Ives, *The Soldier's Dream of Home*, lithograph; collection of the author.

25. Lucy Pier Stevens, diary entry for December 20, 1864, provided by email by Vicki Adams Tongate (the original diary is held at Southern Methodist University).

26. Divine, Souders, and Souders, *"To Talk Is Treason,"* 94.

27. Neely and Holzer, *Union Image*, 91–97; Fahs, "Picturing the Civil War."

28. Neely and Holzer, *Union Image*, 93–94; Schantz, *Awaiting the Heavenly Country*, 163–79. On soldiers holding pictures of their loved ones as they died, see Faust, *This Republic of Suffering*, 11–12.

29. Boyd, *Patriotic Envelopes*, 82. One example of a *carte de visite* is in the collection of the author. Civil War photograph collector Ronald S. Coddington owns two *cartes de visite* of a Pennsylvania soldier who tried to create his own versions of these scenes. In one the soldier pretends to sleep with a letter in his hand, ostensibly dreaming of his wife who sent it. In the other, the photographer superimposed a woman hovering over the soldier as he poses asleep. Presumably the woman is his wife, about whom he always dreams. These images appeared in Coddington, "Comforting Spirit," 72.

30. Allen and Bohannon, *Campaigning with "Old Stonewall,"* 173.

31. Tappan, *Russell M. Tuttle*, 147–48.

32. James M. Harrison to mother, January 14, 1863, Harrison Letters, UAK. For other soldiers who wrote home about having the soldier's dream, see Nat S. Turner, *Southern Soldier's Letters Home*, 100; Blair, *Politician Goes to War*, 195; Barber and Swinson, *Charles Barber*, 63, 161.

33. Kimmel and Musick, *"I Am Busy Drawing Pictures,"* 108–10.

34. Hight, *Fifty-Eighth Indiana*, 414.

35. This is not to say that culture had no influence on what soldiers saw in their dreams.

36. Burstein, *Lincoln Dreamt He Died*, 225.

37. See Fussell, *Great War and Modern Memory*.

38. The World War I and World War II advertisements and postcards described here have all appeared on eBay between August 2013 and November 2015. Some are in the collection of the author.

39. *Raleigh Daily Progress*, October 24, 1863.

40. Sanders, *Strange Tales*, 56–57; Burstein, *Lincoln Dreamt He Died*, 189–191; *Athens Post* (GA), February 8, 1850. On March 2, 1861, *Harper's Weekly* published a two-page spread entitled "The Dreamer at Moultrie—1776 and 1861" that similarly appealed to Southerner soldiers to remember the common sacrifices of the Revolutionary generation.

41. Shelbyville *Shelby Volunteer*, November 8, 1860.

42. The story circulated throughout the war years. See, for example, the following Pennsylvania newspapers: Reading *Daily Times*, December 5, 1861; Bellefonte *Central Press*, April 4, 1861; Greencastle *Pilot*, April 14, 1863; Montrose *Independent Republican*, March 28, 1865.

43. Prince, "General McClellan's Dream," 353–55.

44. *Boston Pilot*, May 10, 1862; Spear, *Jeff Davis's Dream*; Croffut and Morris, *History of Connecticut*, 567; Lowry, *Story the Soldiers Wouldn't Tell*, 49–50. A cartoon entitled, "The Hand-Writing on the Walls at Richmond; or, The Dream of the Rebel Bill-Poster, Jeff Davis," which appeared in *Harper's Weekly* on March 22, 1862, also showed Davis unable to defeat the Yankees and gain Southern independence. The optimism of this early Northern cartoon would soon be shown a bit hollow.

45. *Vanity Fair*, August 17, 1861; *Sacramento Daily Union*, September 7, 1861; Gallman, *Defining Duty*, 95–97, 274.

46. *Millersburg (OH) Holmes County Farmer*, February 11, 1864; *Dayton (OH) Daily Empire*, June 13, 1864; *Ebensburg (PA) Democrat and Sentinel*, June 15, 1864, *Plymouth (IN) Weekly Democrat*, June 16, 1864; *Ebensburg (PA) Democrat and Sentinel*, May 3, 1866.

47. Styple, *Writing and Fighting the Civil War*, 265.

Chapter Seven

1. Helen M. Rauschnabel to Mary Todd Lincoln, 7 May 1861, Lincoln Papers, LC.

2. Weaver, *Thank God My Regiment an African One*, 124–30, 132, 135, 136n56, 140–41, 145, 146n76, 150; Peck, *How Private Peck*, 129.

For a wounded soldier from the Thirty-Eighth Wisconsin Volunteers who dreamed of seeing and hearing Lincoln, see Mary D. Uline, "The Voice: A Lincoln Story Based Upon a True Incident," *Congregationalist*, February 7, 1929, newspaper clipping in "Reminiscences U" file, LFFC.

For dreams of women that foretold the promotion of an officer in their family, see Simon, *Personal Memoirs of Julia Dent Grant*, 90–91; Chittick, *In the Field*, 112.

3. Blackman, *Wild Rose*, 193.

4. *Richmond Enquirer*, July 8, 1864. Wootton published two slightly different versions of the dream after the war. See Wootton, *Mysterious Eternal Facts*, 4–6; *Second Edition*, 6–8. In the postwar versions, Wootton referred to Lincoln as "Booth's special 'pet.'"

5. Henry Mosler Diary, Smithsonian.

6. Washington, *They Knew Lincoln*, 28, 38–40.

7. Gideon Welles, diary entry for April 14, 1865 (probably written April 17), in Gienapp and Gienapp, *Civil War Diary of Gideon Welles*, 623–24; Fehrenbacher and Fehrenbacher, *Recollected Words*, 547n492.

8. Charles Dickens to John Forster, February 4, 1868, in Hartley, *Selected Letters of Charles Dickens*, 418–19.

9. Seward, *Reminiscences*, 255.

10. Dieck, *Life and Public Services*, 669–70; Somers, "Lincoln's Dreams," 15–17. The line that Welles attributed to Grant about Stones River would not have made sense in Grant's telling of the dream since in this account Lincoln recognized that bad events had followed previous occurrences of the dream.

11. *New York Herald*, April 18, 1865; *Philadelphia Press*, April 24, 1865; *Indianapolis Daily Journal*, April 19, 1865; *Cleveland Morning Leader*, April 20, 1865; *Lancaster (OH) Gazette*, April 27, 1865; *San Francisco Bulletin*, May 19, 1865.

12. [Welles], "Lincoln and Johnson," 525; Fox, *Lincoln's Body*, 61.

13. George Templeton Strong, diary entry for April 21, 1865, in Nevins and Thomas, *Diary of Strong*, 3:591; Lewis, *Assassination of Lincoln*, 291; Cyrus O. Poole, "The Religious Convictions of Abraham Lincoln: A Study," newspaper clipping in "Spiritualist" file, LFFC.

14. Welles, *Diary of Gideon Welles*, 2:282. The words "your (my) element" were inserted into the manuscript version in Welles's hand, but it is unknown when the words were added. See the Welles diary entry for April 14, 1865, Welles Papers, LC.

15. Seward, *Seward at Washington*, 274.

16. Marvel, *Lincoln's Autocrat*, 266.

17. See Dieck, *Life and Public Services*, 670; Fox, *Lincoln's Body*, 58–61.

18. Spielberg, *Lincoln*. For one of the children's books, see Smith, *Abe Lincoln's Dream*.

19. Lincoln, "Speech in Independence Hall, Philadelphia, Pennsylvania," February 22, 1861, in *CWL*, 4:240–41.

20. All quoted in Burlingame, *Abraham Lincoln: A Life*, 2:799. See also Buckingham, *Life of Buckingham*, 323. On Lincoln's superstition, spiritualism, and longstanding sense of foreboding, see Wilson, *Honor's Voice*, 188–93; Current, *Lincoln Nobody Knows*, 51–75.

21. Recollection of Le Grand B. Cannon, in Fehrenbacher and Fehrenbacher, *Recollected Words*, 78; Wilson and Davis, *Herndon's Informants*, 679. For a description of how a young Lincoln typically reacted to nightmares, see Whitney, *Life on the Circuit*, 47–48.

22. Lincoln to Mary Todd Lincoln, April 16, 1848 and June 9, 1863, both in *CWL*, 1:466 and 6:256. For brief discussions of Mary's dreams about their sons, see Baker, *Mary Todd Lincoln*, 314; Emerson, *Madness of Mary Lincoln*, 14; Emerson, "Mary Todd Lincoln's Lost Letters," 57.

23. Fox, "Abraham Lincoln's Dreams." Lincoln's law partner William H. Herndon wrote, "His early Baptist training made him a fatalist up to the day of his death, and, listening in boyish wonder to the legends of some toothless old dame led him to believe in the significance of dreams and visions." See Wilson and Davis, *Herndon's Lincoln*, 54.

24. Wilson and Davis, *Herndon's Informants*, 359; Mary Lincoln to Mary Ann Cuthbert, March 24, 1865, and Mary to Abraham Lincoln, April 2, 1865, both in Turner and Turner, *Mary Todd Lincoln*, 207–11. More than a year earlier, on February 10, 1864, the White House stable caught on fire. Lincoln ran out of the White House and tried to save the horses inside, but arrived too late.

25. John Hay, diary entry for December 23, 1863, in Burlingame and Ettlinger, *Inside Lincoln's White House*, 132.

26. Lewis, *Assassination of Lincoln*, 300.

27. Susan Boyce, who knew Lincoln in 1836–1837, claimed sixty years later that he "was a spiritualist and he believed in dreams. He often told me his dreams were prophetic." Boyce's recollections must be read with some caution, however. She also claimed that Lincoln told her, "I was the first woman he ever loved, and that he was sure he could never love any one else as he did me," but that she had rejected his

marriage proposal because she did not love him. Moreover, she recollected incorrectly that Lincoln studied the law in New Salem by borrowing books from William H. Seward. See *Reading (PA) Daily Times and Dispatch*, June 14, 1897, newspaper clipping in LFFC.

28. *Brooklyn Daily Eagle*, May 5, 1865; *New York Times*, May 7, 1865; Somers, "Lincoln's Dreams," 42–43.

29. Washington, D.C. *National Republican*, June 12, 1865. For an early rebuttal to Carpenter's account, see Somers, "Lincoln's Dreams," 45.

30. Brooks, "Personal Recollections," 224–25. As explained below, this account is often mistakenly attributed to John Hay.

31. Carpenter, *Six Months at the White House*, 163–65.

32. Lamon, *Life of Abraham Lincoln*, 476–77. It should be noted that Pennsylvania Democrat Chauncey Forward Black ghostwrote Lamon's *Life of Abraham Lincoln*. Black likely picked the story up from Holland, *Life of Abraham Lincoln*, 245–46, which incorrectly attributed the *Harper's* story to Hay.

33. Lamon, *Recollections*, 112–13. On the discrepancies among the various accounts of this dream, see Fehrenbacher, *Lincoln in Text and Context*, 272–74; Fehrenbacher and Fehrenbacher, *Recollected Words*, 534n280.

34. Lamon, *Recollections*, 114–18.

35. Swanson acknowledges that Lamon might have embellished or even made up the White House funeral dream. Goodwin hedges by stating that Lincoln "purportedly told Ward Lamon" the dream. Current says the dream is "not so well documented," but concludes, "If the story has a pat, made-up quality, it is at least in keeping with Lincoln's well-known propensity to dream and talk about his dreaming." Guelzo rightly points out that the dream was of an assassinated president, not necessarily Lincoln.

Sandburg, *Abraham Lincoln*, 3:823–27; Van Doren Stern, *Life and Writings*, 185; Oates, *With Malice Toward None*, 462–63; Current, *Lincoln Nobody Knows*, 70; Baker, *Mary Todd Lincoln*, 241; Winik, *April 1865*, 204–6; Goodwin, *Team of Rivals*, 728–29; Holzer, *50 Objects*, 318–19; Holzer, *Lincoln Assassinated*, xv–xvii; Guelzo, *Redeemer President*, 428–29; Guelzo, *Fateful Lightning*, 466; Swanson, *Bloody Crimes*, 161–63; Vidal, *Lincoln*, 640; O'Reilly and Dugard, *Killing Lincoln*, 113–14. It appears in other histories as well.

36. Grahame-Smith, *Vampire Hunter*, 367–68 (see also 236–40); Willis, *Lincoln's Dreams*, chap. 4.

37. Millard, *Destiny of the Republic*, 121–22. About a month before his inauguration in 1881, Garfield did dream of a shipwreck in which he survived but his vice president, Chester A. Arthur, drowned. See Burstein, *Lincoln Dreamt He Died*, 222.

38. Ibid., 219–20. Burstein notes that the dream may be embellished or untrue, but the least credible part for him is Mary Lincoln asking her husband whether he believed in dreams since she surely would have known the answer to that question by that point in their relationship.

39. Johnson, *Lincoln* (1988); Moat, *Killing Lincoln* (2013); *Touched by an Angel*, "Beautiful Dreamer" (1998); *Alcoa Presents: One Step Beyond*, "The Day the World Wept" (1960); Jayanti, *Lincoln* (2005); Kane, *Day Lincoln Was Shot* (1998); *Lincoln's Washington at War* (2013). I thank Frank Dello Stritto for e-mailing me about "The Day the World Wept" after seeing me speak about Lincoln's dreams on C-SPAN.

40. Norman Vincent Peale, "Mystic Lincoln," quoted by Sen. Edward J. Thye, February 25, 1957, in "Spiritualist" file, LFFC.

41. Lederer, *Presidential Trivia*, 69; Omoyajowo, *Your Dreams*, 14. After telling the story, Omoyajowo concludes: "As we all know the prophecy was fulfilled in his case." For examples of modern spiritualism books and dream guides that describe this dream, see Savary et al., *Dreams and Spiritual Growth*, 210; Farrell, *Mystical Experiences*, chap. 12; Tull, *Dreams*, 39; Iddrisu, *Understanding Your Dreams*, 6; Kienholz, *Scriptural Lessons*, 237–38; Green, *Psychic Self-Defence*, 81–83; Xiong, *Outline of Parapsychology*, 123; Guiley, *Dreams and Astral Travel*, 71–72; Lord, *Science, Mind and Paranormal Experience*, 227; Allan, *Prophecies*, chap. 20.

42. Stansell incorrectly states that Lincoln made this statement to his Cabinet on April 14, 1865. See Stansell, "Dreams," 249.

43. Lamon, *Recollections*, 114; "The Real Abe Lincoln: Anecdotal Reminiscences: Mr. Lincoln's Strange Presentiments—Curious Dreams at Critical Junctures and His Singular Philosophy Concerning Them," *Chicago Morning News*, August 27, 1887; boxes 21, 25–32, Lamon Papers, HL. In the Fall 2014 issue of *We the People: A Newsletter of the Abraham Lincoln Association*, I argued that Lamon's daughter, Dorothy, had been the one to place Lamon in this story. A few weeks after that article appeared—on January 14, 2015—I discovered a footnote in *Herndon's Informants* pointing to Lamon's 1887 article, which I then obtained through interlibrary loan. In this book I have corrected my mistake.

44. Donald, *Lincoln*, 666n465.

45. Fehrenbacher and Fehrenbacher, *Recollected Words*, 281, 535n294.

46. Lamon to Stanton, April 27, 1865, Lamon Papers; Lamon to Lincoln, March 23, 1865, Lincoln Papers. Lamon claimed to hear the story from Lincoln on several occasions shortly before the assassination (see Lamon, *Recollections*, 113–14), which indicates that he could not have heard the story from Lincoln on April 13, the only day he saw Lincoln that month.

47. Frederick, Maryland *Examiner*, February 4, 1874. The *Waynesboro (PA) Village Record* reprinted the story on Lincoln's birthday a week later, February 12, 1874. The *Examiner* may have picked this story up from another paper, but I have been unable to locate an earlier telling of the story. I have done numerous searches using the Penn State Digital Collections, newspapers.com, newspaperarchive.com, Chronicling America, NYS Historic Newspapers, and several Readex, NewsBank, and ProQuest collections. In these databases, the next newspaper versions of this article appeared in the *Chester (PA) Daily Times*, August 24, 1880, and the *Nebraska Advertiser*, April 29, 1880—after the dream had appeared in *Gleason's Monthly Companion*.

48. "President Lincoln's Dream," 140–41.

49. Ibid., 141; Lamon, *Recollections*, 120; Good, *We Saw Lincoln Shot*, 22–23; Wilson and Davis, *Herndon's Informants*, 359.

50. "President Lincoln's Dream," 141.

51. The ship on the water dream was being discussed publicly in Washington immediately after Lincoln's death. See George Templeton Strong, diary entry for April 21, 1865, in Nevins and Thomas, *Diary of Strong*, 3:591.

52. See, for example, *New Bloomfield (PA) Times*, September 7, 1880; *Nashville Liberal* reproduced in *Washington Post*, November 11, 1883, and the *Troy Times* reproduced in *Herald of Gospel Liberty*, February 14, 1884.

53. Lamon sent letters to about a dozen newspaper editors in 1887 asking them to publish his articles for $25 each. Drafts of the letters survive in his papers at the Huntington Library. I thank Michelle Ganz, archivist at Lincoln Memorial University, for examining the Dorothy Lamon Teillard Collection for any mention of the White House funeral dream.

54. One 1962 article in *Argosy* entitled "Abe Lincoln—Ghost Chaser," claimed that a diary exists from April 11, 1865, stating that "Lincoln often dreams he sees his own corpse laid out in the White House"; however, the original diary has not been located. See "Spiritualist" file, LFFC. If this diary exists, it would be the earliest textual evidence for the dream.

Shortly before this book went to copyediting I discovered a well-researched master's thesis by Lucas R. Somers which argues for the veracity of this dream based on a memoir written by Lamon some time in the 1880s but not published until 2010. Somers maintains that this new source is a bridge between the *Gleason*'s version and that in *Recollections* and "is a credible source for the White House funeral dream." Yet Somers did not notice that some of the language in this "new" version of the story was pilfered from other sources, such as an unrelated story about "a half-witted boy named Jake" that appeared in Carpenter's *Six Months*. This "new" account, in short, shows Lamon doing what he is well known for—pilfering and rewriting stories about Lincoln. In addition, Somers states that in this new version Lamon gave "no specific reference to the date it took place," but Lamon, in fact, claimed that Lincoln reported the dream "only a short time before his death." Thus, a more plausible explanation for this new account is that it was just one step in the progression Lamon took from reading the story in the early 1880s until he finally inserted himself into it in 1887. See Somers, "Lincoln's Dreams," 27–41; O'Connor, *Life of Lincoln*, 464–68.

55. "Lincoln's Birthday Recalls Family History to City Woman," *Minneapolis Star-Journal*, February 12, 1943, newspaper clipping in LFFC.

56. "Colonel W. H. Crook, President's Friend, Dead," (1915) newspaper clipping in LFFC; Crook, *Memories of the White House*, 39–40; Gerry, *Through Five Administrations*, 67–76. On Crook's unreliability, see Hanchett, "Persistent Myths of the Lincoln Assassination," 172–79.

57. "Record of a Dream," Lincoln Association Collection, ALPLM; *CWL*, 8:440. I thank Daniel Stowell for providing me with a copy of this document.

One family in Ypsilanti, Michigan, claimed to have a letter Lincoln wrote in April 1865 in which he said "he had a presentiment that something was going to happen to him or to the government." See "Decatur Woman, 85, Recalls Lincoln," *Illinois State Journal*, February 11, 1940, newspaper clipping in LFFC. To date, the letter has not been located by the Papers of Abraham Lincoln.

For another dream in which Lincoln dreamed of collecting mocking bird eggs, see "Father of W.A. Powel Friend Abe Lincoln," undated newspaper clipping in LFFC.

58. Royster, *Destructive War*, 246; Oates, *With Malice Toward None*, 360.

59. Thomas, *Abraham Lincoln*, 364.

60. Hoffman, "Benjamin P. Thomas," 42–43.

61. After describing the Murfreesboro "dream" and the ship on the water dream, Royster concludes: "Such ties to war put Lincoln into combat in ways beyond his preferring victory and his insisting that the army fight. His empathy, as his contemporaries imagined it, brought him closer to a state of mind wherein Federal victories belonged as much to him as to the soldiers, while the costs in wounds and death fell, as with combatants, on men he knew and finally, after the last dream, on him. Americans who revered Lincoln after his death found in his comprehensive spiritual experience of the war a fitting emblem of the passion and the sensibility of the nation's involvement in combat." See Royster, *Destructive War*, 244.

Some soldiers wished Lincoln would be haunted by the realities of the war in his dreams. "Let him review the past two years, and in his midnight dream, he will see one long line of skeleton forms and weeping widows and orphans moving along in solemn silence, with no voice of consolation or sympathy from them," wrote one New Jersey soldier. See Hennessy, "Lincoln Wins Back His Army," 42.

On Lincoln's sleeplessness, see Powell, *Lincoln Day by Day*, 3:126.

62. Ellis, *Founding Brothers*, 120. This story has been repeated by historians of other eras. Jon Butler, for example, writes that Lincoln had "frequent and tormented dreams," and "numerous premonitions of death, his own as well as those of soldiers on the battlefield." See Butler, *Awash in a Sea of Faith*, 295.

63. Scott, *Visitation of God*, 215; Turner, *Beware the People Weeping*, 82; White, *A. Lincoln*, 675–76; Holzer, Boritt, and Neely, *Lincoln Image*, 149–59; Henry Ward Beecher, "The New Impulse of Patriotism for His Sake," Plymouth Church, Brooklyn, New York, April 23, 1865," in Braden, *Building the Myth*, 39.

64. *Christian Union*, April 17, 1884; Stokes, *D. W. Griffith's The Birth of a Nation*, 166–67; Savage, *Standing Soldiers, Kneeling Slaves*, 126. Regrettably, for some African Americans, this would develop into a "white dream." See Bennett, *Forced into Glory*.

65. Bullard, *Lincoln in Marble and Bronze*, 228–41; Percoco, *Summers with Lincoln*, 57–58.

66. Stanton quoted in Braden, *Building the Myth*, 13; Cullom, "Savior of the Nation," February 12, 1890, ibid., 119; Jonathan P. Dolliver, "The Outline of the Greatness of His Gigantic Figure," February 13, 1905, ibid., 126; William E. Borah, "Lincoln the Orator," November 9, 1911, ibid., 174.

67. Holzer, Boritt, and Neely, *Lincoln Image*, 149.

68. I developed and wrote my interpretation of the significance of Lincoln's dreams before reading Lloyd Lewis's *Myths after Lincoln*. Lewis offers a similar view of Lincoln's dreams, and it is worth quoting here. Of the ship on the water dream, he writes: "Biographers of the man lingered over it, orators grew dramatic with it, superstitious folk took it as evidence that the sad, herculean hero was supernatural, and even Americans who fancied themselves as rationalists cherished it as an instance of Lincoln's superiority in mystic ways." He continues: "Coming when it did, and living as it has, this story of the dream has been one of the reasons—many though they are—for Lincoln's deification in the Republic. It helped make him the American god." See Lewis, *Assassination of Lincoln*, 290.

69. Whitney, *Life on the Circuit*, 599.

70. Jamison, *Recollections of Pioneer*, 43.

Epilogue

1. Recollection of David Dixon Porter, in Fehrenbacher and Fehrenbacher, *Recollected Words*, 366.

2. Messent and Courtney, *Joseph Hopkins Twichell*, 309. Twichell had likened what he saw during the war to a dream as well. See ibid., 13, 125, 145, 149.

3. Tappan, *Russell M. Tuttle*, 216. Many Confederates felt alike. See Lizzie Alsop Diary, April 22, 1865, VHS.

4. Snell, *Dancing Along the Deadline*, 105.

5. Davis and Swentor, *Bluegrass Confederate*, 6; Chamberlain, *Passing of the Armies*, 267. For a recent assessment of the accuracy of Chamberlain's recollections, see Cushman, "Surrender Stories."

6. Sawyer, *Letters from a Civil War Surgeon*, 342; Noble, *Sermon*, 5.

7. William S. Wadham to Edwin M. Stanton, April 26, 1865, Stanton Papers, LC.

8. Deese, *Daughter of Boston*, 347. Virginians had similarly likened John Brown's raid on Harpers Ferry to a dream in 1859. See, for example, Divine et al., *To Talk Is Treason*, 19.

9. Hammond, *Diary of a Union Lady*, 358. Curiously, Lincoln had once likened his own life to Gray's Elegy: "The short and simple annals of the poor." See Herndon, *Herndon's Life of Lincoln*, 1–2.

10. Avary, *Recollections of Stephens*, 141. At least one witness to some of Booth's actions claimed to see one of Booth's conspirators years later in his dreams. See Turner, *Beware the People Weeping*, 230.

11. Greeley, *American Conflict*, 1:554; Nicolay, *Outbreak of Rebellion*, 75.

12. W. F. Hutchinson, "Life on the Texan Blockade," in *Personal Narratives of Events*, 5; Cashin, *First Lady of the Confederacy*, 282.

13. Messent and Courtney, *Joseph Hopkins Twichell*, 159; Kirk, *Fifteenth Pennsylvania Cavalry*, 245–46.

14. Dean, *Shook Over Hell*, 61–62.

15. Ibid., 101–4, 109–13, 128, 131, 137, 144, 153–56, 168, 170. The quote is from page 106. Some modern psychiatrists believe that post-traumatic stress dreams differ from ordinary nightmares in significant ways, including "their content, their repetitive quality, their time of occurrence, and their underlying biology insofar as we know it." See Hartmann, "Who Develops PTSD Nightmares and Who Doesn't," in Barrett, *Trauma and Dreams*, 100–113 (quotation from 105). Unfortunately, historians could never test these distinctions in Civil War soldiers. In many ways we should not even contemplate comparing the dream reports of Civil War veterans with those of later wars, especially Vietnam, since modern veterans' dreams are collected by psychiatrists in great detail and for particular therapeutic purposes, whereas Civil War soldiers' dreams were recorded almost exclusively for private, nonpsychiatric reasons.

16. Kroll and Moran, "White Papers," 249.

17. Macsherry, *Pastime*, 252.

18. Sadly, Woodford died within a week of arriving home. Gordon, *Broken Regiment*, 180–81; Dean, *Shook Over Hell*, 151–53. See also Lowry, *Tarnished Eagles*, 93.

19. Carter, *Magnolia Journey*, 23, 77.

20. Quoted in Faust, *This Republic of Suffering*, 196–97. It should be noted that Bierce was not typical of postwar veteran writers. See Hess, *Union Soldier in Battle*, chap. 9.

21. Whitman, *Leaves of Grass*, 358.

22. Royster, *Destructive War*, 246.

23. Alsop diary entries for July 10, 1865, and February 7, 1866.

24. Quoted in Taliaferro, *All the Great Prizes*, 539–40.

25. Niven, *Chase Papers*, 1:695.

Lincoln has even appeared to people throughout the world in later generations. During World War II, the American president appeared as a vision to a young Czech boy who was suffering in a concentration camp. In the vision Lincoln told the boy things that echoed Lincoln's speeches from the 1850s: "You never forget: All men are created equal. This is true for all men for all times. And these men who would do this thing to you, who put you in here, they're no better than you. You are their equal, because *all men are created equal.* You keep remembering this, and you persevere, you'll be all right." See Ferguson, *Land of Lincoln*, 272.

26. Avary, *Recollections of Stephens*, 346–47.

27. Ibid., 163–64.

28. Ibid., 478.

29. Ibid., 479–80.

30. Ibid., 488.

31. Ibid., 500, 505, 531.

32. Ibid., 99, 345–47.

33. Chamberlayne to Sally Gay (Grattan) Kean, November 18, 1868, Chamberlayne Papers, VHS.

34. Chamberlayne, *Ham Chamberlayne*, viii–ix.

35. Huidekoper to S. Weir Mitchell, February 10, 1906, Mitchell Papers, CP. For an account of Huidekoper's wounding, see Ladd and Ladd, *Bachelder Papers*, 2:954. For a Confederate amputee who awoke from a pleasant dream of home in tears from the pain of his missing limb, see Miller, *Empty Sleeves*, 120.

Note on Method

1. Sobel, *Teach Me Dreams*, 55–56; Gerona, *Night Journeys*, 21–27. Gerona points out that historians Winthrop Jordan, Gary Nash, and Jean Soderland have also relied on this dream, with Jordan offering a similar interpretation "based on the fact that a psychiatrist agreed with him that the pot could be read as a black woman." For his part, the dreamer interpreted the dream as a message from God "to lett black negroes or pots alone," and he thereafter chose not to purchase a slave. He attributed no sexual meaning to the dream as later historians have done.

2. Burstein, *Lincoln Dreamt He Died*, 45. On dream books in this period, see Lears, *Something for Nothing*, 55, 65, 137, 149. To even begin to make these sorts of connections,

one would have to know that the dreamer had read a particular dream book and knew the symbols before having the dream.

3. Friedman, *Enclosed Garden*, 41–45.

4. Charlotte Beradt wrote of dreams under Nazi oppression: "Dreams of this nature also employ imagery, but it is an imagery whose symbols need no interpretation and whose allegories need no explanation; at best, one may decipher its code. These dreams adopt forms and guises which are no more complicated than the ones used in caricature or political satire, and the masks they assume are just as transparent as those worn at carnivals." See Beradt, *Third Reich of Dreams*, 16. My understanding of "dream interpretation" in this book is similar to Beradt's.

5. Burstein, *Lincoln Dreamt He Died*, 59. Gerona offers a helpful explanation of how Quaker dreams got into print. See Gerona, *Night Journeys*, 27–30.

6. Hess, *Union Soldier in Battle*, 161.

7. Plane, *Dreams and the Invisible World*, 12–13. Each chapter discusses a few other dreams in addition to the central dream of the chapter. Chap. 3, for example, focuses on the dreams of four men.

8. Gerona, *Night Journeys*, 6.

9. Sobel, *Teach Me Dreams*, 3.

10. Burstein, *Lincoln Dreamt He Died*, 269. Burstein's chapter on the Civil War discusses about two dozen dreams, not all of which were from the war years, and some of which were published anonymously in newspapers (which means they may not have been actual dreams).

11. Not all dreams that I discovered are included in this book.

12. Shermer, *The Believing Brain*, 257.

13. On the importance of correspondence to soldiers and their families, see Bonner, *Soldier's Pen*, 3–47. Of course, soldiers and their wives were not *always* entirely honest and forthcoming in their letters. For discussion of this aspect of their correspondence, see Gallman, *Mastering Wartime*, chap. 3. Still, Gallman reveals the importance of "correspondence to ease the emotional burdens of separation" (quotation from 71).

14. Nielsen, "Nightmares," in Barrett and McNamara, *Encyclopedia*, 463–65; Gackenbach, "Video Game Play as Nightmare Protection," 222–23. On the unique characteristics of PTSD nightmares—and how they differ from typical nightmares, see van der Kolk et al., "Nightmares and Trauma," 187–90.

Bibliography

Primary Sources

Manuscripts

Carlisle, Pa.
    U.S. Army Military History Institute
        Civil War Times Illustrated Collection
            Charles C. Perkins Diaries
            Diary of Delos Phillips
Chapel Hill, N.C.
    University of North Carolina
        Southern Historical Collection
            William H. Haigh Papers
            Elias Winans Price Papers
Charleston, S.C.
    South Carolina Historical Society
        Patterson-Dye Correspondence (SCHS 1249)
Durham, N.C.
    Duke University
        Motsinger Family Papers
Durham, N.H.
    University of New Hampshire
        Leander Harris Collection
Fayetteville, Ark.
    University of Arkansas
        James M. Harrison Letters
Fort Wayne, Ind.
    Allen County Public Library
        Lincoln Financial Foundation Collection
Harrogate, Tenn.
    Lincoln Memorial University
        Dorothy Lamon Teillard Collection
Iowa City, Iowa
    University of Iowa Libraries
        Charles Thomas Ackley Civil War Letters
        William Titus Rigby Letters
        Shelton Family Papers
        Sterns Family Papers

Lexington, Va.
  Washington & Lee University
    Alexander Sterrett Paxton Papers
Madison, Wisc.
  Wisconsin Historical Society
    H. H. Bennett Papers (MSS 935)
Milwaukee, Wisc.
  University of Wisconsin-Milwaukee
    Miles Butterfield Papers
Mount Desert, Maine
  Mount Desert Island Historical Society
    James M. Parker Papers
Newport, R.I.
  Naval War College
    Naval Historical Collection
      Timothy F. Murphy Papers
Newport News, Va.
  The Mariners' Museum Library
    H. E. Coleman Letter (MS0319)
    William McBlair Papers (MS18)
    Samuel Gilbert Webber Letters (MS0080)
New York, N.Y.
  Gilder Lehrman Institute of American History
    Civil War Broadsides, Posters, and Prints (GLC08442)
    George W. Clark Collection (GLC06167)
    Gustave Cook Collection (GLC02570)
    Gibson Collection of Civil War Soldiers Archives (GLC03523)
    John Jones Collection (GLC05981)
    Joseph Jones Collection (GLC02739)
    George W. Tillotson Collection (GLC04558)
    Lysander Wheeler Collection (GLC07460)
  New-York Historical Society
    War Letters, 1861–1865
Philadelphia, Pa.
  The College of Physicians
    S. Weir Mitchell Papers
  Historical Society of Pennsylvania
    Sidney George Fisher Collection
  Union League of Philadelphia
    Alexander Wallace Givens Diary
  University of Pennsylvania
    Harriet M. Buss Papers
    Henry Inch Cowan Letters
Richmond, Va.
  Library of Virginia

Sophia Stockett Sellman Letters
Virginia Historical Society
Lizzie Alsop Diary
Aylett Family Papers
John Bennett Papers
Bolton Family Papers
John Hampden Chamberlayne Papers
Rose Family Papers
War Record of Doctor James McClure Scott
Thom Family Papers
Wynne Family Papers
San Marino, Calif.
The Huntington Library
Robert Alonzo Brock Collection
Ward Hill Lamon Papers
South Windsor, Conn.
Wood Memorial Library
Erastus W. Burnham Collection
Springfield, Ill.
Abraham Lincoln Presidential Library and Museum
Abraham Lincoln Association Collection
Tallahassee, Fla.
Florida State Archives
Louis James M. Boyd Papers
Florida State University
Roderick Gaspero and James Kirkpatrick Shaw Papers
Washington, D.C.
Library of Congress
Samuel J. Gibson Diary and Correspondence
Abraham Lincoln Papers
Edwin M. Stanton Papers
Gideon Welles Papers
WPA Slave Narratives
National Archives and Records Administration
Combined Military Service Records
Records of the Judge Advocate General (Army) (RG 153)
U.S. Census (1860)
Smithsonian Institution
Henry Mosler Civil War Diary
Williamsburg, Va.
College of William and Mary
James F. Clarke Account Books

Periodicals

American Journal of Insanity
American Journal of the Medical Sciences
Atlantic Monthly
Godey's Lady's Book
Harper's Weekly
Vanity Fair

Published Primary Sources

Abbott, Horace R. *My Escape from Belle Isle: A Paper Prepared and Read Before Michigan Commandery of the Military Order of the Loyal Legion of the United States, December 5, 1889.* Detroit: Winn & Hammond, 1889.

Allen, Randall, and Keith S. Bohannon, eds. *Campaigning with "Old Stonewall": Confederate Captain Ujanirtus Allen's Letters to His Wife.* Baton Rouge: Louisiana State University Press, 1998.

American Slavery As It Is: Testimony of a Thousand Witnesses. New York: American Anti-Slavery Society, 1839.

Ames, Blanche Butler, comp. *Chronicles from the Nineteenth Century: Family Letters of Blanche Butler and Adelbert Ames.* 2 vols. Clinton, Mass.: Colonial Press, 1957.

Anderson, John Q., ed. *Brokenburn: The Journal of Kate Stone, 1861–1868.* 1955; reprint, Baton Rouge: Louisiana State University Press, 1995.

Andrews, William L., ed. *Sisters of the Spirit: Three Black Women's Autobiographies of the Nineteenth Century.* Bloomington: Indiana University Press, 1986.

Ashton, Susanna, ed. *I Belong to South Carolina: South Carolina Slave Narratives.* Columbia: University of South Carolina Press, 2010.

Avary, Myrta Lockett, ed. *Recollections of Alexander H. Stephens.* New York: Doubleday, Page & Co., 1910.

[Bacon, William Johnson]. *Memorial of William Kirkland Bacon, Late Adjutant of the Twenty-Sixth Regiment of New York State Volunteers.* Utica: Roberts, 1863.

Baer, Elizabeth R., ed. *Shadows on My Heart: The Civil War Diary of Lucy Rebecca Buck of Virginia.* Athens: University of Georgia Press, 1997.

Baker, T. Lindsay, ed. *Confederate Guerilla: The Civil War Memoir of Joseph M. Bailey.* Fayetteville: University of Arkansas Press, 2007.

Barber, Lucius W. *Army Memoirs of Lucius W. Barber, Company "D," 15th Illinois Volunteer Infantry.* Chicago: J. M. W. Jones Stationery and Printing Co., 1894.

Barber, Raymond G., and Gary E. Swinson, ed. *The Civil War Letters of Charles Barber, Private, 104th New York Volunteer Infantry.* Torrance, Calif.: Gary E. Swinson, 1991.

Barnet, James, ed. *The Martyrs and Heroes of Illinois in the Great Rebellion*, 2nd ed. Chicago: J. Barnet, 1866.

Barnum, Phineas Taylor. *The Humbugs of the World.* New York: Carleton, 1866.

Bartholow, Roberts. *A Manual of Instructions for Enlisting and Discharging Soldiers.* Philadelphia: J. B. Lippincott, 1864.

———. *Spermatorrhoea: It's Causes, Symptoms, Results, and Treatment.* New York: William Wood, 1870.

Basler, Roy P., et al., eds. *The Collected Works of Abraham Lincoln.* 9 vols. New Brunswick, N.J.: Rutgers University Press, 1953–1955.

Bauer, K. Jack, ed. *Soldiering: The Civil War Diary of Rice C. Bull, 123rd New York Volunteer Infantry.* San Rafael, Calif.: Presidio, 1977.

Bearss, Edwin C., ed. *The Civil War Letters of Major William G. Thompson of the 20th Iowa Infantry Regiment.* Fayetteville, Ark.: Washington County Historical Society, 1966.

Beck, E. W. H. "Letters of a Civil War Surgeon." *Indiana Magazine of History* 27 (June 1931): 132–63.

Bee, Robert L., ed. *The Boys from Rockville: Civil War Narratives of Sgt. Benjamin Hirst, Company D, 14th Connecticut Volunteers.* Knoxville: University of Tennessee Press, 1998.

Bergeron, Paul H., ed. *The Papers of Andrew Johnson: Volume 15, September 1868–April 1869.* Knoxville: University of Tennessee Press, 1998.

Berlin, Ira, et al., eds. *Freedom: A Documentary History of Emancipation, 1861–1867: Series I, Volume I: The Destruction of Slavery.* New York: Cambridge University Press, 1985.

———. *Freedom: A Documentary History of Emancipation, 1861–1867, Series I, Volume II: The Wartime Genesis of Free Labor: The Upper South.* New York: Cambridge University Press, 1993.

———. *Freedom: A Documentary History of Emancipation, 1861–1867, Series I, Volume III: The Wartime Genesis of Free Labor: The Lower South.* New York: Cambridge University Press, 1990.

———. *Freedom: A Documentary History of Emancipation, 1861–1867, Series II: The Black Military Experience.* New York: Cambridge University Press, 1982.

Berlin, Jean V., ed. *A Confederate Nurse: The Diary of Ada W. Bacot, 1860–1863.* Columbia: University of South Carolina Press, 2000.

Billings, John D. *Hardtack and Coffee, or, The Unwritten Story of Army Life.* Boston: George M. Smith, 1887.

Bingham, Luther Goodyear, comp. *The Little Drummer Boy, Clarence D. McKenzie: The Child of the Thirteenth Regiment, N.Y.S.M., and the Child of the Mission Sunday School.* New York: Reformed Protestant Dutch Church, 1861.

Birdwhistell, Jack, ed. "Extracts from the Diary of B. F. Hungerford, a Kentucky Baptist Pastor during the Civil War." *Baptist History and Heritage* 14 (Spring 1979): 24–31.

Blair, William A., ed. *A Politician Goes to War: The Civil War Letters of John White Geary.* University Park: Pennsylvania State University Press, 1995.

Blaisdell, Bob, ed. *Civil War Letters: From Home, Camp & Battlefield.* Mineola, N.Y.: Dover, 2012.

Blakeman, A. Noel, ed. *Personal Recollections of the War of the Rebellion: Addresses Delivered before the Commandery of the State of New York, Military Order of the Loyal Legion of the United States,* 2nd ser. New York: G. P. Putnam's Sons, 1897.

Blassingame, John W., ed. *Slave Testimony: Two Centuries of Letters, Speeches, Interviews, and Autobiographies.* Baton Rouge: Louisiana State University Press, 1977.

Blight, David W., ed. *A Slave No More: Two Men Who Escaped to Freedom, Including Their Own Narratives of Emancipation.* New York: Harcourt, 2007.

———. *When This Cruel War Is Over: The Civil War Letters of Charles Harvey Brewster.* Amherst: University of Massachusetts Press, 1992.

Blomquist, Ann K., and Robert A. Taylor, ed. *This Cruel War: The Civil War Letters of Grant and Malinda Taylor, 1862–1865.* Macon, Ga.: Mercer University Press, 2000.

Bond, Natalie Jenkins, and Osmun Latrobe Coward, eds. *The South Carolinians: Colonel Asbury Coward's Memoirs.* New York: Vantage Press, 1968.

Boney, F. N., ed. *A Union Soldier in the Land of the Vanquished: The Diary of Sergeant Mathew Woodruff, June–December, 1865.* University Station: University of Alabama Press, 1969.

Bonner, Robert E., ed. *The Soldier's Pen: Firsthand Impressions of the Civil War.* New York: Hill and Wang, 2006.

Braden, Waldo W., ed. *Building the Myth: Selected Speeches Memorializing Abraham Lincoln.* Urbana: University of Illinois Press, 1990.

Britton, Ann Hartwell, and Thomas J. Reed, eds. *To My Beloved Wife and Boy at Home: The Letters and Diaries of Orderly Sergeant John F. L. Hartwell.* Madison, Wisc.: Fairleigh Dickinson University Press, 1997.

Broadhead, Sarah M. *The Diary of a Lady of Gettysburg, Pennsylvania, from June 15 to July 15, 1863.* 1863; reprint, Hershey, Pa.: Gary T. Hawbaker, 1990.

Brooks, Noah. "Personal Recollections of Abraham Lincoln." *Harper's New Monthly Magazine* 31 (July 1865): 222–30.

Brown, William Wells. *Narrative of William W. Brown, an American Slave.* London: Charles Gilpin, 1849.

Bryan Jr., Charles F. and Nelson D. Lankford, eds. *Eye of the Storm: A Civil War Odyssey.* New York: Free Press, 2000.

Burlingame, Michael, and John R. Turner Ettlinger, eds. *Inside Lincoln's White House: The Complete Civil War Diary of John Hay.* Carbondale: Southern Illinois University Press, 1997.

Carmichael, Peter S. "One Man's Turning Point." *Civil War Times* 42 (August 2003): 66–73.

Carpenter, Francis B. *Six Months at the White House with Abraham Lincoln.* New York: Hurd and Houghton, 1866.

Carter, Joseph C., ed. *Magnolia Journey: A Union Veteran Revisits the Former Confederate States, Arranged from Letters of Correspondent Russell H. Conwell to the Daily Evening Traveller (Boston, 1869).* University: University of Alabama Press, 1974.

Chamberlain, Joshua Lawrence. *"Bayonet! Forward": My Civil War Reminiscences.* Gettysburg: Stan Clark Military Books, 1994.

———. *The Passing of the Armies: An Account of the Final Campaign of the Army of the Potomac, Based upon Personal Reminiscences of the Fifth Army Corps.* 1915; reprint, Gettysburg: Stan Clark Military Books, 1994.

Chamberlayne, C. G., ed. *Ham Chamberlayne—Virginian: Letters and Papers of an Artillery Officer in the War for Southern Independence, 1861–1865.* Richmond: Dietz, 1932.

Chesson, Michael B., ed. *The Journal of a Civil War Surgeon.* Lincoln: University of Nebraska Press, 2003.

Chittick, Geraldine Frances, ed. *In the Field: Doctor Melvin John Hyde, Surgeon, 2nd Vermont Volunteers.* Newport, Vt.: Vermont Civil War Enterprises, 1999.

Churchill, James O. *War Papers and Personal Reminiscences, 1861–1865.* St. Louis: Becktold, 1892.

Clark, Grata J., and Jeffrey S. Clark, eds. *A Soldier's Dream of Home: The Civil War Letters of John C. Hughes to His Wife, Harriet.* Fort Worth, Tex.: Arcadia-Clark, 1996.

Clark, Leach. "Dreams That Come to Pass: A Thirty-Sixth Illinois Soldier's Dream and Its Strange Fulfillment." *Bivouac* (1884): 330–332.

Cockrell, Thomas D., and Michael B. Ballard, eds. *A Mississippi Rebel in the Army of Northern Virginia: The Civil War Memoirs of Private David Holt.* Baton Rouge: Louisiana State University Press, 1995.

Collier, Ellen C., ed. *Letters of a Civil War Soldier: Chandler B. Gillam, 28th New York Volunteers, with Diary of W. L. Hicks.* Bloomington, Ind.: Xlibris, 2005.

Colton, J. Ferrell, and Antoinette G. Smith, eds. *Column South: With the Fifteenth Pennsylvania Cavalry from Antietam to the Capture of Jefferson Davis.* Flagstaff: J. F. Colton, 1960.

Cooney, Charles F., ed. *Common Soldier, Uncommon War: Life as a Cavalryman in the Civil War.* Baltimore: Port City Press, 1994.

Crewdson, Robert H., ed. *Love and War: A Southern Soldier's Struggle Between Love and Duty.* Buena Vista, Va.: Mariner Publishing, 2009.

Crist, Lynda Lasswell, Suzanne Scott Gibbs, Brady L. Hutchison, and Elizabeth Henson Smith, eds. *The Papers of Jefferson Davis: Volume 8, 1862.* Baton Rouge: Louisiana State University Press, 1995.

Crofts, Daniel W., ed. "Southampton County Diarists in the Civil War Era: Elliott L. Story and Daniel W. Cobb." *Virginia Magazine of History and Biography* 98 (October 1990): 537–612.

Crook, W. H. *Memories of the White House: The Home Life of Our Presidents from Lincoln to Roosevelt.* Edited by Henry Rood. Boston: Little, Brown and Co., 1911.

Crow, Terrell Armistead, and Mary Moulton Barden, eds. *Live Your Own Life: The Family Papers of Mary Bayard Clarke, 1854–1886.* Columbia: University of South Carolina Press, 2003.

Culpepper, Marilyn Mayer, comp. *Women of the Civil War South: Personal Accounts from Diaries, Letters and Postwar Reminiscences.* Jefferson, N.C.: McFarland, 2003.

Cumming, Kate. *Journal of Hospital Life in the Confederate Army of Tennessee from the Battle of Shiloh to the End of the War.* Louisville: John P. Morton, 1866.

Curran, Robert Emmett, ed. *John Dooley's Civil War: An Irish American's Journey in the First Virginia Infantry Regiment.* Knoxville: University of Tennessee Press, 2012.

Cuttino, George P., ed. *Saddle Bag and Spinning Wheel: Being the Civil War Letters of George W. Peddy, MD, Surgeon, 56th Georgia Volunteer Regiment, CSA.* Macon, Ga.: Mercer University Press, 1981.

Daly, Robert W., ed. *Aboard the USS Florida, 1863–1865: The Letters of Paymaster William Frederick Keeler, U.S. Navy, to His Wife, Anna.* Annapolis, Md.: United States Naval Institute, 1968.

———. *Aboard the USS Monitor: 1862: The Letters of Acting Paymaster William Frederick Keeler, U.S. Navy, to His Wife, Anna.* Annapolis, Md.: United States Naval Institute, 1964.

Davis, James A., ed. *"Bully for the Band!": The Civil War Letters and Diary of Four Brothers in the 10th Vermont Infantry Band.* Jefferson, N.C.: McFarland, 2012.

Davis Jr., Robert S. "Selective Memories of Civil War Atlanta: The Memoir of Sallie Clayton." *Georgia Historical Quarterly* 82 (Winter 1998): 735–50.

Davis, William C., and Meredith L. Swentor, eds. *Bluegrass Confederate: The Headquarters Diary of Edward O. Guerrant.* Baton Rouge: Louisiana State University Press, 1999.

Day, Lewis W. *Story of the One Hundred and First Ohio Infantry: A Memorial Volume.* Cleveland: W. M. Bayne, 1894.

Deese, Helen R., ed. *Daughter of Boston: The Extraordinary Diary of a Nineteenth-Century Woman, Caroline Healey Dall.* Boston: Beacon Press, 2005.

De Haes Janvier, Francis. *The Sleeping Sentinel.* Philadelphia: T. B. Peterson, 1863.

Denison, F., ed. *The Evangelist: Or Life and Labors of Rev. Jabez Swan.* 2nd ed. Waterford, Conn.: William L. Peckham, 1873.

Diamond, E. Grey, and Herman Hattaway, eds. *Letters from Forest Place: A Plantation Family's Correspondence, 1846–1881.* Jackson: University Press of Mississippi, 1993.

Dieck, Herman. *The Most Complete and Authentic History of the Life and Public Services of General U.S. Grant.* Philadelphia: Thayer, Merriam and Co., 1885.

Divine, John E., Bronwen C. Souders, and John M. Souders, eds. *"To Talk is Treason": Quakers of Waterford, Virginia on Life, Love, Death and War in the Southern Confederacy.* Waterford, Va.: Waterford Foundation, 1996.

Donald, David Herbert, ed. *Gone for a Soldier: The Civil War Memoirs of Private Alfred Ballard.* Boston: Little, Brown and Co., 1975.

Donald, Robert Bruce, ed. *Manhood and Patriotic Awakening in the American Civil War: The John E. Mattoon Letters, 1859–1866.* Lanham, Md.: Hamilton Books, 2008.

Douglass, Frederick. *My Bondage and My Freedom.* New York: Miller, Orton and Mulligan, 1855.

Drake, J. Madison. *Fast and Loose in Dixie.* New York: The Author's Publishing Company, 1880.

Duncan, Russell, ed. *Blue-Eyed Child of Fortune: The Civil War Letters of Colonel Robert Gould Shaw.* Athens: University of Georgia Press, 1992.

East, Charles, ed. *Sarah Morgan: The Civil War Diary of a Southern Woman.* New York: Touchstone, 1991.

Eckert, Edward K. *"Fiction Distorting Fact": The Prison Life, Annotated by Jefferson Davis.* Macon, Ga.: Mercer University Press, 1987.

Elder III, Donald C., ed. *Love Amid the Turmoil: The Civil War Letters of William and Mary Vermilion.* Iowa City: University of Iowa Press, 2003.

Evans, Robert G., ed. *The 16th Mississippi Infantry: Civil War Letters and Reminiscences.* Jackson: University of Mississippi Press, 2002.

Everest, C. "The Soldier's Vision." Philadelphia: Lee and Walker, 1862.

Everson, Guy R., and Edward W. Simpson Jr., ed. *"Far, Far from Home": The Wartime Letters of Dick and Tally Simpson, Third South Carolina Volunteers.* New York: Oxford University Press, 1994.

Fain, John N., ed. *Sanctified Trial: The Diary of Eliza Rhea Anderson Fain, a Confederate Woman in East Tennessee.* Knoxville: University of Tennessee Press, 2004.

Favill, John Marshall. *The Diary of a Young Officer Serving with the Armies of the United States During the War of the Rebellion.* Chicago: R. R. Donnelley, 1909.

Fehrenbacher, Don E., and Virginia Fehrenbacher, eds. *Recollected Words of Abraham Lincoln.* Sanford: Stanford University Press, 1996.

Fleming, Francis P. *Memoir of Capt. C. Seton Fleming, of the Second Florida Infantry, C.S.A.* Jacksonville: Times-Union Publishing House, 1881.

Foroughi, Andrea R., ed. *Go If You Think It Your Duty: A Minnesota Couple's Civil War Letters.* St. Paul: Minnesota Historical Society Press, 2008.

Gardner, Eric, ed. *"The Complete Fortune Teller and Dream Book:* An Antebellum Text 'By Chloe Russel, A Woman of Colour.'" *New England Quarterly* 78 (June 2005): 259–88.

Gerry, Margarita Spalding, ed. *Through Five Administrations: Reminiscences of Colonel William H. Crook, Body-Guard to President Lincoln.* New York: Harper and Brothers, 1910.

Gienapp, William E., and Erica L. Gienapp, eds. *The Civil War Diary of Gideon Welles, Lincoln's Secretary of the Navy: The Original Manuscript Edition.* Urbana: University of Illinois Press, 2014.

Good, Timothy S., ed. *We Saw Lincoln Shot: One Hundred Eyewitness Accounts.* Jackson: University Press of Mississippi, 1995.

Goodrich, S. G. *The Fourth Reader for the Use of Schools.* Boston: Otis, Broaders, and Co., 1839.

Gordon, John B. *Reminiscences of the Civil War.* New York: Charles Scribner's Sons, 1911.

Greeley, Horace. *The American Conflict: A History of the Great Rebellion in the United States of America, 1860–'64.* 2 vols. Hartford: O. D. Case, 1865.

Greenberg, Kenneth S., ed. *The Confessions of Nat Turner and Related Documents.* Boston: Bedford/St. Martin's, 1996.

Grimes, William. *Life of William Grimes, the Runaway Slave.* New York: [W. Grimes], 1825.

Gwin, Minrose C., ed. *A Woman's Civil War: A Diary with Reminiscences of the War from March 1862.* Madison: University of Wisconsin Press, 1992.

Hallock, Judith Lee, ed. *The Civil War Letters of Joshua K. Callaway.* Athens: University of Georgia Press, 1997.

Hammond, Harold Earl, ed. *Diary of a Union Lady, 1861–1865.* 1962; reprint, Lincoln: University of Nebraska Press, 2000.

Hartley, Jenny, ed. *The Selected Letters of Charles Dickens.* New York: Oxford University Press, 2012.

Hassler, William W., ed. *The General to His Lady: The Civil War Letters of William Dorsey Pender to Fanny Pender.* Chapel Hill: University of North Carolina Press, 1965.

Hedrick, David T., and Gordon Barry Davis Jr., eds. *I'm Surrounded by Methodists: Diary of John H. W. Stuckenberg, Chaplain of the 145th Pennsylvania Volunteer Infantry*. Gettysburg: Thomas Publications, 1995.

Herndon, William Henry. *Herndon's Life of Lincoln*. Edited by Henry Steele Commager. 1942; reprint, New York: Da Capo, 1983.

Hitchcock, Roswell D. *Hitchcock's New and Complete Analysis of the Holy Bible*. New York: A. J. Johnson, 1870.

Holland, Josiah Gilbert. *The Life of Abraham Lincoln*. Springfield, Mass.: Gurdon Hill, 1866.

Holzer, Harold, ed. *President Lincoln Assassinated!!: The Firsthand Story of the Murder, Manhunt, Trial, and Mourning*. New York: Library of America, 2014.

Holzhueter, John O., ed. "William Wallace's Civil War Letters: The Virginia Campaign." *Wisconsin Magazine of History* 57 (Autumn 1957): 28–59.

Howe, Julia Ward. "Battle Hymn of the Republic." *Atlantic Monthly* 9 (February 1862): 145.

———. "Battle Hymn of the Republic." *To-Day: The Monthly Magazine of Scientific Socialism* 3 (February 1885): 88.

———. "Reminiscences of Julia Ward Howe. VI. James Freeman Clarke; In War Time; Boston Radical Club." *Atlantic Monthly* 83 (May 1899): 701–12.

Hughes Jr., Nathaniel Cheairs, ed. *The Civil War Memoir of Philip Daingerfield Stephenson, D. D.* Baton Rouge: Louisiana State University Press, 1998.

Humez, Jean McMahon, ed. *Gifts of Power: The Writings of Rebecca Jackson, Black Visionary, Shaker Eldress*. Amherst: University of Massachusetts Press, 1981.

Hyatt, Hudson, ed. "Captain Hyatt: Being the Letters Written during the Years 1863–1864, to His Wife, Mary, by Captain T. J. Hyatt, 126th Ohio Volunteer Infantry." *Ohio Archeological and Historical Quarterly* 53 (April–June 1944): 166–83.

Innes, C. L., ed. *Slave Life in Virginia and Kentucky: A Narrative by Francis Fredric, Escaped Slave*. Baton Rouge: Louisiana State University Press, 2010.

Jackson, Alto Loftin, ed. *So Mourns the Dove: Letters of a Confederate Infantryman to His Family*. New York: Exposition Press, 1965.

Jacobs, Harriet. *Incidents in the Life of a Slave Girl*. Boston: n.p., 1861.

Jamison, Matthew H. *Recollections of Pioneer and Army Life*. Kansas City: Hudson Press, 1911.

Johansson, M. Jane, ed. *Widows by the Thousand: The Civil War Letters of Theophilus and Harriet Perry, 1862–1864*. Fayetteville: University of Arkansas Press, 2000.

Johnson, Clifton H., ed. *God Struck Me Dead: Religious Conversion Experiences and Autobiographies of Ex-Slaves*. Philadelphia: Pilgrim Press, 1969.

Johnston Jr., Terry A., ed. *"Him on the One Side and Me on the Other": The Civil War Letters of Alexander Campbell, 79th New York Infantry Regiment and James Campbell, 1st South Carolina Battalion*. Columbia: University of South Carolina Press, 1999.

Jones, Charles C. *The Religious Instruction of the Negroes in the United States*. Savannah: Thomas Purse, 1842.

Jones, J. B. *A Rebel War Clerk's Diary at the Confederate States Capital*. 2 vols. Philadelphia: J. B. Lippincott, 1866.

Jones, James B., ed. *Tennessee in the Civil War: Selected Contemporary Accounts of Military and Other Events, Month by Month.* Jefferson, N.C.: McFarland, 2011.

Jordan Jr., William B., ed. *The Civil War Journals of John Mead Gould, 1861–1866.* Baltimore: Butternut and Blue, 1997.

Kallgren, Beverly Hayes, ed. *Abial and Anna: The Life of a Civil War Veteran as Told in Family Letters.* Orono: University of Maine Press, 1996.

Kass, Amy A., Leon R. Kass, and Diana Schaub, eds. *What So Proudly We Hail: The American Soul in Story, Speech, and Song.* Newark, Del.: ISI Books, 2011.

Kidd, J. H. *Personal Recollections of a Cavalryman with Custer's Michigan Cavalry Brigade in the Civil War.* Ionia, Mich.: Sentinel, 1908.

Kimmel, Ross M., and Michael P. Musick, eds. *"I Am Busy Drawing Pictures": The Civil War Art and Letters of Private John Jacob Omenhausser, CSA.* Annapolis: Friends of the Maryland State Archives, 2014.

King, Wilma, ed. *A Northern Woman in the Plantation South: Letters of Tryphena Blanche Holder Fox, 1856–1876.* Columbia: University of South Carolina Press, 1993.

Kiper, Richard L., ed. *Dear Catharine, Dear Taylor: The Civil War Letters of a Union Soldier and His Wife.* Lawrence: University Press of Kansas, 2002.

Knight, James R., ed. *Letters to Anna: The Civil War through the Eyes and Heart of a Soldier.* Nashville: Cold Tree Press, 2007.

Kroll, Kathleen, and Charles Moran, eds. "The White Papers." *Massachusetts Review* 18 (Summer 1977): 248–70.

Krynski Elizabeth, and Kimberly Little, eds. "Hannah's Letters: The Story of a Wisconsin Family, 1856–1864, Part II." *Wisconsin Magazine of History* 74 (Summer 1991): 272–96.

———. "Hannah's Letters: The Story of a Wisconsin Family, 1856–1864, Part III." *Wisconsin Magazine of History* 74 (Autumn 1991): 162–95.

Kundahl, George G., ed. *The Bravest of the Brave: The Correspondence of Stephen Dodson Ramseur.* Chapel Hill: University of North Carolina Press, 2010.

Laas, Virginia Jeans, ed. *Wartime Washington: The Civil War Letters of Elizabeth Blair Lee.* Urbana: University of Illinois Press, 1991.

Ladd, David L., and Audrey J. Ladd, eds. *The Bachelder Papers: Gettysburg in Their Own Words.* 3 vols. Dayton, Ohio: Morningside, 1994.

Lamon, Ward Hill. *The Life of Abraham Lincoln: From His Birth to His Inauguration as President.* Boston: J. R. Osgood, 1872.

———. *Recollections of Abraham Lincoln, 1847–1865.* Edited by Dorothy Lamon Teillard. 1895; reprint, Washington, D.C.: Published by the Editor, 1911.

Lane, Mills, ed. *Times That Prove People's Principles: Civil War in Georgia, A Documentary History.* Savannah: Beehive Press, 1993.

Lanman, Charles, ed. *Journal of Alfred Ely, A Prisoner of War in Richmond.* New York: D. Appleton, 1862.

Larimer, Charles F., ed. *Love and Valor: The Intimate Civil War Letters Between Captain Jacob and Emeline Ritner.* Western Springs, Ill.: Sigourney Press, 2000.

Lee, Jarena. *Religious Experience and Journal of Mrs. Jarena Lee, Giving an Account of Her Call to Preach the Gospel.* Philadelphia: privately printed, 1849.

Lee, Natalie H., ed. *Dear Isa, Dear Johna: The Civil War Correspondence of One of Ohio's Hundred Days' Men, First Sergeant John A. Brown, 148th Ohio National Guard.* Dexter, Mich.: Thomson-Shore, 1998.

Levstik, Frank, ed. "The Civil War Diary of Colonel Albert Rogall." *Polish American Studies* 27 (Spring/Autumn 1970): 33–79.

Long, A. L. *Memoirs of Robert E. Lee.* New York: J. M. Stoddart, 1887.

Longacre, Edward G., ed. " 'Come Home Soon and Dont Delay': Letters from the Home Front, July, 1861." *Pennsylvania Magazine of History and Biography* 100 (July 1976): 395–406.

Looby, Christopher, ed. *The Complete Civil War Journal and Selected Letters of Thomas Wentworth Higginson.* Chicago: University of Chicago Press, 2000.

Lowe, Richard, ed. *A Texas Cavalry Officer's Civil War: The Diary and Letters of James C. Bates.* Baton Rouge: Louisiana State University Press, 1999.

Lowry, Thomas P., ed. *Swamp Doctor: The Diary of a Union Surgeon in the Virginia and North Carolina Marshes.* Mechanicsburg, Pa.: Stackpole Books, 2001.

Macsherry, Helen Drury, ed. *Pastime: Life & Love on the Homefront During the Civil War, 1861–1865: Shriver Family Diaries & Letters, Union Mills, Maryland.* Westminster, Md.: Union Mills Homestead Foundation, 2013.

Maness, Donald C., and H. Jason Combs, eds. *Do They Miss Me at Home?: The Civil War Letters of William McKnight, Seventh Ohio Volunteer Cavalry.* Athens: Ohio University Press, 2010.

Mannis, Jedediah, and Galen R. Wilson, eds. *Bound to Be a Soldier: The Letters of Private James T. Miller, 111th Pennsylvania Infantry, 1861–1864.* Knoxville: University of Tennessee Press, 2001.

Martin, Kenneth R., and Ralph Linwood Snow, eds. *"I Am Now a Soldier": The Civil War Diaries of Lorenzo Vanderhoef.* Snow, Me.: Patten Free Library, 1990.

McCalmont, Alfred B. *Extracts from Letters Written by Alfred B. McCalmont.* Franklin, Pa.: privately printed, 1908.

McDonald, Laurie B., ed. *14 Letters to a Friend: The Wartime Ordeal of Captain DeWitt Clinton Fort.* Edinburg, Tex.: privately printed, 2007.

McElroy, John. *Andersonville: The Story of Rebel Military Prisons.* Toledo: D. R. Locke, 1879.

McIntosh, James T., et al., eds. *The Papers of Jefferson Davis: Volume 3, July 1846–December 1848.* Baton Rouge: Louisiana State University Press, 1981.

McMurry, Richard M., ed. *Footprints of a Regiment: A Recollection of the 1st Georgia Regulars, 1861–1865.* Marietta, Ga.: Longstreet Press, 1992.

——. *An Uncompromising Secessionist: The Civil War of George Knox Miller, Eighth (Wade's) Confederate Cavalry.* Tuscaloosa: University of Alabama Press, 2007.

Messent, Peter, and Steve Courtney, eds. *The Civil War Letters of Joseph Hopkins Twichell: A Chaplain's Story.* Athens: University of Georgia Press, 2006.

Miller, Brian Craig, ed. *"A Punishment on the Nation": An Iowa Soldier Endures the Civil War.* Kent, Ohio: Kent State University Press, 2012.

Miller, John D., ed. "An Alabama Merchant in Civil War Richmond: The Harvey Wilkerson Luttrell Letters, 1861–1865." *Alabama Review* 58 (July 2005): 176–206.

Miller, Randall M., ed. *"Dear Master": Letters of a Slave Family*, 2nd ed. Athens: University of Georgia Press, 1990.

Mohr, James C., ed. *The Cormany Diaries: A Northern Family in the Civil War.* Pittsburgh: University of Pittsburgh Press, 1982.

Moneyhon, Carl H., ed. "Life in Confederate Arkansas: The Diary of Virginia Davis Gray, 1863–1865, Part I." *Arkansas Historical Quarterly* 42 (Spring 1983): 134–69.

Moore, Frank, comp. *The Civil War in Song and Story, 1861–1865.* New York: P. F. Collier, 1889.

———. *Lyrics of Loyalty.* New York: George P. Putnam, 1864.

Nanzig, Thomas P., ed. *The Civil War Memoirs of a Virginia Cavalryman: Lt. Robert T. Hubard, Jr.* Tuscaloosa: University of Alabama Press, 2007.

Nevins, Allan, and Milton Halsey Thomas, eds. *The Diary of George Templeton Strong.* 4 vols. New York: Macmillan, 1952.

Newsome, Hampton, John Horn, and John G. Selby, eds. *Civil War Talks: Further Reminiscences of George S. Bernard and His Fellow Veterans.* Charlottesville: University of Virginia Press, 2012.

Nicolay, John G. *The Outbreak of Rebellion.* New York: Charles Scribner's Sons, 1881.

Nisbet, James Cooper. *Four Years on the Firing Line.* Chattanooga: Imperial Press, 1914.

Niven, John, et al., eds. *The Salmon P. Chase Papers.* 5 vols. Kent, Ohio: Kent State University Press, 1993–1998.

Noble, Mason. *Sermon Delivered in the United States Naval Academy, on the Day of the Funeral of the Late President, Abraham Lincoln.* Newport, R.I.: George T. Hammond, 1865.

Northrop, John Worrell. *Chronicles from the Diary of a War Prisoner in Andersonville and Other Military Prisons of the South in 1864.* Wichita: Wining Printery, 1904.

Northup, Solomon. *Twelve Years a Slave.* New York: Miller, Orton and Mulligan, 1855.

O'Connor, Bob, ed. *The Life of Abraham Lincoln as President.* West Conshohocken, Pa.: Mont Clair Press, 2010.

Offenberg, Richard F., and Robert Rue Parsonage, eds. *The War Letters of Duren F. Kelley, 1862–1865.* New York: Pageant, 1967.

Ordronaux, John. *Hints on the Preservation of Health in the Armies.* New York: Appleton, 1861.

Orr, Kelly and Mary Davies Kelly. *Dream's End: Two Iowa Brothers in the Civil War.* New York: Kodansha, 1998.

Pease, Theodore Calvin, and James G. Randall, eds. *The Diary of Orville Hickman Browning.* 2 vols. Springfield: Illinois State Historical Library, 1925.

Peck, George W. *How Private Geo. W. Peck Put Down the Rebellion, or the Funny Experiences of a Raw Recruit.* Chicago: Belford, Clarke & Co., 1887.

Personal Narratives of Events in the War of the Rebellion: Being Papers Read Before the Rhode Island Soldiers and Sailors Historical Society, 3rd ser., no. 1. Providence: The Society, 1883.

Poremba, David Lee, ed. *If I Am Found Dead: Michigan Voices from the Civil War.* Ann Arbor: Ann Arbor Media Group, 2006.

Porter, Horace. *Campaigning with Grant.* New York: Century, 1897.

Post, Lydia Minturn, ed. *Soldiers' Letters from Camp, Battle-Field and Prison.* New York: Bunce & Huntington, 1865.

Powell, Walter L., ed. *Letters from the Storm: The Intimate Civil War Letters of Lt. J. A. H. Foster, 155th Pennsylvania Volunteers.* Chicora, Pa.: Firefly Publications, 2010.

Pratt, Harry E., ed. "Civil War Letters of Brigadier General William Ward Orme, 1862–1866." *Journal of the Illinois State Historical Society* 23 (July 1930): 246–316.

"President Lincoln's Dream." *Gleason's Monthly Companion* 9 (March 1880): 140–41.

Preston, R. A. "A Letter from a British Military Observer of the American Civil War." *Military Affairs* (Summer 1952): 49–60.

Racine, Philip N., ed. *"Unspoiled Heart": The Journal of Charles Mattocks of the 17th Maine.* Knoxville: University of Tennessee Press, 1994.

Ransom, John L. *John Ransom's Diary.* 1881; reprint, New York: Dell, 1964.

Rattenbury, Richard C., ed. *From Wisconsin to the Sea: The Civil War Letters of Sergeant John V. Richards, Thirty-First Regiment of Wisconsin Volunteer Infantry, 1862–1865.* Houston: D. Armstrong, 1986.

Rausch, David A., ed. "Civil War Medicine: A Patient's Account." *Pennsylvania Folklife* 26 (1977): 46–48.

Ray, Johnette Highsmith, ed. "Civil War Letters from Parsons' Texas Cavalry Brigade." *Southwestern Historical Quarterly* 69 (October 1965): 210–23.

Reid, Richard M., ed. *Practicing Medicine in a Black Regiment: The Civil War Diary of Burt Green Wilder, 55th Massachusetts.* Amherst: University of Massachusetts Press, 2010.

Richards, Caroline Cowles. *Village Life in America, 1852–1872, Including the Period of the American Civil War as Told in the Diary of a School-Girl.* 1913; reprint, Williamstown, Mass.: Corner House, 1972.

Riley, Glenda, ed. "Civil War Wife: The Letters of Harriet Jane Thompson, Part I." *Annals of Iowa* 44 (Winter 1978): 214–31.

———. "Civil War Wife: The Letters of Harriet Jane Thompson, Part II." *Annals of Iowa* 44 (Spring 1978): 296–314.

Robertson, Mary D., ed. *Lucy Breckinridge of Grove Hill: The Journal of a Virginia Girl, 1862–1864.* Kent, Ohio: Kent State University Press, 1979.

Robertson Jr., James I., ed. "An Indiana Soldier in Love and War: The Civil War Letters of John V. Hadley." *Indiana Magazine of History* 59 (September 1963): 189–208.

Roemer, Jacob. *Reminiscences of the War of the Rebellion, 1861–1865.* Flushing, N.Y.: n.p., 1897.

Sargent, Epes. *The Standard Speaker; Containing Exercises in Prose and Poetry for Declamation in Schools, Academies, Lyceums, Colleges.* Philadelphia: Thomas, Cowperthwait and Co., 1852.

Sawyer, Charles Carroll. "I Dreamed My Boy Was Home Again." Brooklyn: Sawyer and Thompson, 1863.

Sawyer, Merrill C., Betty Sawyer, and Timothy C. Sawyer, eds. *Letters from a Civil War Surgeon: The Letters of Dr. William Child of the Fifth New Hampshire Volunteers*. Solon, Me.: Polar Bear, 2001.

Schultz, Jane E., ed. *This Birth Place of Souls: The Civil War Nursing Diary of Harriet Eaton*. New York: Oxford University Press, 2011.

Sears, Stephen W., ed. *For Country, Cause & Leader: The Civil War Journal of Charles B. Haydon*. New York: Ticknor & Fields, 1993.

Seward, Frederick W. *Reminiscences of a War-Time Statesman and Diplomat, 1830–1915*. New York: G. P. Putnam's Sons, 1916.

———. *Seward at Washington as Senator and Secretary of State: A Memoir of His Life, with Selections from His Letters, 1861–1872*. New York: Derby and Miller, 1891.

Shepherd, Henry E. *Narrative of Prison Life at Baltimore and Johnson's Island, Ohio*. Baltimore: Commercial, 1917.

Sherman, William Tecumseh. *Memoirs of Gen. William T. Sherman*. 2 vols. New York: D. Appleton, 1891.

Silber, Nina, and Mary Beth Sievers, eds. *Yankee Correspondence: Civil War Letters between New England Soldiers and the Home Front*. Charlottesville: University Press of Virginia, 1996.

Silliker, Ruth L., ed. *The Rebel Yell and the Yankee Hurrah: The Civil War Journal of a Maine Volunteer*. Camden, Me.: Down East Books, 1985.

Simon, John Y., ed. *The Personal Memoirs of Julia Dent Grant*. New York: G. P. Putnam's Sons, 1975.

Skipper, Marti, and Jane Taylor, eds. *A Handful of Providence: The Civil War Letters of Lt. Richard Goldwaite, New York Volunteers, and Ellen Goldwaite*. Jefferson, N.C.: McFarland, 2004.

Snell, Mark A., ed. *Dancing Along the Deadline: The Andersonville Memoir of a Prisoner of the Confederacy*. Novato, Calif.: Presidio, 1996.

Spear, Frank. *Jeff Davis's Dream*. New York: J. Wrigley, 1862.

Stevens, George T. *Three Years in the Sixth Corps*. Albany: S. R. Gray, 1866.

Steward, Austin. *Twenty-Two Years a Slave, and Forty Years a Freeman*. Rochester, N.Y.: William Alling, 1857.

Stewart, William H. *A Pair of Blankets: War-Time History in Letters to the Young People of the South*. 1911; reprint, Wilmington, N.C.: Broadfoot, 1990.

Styple, William B., ed. *Writing and Fighting the Civil War: Soldier Correspondence to the New York Sunday Mercury*. Kearny, N.J.: Belle Grove, 2000.

Swank, Walbrook D., ed. *Confederate Letters and Diaries, 1861–1865*. Shippensburg, Pa.: Burd Street Press, 1992.

Taber, Thomas R., ed. *Hard Breathing Days: The Civil War Letters of Cora Beach Benton, Albion, New York, 1862–1865*. Albion, N.Y.: Almeron Press, 2003.

Tappan, George H., ed. *The Civil War Journal of Lt. Russell M. Tuttle*. Jefferson, N.C.: McFarland, 2006.

Tatum, Margaret Black, ed. "'Please Send Stamps': The Civil War Letters of William Allen Clark, Part II." *Indiana Magazine of History* 91 (June 1995): 81–108.

Taylor, Yuval, ed. *I Was Born a Slave: An Anthology of Classic Slave Narratives*. 2 vols. Chicago: Lawrence Hill Books, 1999.

Thoreau, Henry D. *A Week on the Concord and Merrimack Rivers*. Rev. ed. 1849; Boston: Ticknor and Fields, 1868.

Toalson, Jeff, ed. *Send Me a Pair of Old Boots and Kiss My Little Girls: The Civil War Letters of Richard and Mary Watkins, 1861–1865*. New York: iUniverse, 2009.

Turner, Justin G., and Linda Levitt Turner, eds. *Mary Todd Lincoln: Her Life and Letters*. New York: Alfred A. Knopf, 1972.

Turner, Nat S. *A Southern Soldier's Letters Home: The Civil War Letters of Samuel A. Burney, Cobb's Georgia Legion, Army of Northern Virginia*. Macon, Ga.: Mercer University Press, 2002.

The Visions of Joseph Hoag & Daniel Barker. Also, A Prophecy of Stephen Grellet. Carthage, Ind.: David Marshall, 1889.

Weaver, Clare P., ed. *Thank God My Regiment an African One: The Civil War Diary of Colonel Nathan W. Daniels*. Baton Rouge: Louisiana State University Press, 1998.

Welles, Edgar T., ed. *Diary of Gideon Welles: Secretary of the Navy under Lincoln and Johnson*, 3 vols. Boston: Houghton Mifflin, 1911.

Welles, Gideon. "Lincoln and Johnson." *The Galaxy: A Magazine of Entertaining Reading* 13 (April 1872): 521–32.

Wharton. H. M., ed. *War Songs and Poems of the Southern Confederacy, 1861–1865*. n.p., 1904.

White, Jonathan W., Katie Fisher, and Elizabeth Wall, eds. "The Civil War Letters of Tillman Valentine, Third U.S. Colored Troops." *Pennsylvania Magazine of History and Biography* 139 (April 2015): 171–88.

White, Russell C., ed. *The Civil War Diary of Wyman S. White: First Sergeant of Company F, 2nd United States Sharpshooter Regiment, 1861–1865*. Baltimore: Butternut and Blue, 1993.

Whitman, Walt. *Leaves of Grass: The Deathbed Edition*. New York: Book of the Month Club, 1992.

———. *Memoranda During the War*. Camden, N.J.: New Republic Print, 1875.

Whitney, Henry Clay. *Life on the Circuit with Lincoln*. Boston: Estes and Lauriat, 1892.

Wiley, Bell Irvin, ed. *Letters of Warren Akin, Confederate Congressman*. 1959; reprint, Athens: University of Georgia Press, 2010.

Wilkinson, Warren. *Mother, May You Never See the Sights I Have Seen*. New York: Harper and Row, 1990.

Williams, John A. B. *Leaves from a Trooper's Diary*. Philadelphia: n.p., 1869.

Wilson, Douglas L., and Rodney O. Davis, eds. *Herndon's Informants: Letters, Interviews and Statements about Abraham Lincoln*. Urbana: University of Illinois Press, 1998.

———. *Herndon's Lincoln*. Urbana: University of Illinois Press, 2006.

Woodward, C. Vann, ed. *Mary Chesnut's Civil War*. New Haven: Yale University Press, 1981.

Wooton, G. D. *Mysterious Eternal Facts. My Two Dreams, The First during the Late War; The Second on 5th March, 1877*. Richmond: Daniel Murphy, 1877.

———. *Second Edition of My Strange, Mysterious Dreams, Enlarged with Wonders and Charms*. Richmond: n.p., 1877.

The Wreath: A Collection of Poems from Celebrated English Authors. Hartford, Conn.: Silas Andrus, 1821.

Wynne, Lewis N., and Robert A. Taylor, eds. *This War So Horrible: The Civil War Diary of Hiram Smith Williams.* Tuscaloosa: University of Alabama Press, 1993.

Yacovone, Donald, ed. *Freedom's Journey: African American Voices of the Civil War.* Chicago: Lawrence Hill Books, 2004.

Regimental Histories

Abbott, Stephen G. *The First Regiment New Hampshire Volunteers in the Great Rebellion.* Keene, N.H.: Sentinel, 1890.

Anderson, John. *The Fifty-Seventh Regiment of Massachusetts Volunteers in the War of the Rebellion.* Boston: E. B. Stillings, 1896.

Bartlett, A. W. *History of the Twelfth Regiment New Hampshire Volunteers in the War of the Rebellion.* Concord: Ira C. Evans, 1897.

Bennett, L. G., and William M. Haigh. *History of the Thirty-Sixth Regiment Illinois Volunteers, during the War of the Rebellion.* Aurora, Ill.: Knickerbocker and Hodder, 1876.

Best, Isaac O. *History of the 121st New York State Infantry.* Chicago: Jas. H. Smith, 1921.

Boies, Andrew J. *Record of the Thirty-Third Massachusetts Volunteer Infantry, from Aug. 1862 to Aug. 1865.* Fitchburg, Mass.: Sentinel, 1880.

Bolton, H. W. *History of the Second Regiment Illinois Volunteer Infantry from Organization to Muster-Out.* Chicago: R. R. Donnelley and Sons, 1899.

Bruce, George Anson. *The Twentieth Regiment of Massachusetts Volunteer Infantry, 1861–1865.* Boston: Houghton Mifflin, 1906.

Bryant, Edwin E. *History of the Third Regiment of Wisconsin Veteran Volunteer Infantry, 1861–1865.* Madison: Veteran Association of the Regiment, 1891.

Burrage, Henry Sweetser. *History of the Thirty-Sixth Regiment Massachusetts, 1862–1865.* Boston: Rockwell and Churchill, 1884.

Carpenter, George N. *History of the Eighth Regiment Vermont Volunteers, 1861–1865.* Boston: Deland & Barta, 1886.

Clark, James H. *The Iron Hearted Regiment: Being an Account of the Battles, Marches and Gallant Deeds Performed by the 115th Regiment N.Y. Vols.* Albany: J. Munsell, 1865.

Cogswell, Leander W. *A History of the Eleventh New Hampshire Regiment, Volunteer Infantry in the Rebellion War, 1861–1865.* Concord: Republican Press Association, 1891.

Coker, James Lide. *History of Company G, Ninth S.C. Regiment, Infantry, S.C. Army, and of Company E, Sixth S.C. Regiment, Infantry, S.C. Army.* Greenwood, S.C.: Attic Press, 1979.

Craft, David. *History of the One Hundred Forty-First Regiment, Pennsylvania Volunteers, 1862–1865.* Towanda, Pa.: Reporter-Journal, 1885.

Davenport, Alfred. *Camp and Field Life of the Fifth New York Volunteer Infantry, Duryee Zouaves.* New York: Dick and Fitzgerald, 1879.

Davis, Washington. *Camp-Fire Chats of the Civil War.* Detroit: W. H. Boothroyd, 1887.

Denny, J. Waldo. *Wearing the Blue in the Twenty-Fifth Mass. Volunteer Infantry, With Burnside's Coast Division, 18th Army Corps, and Army of the James.* Worcester, Mass.: Putnam and Davis, 1879.

Derby, William P. *Bearing Arms in the Twenty-Seventh Massachusetts Regiment of Volunteer Infantry During the Civil War, 1861–1865.* Boston: Wright & Potter, 1883.

Eddy, Richard. *History of the Sixteenth Regiment New York State Volunteers.* Philadelphia: Crissy and Markley, 1864.

Emilio, Luis F. *History of the Fifty-Fourth Regiment of Massachusetts Volunteer Infantry, 1863–1865.* 2nd ed. Boston: Boston Book Company, 1894.

Emmerton, James A. *A Record of the Twenty-Third Regiment Mass. Vol. Infantry in the War of the Rebellion, 1861–1865.* Boston: William Ware, 1866.

Floyd, David Bittle. *History of the Seventy-Fifth Regiment of Indiana Infantry Volunteers.* Philadelphia: Lutheran Publication Society, 1893.

Floyd, Fred C. *History of the Fortieth (Mozart) Regiment New York Volunteers.* Boston: F. H. Gilson, 1909.

Gordon, Leslie J. *A Broken Regiment: The 16th Connecticut's Civil War.* Baton Rouge: Louisiana State University Press, 2014.

Gould, John M. *History of the First-Tenth-Twenty-Ninth Maine Regiment.* Portland, Me.: Stephen Berry, 1871.

Green, Robert M., comp. *History of the One Hundred and Twenty-Fourth Regiment Pennsylvania Volunteers in the War of the Rebellion, 1862–1863.* Philadelphia: Wane Bros., 1907.

Hall, Henry, and James Hall, *Cayuga in the Field: A Record of the 19th N.Y. Volunteers, all the Batteries of the 3d New York Artillery, and the 75th New York Volunteers.* Auburn, N.Y.: Truair, Smith and Co., 1873.

Hard, Abner. *History of the Eighth Cavalry Regiment Illinois Volunteers, During the Great Rebellion.* Aurora, Ill.: n.p., 1868.

Hartman, David W., and David Coles, comps. *Biographical Rosters of Florida's Confederate and Union Soldiers, 1861–1865,* 6 vols. Wilmington, N.C.: Broadfoot, 1995.

Haynes, E. M. *A History of the Tenth Regiment, Vt. Vols.* Rutland, Vt.: Tuttle Company, 1894.

Hight, John J. *History of the Fifty-Eighth Regiment of Indiana Volunteer Infantry.* Princeton, Ind.: Press of the Clarion, 1895.

Hopkins, William P. *The Seventh Regiment Rhode Island Volunteers in the Civil War, 1861–1865.* Providence: Snow & Farnham, 1903.

Hull, Isaac. *History of the Ninety-Seventh Regiment New York Volunteers, ("Conkling Rifles,") In the War for the Union.* Utica, N.Y.: L. C. Childs and Son, 1890.

Hutchinson, Nelson V. *History of the Seventh Massachusetts Volunteer Infantry in the War of the Rebellion of the Southern States against the Constitutional Authority, 1861–1865.* Taunton, Mass.: The Regimental Association, 1890.

Hyde, William L. *History of the One Hundred and Twelfth Regiment N.Y. Volunteers.* Fredonia, N.Y.: W. McKinstry, 1866.

Jackman, Lyman. *History of the Sixth New Hampshire Regiment in the War for the Union.* Concord, N.H.: Republican Press Association, 1891.

Kimbell, Charles B. *History of Battery "A" First Illinois Light Artillery Volunteers.* Chicago: Cushing, 1899.

King, David H., A. Judson Gibbs, and Jay H. Northup, comps. *History of the Ninety-Third Regiment, New York Volunteer Infantry, 1861–1865.* Milwaukee: Swain and Tate, 1895.

Kirk, Charles H., ed. *History of the Fifteenth Pennsylvania Volunteer Cavalry which was Recruited and Known as the Anderson Cavalry in the Rebellion of 1861–1865.* Philadelphia: n.p., 1906.

Little, Henry F. W. *The Seventh Regiment New Hampshire Volunteers in the War of the Rebellion.* Concord, N.H.: Ira C. Evans, 1896.

McGee, B. F. *History of the 72d Indiana Volunteer Infantry of the Mounted Lightning Brigade.* LaFayette, Ind.: S. Vater, 1882.

McMorries, Edward Young. *History of the First Regiment Alabama Volunteer Infantry C.S.A.* Montgomery, Ala.: Brown, 1904.

McMurray, W. J. *History of the Twentieth Tennessee Regiment Volunteer Infantry, C.S.A.* Nashville: n.p., 1904.

A Memorial of the Great Rebellion: Being a History of the Fourteenth Regiment New-Hampshire Volunteers, Covering Its Three Years of Service, with Original Sketches of Army Life, 1862–1865. Boston: Franklin Press, 1882.

Merrill, J. W. comp., *Records of the 24th Independent Battery, N.Y. Light Artillery U.S.V.* Perry, N.Y.: Ladies' Cemetery Association, 1870.

Muffly, J. W., ed. *The Story of Our Regiment: A History of the 148th Pennsylvania Vols.* Des Moines, Iowa: Kenyon Printing and Mfg. Co., 1904.

Nanzig, Thomas P. *3rd Virginia Cavalry.* Lynchburg, Va.: H. E. Howard, 1989.

Neal, W. A., ed. *An Illustrated History of the Missouri Engineer and the 25th Infantry Regiments.* Chicago: Donohue and Henneberry, 1889.

Nesbit, John W., comp. *General History of Company D, 149th Pennsylvania Volunteers and Personal Sketches of the Members.* Philadelphia: Oakdale Printing, 1908.

Parker, John L., and Robert G. Carter. *Henry Wilson's Regiment: History of the Twenty-Second Massachusetts Infantry, the Second Company Sharpshooters, and the Third Light Battery, in the War of the Rebellion.* Boston: Rand Avery, 1887.

Partridge, Charles A., ed. *History of the Ninety-Sixth Regiment Illinois Volunteer Infantry.* Chicago: Brown, Pettibone and Co., 1887.

Proceedings of the Twenty-First Wisconsin Regiment Association, at its Thirteenth Annual Reunion, Held at Appleton, Wisconsin, Wednesday and Thursday, July 18–19, 1900. Waupaca, Wisc.: Record Book and Job Print, 1900.

Reid, J. W. *History of the Fourth Regiment of S.C. Volunteers, from the Commencement of the War until Lee's Surrender.* Greenville, S.C.: Shannon & Co., 1892.

Report of the Proceedings of the Association of the Fifty-Fifth Illinois Veteran Volunteer Infantry, at their First Reunion Held at Canton, Ill., Oct. 30, & 31, 1884. Chicago: James Guilbert, 1885.

Rodenbough, Theo. F., Henry C. Potter, and William P. Seal, comps. *History of the Eighteenth Regiment of Cavalry Pennsylvania Volunteers (163d Regiment of the Line), 1862–1865.* New York: Wynkoop Hallenback Crawford Co., 1909.

Rood, Hosea Whitford. *Story of the Service of Company E: and the Twelfth Wisconsin Regiment, Veteran Volunteer Infantry, in the War of the Rebellion*. Milwaukee: Swain and Tate, 1893.

Salmon, Verel R. *Common Men in the War for the Common Man: History of the 145th Pennsylvania Volunteers from Organization through Gettysburg*. [n.p.]: Xlibris, 2013.

Schmidt, Lewis G. *A Civil War History of the 147th Pennsylvania Regiment*. Allentown, Pa.: Lewis G. Schmidt, 2000.

Shaw, Horace H., and House, Charles J. *The First Maine Heavy Artillery, 1862–1865*. Portland, Me.: n.p. 1903.

Small, A. R. *The Sixteenth Maine Regiment in the War of the Rebellion, 1861–1865*. Portland, Me.: B. Thurston, 1886.

Smith, H. I. *History of the Seventh Iowa Veteran Volunteer Infantry during the Civil War*. Mason City: E. Hitchcock, 1903.

Smith, John Thomas. *A History of the Thirty-First Regiment of Indiana Volunteer Infantry in the War of the Rebellion*. Cincinnati: Western Methodist Book Concern, 1900.

Sperry, Andrew F. *History of the 33d Iowa Infantry Volunteer Regiment, 1863–6*. Des Moines, Iowa: Mills, 1866.

Stanyan, John M. *A History of the Eighth Regiment of New Hampshire Volunteers including its Service as Infantry, Second N.H. Cavalry, and Veteran Battallion in the Civil War of 1861–1865*. Concord, N. H.: Ira C. Evans, 1892.

Stewart, Nixon B. *Dan McCook's Regiment, 52nd O.V.I.: A History of the Regiment, Its Campaigns and Battles*. Alliance, Ohio: Review Print, 1900.

Stewart, Robert Laird. *History of the One Hundred and Fortieth Regiment Pennsylvania Volunteers*. 1912.

The Story of the Fifty-Fifth Regiment Illinois Volunteer Infantry in the Civil War, 1861–1865. Clinton, Mass.: W. J. Coulter, 1887.

Strong, W. W., et al. *History of the 121st Regiment Pennsylvania Volunteers*. Rev. ed. Philadelphia: Catholic Standard and Times, 1906.

Survivors' Association. *History of the 118th Pennsylvania Volunteers, Corn Exchange Regiment, From Their First Engagement at Antietam to Appomattox*. Philadelphia: J. L. Smith, 1905.

Thompson, B. F. *History of the 112th Regiment of Illinois Volunteer Infantry, in the Great War of the Rebellion, 1862–1865*. Toulon, Ill.: Stark County News Office, 1885.

Thompson, S. Millett. *Thirteenth Regiment of New Hampshire Volunteer Infantry in the War of the Rebellion, 1861–1865*. Boston: Houghton Mifflin, 1888.

Tobie, Edward Parsons. *History of the First Maine Cavalry, 1861–1865*. Boston: Emery and Hughes, 1887.

Vincent L. Burns. *The Fifth New York Cavalry in the Civil War*. Jefferson, N.C.: McFarland, 2013.

Wall, H. C. *Historical Sketch of the Pee Dee Guards. Co. D, 23d N.C. Regiment from 1861 to 1865*. Raleigh, N.C.: Edwards, Broughton & Co., 1876.

Wallace, William W., et al. *History of the One Hundred and Twenty-Fifth Regiment Pennsylvania Volunteers, 1862–1863*. Philadelphia: J. B. Lippincott, 1906.

Wilkinson, Warren, and Steven E. Woodworth. *A Scythe of Fire: A Civil War Story of the Eighth Georgia Infantry Regiment*. New York: William Morrow, 2002.

Woodward, E. M. *Our Regiment [Regimental History of the Second Pennsylvania Reserves]*. Philadelphia: John E. Potter, 1865.

Worsham, W. J. *The Old Nineteenth Tennessee Regiment, C.S.A., June, 1861–April, 1865*. Knoxville: Press of Paragon Printing Company, 1902.

Zeller, Paul G. *The Second Vermont Volunteer Infantry Regiment, 1861–1865*. Jefferson, N.C.: McFarland, 2002.

Digital Newspaper Databases

Chronicling America   NYS Historic Newspapers
GenealogyBank   Penn State Digital Collections
NewsBank   ProQuest
Newspaperarchive.com   Readex
Newspapers.com

Microfilmed Newspapers

Chicago Morning News
Cincinnati *Western Christian Advocate*
Richmond Enquirer

Secondary Sources

Books

Adams, Michael C. C. *Living Hell: The Dark Side of the Civil War*. Baltimore: Johns Hopkins University Press, 2014.

Allan, Tony. *Prophecies: 4,000 Years of Prophets, Visionaries and Predictions*. London: Watkins, 2011.

Andrews, J. Cutler. *The North Reports the Civil War*. Pittsburgh: University of Pittsburgh Press, 1955.

Archer, Jermaine O. *Antebellum Slave Narratives: Cultural and Political Expressions of Africa*. New York: Routledge, 2009.

Baker, Jean H. *Mary Todd Lincoln: A Biography*. New York: W. W. Norton, 1989.

Bennett Jr., Lerone. *Forced into Glory: Abraham Lincoln's White Dream*. Chicago: Johnson, 2000.

Beradt, Charlotte. *Third Reich of Dreams*. Chicago: Quadrangle Books, 1968.

Berlin, Ira. *Generations of Captivity: A History of African-American Slaves*. Cambridge, Mass.: Harvard University Press, 2003.

Berry II, Stephen W. *All That Makes a Man: Love and Ambition in the Civil War South*. New York: Oxford University Press, 2003.

Blackman, Ann. *Wild Rose: Rose O'Neale Greenhow, Civil War Spy*. New York: Random House, 2005.

Bogard, Paul. *The End of Night: Searching for Natural Darkness in an Age of Artificial Light*. New York: Little, Brown and Co., 2013.

Boyd, Steven R. *Patriotic Envelopes of the Civil War: The Iconography of Union and Confederate Covers*. Baton Rouge: Louisiana State University Press, 2010.

Bradford, Sarah H. *Harriet: The Moses of Her People.* New York: Geo. R. Lockwood and Son, 1886.

———. *Scenes in the Life of Harriet Tubman.* Auburn, N.Y.: W. J. Moses, 1869.

Brown, Ras Michael. *African-Atlantic Cultures and the South Carolina Lowcountry.* New York: Cambridge University Press, 2012.

Buckingham, Samuel G. *The Life of William A. Buckingham, The War Governor of Connecticut* Springfield, Mass.: W.F. Adams, 1894.

Bullard, F. Lauriston. *Lincoln in Marble and Bronze.* New Brunswick, N.J.: Rutgers University Press, 1952.

Burlingame, Michael. *Abraham Lincoln: A Life.* 2 vols. Baltimore: Johns Hopkins University Press, 2009.

Burstein, Andrew. *Lincoln Dreamt He Died: The Midnight Visions of Remarkable Americans from Colonial Times to Freud.* New York: Palgrave Macmillan, 2013.

Butler, Jon. *Awash in a Sea of Faith: Christianizing the American People.* Cambridge, Mass: Harvard University Press, 1990.

Cashin, Joan E. *First Lady of the Confederacy: Varina Howell Davis's Civil War.* Cambridge, Mass.: Harvard University Press, 2006.

Chireau, Yvonne P. *Black Magic: Religion and the African American Conjuring Tradition.* Berkeley: University of California Press, 2003.

Cimprich, John. *Fort Pillow: A Civil War Massacre, and Public Memory.* Baton Rouge: Louisiana State University Press, 2005.

Clarke, Frances M. *War Stories: Suffering and Sacrifice in the Civil War North.* Chicago: University of Chicago Press, 2011.

Clifford, Deborah Pickman. *Mine Eyes Have Seen the Glory: A Biography of Julia Ward Howe.* Boston: Little, Brown and Co., 1979.

Coffin, Howard. *Full Duty: Vermonters in the Civil War.* Woodstock, Vt.: Countryman Press, 1995.

Conrad, Earl. *Harriet Tubman.* Washington, D.C.: Associated Publishers, 1943.

Creel, Margaret Washington. *"A Peculiar People": Slave Religion and Community-Culture Among the Gullahs.* New York: New York University Press, 1988.

Croffut, W. A., and John M. Morris. *Military and Civil History of Connecticut during the War of 1861–65.* New York: Ledyard Bill, 1868.

Crowley, William J. *Tennessee Cavalier in the Missouri Cavalry: Major Henry Ewing, C.S.A., of the St. Louis Times, A Biographical Sketch.* Columbia, Mo.: Kelly Press, 1978.

Current, Richard N. *The Lincoln Nobody Knows* 1958; reprint. New York: Hill and Wang, 1963.

Dean Jr., Eric T. *Shook Over Hell: Post-Traumatic Stress, Vietnam, and the Civil War.* Cambridge, Mass.: Harvard University Press, 1997.

Deyle, Steven. *Carry Me Back: The Domestic Slave Trade in American Life.* New York: Oxford University Press, 2005.

Dobak, William A. *Freedom by the Sword: The U.S. Colored Troops, 1862–1867.* Washington, D.C.: Center of Military History, 2011.

Donald, David Herbert. *Lincoln.* New York: Simon and Schuster, 1996.

Drago, Edmund L. *Confederate Phoenix: Rebel Children and Their Families in South Carolina.* New York: Fordham University Press, 2008.

Ellis, Joseph J. *Founding Brothers: The Revolutionary Generation.* New York: Random House, 2000.

Emerson, Jason. *The Madness of Mary Lincoln.* Carbondale: Southern Illinois University Press, 2007.

Fahs, Alice. *The Imagined Civil War: Popular Literature of the North & South, 1861–1865.* Chapel Hill: University of North Carolina Press, 2001.

Farrell, Jack. *Mystical Experiences.* San Francisco: Untreed Reads, 2012.

Faust, Drew Gilpin. *This Republic of Suffering: Death and the American Civil War.* New York: Knopf, 2006.

Fehrenbacher, Don E. *Lincoln in Text and Context: Collected Essays.* Stanford: Stanford University Press, 1987.

Ferguson, Andrew. *Land of Lincoln: Adventures in Abe's America.* New York: Atlantic Monthly Press, 2007.

Fischer, David Hackett. *Albion's Seed: Four British Folkways in America.* New York: Oxford University Press, 1989.

———. *Liberty and Freedom: A Visual History of America's Founding Ideas.* New York: Oxford University Press, 2005.

Foote, Lorien. *The Gentlemen and the Roughs: Violence, Honor, and Manhood in the Union Army.* New York: New York University Press, 2010.

Fox, Richard Wightman. *Lincoln's Body: A Cultural History.* New York: W. W. Norton, 2015.

Frank, Lisa Tendrich. *The Civilian War: Confederate Women and Union Soldiers during Sherman's March.* Baton Rouge: Louisiana State University Press, 2015.

Frey, Sylvia R., and Betty Wood. *Come Shouting to Zion: African American Protestantism in the American South and British Caribbean to 1830.* Chapel Hill: University of North Carolina Press, 1998.

Friedman, Jean E. *The Enclosed Garden: Women and Community in the Evangelical South, 1830–1900.* Chapel Hill: University of North Carolina Press, 1985.

Fussell, Paul. *The Great War and Modern Memory.* New York: Oxford University Press, 1975.

Futch, Ovid L. *History of Andersonville Prison.* Rev. ed. Gainesville: University Press of Florida, 2011.

Gallman, J. Matthew. *Defining Duty in the Civil War: Personal Choice, Popular Culture, and the Union Home Front.* Chapel Hill: University of North Carolina Press, 2015.

———. *Mastering Wartime: A Social History of Philadelphia During the Civil War.* New York: Cambridge University Press, 1990.

Genovese, Eugene D. *Roll, Jordan, Roll: The World the Slaves Made.* New York: Pantheon, 1972.

Gerona, Carla. *Night Journeys: The Power of Dreams in Transatlantic Quaker Culture.* Charlottesville: University of Virginia Press, 2004.

Glover, Waldo F. *Abraham Lincoln and the Sleeping Sentinel of Vermont.* Montpelier: Vermont Historical Society, 1936.

Goodwin, Doris Kearns. *Team of Rivals: The Political Genius of Abraham Lincoln.* New York: Simon and Schuster, 2005.

Gray, Michael P. *The Business of Captivity: Elmira and Its Civil War Prison.* Kent, Ohio: Kent State University Press, 2001.

Green, David. *Psychic Self-Defence: The Health and Safety of Spirituality.* Raleigh, N.C.: Lulu, 2012.

Grimsted, David. *American Mobbing, 1828–1861: Toward Civil War.* New York: Oxford University Press, 1998.

Guelzo, Allen C. *Abraham Lincoln: Redeemer President.* Grand Rapids, Mich.: William B. Eerdmans, 1999.

———. *Fateful Lightning: A New History of the Civil War and Reconstruction.* New York: Oxford University Press, 2012.

———. *Gettysburg: The Last Invasion.* New York: Alfred A. Knopf, 2013.

Guiley, Rosemary. *Dreams and Astral Travel.* New York: Chelsea House, 2009.

Hall, David D. *Worlds of Wonder; Days of Judgment: Popular Religious Belief in Early New England.* Cambridge, Mass.: Harvard University Press, 1990.

Hatch, Nathan O. *The Democratization of American Christianity.* New Haven, Conn.: Yale University Press, 1989.

Henn, William F. *The Civil War and Pike County.* 2nd ed. Milford, Pa.: Pike County Historical Society, 2000.

Hess, Earl J. *The Union Soldier in Battle: Enduring the Ordeal of Combat.* Lawrence: University Press of Kansas, 1997.

Heyrman, Christine Leigh. *Southern Cross: The Beginnings of the Bible Belt.* New York: Alfred A. Knopf, 1997.

Hinman, Wilbur F. *The Story of the Sherman Brigade.* Alliance, Ohio: privately printed, 1897.

Hobson, J. Allan. *Dreaming: A Very Short Introduction.* New York: Oxford University Press, 2005.

Holzer, Harold. *The Civil War in 50 Objects.* New York: Viking, 2013.

Holzer, Harold, Gabor S. Boritt, and Mark E. Neely Jr. *The Lincoln Image: Abraham Lincoln and the Popular Print.* New York: Scribner, 1984.

Hong Xiong, Jesse. *The Outline of Parapsychology.* Lanham, Md.: University Press of America, 2009.

Hughes, Amy E. *Spectacles of Reform: Theater and Activism in Nineteenth-Century America.* Ann Arbor: University of Michigan Press, 2012.

Iddrisu, Alhassan. *Understanding your Dreams: A Divine Revelation.* Bloomington, Ind.: Trafford, 2012.

Jabour, Anya. *Scarlett's Sisters: Young Women in the Old South.* Chapel Hill: University of North Carolina Press, 2009.

———. *Topsy-Turvy: How the Civil War Turned the World Upside Down for Southern Children.* Chicago: Ivan R. Dee, 2010.

Johnson, Walter. *River of Dark Dreams: Slavery and Empire in the Cotton Kingdom.* Cambridge, Mass.: Harvard University Press, 2013.

Jones, J. W. *The Story of American Heroism.* Springfield, Ohio: Werner, 1897.

Jordan, Brian Matthew. *Marching Home: Union Veterans and Their Unending Civil War.* New York: Liveright, 2014.

Kienholz, Don. *Scriptural Lessons from the Civil War.* Bloomington, Ind.: WestBow, 2012.

Lane, Roger. *Violent Death in the City: Suicide, Accident, and Murder in Nineteenth-Century Philadelphia.* 2nd ed. Columbus: Ohio State University Press, 1999.

Larson, Kate Clifford. *Bound for the Promised Land: Harriet Tubman, Portrait of an American Hero.* New York: Ballantine Books, 2004.

Lears, Jackson. *Something for Nothing: Luck in America.* New York: Viking, 2003.

Lederer, Richard. *Presidential Trivia: The Feats, Fates, Families, Foibles, and Firsts of Our American Presidents.* Salt Lake City: Gibbs Smith, 2007.

Lehman, James O., and Steven M. Nolt. *Mennonites, Amish, and the American Civil War.* Baltimore: Johns Hopkins University Press, 2007.

Leonard, Arthur Glyn. *The Lower Niger and Its Tribes.* London: Macmillan, 1906.

Lewis, Lloyd. *The Assassination of Lincoln: History and Myth.* Formerly titled *Myths after Lincoln.* 1929; reprint. New York: MJF Books, 1994.

Lilienfeld, Scott O., Steven Jay Lynn, John Ruscio, and Barry L. Beyerstein. *50 Great Myths of Popular Psychology: Shattering Widespread Misconceptions about Human Behavior.* West Sussex, UK: Wiley Blackwell, 2010.

Linderman, Gerald F. *Embattled Courage: The Experience of Combat in the American Civil War.* New York: Free Press, 1987.

Lord, Eric. *Science, Mind and Paranormal Experience.* Raleigh, N.C.: Lulu, 2009.

Lowry, Thomas P. *Don't Shoot That Boy: Abraham Lincoln and Military Justice.* Mason City, Iowa: Savas Publishing, 1999.

———. *Merciful Lincoln: The President and Military Justice.* n.p., 2009.

———. *The Story the Soldiers Wouldn't Tell: Sex in the Civil War.* Mechanicsburg, Pa.: Stackpole Books, 1994.

———. *Tarnished Eagles: The Courts-Martial of Fifty Union Colonels and Lieutenant Colonels.* Mechanicsburg, Pa.: Stackpole, 1997.

Lyerly, Cynthia Lynn. *Methodism and the Southern Mind, 1770–1810.* New York: Oxford University Press, 1998.

Manning, Chandra. *What This Cruel War Was Over: Soldiers, Slavery, and the Civil War.* New York: Random House, 2007.

Marvel, William. *Andersonville: The Last Depot.* Chapel Hill: University of North Carolina Press, 1994.

———. *Lincoln's Autocrat: The Life of Edwin Stanton.* Chapel Hill: University of North Carolina Press, 2015.

Mauro, Charles V. *A Southern Spy in Northern Virginia: The Civil War Album of Laura Ratcliffe.* Charleston, S.C.: History Press, 2009.

McClurken, Jeffrey W. *Take Care of the Living: Reconstructing Confederate Veteran Families in Virginia.* Charlottesville: University of Virginia Press, 2009.

McPherson, James M. *For Cause and Comrades: Why Men Fought in the Civil War.* New York: Oxford University Press, 1997.

McWhirter, Christian. *Battle Hymns: Music and the American Civil War.* Chapel Hill: University of North Carolina Press, 2012.

Meier, Kathryn Shively. *Nature's Civil War: Common Soldiers and the Environment in 1862 Virginia.* Chapel Hill: University of North Carolina Press, 2013.

Miles, Dudley H., ed. *Photographic History of the Civil War*, 10 vols. New York: Review of Reviews, 1911.

Millard, Candice. *Destiny of the Republic: A Tale of Madness, Medicine, and the Murder of a President.* New York: Doubleday, 2011.

Miller, Brian Craig. *Empty Sleeves: Amputation in the Civil War South.* Athens: University of Georgia Press, 2015.

Mintz, Steven, and Susan Kellogg. *Domestic Revolutions: A Social History of American Family Life.* New York: Free Press, 1988. '

Mitchell, Reid. *Civil War Soldiers: Their Expectations and Their Experiences.* New York: Simon and Schuster, 1988.

Morris, David J. *The Evil Hours: A Biography of Post-Traumatic Stress Disorder.* Boston: Eamon Dolan, 2015.

Neely Jr., Mark E., and Harold Holzer. *The Union Image: Popular Prints of the Civil War North.* Chapel Hill: University of North Carolina Press, 2000.

Neely Jr., Mark E., Harold Holzer, and Gabor S. Boritt. *The Confederate Image: Prints of the Lost Cause.* Chapel Hill: University of North Carolina Press, 1987.

Nelson, Scott, and Carol Sheriff. *A People at War: Civilians and Soldiers in America's Civil War, 1854–1877.* New York: Oxford University Press, 2008.

Nolen, Charles H. *African American Southerners in Slavery, Civil War and Reconstruction.* Jefferson, N.C.: McFarland, 2001.

O'Reilly, Bill, and Martin Dugard. *Killing Lincoln: The Shocking Assassination That Changed America Forever.* New York: Henry Holt, 2011.

Oates, Stephen B. *With Malice Toward None: The Life of Abraham Lincoln.* New York: Mentor, 1978.

Omoyajowo, Akinyele. *Your Dreams: An Introductory Study.* Ibadan, Nigeria: Daystar Press 1965.

Owen, Christopher H. *The Sacred Flame of Love: Methodism and Society in Nineteenth-Century Georgia.* Athens: University of Georgia Press, 1998.

Paludan, Phillip Shaw. *"A People's Contest": The Union and Civil War, 1861–1865.* New York: Harper and Row, 1988.

Paperno, Irina. *Stories of the Soviet Experience: Memoirs, Diaries, Dreams.* Ithaca, N.Y.: Cornell University Press, 2009.

Percoco, James A. *Summers with Lincoln: Looking for the Man in the Monuments.* New York: Fordham University Press, 2008.

Phipps, Sheila R. *Genteel Rebel: The Life of Mary Greenhow Lee.* Baton Rouge: Louisiana State University Press, 2004.

Pinsker, Matthew. *Lincoln's Sanctuary: Abraham Lincoln and the Soldiers' Home.* New York: Oxford University Press, 2003.

Pitts, Lulie. *History of Gordon County, Georgia.* Calhoun, Ga.: Press of the Calhoun Times, 1934.

Plane, Ann Marie. *Dreams and the Invisible World in Colonial New England: Indians, Colonists, and the Seventeenth Century.* Philadelphia: University of Pennsylvania Press, 2014.

Powell, C. Percy. *Lincoln Day by Day: A Chronology, 1809–1865,* 3 vols. Washington, D.C.: Lincoln Sesquicentennial Commission, 1960.

Puckett, Newbell Niles. *Folk Beliefs of the Southern Negro.* Chapel Hill: University of North Carolina Press, 1926.

Rable, George C. *Civil Wars: Women and the Crisis of Southern Nationalism.* Urbana: University of Illinois Press, 1989.

———. *Fredericksburg! Fredericksburg!* Chapel Hill: University of North Carolina Press, 2002.

———. *God's Almost Chosen Peoples: A Religious History of the American Civil War.* Chapel Hill: University of North Carolina Press, 2010.

Raboteau, Albert J. *Slave Religion: The "Invisible Institution" in the Antebellum South.* New York: Oxford University Press, 1978.

Ramold, Steven J. *Across the Divide: Union Soldiers View the Northern Home Front.* New York: New York University Press, 2013.

———. *Baring the Iron Hand: Discipline in the Union Army.* DeKalb: Northern Illinois University Press, 2010.

Rawlings, Kevin. *We Were Marching on Christmas Day: A History and Chronicle of Christmas during the Civil War.* Baltimore: Toomey Press, 1996.

Reardon, Carol A. *Pickett's Charge in History and Memory.* Chapel Hill: University of North Carolina Press, 1997.

———. *With a Sword in One Hand and Jomini in the Other: The Problem of Military Thought in the Civil War North.* Chapel Hill: University of North Carolina Press, 2012.

Rediker, Marcus. *The Slave Ship: A Human History.* New York: Penguin, 2007.

Rhea, Gordon C. *The Battles for Spotsylvania Court House and the Road to Yellow Tavern, May 7–12, 1864.* Baton Rouge: Louisiana State University Press, 1997.

Roark, James L. *Masters without Slaves: Southern Planters in the Civil War and Reconstruction.* New York: W. W. Norton, 1977.

Roberts, Giselle. *The Confederate Belle.* Columbia: University of Missouri Press, 2003.

Robertson Jr., James I. *Stonewall Jackson: The Man, the Soldier, the Legend.* New York: Macmillan, 1997.

Royster, Charles. *The Destructive War: William Tecumseh Sherman, Stonewall Jackson, and the Americans.* New York: Random House, 1991.

Sandburg, Carl. *Abraham Lincoln,* 3 vols. 1936; reprint, New York: Dell, 1959.

Sanders, Michael. *Strange Tales of the Civil War.* Shippensburg, Pa.: Burd Street Press, 2001.

Savage, Kirk. *Standing Soldiers, Kneeling Slaves: Race, War, and Monument in Nineteenth-Century America.* Princeton, N.J.: Princeton University Press, 1997.

Savary, Louis M., Patricia H. Berne, and Strephon Kaplan Williams. *Dreams and Spiritual Growth: A Judeo-Christian Way of Dreamwork, Including 37 Dreamwork Techniques.* Mahwah, N.J.: Paulist Press, 1984.

Schantz, Mark S. *Awaiting the Heavenly Country: The Civil War and America's Culture of Death.* Ithaca: Cornell University Press, 2008.

Scott, Sean A. *A Visitation of God: Northern Civilians Interpret the Civil War.* New York: Oxford University Press, 2010.

Sensbach, Jon F. *Rebecca's Revival: Creating Black Christianity in the Atlantic World.* Cambridge, Mass.: Harvard University Press, 2005.

Sernett, Milton C. *Harriet Tubman: Myth, Memory, and History.* Durham: Duke University Press, 2007.

Shermer, Michael. *The Believing Brain: From Ghosts to God to Politics and Conspiracies: How We Construct Beliefs and Reinforce Them as Truths.* New York: Times, 2011.

Silber, Nina. *Daughters of the Union: Northern Women Fight the Civil War.* Cambridge, Mass.: Harvard University Press, 2005.

Smith, Mark M. *Listening to Nineteenth-Century America.* Chapel Hill: University of North Carolina Press, 2001.

Sobel, Mechal. *Teach Me Dreams: The Search for Self in the Revolutionary Era.* Princeton, N.J.: Princeton University Press, 2000.

———. *Trabelin' On: The Slave Journey to an Afro-Baptist Faith.* Westport, Conn.: Greenwood Press, 1979.

Stauffer, John, and Benjamin Soskis. *The Battle Hymn of the Republic: A Biography of the Song that Marches On.* New York: Oxford University Press, 2013.

Stokes, Melvyn. *D. W. Griffith's "The Birth of a Nation": A History of "The Most Controversial Film of All Time."* New York: Oxford University Press, 2007.

Swanson, James L. *Bloody Crimes: The Chase for Jefferson Davis and the Death Pageant for Lincoln's Corpse.* New York: William Morrow, 2010.

Swisher, James K. *Prince of Edisto: Brigadier General Micah Jenkins, C.S.A.* Berryville, Va.: Rockbridge Publishing Company, 1996.

Taliaferro, John. *All the Great Prizes: The Life of John Hay, From Lincoln to Roosevelt.* New York: Simon and Schuster, 2013.

Tarter, Brent. *Daydreams and Nightmares: A Virginia Family Faces Secession and War.* Charlottesville: University of Virginia Press, 2015.

Taves, Ann. *Fits, Trances, and Visions: Experiencing Religion and Explaining Experience from Wesley to James.* Princeton, N.J.: Princeton University Press, 1999.

Thomas, Benjamin P. *Abraham Lincoln: A Biography.* 1952; reprint, New York: Modern Library, 1968.

Tull, Mary Herd. *Dreams: Mind Movies of the Night.* Brookfield, Conn.: Millbrook Press, 2000.

Turner, Thomas Reed. *Beware the People Weeping: Public Opinion and the Assassination of Abraham Lincoln.* Baton Rouge: Louisiana State University Press, 1982.

Van Doren Stern, Philip. *The Life and Writings of Abraham Lincoln.* New York: Modern Library, 1942.

Walker, Scott. *Hell's Broke Loose in Georgia: Survival in a Civil War Regiment.* Athens: University of Georgia Press, 2005.

Walsh, Chris. *Cowardice: A Brief History.* Princeton, N.J.: Princeton University Press, 2014.

Washington, John E. *They Knew Lincoln.* New York: E. P. Dutton, 1942.

Weiss, Joseph. *How Psychotherapy Works: Process and Technique.* New York: Guilford, 1993.

Weiss Jr., William R. *The Catalog of Union Civil War Patriotic Covers.* n.p., 1995.

Wells, Cheryl A. *Civil War Time: Temporality and Identity in America, 1861–1865.* Athens: University of Georgia Press, 2005.

White, Jonathan W. *Emancipation, the Union Army, and the Reelection of Abraham Lincoln.* Baton Rouge: Louisiana State University Press, 2014.

White Jr., Ronald C. *A. Lincoln: A Biography.* New York: Random House, 2009.

Whitney, Annie Weston, and Caroline Canfield Bullock, comps. *Folk-Lore from Maryland.* New York: American Folk-Lore Society, 1925.

Wiley, Bell Irvin. *The Life of Billy Yank: The Common Soldier of the Civil War.* New York: Bobbs-Merrill, 1952.

Wilson, Douglas L. *Honor's Voice: The Transformation of Abraham Lincoln.* New York: Knopf, 1998.

Winik, Jay. *April 1865: The Month that Saved America.* New York: Perennial, 2001.

Woodworth, Stephen E. *While God Is Marching On: The Religious Life of Civil War Soldiers.* Lawrence: University Press of Kansas, 2001.

Edited Volumes

Barrett, Deirdre, ed. *Trauma and Dreams.* Cambridge: Mass.: Harvard University Press, 1996.

Barrett, Deirdre, and Patrick McNamara, eds. *Encyclopedia of Sleep and Dreams: The Evolution, Function, Nature, and Mysteries of Slumber.* 2 vols. Santa Barbara: Greenwood, 2012.

Bulkeley, Kelly, Kate Adams, and Patricia M. Davis, eds. *Dreaming in Christianity and Islam: Culture, Conflict, and Creativity.* New Brunswick, N.J.: Rutgers University Press, 2009.

Clinton, Catherine, ed. *Southern Families at War: Loyalty and Conflict in the Civil War South.* New York: Oxford University Press, 2000.

Hornsby Jr., Alton, ed. *A Companion to African American History.* Malden, Mass.: Blackwell, 2005.

Moreno, Paul D., and Johnathan O'Neill, eds. *Constitutionalism and the Civil War: Prelude and Legacy.* New York: Fordham University Press, 2013.

Plane, Ann Marie, and Leslie Tuttle, eds. *Dreams, Dreamers, and Visions: The Early Modern Atlantic World.* Philadelphia: University of Pennsylvania Press, 2013.

Stowell, Daniel W., ed. *In Tender Consideration: Women, Families, and the Law in Abraham Lincoln's Illinois.* Urbana: University of Illinois Press, 2002.

Whites, LeeAnn, and Alecia P. Long, eds. *Occupied Women: Gender, Military Occupation and the American Civil War.* Baton Rouge: Louisiana State University Press, 2009.

Dissertations and Theses

Gerleman, David J. "Unchronicled Heroes: A Study of Union Cavalry Horses in the Eastern Theater; Care, Treatment, and Use 1861–1865." Ph.D. diss., Southern Illinois University, 1999.

Somers, Lucas R. "Lincoln's Dreams: An Analysis of the Sixteenth President's 'Night Terrors' and Other Chimeras." M.A. thesis, Western Kentucky University, 2015.

Willet, Adrian Schultze Buser. "Our House Was Divided: Kentucky Women and the Civil War." Ph.D. diss., Indiana University, 2008.

Articles and Blogs

Barrett, Deirdre, et al. "Content of Dreams from WWII POWs." *Imagination, Cognition and Personality* 33 (2013–2014): 193–204.

Berlin, Ira. "Time, Space, and the Evolution of Afro-American Society on British Mainland North America." *American Historical Review* 85 (February 1980): 44–78.

Burch, Wanda. "The Home Voices Speak Louder Than Drums." *New York History Blog* (April 30, 2012), www.newyorkhistoryblog.com/ (accessed May 29, 2015).

Burlingame, Michael. "'A Sin against Scholarship': Some Examples of Plagiarism in Stephen B. Oates's Biographies of Abraham Lincoln, Martin Luther King, Jr., and William Faulkner." *Journal of Information Ethics* 3 (Spring 1994): 48–57.

Coddington, Ronald S. "Comforting Spirit." *Military Images* 34 (Autumn 2016): 72.

Cozzens, Peter. "Survival in an Alabama Slammer." *America's Civil War* 24 (March 2011): 54–59.

Cushman, Stephen. "Surrender Stories: The Origins and Evolution of Joshua Lawrence Chamberlain's Account of the Historic Salute to Confederate Troops at Appomattox." *Civil War Monitor* 5 (Spring 2015): 58–65, 76–77.

Ekirch, A. Roger. "Sleep We Have Lost: Pre-Industrial Slumber in the British Isles." *American Historical Review* 105 (April 2001): 343–86.

Emerson, Jason. "Mary Todd Lincoln's Lost Letters." *Civil War Times* 46 (October 2007): 54–60.

Fahs, Alice. "Picturing the Civil War 2: Sentimental Soldiers," http://picturinghistory .gc.cuny.edu/?p=916 (accessed December 29, 2014).

Ferguson, Jack D. "The Furnace of Dreams: An Account of Soldiers, Pastors, and Chaplains during the American Civil War." *Concordia Institute Historical Quarterly* 86 (Winter 2013): 24–65.

Fitzpatrick, Michael F. "Jubal Early and the Californians." *Civil War Times Illustrated* 37 (May 1998): 50–61.

Fox, Richard Wightman. "Abraham Lincoln's Dreams, Authentic and Inauthentic." *From Out of the Top Hat: A Blog from the Abraham Lincoln Presidential Library & Museum.* (January 10, 2011), http://www.alplm.org/ (accessed June 12, 2013).

Gackenbach, Jayne. "Video Game Play as Nightmare Protection: A Preliminary Inquiry with Military Gamers." *Dreaming* 21 (December 2011): 221–45.

Gorn, Elliott J. "'Gouge and Bite, Pull Hair and Scratch': The Social Significance of Fighting in the Southern Backcountry." *American Historical Review* 90 (February 1985): 18–43.

Hanchett, William. "Persistent Myths of the Lincoln Assassination." *Lincoln Herald* 99 (1997): 172–79.

Hartwig, D. Scott. "1st Minnesota Infantry: 'No More Gallant Deed.'" *America's Civil War* 14 (July 2001): 38–45.

Hennessy, John J. "Lincoln Wins Back His Army." *Civil War Times Illustrated* 39 (February 2001): 34–42, 65.

Hoffman, John. "Benjamin P. Thomas." *Journal of the Abraham Lincoln Association* 19 (Summer 1998): 15–54.

Johnson, Martin P. "Did Abraham Lincoln Sleep with His Bodyguard?: Another Look at the Evidence." *Journal of the Abraham Lincoln Association* 27 (Summer 2006): 42–55.

Jones, James P., ed. "'Your Left Arm': James H. Wilson's Letters to Adam Badeau." *Civil War History* 12 (September 1966): 230–45.

Lilienfeld, Scott O. James M. Wood, and Howard N. Garb. "What's Wrong with This Picture?" *Scientific American* 285 (May 2001): 80–87.

Melish, Joanne Pope. Review of *Teach Me Dreams: The Search for Self in the Revolutionary Era*, by Mechal Sobel. *Journal of the Early Republic* 22 (Summer 2002): 304–6.

Merrill, James M. "Men, Monotony, and Mouldy Beans—Life on Board Civil War Blockaders." *American Neptune* 16 (January 1956): 49–59.

Nicholson, Christie. "Strange but True: Less Sleep Means More Dreams." September 20, 2007, http://www.scientificamerican.com/article/strange-but -true-less-sleep-means-more-dreams/ (accessed May 20, 2015).

Nielsen, Tore, et al. "Partial REM-Sleep Deprivation Increases the Dream-Like Quality of Mentation from REM Sleep and Sleep Onset." *Sleep* 28 (September 2005): 1083–89.

Orr, Timothy J. "The Outcome of a Maimed Consciousness." March 24, 2014. *Tales from the Army of the Potomac* blog, http://talesfromaop.blogspot.com/2014/03/the -outcome-of-maimed-consciousness.html (accessed March 24, 2014).

Prince, Walter F. "General McClellan's Dream," *Journal of the American Society for Psychical Research* 11 (June 1917): 353–55.

Rozear, Marvin P., et al. "R. E. Lee's Stroke." *Virginia Magazine of History and Biography* 98 (April 1990): 291–308.

Silber, Nina. "Intemperate Men, Spiteful Women, and Jefferson Davis: Northern Views of the Defeated South." *American Quarterly* 41 (December 1989): 614–35.

Stansell, Christine. "Dreams." *History Workshop Journal* 62 (Autumn 2006): 241–52.

Thornton, John K. "African Dimensions of the Stono Rebellion." *American Historical Review* 96 (October 1991): 1101–13.

van der Kolk, Bessel, et al. "Nightmares and Trauma: A Comparison of Nightmares after Combat with Lifelong Nightmares in Veterans." *American Journal of Psychiatry* 141 (February 1984): 187–90.

Vande Kemp, Hendrika. "The Dream in Periodical Literature, 1860–1910." *Journal of the History of the Behavioral Sciences* 17 (January 1981): 88–113.

Zettler, B. M. *War Stories and School-Day Incidents for the Children.* New York: Neale, 1912.

Fiction

Browne, Martha Griffith. *Autobiography of a Female Slave.* New York: Redfield, 1857.

Grahame-Smith, Seth. *Abraham Lincoln: Vampire Hunter.* New York: Grand Central, 2010.

Smith, Lane. *Abe Lincoln's Dream.* New York: Roaring Brook Press, 2012.

Vidal, Gore. *Lincoln: A Novel.* New York: Random House, 1984.

Willis, Connie. *Lincoln's Dreams.* New York: Bantam Books, 1987.

Movies and Television Shows

Christianson, Bob. *Lincoln.* Directed by Lamont Johnson. NBC, 1988.

Greenwald, Robert. *The Day Lincoln Was Shot.* Directed by Thomas John Kane. TNT, 1998.

Jendresen, Erik. *Killing Lincoln.* Directed by Adrian Moat. Richmond, VA: National Geographic Channel, 2013.

Kushner, Tony. *Lincoln.* DVD. Directed by Steven Spielberg. Burbank, CA: Walt Disney Studios Motion Pictures, 2013.

Lincoln. Directed by Vikram Jayanti. Farmington, Ky.: History Channel, 2005.

Lincoln's Washington at War. Directed by Molly Hermann. Smithsonian Channel, 2013.

Marcus, Lawrence B. "The Day the World Wept: The Lincoln Story," *Alcoa Presents: One Step Beyond,* season 2, episode 21, directed by John Newland, aired February 9, 1960 (Culver City, Calif.: Metro-Goldwyn-Mayer Studios, 1960).

Williamson, Martha. "Beautiful Dreamer," *Touched by an Angel,* season 5, episode 6, directed by Peter H. Hunt, aired October 25, 1998 (Washington, D.C.: CBS Productions, 1998).

Index

Adams, Michael C. C., xxiv

African Americans, xviii, 75, 87, 116, 148, 162, 169, 179; dream beliefs and practices of, 91–100, 106, 114, 211n46, 211n49, 212n59, 213n68; dreams about by whites, 45, 49, 66, 70, 72–74, 185, 227n1; dreams about emancipation, 49, 82, 87, 90; dreams of, 47, 81–97, 151, 186, 212n57; escape from slavery, 87–89; and night, 8, 84–87, 193n37; soldiers, 9, 47, 73, 87, 122, 195n2. *See also* slaves

Akin, Warren, 80, 116

alcohol and drunkenness, xx, 9, 16, 30, 193n31, 196n27; in dreams, 96

American Revolution, xxiv, 20, 57, 141–43, 168, 185–87, 219n40. *See also* Washington, George

Antebellum America: dream sharing and interpretations in, xv, 59, 63, 84, 96–97, 105; dreams about, 38, 77, 91, 101, 183; night and sleep during, 10, 16, 46; popular culture during, 124, 128, 141; views of death and providence, 103–4, 110, 115

Arnold, Benedict, 57, 141

Basler, Roy P., 166

Battles: Antietam, xiv, 101, 128, 152; Appomattox, 74, 173; Atlanta Campaign, 17, 20, 75, 106–7, 131, 134; Big Bethel, 62; Bull Run, First Battle of, xviii, 39, 46, 101, 144, 152; Bull Run, Second Battle of, 101; Chancellorsville, 80, 101–2, 109, 111, 182, 215n41; Chickamauga, 109, 122; Cold Harbor, 105, 177; Corinth, 112, 114; Fort Fisher, 108; Fort Sumter, 152;

Fort Wagner, 106, 177; Fredericksburg, xx, 8, 11, 17–18, 110, 131, 144, 182; Gaines Mill, 111; Gettysburg, 20, 43, 48, 105, 111, 130, 152, 163, 170, 176, 183; Overland Campaign, xvii, xix–xxii, 20, 105–7, 193n36; New Hope Church, 107; Peninsula Campaign, xv, 19, 63, 121–23, 144; Petersburg, xxii, 17, 23, 87, 108, 111, 130; Resaca, 114; Saylor's Creek, 178; Shenandoah Valley Campaign, 101, 182; Shiloh, 108; Spotsylvania, xxi; Stones River (Murfreesboro), 152, 154, 166–67, 178, 220n10, 225n61; Vicksburg, 71, 75, 112, 152; White Hall, 106; Wilderness, 102, 108, 110; Wilmington, 152, 155

Beecher, Henry Ward, 169

Bible: allusions to, 15, 24, 91, 137, 150, 169–70, 213n2; and dreams, 100, 124, 160; Jesus Christ, xii, 93, 102, 122–23, 157, 169–70, 174; Joseph, 91, 100; read or understood by soldiers, 7, 100, 104; read by women, 106, 114, 185; as understood by slaves, 87, 91, 100. *See also* Christianity; Sabbath; Satan

birds: in dreams, 81, 88, 93; as symbols, 106

bizarre dreams, xxii–xxiii, 41, 48, 62, 67, 72, 76–78, 96

black soldiers. *See* African Americans

Booth, John Wilkes, 57, 151, 164, 169, 174, 220n4, 226n10

Boritt, Gabor S., 170

Brooks, Noah, 158–59

Brown, John, xi–xii, 81–82, 111, 226n8

Brown, William Wells, 82, 87